W9-CRK-829

Map 1
Pingelap Atoll

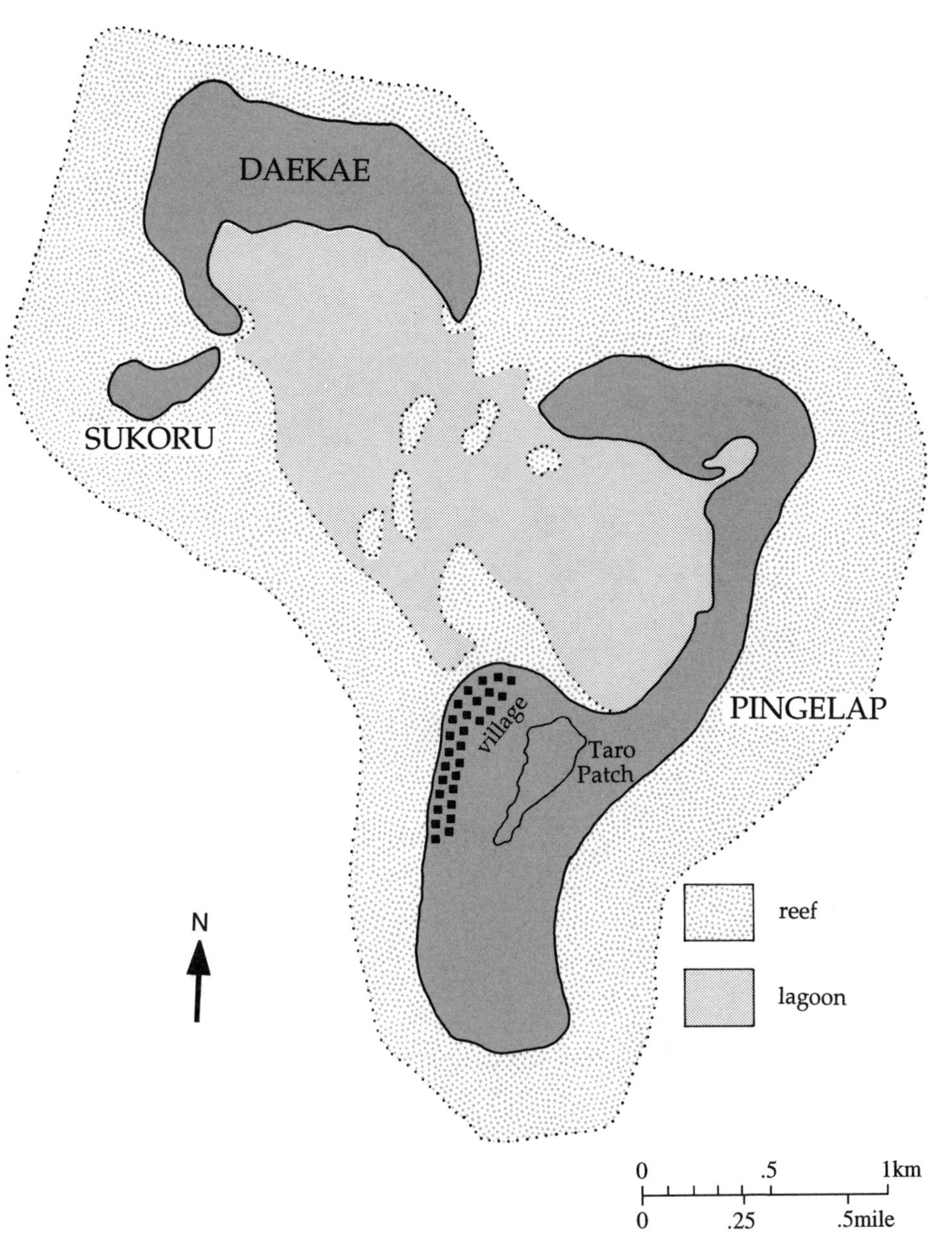

Bountiful Island

A Study of Land Tenure on a Micronesian Atoll

David Damas

Wilfrid Laurier University Press

Canadian Cataloguing in Publication Data

Damas, David, 1926-
Bountiful island : a study of land tenure on a Micronesian atoll

Includes bibliographical references and index.
ISBN 0-88920-239-7

1. Pingelapese (Micronesian people) – Social life and customs. 2. Land tenure – Micronesia (Federated States) – Pingelap. 3. Pingelap (Micronesia) – Social life and customs.
4. Ethnology – Micronesia (Federated States) – Pingelap. I. Title.

DU568.D35 1994 306.3′2′09966 C94-930419-0

Wilfrid Laurier University Press
Waterloo, Ontario, Canada
N2L 3C5

Cover design by Jose Martucci, Design Communications

Cartography by Pam Schaus

Printed in Canada

Bountiful Island: A Study of Land Tenure on a Micronesian Atoll has been produced from a manuscript supplied in electronic form by the author.

In memory of Albert

who made it possible

Contents

Illustrations

Maps

MAP

Figures

FIGURE

Tables

TABLE

Canoes on beach

Scene along main road of Pingelap

Copra drying

Food gifts at ceremony

Scene showing lagoon and islands of Pingelap

The taro patch of Pingelap

Acknowledgements

For one moving into a new cultural area late in career I was surprised at some of the responses received in answer to my inquiries by colleagues who had preceded me. There were those who displayed an unexpected territoriality, blocking out large areas of the Pacific for their future study or for the future study of their students. Then there were those who expressed the view that with the large number of anthropological theses and publications that had been produced there was little left to do in the area. While I was somewhat discouraged by these negative reactions, on balance, those who were helpful and encouraging far outnumbered such naysayers, as indicated below.

My original plan had been to study a Polynesian outlier in the then-British Solomon Islands Protectorate. Roger Green and Tim Bayliss-Smith gave encouragement to me in this plan. With negative response from the government in that region I turned my interests in a new direction. Ivan Brady first suggested that I explore the possibility of research in the U.S. Trust Territory of the Pacific, and he has continued to offer encouragement through the years. Saul Riesenberg suggested Ngatik and Pingelap atolls as appropriate places for my study. Bruce VanDyke sent a tape from Ngatik to aid me in my decision, but it was Dr. Newton E. Morton whose descriptions of Pingelap were most instrumental in my choosing that atoll for study, a decision which proved most fortunate. Dr. Morton provided me with copies of his genealogies and offered advice and provided valuable information whenever I passed through Hawaii on my trips to Micronesia. Others whom I met with in Hawaii have been sources of psychological and professional support. Most prominent of these have been William Alkire, E.H. Bryan, Jr., Roland Force, Ward Goodenough, Robert Kiste, Leonard Mason, Norman Meller, Kenneth Regh, and foremost, John and Mary Thomas, whose friendship has been a source of comfort since our meeting in 1975.

Several individuals who served as assessors for grant proposals have been an undoubted help in my securing funds for my Micronesian researches but they are, of course, anonymous. In this regard I wish to express my gratitude to those sources of support. For my 1975-76, 1980, and 1982-83 studies, grants and fellowships from the Social Sciences and Humanities Research Council (formerly The Canada Council) provided funds. The Arts Research Board of McMaster University furnished a travel grant for my 1978 trip to Micronesia.

Anyone attempting to explore the documentary history of Micronesia must struggle with the problem of the polyglot nature of the sources. In this regard I have been helped by the translation of Japanese publications by Chris Pearce, by the translation of the French by Diane Dyer, and the German by Thomas E. Willey. Douglas Davidson provided help and instruction for rendition of botanical taxonomy.

To single out the gracious and hospitable people of Pingelap and Mwaekil and their colonies in Pohnpei would seem to be almost an injustice. Certain individuals, however, proved to be especially helpful in my work. The late Yeshua Kelly provided me with entrée into the community and served as interpreter. Also serving as interpreter was Ishmael Edward. Person Samson worked for me both as a field assistant in many capacities, and as interpreter. Most notable among my Pingelapese informants were the now deceased Alik Dison, and Kuhan Edward. Albert Diapolous was my most able and valuable informant. Olid Mora helped with identifying ownership of plots on Sokehs Island. Max Lebehn served as interpreter in the Mwaekil colony in Sokehs, and Lincoln Lebehn on Mwaekil atoll.

Regarding preparation of the manuscript for publication, I am indebted to Robert M. Netting, Michael D. Lieber, and several anonymous reviewers for improvements. Finally, I am most grateful to Delia Gerner, members of the Social Sciences Word Processing Centre, and Janis Weir at McMaster University who struggled to convert my poor typing and poorer handwriting through several drafts in order to transform my rough copy into a readable version.

This book has been published with the help of a grant from the Social Science Federation of Canada, using funds provided by the Social Sciences and Humanities Research Council of Canada.

CHAPTER 1

First Impressions of Pingelap and Conceptual Background

Located halfway between the high islands of Pohnpei and Kosrae[1] in the Eastern Carolines, at 6°13′ N and 160°42′ E, Pingelap atoll lies in a belt of heavy rainfall and high humidity, which conditions are relieved somewhat from October to April by fresh northeast trade winds (Wiens 1962: 136-62; Alkire 1978: 12-13). As a representative of atolls, Pingelap is unusual in its small total diametre and tiny lagoon. Instead of presenting a classic picture of a string of narrow islets surrounding an expansive lagoon and extending beyond the horizon, the three islands of Pingelap are to the viewer all plainly in sight. The lagoon itself is only a mile across and its area is actually smaller than the less than three quarters of a square mile of land area. The length of the atoll in high tide is only two and one half miles, though the reef extends some distance outward and is largely visible during the ebb periods.[2]

The Atoll and Its People

My first sight of Pingelap came from the deck of a small sailing vessel, and I had all the symptoms of a staggering seaman struggling for his land legs when first I came ashore. But, until the completion of an air strip in 1982, the usual transportation was provided by a diesel-powered field trip ship which, though scheduled to arrive monthly, came less frequently during the years of my study, 1975-83. If the visitor arrives on a sunny day in the trade wind season, the scene will conform to those postcard pictures of Pacific islands with blue skies, bluer seas, a thin strip of brilliantly shining sand surmounted by a uniformly thick forest with palms swaying in the breezes which cool the visitor until he steps ashore. If, on the other hand, he arrives as I did during the season of calms and squalls, under overcast skies and when the tide is at ebb, the scene is less

Notes to Chapter 1 are on pp. 245-46.

inviting. Two hundred yards of dirty brown coral reef, strewn with a number of huge blocks of cement scattered wildly about and giving evidence of the destructive force of a typhoon, separate the sea from the shore. The heat and humidity are stifling. If the tide happens to be running in, the visitor coming from the ship in one of the whaleboats of the atoll is given a wild ride through a narrow gap in the reef before climbing out for a careful walk over the remaining coral surface to the beach. If the tide is running out there is an even fiercer struggle for the crewmen to force the craft through the chute before quieter inner waters are reached.

On the beach several palm-roofed boat shelters shading outrigger canoes can be seen. The beach is separated from higher ground by a three-foot-high cement seawall which is broken by a staircase. At ship time this entry to the village is lined with women resplendent in clean white dresses and adorned with flowers, making a sharp contrast to the men who have accompanied you ashore garbed in rough work clothes or in various states of undress. The clamour is considerable as numbers of Pingelapese return from, or leave for the colonies on Pohnpei with every visit of the ship.

From the ship, only glimpses of the whitewashed church, an impressive structure indeed, can be seen through the thick foliage to give indication of the village. But as one climbs to the level of the road and gets beyond the trees that line the beach, other buildings come into view. The road runs the length of the main part of the village, parallel for the most part to the shoreline. It is terminated at the south end by the church and lined on the landward side by dwelling houses, usually one storey in height and built of cement blocks with corrugated iron roofs. One of the few two-storey structures which rise above the others is the Community House, faced by a bold sign stating "Pingelap Municipality Incorporated 1946."

A few dwellings are also located on the seaward side of the road. They are interspersed with open-sided thatch-roofed structures. Some of these, with their open hearths, are the cooking shelters, while others, complete with raised grates of steel mesh, are the copra drying places. Coconut palms bent towards the sea and stilted pandanus grow between the road and the sea wall. On the landward side of the road, amongst the dwellings, majestic breadfruit trees grow, their sheetlike roots rising to blend into the thick trunks and their broad leaves forming a canopy many feet above. The road itself, smooth, hard-packed coral sand lined with whitewashed stones, continues to the north before becoming lost from sight among the houses as it bends eastward. Later, one discovers other houses hidden in the forest of the interior. Between them and the village proper is a path which runs about parallel to the main road. Located along this path are the four screened chapels, and somewhat removed from it, the cement-slab nursing station and quarters for the resident paramedic.

Exploring further inland one will quickly reach the large taro[3] patch immediately behind the island's one prominent hill that features so strongly in the traditions of the atoll as a refuge from tidal waves. On sunny days one emerges from the shade into a burst of light that reveals the large open area of the patch, the muddy surface of which is recessed some feet below the surrounding path and mounds of earth. Thousands of plants with tall stalks and broad green leaves rise above that surface to about the height of a man. Beyond the patch sections of the island are largely cleared of underbrush but deeply shaded, for the interior is a dark cathedral of trees. Further from the patch and the village, and especially on the two islands across the lagoon, undergrowth sprouts from the hard and often rocky surface. In places bush knives are needed to penetrate the thickets. Wherever one walks on any of the three islands, the ubiquitous rows of piled dead palm fronds and coconut husks divide the land into seemingly countless sections. Thus, one is aware early of the concern with land ownership on Pingelap. These rows mark the boundaries of individual plots. Most of the plots are linear and they run transversely from the lagoon to the sea in the narrower parts of the main island. Elsewhere, the lots assume a variety of shapes: rectangles, squares, trapezoids, and wedges. Here and there, usually at the ends of plots, there are excavations 20 or more feet across that are sites for several aroid plants whose upper leaves rise a little above the mounds of excavated earth surrounding them. On the main island, dry land taro plants banked with coconut husks for fertilizer are scattered here and there. Mixed among coconut and breadfruit trees, and those which do not bear fruit, rise the tall male pandanus trees, their straight slender trunks and small surmounting crowns contrasting to the squat, propped, fruit-bearing female trees growing along the beach.

Some landmarks or special features distinguish certain locales on the islands of the atoll. Near the south end of the main island blackened cement structures mark the site of Japanese occupation during World War II. Nearby is a large bomb crater giving testimony to the American air raids of that war. During my first stay on Pingelap in 1975-76 there were still some signs of the effects of the typhoon of 1972. In particular, on Daekae, the larger of the two islands across the lagoon, many naked brown trunks of dead breadfruit trees showed the effects of tidal wave salt water on plant growth.

A mangrove swamp fringes the inlet that nearly bisects the long neck of the main island near its northern extremity. The gap between that peninsula and Daekae forms a chute through which the winds rush during the months of trades, often making the waters of the lagoon too rough for small craft. But the fringing reef shelters the shores from the direct action of the surf, except in the most severe storms, which come out of the southwest and the west. On the eastern shores the surf line forms some distance from the beach, and the waters that cover the reef (except at ebb periods) are usually smooth even during the times of normal northeast trade wind activity.

Apart from their visual impressions, visitors to Pacific islands can often recall those of smell. In this regard Pingelap must rate among the more pleasant places in the area. It is only during the breadfruit season, from May to September, when the ripe fruit rots on the ground and attracts clouds of flies, that any offensive odour is present. There is not, for instance, the ever-present smell of rotting vegetation that I noted on the high island of Pohnpei.

For me, more vivid than the impressions of either sight or smell were those of skin and ears. The heat and humidity are less intense during the season of the trades, especially when one walks to the windward, or eastern, shore of the main island, but the cooling breezes penetrate less than 100 yards into the wooded interior. On the leeward side, where the village stands, it is only in the higher trees that one can see the effects of the trades.

But auditory impressions are by far the most intense memories of my stays on Pingelap. Any dream of an idyllic isle, where only the swishing of palms in the trades and the subdued roar of the surf can be heard, must be abandoned if one visits Pingelap. During the night a variety of sounds frequently broke my sleep, for the night air is punctured by the sounds of barking dogs, squealing pigs, crowing roosters, who begin their activities hours before the first hint of daylight. Some nights domestic quarrels add spice, and in my neighbourhood there was a woman who moaned loudly during the night for she never seemed to find a comfortable position for sleep. An apparently tubercular man would awake and engage in a paroxysm of coughing at any time. The nights from January through June are broken by the yells of the lookout for the torch fishing who call the crews as the moon sets. Instead of waking individual fishermen, perhaps by visiting the house of each, the shouting from the beach continues until the entire village awakens. Then the animal noises reach a new crescendo and a number of conversations begin within and between houses after which there was usually a period of relative quiet as people got back to sleep for whatever remained of the night.

With dawn the roosters take over in earnest and shortly a shell trumpet awakens whoever might still be sleeping and sets off another chorus of dogs, pigs, roosters, and soon, the shouting of adults and children. These sounds signify the beginning of another day's routine. The shell trumpet is blown to call people to the morning services in each of the chapels which represent the four *pwekil(s)* or quasi-political divisions of the village. After a spell of hymn-singing and some discussions, the men usually disperse to various tasks. Some go to the edge of the reef in their canoes, where they drop lines to catch the large tuna. Others walk to the interior to collect coconuts. Still others begin uprooting plants in the taro patch. On some days there are activities that involve larger numbers of workers, such as the manpower of each of the four sections, or of smaller groups of men, taking part in house-building or tree-cutting for canoe material. Women usually occupy themselves in or near their houses, but occasionally there are work projects such as cleaning the road that involve a number of them. Ordinarily the streets are clear of adults during the daylight hours, but children can be heard and seen playing at any time. A visitor who walks into the interior may not encounter people for a time, but eventually there will be a man, or a man and wife, gathering coconuts or stripping the husks from the nuts with sharpened sticks or metal tools. Very often they will either offer a drinking nut or climb a tree to secure one. Women can also be encountered carrying heavy back loads of grass used for mulching taro.

A sojourner who spends even a few days on Pingelap will quickly form some very definite and inescapable impressions of the people and their activities. The average male is about five feet three or four inches in height and women are seldom over five feet. Skin colour varies rather widely from light brown to nearly black for those men who sit for hours in their canoes under the sun fishing for tuna, or for those children who run about naked or nearly so. There is visible evidence of racial intermixture, with Japanese or Caucasians in some families; and one family is clearly part Melanesian. Somatic types vary quite widely with linear, stocky, to definitely heavy builds in evidence.

Some of the health problems of the Pingelapese show their marks on bodies. There is a high incidence of leprosy, and one can see depigmented skin[4] on legs and arms and some disfigurement of lips and faces. Fortunately, because of the application of advanced medical treatments in Micronesia during the American period, the disease is held in remission from those most obvious symptoms in recently contracted cases. Noticeable are the cases of achromatopsia (colour-blindness combined with extreme sensitivity to light). Its victims are those natives one sees wearing sunglasses even on cloudy days. In speaking with the Peace Corps volunteer and his native successor, who acted as paramedics on the atoll, I learned that Pingelapese are also prone to tropical skin infections and intestinal parasites, and they seem to have their share or more of heart disease and diabetes. Cancer is also known on the atoll. During Japanese times venereal disease was likely a health problem, as will be discussed in the next chapter.

With regard to bodily adornment, men often dress in ragged shorts or, at times in the trademark of Pacific wardrobes, the lavalava or coloured wrap-around cloth garment that covers from waist to knee. Fishermen wear pandanus straw hats. Some people go barefoot while others wear the *zori* or Japanese-style sandal, which is held on the foot by gripping a strap between the great and second toe. Women often wear full dress but they also appear in public in a combination of immaculately laundered white brassieres and highly coloured print skirts. On Sundays men wear white dress shirts open at the throat, long black trousers, and a few own black dress oxfords.

Pingelapese try to bathe at least once daily. Aside from seeking relief from the heat and humidity, there is an obvious effort to keep bodies clean. Each house has some sort of catchment system which usually consists of eavestroughs that drain corrugated iron roofs and pour rainwater into cement cisterns built either on the outside or within the dwellings. Aside from use of these cisterns for drinking and cooking water, most houses have shower arrangements.

One is struck early by certain external characteristics of the Pingelapese. The level of energy expended is truly remarkable. Whether out of a sense of economic necessity, some sort of work ethic, or in part due to the high carbohydrate diet, or perhaps to some constitutional predisposition, the people are active the day long and to a great age. I found that the notion of 8 hours of the 24 being allotted to sleep was unknown and I think that few people enjoy that much rest. Very seldom could people be seen sitting idle for any length of time, though perhaps some of those in extreme old age may have done so within their houses.

Pingelapese can be characterized as energetic, expansive to the degree of boisterousness, hearty, good-humoured, and affectionate. To any outsider the most indelible memory is one of their considerateness and hospitality. The good, or ideal, person on Pingelap is the one who is *sadek*, kind. Very often I was asked by various people as to whether the Pingelapese were being kind to me. It was easy to answer in the affirmative. There were few departures from that ideal of behaviour as applied to me during my stays on the atoll.

Very prominent among the impressions of life on the atoll for any visitor is the influence of Christianity. The American Board of Commissioners for Foreign Missions (ABCFM), a Congregationalist sect, is the most pervasive aspect of non-indigenous culture. Indeed, that church has replaced several native institutions in their functions, and attempts by other sects to get established on Pingelap have met with strong opposition. The morning chapel sessions drew nearly all members of the congregation each day during my early stays on the atoll with only those fishermen who left before dawn being exempt from attendance.[5] In addition to the prayers and hymn-singing, these meetings often serve as times of discussion of work projects and of civil affairs for each of the four sections [*pwekil(s)*] of the village which they represent. Other church functions include meetings several nights a week, and thrice daily services on Sunday when all work, including cooking, is suspended.[6] At these services women, girls and small children sit in pews on the left side of the church, while men and older boys occupy those to the right. The choir is impressively harmonious and is seated behind the pulpit. Each service is characterized by a series of short sermons given by the elders of the church and by several of the younger men.

The most strictly enforced rules of the church are those forbidding smoking, drinking of alcoholic beverages, participating in extra-marital and even pre-marital sexual relations, and working on Sundays. Adults carry a card which certifies that they are Christians in good standing. This card is withdrawn when one of the above sins is suspected, but can be restored after a period of good behaviour.

Christianity spills over to some extent into the traditional food prestation ceremonies that enliven Pingelap life, since they are often preceded by prayer. These occasions seem to be without number, and I am sure that the following list omits several. Of those that I can account for, occasions of prestation which mark the yearly economic cycle such as that of the *derak* or estate settlement ceremony will be discussed in later chapters. I have also written of ceremonies of this nature that celebrate the transfer of titles, as well as those that cement ties within the extended family and within the larger patrilineally oriented unit of the *keinek* (Damas 1981: 1983a). Each boy's first birthday is also an occasion for food distribution, and formerly, at least there was the *kousahkis* event which the paramount chief could call at any time to test the community's productivity over a given period. Another ceremony is the *irirpwe* when the paramount chief has recovered from serious illness or injury.

Other events that mark points of the year's cycle include the athletic contests between the four sections of the village at New Year's and on the

American Independence Day. These contests have their history deep in traditional times (Morton et al. 1973a) though the dates of occurence or celebration and several of the events are clearly American in origin. Combined with the New Year's contests at the beginning of 1976 was a three-day relaxation of the local ordinance against alcoholic drinks, and a large part of the population was intoxicated on home brew made from sugar and yeast during much of that time. I was dimly aware of some unusual behaviour but missed exhibitions of transvestism of which I was told many months later, due to my own degree of participation in the bacchanalian aspect of the celebrations.

Field Work Motives and the Evolution of the Land Tenure Study

It would be most appropriate if I could state that my chief motivation for visiting Pingelap was from the beginning an abiding interest in studying land tenure under atoll conditions. Such was not the case, for it was only after I reached Pingelap that I began to appreciate the pervasiveness of land tenure concerns under such conditions. Other motives, both personal and professional, were more prominent in my feelings and my thinking when I chose Pingelap as the site for my study. I have always felt that anthropologists are too sensitive in their response when accused of preoccupation with the exotic. In my view it is to a large extent the spirit of adventure that enables the field worker to endure situations which often entail hardship. I readily admit to boyhood fantasies and dreams about travelling by dogsled and sleeping in snowhouses, as well as living on some tropic isle complete with white sands, tall trees, and comely, brown-skinned maidens.

After having spent considerable time in trying to realize both adventurous and professional objectives in the Arctic, I turned to the tropics to pursue them further. Aside from the motives of fulfilling romantic boyhood dreams I also sought to expand my education in anthropology. Having devoted 15 years to the study of hunting peoples with traditionally sparse settlement and bilateral kinship systems, I found that both my social anthropological interests and my interest in economics and ecology were limited in realization. I wanted to move to another level of economy, more densely concentrated populations and more complex social systems. Micronesia seemed to offer what I wanted. Pingelap in particular emerged as a good choice for a study after I had narrowed the various possibilities. Fischer and Fischer (1957) had reported the existence of double descent for that atoll, though details were lacking. It looked as if Pingelap would not only introduce me to the mysteries of descent systems but also present an opportunity to explore one of the most rare types of kinship structure. My previous research in the Canadian Arctic had stirred interest in the interaction of ecology and history. In Micronesia the occurrence of double descent, and more especially, the apparent uniqueness of patrilineal forms in a region dominated by matrilineal systems suggested independent development under conditions of isolation and an atoll environment. This apparent set of circumstances promised some intriguing problems. Accordingly, I hoped that in addition to fulfilling my own educational objectives, I could also make some contribution to social anthropological and ethnological theory.

In recent years field work strategies and techniques have become a separate study in anthropology and one that doubtlessly has been exceedingly useful to young field workers. In my own case, however, it was only at the very beginning of my career that I considered myself qualified to give meaningful advice to fellow anthropologists about how to do field work. It may be useful, however, to consider the emergence of interest, and the procedures which followed in the land tenure study.

While I did get some information on descent emphases during my first visit to Micronesia and Pingelap in 1975-76, it was only in 1980 that distinctions among descent, succession and inheritance became clear to me.[7] I also found early in my studies that much of the social fabric of Pingelap involved elements other than descent. The study of genealogies which grew out of my interest in descent and allied phenomena, especially adoption practices, drew me into considerations of land inheritance as they related to kinship. But even before I had gone far in my genealogical work, I had begun the survey of the islands of the atoll. The presence of hundreds of very visible boundaries on the land and of well-marked sections and rows in the taro patch begged examination. I felt that I must measure these in order to fulfill a basic ethnographic responsibility, regardless of whatever theoretical significance the survey might have. The survey of the islands of the atoll took much of my time between early October 1975 and late April 1976. This survey was carried out with the aid of a Brunton compass and by pacing off distances. Person Samson supplied me with ownership information which he elicited from individuals.

The Pingelapese were very cooperative and followed my survey with considerable interest. The existence of land disputes stimulated a concern with precise recording of the division of land. There was also a concern with capturing elements of traditional culture for their own sake, for the Pingelapese of the 1970s and 1980s were conscious of the gradual sloughing off of traditional practices and expressed to me regret with their passing.

Before the mapping was completed, I began collecting land ownership histories and continued this pursuit until my departure in July of 1976. By the end of my first visit I had also begun to explore the complexities of the system of stewardship, or *kohwa*, as it operated on the atoll and I resumed that study on my return in the summer of 1978. Also, during my two months' stay on Pingelap that summer I made a number of corrections in my charts, updated them with recent transactions, and expanded my corpus of case histories. In addition, I collected considerable data on the *derak* or estate-division ceremony during that visit.

I was able to reach Pingelap for only two very brief periods in 1980 and 1983, but while living on Pohnpei I documented the histories of land tenure in the two Pingelapese colonies there during my visits in those years. As well, in

1980 I had access to records of the Ponape District Court regarding land tenure disputes and decisions which involved Pingelapese.

Studies of Population Pressures on Land Tenure Practices

Before embarking on discussion of Pingelapese land tenure, it is advantageous to explore the background of studies which confronted similar problems. Two quite contrasting interpretations of the effects of population pressures on land tenure emerge from the literature of the New Guinea Highlands. On the one hand, Meggitt (1958,1965) saw the hardening of patrilineality in land tenure with such increased pressures. His position appears to have two difficulties. The first relates to the definition of descent, or more specifically, agnation, as it applies to the region (Strathern 1968). The second involves conflicting evidence from among the tribes considered, especially the Chimbu (Brookfield and Brown 1963) where under intense population pressure "agnatic concepts of recruitment may not be stiffened but abandoned" (Strathern 1968: 41). Rappaport (1967: 26-27) largely supports Meggitt but also attempts to reconcile the latter's views with those of Brookfield and Brown in an intricate argument, while enlisting the variable of warfare in the equation of land tenure and population pressure. Hallpike (1977: 230-31, 1986: 106-108) on the other hand, argues that warfare is endemic throughout the highlands regardless of degree of pressures on land. Continuing the debate, Brown and Podolefsky (1976) survey information from 17 New Guinea societies. Among their conclusions is that the tendency for individual ownership of land is strongly correlated with high population density, but that on closer examination it is really agricultural intensity rather than population density which affects land tenure organizations in the area. At the same time, there is an indirect linkage with the latter variable (Brown and Podolefsky 1976: 221). Further, they found the closest correlation to exist between land tenure and length of fallow. They would not, however, endorse a causative direction between population growth and intensification of agriculture, but rather, they consider that the "relationship is interactional" (1976: 229).

While adopting a cautious appraisal of available data Feil (1987) argues that there should be a serious attempt to separate developments in the eastern highlands from those in the western highlands. While associating contrasts in human population group sizes and densities with intensification of agriculture, he adds that pig populations "are critical to any assessment of intensification of production" (1987: 44). Raising pigs for exchange purposes provides the motivation for developing agricultural systems of high intensity. Further, he argues that "agriculture itself is almost epiphenomenal (or at least a dependent variable) to the concern with pig husbandry" (1987: 40) and that pig husbandry relates mainly to the realm of "social production" rather than to subsistence production in the western highlands (1987: 58). Feil also purportedly rejects ecological explanations of warfare in the highlands as a whole while developing an intricate argument based on differential historical changes as accounting for the greater intensity of warfare in the eastern as compared to western highlands.

Turning to another part of the world where land tenure questions have been examined with perception, Netting (1969) argued that in Nigeria high population densities correlated with adoption of intensive agriculture, dispersed settlement, nuclear families, and individual land tenure in the case of the Kofyar; and, low population density, shifting agriculture, nucleated settlement, extended families, and communal land tenure for the Igbo. He also pointed out that those Kofyar living in regions of most overworked soil were the first to engage in migration, and he posed a " 'tipping point' when rural population density reaches between 200 and 500 persons per square mile" when intensification of agriculture occurs (1969: 109). Again, as in the Brown and Podolefsky study, the correlation between shortening of the fallow period and increased population pressures was strong, and a good indicator of intensification of farming in regions where shifting cultivation is the norm. The same author's study of a Swiss alpine village documents how the introduction of the potato not only was instrumental in population growth but also allowed for greater intensification of agriculture in order to cope with expanding populations as they achieved higher caloric yields per unit of land (Netting 1981: 164).

For a geographical area which incorporates that of the present study, Goodenough (1955) developed a hypothesis which related population density and descent emphases in the Malayo-Polynesian culture area. Goodenough presumes an original bilocal, social structure with bilateral kindreds and without unilineal descent groups. He felt that appearance of unilineal descent, either patrilineal or matrilineal, in Oceania related to changes in residence practices and correlated with conditions of arable land. With increased pressures on land inequalities in land distribution result, unless non-unilineal descent units are retained. Goodenough draws much of his argument from the example of non-unilineal descent in the Gilberts, and the articulation of such units to land tenure there seems clear-cut (Lambert 1971; Lundsgaarde 1974a). Their apparent utility appears to conform more to the arguments of Brookfield and Brown than those of Meggitt for New Guinea in that opportunities for optation or shifts in residential or other personnel alignments are advantageous in increasing land holdings or use opportunities. Both sets of examples are posited as responses to overpopulation. Other means of achieving such optation have been cited under basically patrilineal situations for Polynesia with the *hapu* of the Maori (Best 1924: Firth 1929) and the Mangaiian *kopu* (Buck 1934) being examples of non-unilineal elements being incorporated in the context of land ownership, use, and inheritance. Sources for the Central and Western Carolines (Goodenough 1961; Alkire 1974; Severance 1976) as well as the Marshalls (Tobin 1967; Kiste 1967; Rynkiewich 1972; Pollock 1970, 1974) note bilateral or cognatic deviations from matrilineal bases which produce conditions for optation in land tenure. Another solution to pressures on land appears to have occurred on Yap where an apparently original matrilineal land tenure system has been modified by parallel development of patrilineally oriented units also associated with land ownership, though alternative interpretations have been offered (Schneider 1953, 1962, 1984; Lingenfelter 1975; Labby 1976).

Collier sought to reconcile the positions of Meggitt and Goodenough regarding the direction of adaptations of land tenure systems to conditions of crowding with his "curvilinear hypothesis" (Collier 1975: 50). He saw an intensification of unilineality in land tenure during one phase of population expansion which is followed by increasing individuation as pressures become more severe. In his Tzotil example he used a comparison of several communities to back this hypothesis, but in the end most intense pressure resulted in emigration for wage labour, thus providing a *deus ex machina* for the problem. Indeed, the literature of land tenure has for some time dealt with such acculturative factors as codification (Crocombe 1971), and more recently with migration for wage labour (Greene 1981; Hecht 1984; G. T. Harris 1985; Connell 1986) and cash-cropping (Rodman 1987). While he made tentative attempts to resolve more broadly based problems of land tenure, Collier also sees difficulty in applying his hypothesis cross-culturally and favours the controlled comparison method (1975: 59) in order to control variables.

Such control is achieved to great extent by Alkire (1978) in his focus on coral isolates which corresponds closely to the concerns of the present study. Alkire indicates the importance of taro cultivation in intensification of agriculture on such coral islands and atolls, and he also notes the catastrophic effects of droughts and typhoons on crops as well as on human populations. But most interesting in the context of this study are his statements regarding the effects of pressures on land as they affect land tenure practices:

> The underlying pattern of land and resource control common in Oceania was based on corporate control. Kin groups, either lineages or ramages, held land jointly and reallocated it among the group's members for exploitation and use. The ramage form of organization, of course, often permits one to claim membership in more than one land holding group. Alliances of various types could also increase an individual's options. For example on both Nauru and Niue a stated consideration in negotiation of marriage was possible access to resource areas the marriage would permit. Periods of resource shortages brought both internal and external pressures on those groups for redistribution. Collectivization or further individuation of holdings were contrasting options. By individuation is meant the transfer of effective control from the larger corporate units into the hands of individuals (Alkire 1978: 91).

Thus, in addition to the solutions of individuation and optation which have been featured in the thinking of the above-mentioned scholars, Alkire indicates other possibilities. In his doing so, however, we are left with the problem of what conditions determine which of the contrasting options that is selected.

In summarizing a collection of studies of Oceanic land tenure, most of which concerned coral atolls or islands, Lundsgaarde remarks "we have reached the point in studies of Pacific land tenure systems which separates a past phase dominated by particularistic studies of individual societies from an emerging phase which adds a generalizing dimension" (1974b: 266). Unfortunately, interest in land tenure in Oceania has faded since the time of

Lingenfelter's statement and there has been little advance into the second or generalizing phase. Certainly the "wide variety and diversity of land tenure systems found in Oceania represent a formidable challenge" (ibid.) for such attempts. The same author does make a bold generalization when he says "there are no societies in Oceania that can be said to allow persons to hold a fee simple estate interest in land" (1974b: 270). He goes on to say that the lack of rights to disposal disqualifies any Pacific system from a fee simple status. There will be occasion to examine this and other points made by the above authors during the course of this study.

Objectives, Orientation, and Procedures

Taking into account some of the questions raised in the above discussion as they may apply to Pingelap, the problems to be addressed here can be stated simply as follows: (1) to ascertain the degree to which the evolution of the Pingelapese land tenure system can be linked to expanding populations; (2) to assess the degree to which the system that has evolved has accommodated or continues to accommodate the expanding populations; (3) to evaluate the role of emigration and other acculturative factors on the land tenure practices of the total Pingelap population, and finally; (4) to examine the system against the backdrop of other studies of land tenure systems operating under conditions of population expansion.

Either explicitly or implicitly, every anthropologist carries certain orientational biases or convictions in addressing any problem or series of problems. All land tenure studies, rooted as they are in the earth and being involved in relations between economic activities and society and culture, should be considered within the theoretical framework of *cultural* or *human ecology*. While *cultural ecology* has perhaps faded from the forefront of current theoretical interests, it must remain as a basic and vital approach to the "human whole" (Redfield 1955). During a time of peak interest in *cultural ecology*, I (Damas 1969) agreed with Rogers (1969: 24) that "explanations in terms of environmental conditions and technological levels are . . . approaching an extreme position." Indeed, I felt then that the original formulations of Steward (1955) and such studies as that of Sahlins (1958) must be modified. Likewise, the *cultural materialism* of M. Harris (1968) has seemed to me to be too extreme an endorsement of what I see as economic determinism. What I did not envision was the rapid fall of cultural ecology from its central position in the anthropology of that time (Netting 1982). I underestimated the force of style or fashion. That is, the overpowering force of hell-bent-for-leather endorsement of certain approaches which are then abandoned when they alone do not solve all of the fascinating and often perplexing problems of anthropology.[8] In my earlier statement (Damas 1969: 10), I suggested adoption of a *new ethnology* which "combines ecological and historical methods, together with attempts to understand the effects of ideology on society." I have tried to combine such approaches here but in the attempt have come to realize the difficulties inherent in such a procedure. The strongest advocates of each of these approaches will in some ways find my attempts to be inadequate.

My approach and methods will not satisfy fully those who espouse the orientation of *ecological anthropology* (Vayda and Rappaport 1976). Although I have tried to quantify elements of Pingelapese land tenure, time and energy limitations prevented me from achieving the meticulous treatments of the animal ecologists. I am also somewhat skeptical as to the extent to which a more minute examination of the environment and economy of Pingelap would have yielded substantially different results from those achieved here.

With regard to the ideological dimension, and without delving into questions of causal direction, one might expect that traditional beliefs and rituals of the Pingelapese must articulate with, or enter into, their land tenure system. But after 100 years of Christianity much of that aspect of culture is lost, and it is my contention that the land tenure system maintains itself largely in economic and sociological terms without the support of traditional religion and with only superficial connection with Christian beliefs.

Those exponents of the *ethnoscientific* and related *ethnoecological* approaches (Conklin 1957; Frake 1962; Sturtevant 1964; Johnson 1974) will find my application to be incomplete. For while I have catalogued plants (see Appendix) and other elements of the environment in native terms, I have not gone far into the cognitive significance of such nomenclature. This is due more to limitations of time and training rather than any criticism of that orientation. I have tried to enter into the cognitive world of the Pingelapese by seeking to find a normative set of conventions or ideals of land tenure practices on the basis of informant statements. Advocates of *symbolic anthropology* (Dolgin et al. 1977) will find these attempts of mine to be inadequate, for I have made only the first step in their progression of analysis. While I have tried to abstract a normative system, I have not dealt with the level of the "cultural system." I did not find, as suggested by Schneider (1972: 38), that the world of symbols and meaning "can be easily abstracted" from the normative level. My difficulty here concerns the fact that in my attempts to discover the ideal system of the conventions and customs of land tenure, I found it was necessary to extrapolate and indeed, take leaps of faith to augment statements of informants.[9] I felt that I was promoting a partly artificial set of precepts. For me to move even further up the ladder of abstraction on the basis of material available seems perilous.

My historical treatment of the land tenure system of Pingelap will satisfy neither those historians who would rely exclusively on documents, nor those anthropologists who reconstruct myth as history or history as myth or history as metaphor (Rosaldo 1980; Sahlins 1981, 1985). My inclusion of legendary accounts is not due to any great faith in their historical accuracy but rather to the paucity of documentation for the earlier phases of Pingelapese history and the total lack of archaeology of the atoll. I do not attempt to grasp the symbolic content of these accounts, partly, I suppose because of lack of imagination, but also because of skepticism about the results of such studies (cf. Shankman 1986).

If, then, my utilization of aspects of several approaches in my attempts to understand the land tenure practices of the Pingelapese will not meet the standards of their most dedicated adherents, what merit or justification is there in employing the combinations of elements of such approaches that I have selected? First, with regard to ecology, I hope that my attempts to document the characteristics of the environment and economy of the atoll, following native categories as closely as I am able, will provide substantial background for analysis of the land tenure system, even though I do not employ input-output equations or flow charts. The reader will have to judge the adequacy of these data in terms of the problems at hand. While I conceive of the Pingelapese land tenure system as being understandable in economic terms to a large extent, I shall discuss the various rituals which accompany the yearly cycle of agriculture and fishing, as well as ritual involved in validating claims to land to the extent to which they survived to the time of my study. My use of norms of land tenure, or my attempts to depict the "pragmatic design" (Nadel 1957: 140) as I perceive it to be understood by the Pingelapese, is in the spirit of providing a framework of organization within which observed and statistically derived information becomes more intelligible.

I hope that throughout my historical treatment of land tenure on Pingelap there is an appropriate consideration of the dynamic character of the evolving system. This dynamism can be seen in the early history of the atoll, which is accessible only through legend and genealogies, when largely internally inspired change occurred. It is visible also in later times when externally promoted demographic changes and emigration which affected land tenure can be subjected to greater control.

There is another orientation which I will follow in this study. That is the *method of controlled comparison* as developed by my teacher, Fred Eggan, who writes of that approach as follows:

> My own preference is for the utilization of the comparative method on a smaller scale and with as much control over the frame of comparison as is possible to secure. It has seemed natural to utilize regions of relatively homogeneous culture or to work within social or cultural types and to further control the ecology and the historical factors so far as it is possible to do so (Eggan 1954: 747).

Here I shall try to apply this method by first comparing results from Pingelap with those from its nearest atoll neighbor, Mwaekil, and then by expanding the comparisons to other Micronesian atolls which share both elements of common heritage and similar ecological conditions, though showing some variability. While comparisons on such a scale is a chief objective of this study, applying this focus does not preclude the possibility of attempting more tentative generalizations about land tenure on wider dimensions.

The sequence of procedures which I shall use in attempting to achieve these objectives can be seen in the table of contents. I shall first explore the history of the atoll with special emphasis on events and processes that bear on the problems of land tenure, while at the same time providing an ethnographic background. Following will be a description of the environment and economy of

Pingelap. After that an outline of the spatial and normative dimensions of land tenure will be presented. Then I shall examine case history material which will reveal the operation of the system of land inheritance on the atoll. Consideration of the ceremonial affirmation of land distribution follows. Land tenure in the Pingelapese colonies is the subject of the next chapter. Then another perspective, that of the relationship of land tenure on the atoll to the outside world, will be employed. In the final chapter I will first summarize my findings on Pingelap and then attempt a gradually widening series of comparisons in order to relate my study to the general theory of land tenure in restricted space.

CHAPTER 2

History and Culture of Pingelap

If the estimate of Morton et al. (1972a: 360)[1] for original settlement of Pingelap at 1 000 years B.P. is to be accepted, it means that a period of about 800 years passed before European contact occurred during a visit to the atoll by Duperrey in 1824 (Eilers 1934: 409-12). Until archaeological data are available to fill out the picture, the ethnologist is wholly reliant on the oral traditions of the Pingelapese for this entire period. The status of oral tradition in providing accounts of precontact histories is represented by two extremes. At the negative pole is Lowie (1915: 598) who stated that he could not "attach to oral tradition any historical value whatsoever under any conditions whatsoever." Such skepticism was endorsed by later generations of social anthropologists, but an exception is Raymond Firth (1961) who explored the oral history of Tikopia despite expressing some qualifications regarding its validity.[2]

At the other extreme is the view of traditionalists among native peoples who accept such accounts as accurate portrayals of their history. There are some Pingelapese who do so regard their oral traditions, while others attest to more qualified endorsements. I take a position somewhere between the extremes in that I would regard total rejection of such traditions in the absence of more concrete sources of evidence as unwarranted and crippling disdain. On the other hand, in employing such accounts I try to apply a reasonably critical approach in evaluating their significance.

The Settlement of Pingelap

The legendary history of Pingelap is well represented in the work of Newton Morton and his associates (Morton et al. 1973) and especially Jane Hurd (1977). Hurd and Morton worked largely with informants of a generation previous to that I contacted only five years later, since most of the former were

---

Notes to Chapter 2 are on pp. 246-47.

deceased at the times of my study. I have been able to add some legends to the ones referred to by Hurd and Morton. For instance, from my chief informant I heard the following myth of origin for the atoll and its population:

> A reef broke through the surface of the sea and a turtle and a fish, *kahil*, appeared on the reef and caused a commotion of waves moving against the rocks which in turn became sand lodged on the stone. Then the spirit Nahwehlap appeared on the pile of sand. He then went to Kosrae, married a Kosraen royal spirit and returned to Pingelap to stay and reproduce. Over the generations their descendants became less and less spiritlike and more and more humanlike until the native Pingelapese emerged from the process. Nahwehlap continued as the spirit of the *nahlaihmw* or priest of the sea.

The more widely known version of the settlement of Pingelap is recorded by Hurd (1977: 111-36) as "Duen Tapida en Wein Pingelap," or "How Pingelap Began." This legend features a pair of brothers from Yap discovering a pile of sand where they encountered two women. The land was described as being vast and hence the name, Pingelap, which is translated as "Big News." Later one of the brothers travelled to Kosrae, an event which began the long association with that island in the legendary history. The legend continues with the son of one of the brothers coming from Yap bringing news of the search for the missing navigators. This prompted a return to Yap, and eventually to Pingelap, where the first children, three girls and a boy were born. The boy, Iengirsandeir, became the first *nahnmariki* (paramount chief) and the three daughters were the wellspring of all the succeeding people of Pingelap.

Certain features of these tales beg comment. In the first account it is interesting to note that there is an understanding that the action of waves on coral produces soil and thus the possibility of plant growth to support human life. It is also noteworthy that the transition from spirit forms to human forms was a gradual process. As in the folk tales of many peoples, in Pingelap traditions, spirits interact freely with humans and changes in identity from one to the other form are common.

In the second account one is struck by the extent of the new land discovered and its barren nature, characteristics which stand in sharp contrast to Pingelap's small area and lush vegetation. This myth depicts Yap as the point of origin for the first Pingelapese population, but Morton et al. (1973: 322) suppose that this Yap is not necessarily the island of that name today, but rather is the habitat of the gods throughout much of Micronesian mythology. Certainly there is little similarity between the society and culture of the two islands that would suggest close historical relationships. Further, despite the closer linguistic relationships with Pohnpei, Kosrae is mentioned more frequently in the legendary history of Pingelap. Indeed, one myth has the settlement of Pohnpei coming from Kosrae via Pingelap. Only through archaeology can we hope to resolve such discrepancies. Another interesting aspect to the second of these origin myths is the descent of the population from three sisters (though the origin of their husbands is obscure), a depiction which is consistent with the population being perceived as originally divided into three matriclans.

According to the tradition told to Morton (Morton et al. 1973: 319), the taro patch was dug during the reign of the second *nahnmariki*, Kaupene. But the account which I have places that event at a time shortly after the settlement of the atoll, before a *nahnmariki* had been chosen. At that time there is said to have been three *kounen kousapw*(s), or heads of major divisions of the atoll; one for Daekae, and one each for Lehpung and Lepier, the northern and southern sections of the main island. In the event of digging the patch, a competition was staged with the men of Lehpung digging from the north near the lagoon, and with the men of Lepier beginning in a section of the island called Sapweino, near the south end of the island. Both parties worked toward a central meeting place.

First the area was cleared of trees. This was very hard work because it meant uprooting breadfruit, coconut, and pandanus trees. The men of each of the two *kousapw*(s) slept only in their men's houses during the period of construction of the patch. The actual loosening of the soil with large branches of mangrove for digging sticks followed. The digging was aided by flooding in order to soften the soil. Flooding was accomplished by digging a channel from the lagoon to allow invasion of salt water. As to the outcome of the competition, the Lepier people soon found that much of the area in the southern part of the island had soil unsuitable for planting taro and eventually they had to be content with a small area to the south of the present-day causeway extending at first to the area used later as the "banana plantation." Eventually their share of the patch shrunk even further to its present limit because of the poor condition of the soil.

When the men of Lepier saw that they were losing in the competition they were angered, and a fight ensued in which the main protagonists were the two *kounen kousapw*(s). The head man of Lehpung is reported to have been very strong and had a left hand with six fingers. He is said to have hit the other with a stick and then flown up into a coconut tree, and afterwards fell down into the section of the village called Mweniap as a ghost. From that time onward people have been forbidden to make loud noises in that part of the village for fear of disturbing that ghost.

The actual construction of the patch is said to have taken only two-and-a-half months. This short time is explained by the original Pingelapese having been very large people with men up to seven feet in height who worked with digging sticks one-and-one-half fathoms in length. After the digging was complete the salt water had to be drained into the lagoon. Then came a period of nearly a year while the rains cleansed the cleared area and muddied it so that planting could begin. My source for this information says that the plantings consisted of four varieties of taro which were brought from mysterious Yap.

Some aspects of this account arouse special interest. Discounting the supernatural elements in the legend, certain details are understandable in the light of later developments and the present-day condition of the taro patch. The coincidence of the causeway with the point where the two teams of diggers met might be rationalization for the contemporary location of that feature. The commencement of the project shortly after settlement is logical in that planting taro requires parts of corms and stalks brought from other places, and these cuttings have short lifetimes after the plant has been uprooted. It is not clear why such a short period is allotted for the project. The giant humans appear to have been created specifically to rationalize this rapid construction period, for this characteristic of the original population does not appear in any of the other traditions collected by either Morton, Hurd, or myself. While the account of the procedures used coincide quite well with later reports regarding renewing the patch after floodings, there is one anomaly. That is the assertion that the salt water was drained to the north into the lagoon. Later attempts to do this resulted in failure because that means of draining works against gravity. But it is interesting to note that further attempts to follow this procedure were tried as late as 1957 (see further discussion in the next chapter). Isolation of males in the men's houses during digging is consistent with sexual abstinence and isolation before or during activities that suggest danger or uncertainty, such as torch-fishing, and indeed, restoration of the taro patch.

The Early Dynasties

The oral history proceeds as accounts centred on the reigns of succeeding paramount chiefs. The accounts are laced with mythical elements, especially appearances of ghosts, but there are some major legendary events which deserve mention. The redivision of the village into four sections or *pwekil*(s); Lehpung into Peruku and Kahkahlia; Lepier into Mweniap and Serkarakapw, is attributed to the time of the third *nahnmariki*, Pakispok (Morton et al. 1973: 319). A raiding expedition to Pohnpei is also supposed to have taken place during the latter's reign, though other accounts put such a raid later in time. This could mean two such expeditions. In the time of the fourth *nahnmariki* a typhoon is supposed to have occurred which not only reduced the population to 30, but also ended the first royal line. From the fifth *nahnmariki*, Mwungesamarou, who is generally agreed to have been a Kosraen, through the sixteenth, there is considerable controversy among Hurd's (1977: 43-51), Morton's (Morton et al. 1973: 319-21), and my own informants as to the island origin of the various chiefs. One version has these chiefs forming a dynasty of Kosraens who were expelled after a battle, perhaps in the early or mid-eighteenth century. Another version divides the era into two series of dynasties, one from Kosrae, beginning with Mwungesamarou, and the other with Gilbertese, from the thirteenth through the sixteenth chiefs, before the Pingelapese were again restored to paramount chieftainship. Still another version has rule by outsiders end with the Kosraen chiefs who occupied the paramount chieftainship only in cases of the fifth and sixth *nahnmariki*(s) after which the royalty reverted to Pingelapese and then, for the thirteenth through the sixteenth, to rule by Gilbertese. Finally, dominance came back to the original inhabitants of the atoll again.

My own chief informant considers that the Kosraen dynasties extended from the fifth chief named by Morton, through the sixteenth, though he does omit one from of the list of Morton. This informant thought that the confusion over Gilbertese and Kosraen dynasties comes from garbling of the usage "Delawan," which some informants interpreted as "Tarawan," or inhabitant of the home atoll of the Gilbertese who were reputed to have landed on Pingelap. His own translation of the term is derived from two words, *dela* or "to come or go" and *wa* "canoe," and refers to any foreigner.

In view of the much stronger cultural and linguistic ties with Pohnpei than with either Kosrae or the Gilberts (Morton et al. 1973: 322) it appears more likely that settlement came from the former high island. On the other hand, Morton notes that "genealogies suggest that Pingelap has been occupied for at least 25 generations, and perhaps longer than 1 000 years. This would give sufficient time for a succession of typhoons, famines, and immigration" (Morton et al. 1972a: 360). While the oral history of the atoll notes only two typhoons of the magnitude to have resulted in depopulation, it appears on the basis of our knowledge of their occurrences in recent years that such disasters must have been much more frequent. In the present century the typhoons of 1905, 1957, and 1972 have been described as being so severe that without outside supplies starvation would have been rife.[3] It seems conceivable then, as suggested by Morton, and agreed to by my chief informant, that Pingelap has been repeatedly completely or nearly completely depopulated and resettled. Such being the likelihood it is also conceivable that earlier occupations may have come from islands other than Pohnpei. If this is the case, however, it seems clear that whenever the most recent resettlement occurred, it must have emanated from Pohnpei, for influences from that direction clearly predominate. Another possibility is suggested by the history of the atoll, since the disaster of the 1770s, from which time recovery of the population from a small survivor group has been accomplished almost entirely from internal growth.

The Great Typhoon and Its Aftermath

The first reasonably well pinpointed occurrence in the history of Pingelap was this typhoon, which Weckler (1949: 42) has taken great pains to date. It seems clear that his description for Mwaekil relates to a contemporaneous event on Pingelap between about 1770 and 1780. Apart from the story of the founding of the taro patch, another event or series of events which has relevance to my central interest here in land tenure is attributed to the period just before this typhoon, variously called Lengkieki or Lenglapalap. Again, there is more than one version. In the version given by Hurd (1977: 35) a reapportionment of land is attributed to the last *nahnmariki* who preceded the 1770s disaster, Semenuhwe. Prior to that time, land is said to have belonged to the *nahnmariki* and everyone worked it, and the taro patch as well, without any ownership boundaries existing in either the patch or on the land. Semenuhwe instructed men to work only in those areas which they now owned. According to this version that chief also laid the basis for land to be transmitted patrilineally from father to son, rather than through the *keinek*(s) or "patrilineages" which serve to transmit the political titles.

I have gotten two separate variations from my own informants regarding shifts in land tenure practices. One informant sees the land as having been owned by "about 20 nobles" and then being redivided by Semenuhwe into plots for all men of the atoll. But there was some contradiction in this testimony regarding the sequence of chiefs which makes this account somewhat suspect. The account of my main informant differs from either of the two preceding statements. In this version the land of the islands of the atoll were first owned by the paramount chief, but that of the taro patch had been previously divided into its major sections. The system of land use in force was called *keliek* and comprised an essentially shifting horticultural and arboricultural arrangement. Three main areas were designated, as follows: (1) Maseirung, or the main part of the principal island; (2) Liken Epin, or the long peninsula that extends from it; (3) the other two islands, Daekae and Sukoru. At any one time one of these sections was being planted, a second was being cleared of weeds, and the third harvested. This system applied to coconuts and dry taro. Not included were pandanus and breadfruit, in which cases one would ask the *nahnmariki* for permission to use the fruit of those trees. According to this version, under Semenuhwe the land was redivided and assigned to individual men. My main informant insists that there was no intermediate division into *keinek* lands, but titled persons got first choices in the division and, ostensibly, got larger shares. At the same time there was for a period a general association between *keinek*(s) and major divisions of the land, the *lepinsapw*(s). For instance, the major *keinek* with which my informant identifies was given two entire *lepinsapw*(s) and part of another. If there is merit to this account, my interpretation is that men of the same *keinek* may have been given adjoining plots. My chief informant also stated that the division of the taro patch into its major sections, *maekah*(s), for each recognized *keinek* came in the time of the paramount chief, Naniok, who is listed by Morton et al. (1973: 320) as being the eighth *nahnmariki* (Semenuhwe being the seventeenth). Morton et al. (1973: 324) have suggested a likely redivision of lands after the disastrous typhoon of the 1770s, but my main informant told me that in the absence of deceased landowners the land and taro rows reverted to relatives within each *keinek*. This interpretation somewhat contradicts his other statements regarding the role of the *keinek* in land tenure.

I shall return later to the question of the relative merits of these various versions of the evolution of the Pingelapese land tenure system. It might be worth mentioning at this point that the reason given by my chief informant for the distribution of land into individual plots by Semenuhwe is that the communal system of labour did not work well, since not everyone did his share. The revised ownership plan was instituted with the expectation that, if men worked their property and became reliant on their own labour for food, shirking would cease. It is difficult to know whether this interpretation is influenced by Protestant ideals of self and of individual achievement and may reflect contact-inspired expectations, or whether it was indeed a genuine product of traditional Pingelapese thinking.

Thirty people are said to have survived the period of starvation that followed the typhoon of the 1770s. Since that same figure is applied to the survivors of the earlier catastrophe which is mentioned in the oral history, it may represent a mythical number. Morton et al. (1972b: 278) suggest that on the basis of the nineteenth-century recovery rate, the number was probably somewhat higher in the case of the 1770s typhoon. The genealogies show gaps during the first 50 years after this major disaster so that it is difficult to arrive at an exact figure, but it may have been a very small number, given the fecundity of the post-typhoon population, especially that of some of the polygynous paramount chiefs. For example Mwanenised, the second post-typhoon paramount chief had 10 children, an accomplishment which earned him the posthumous name of "Backbone of Pingelap" (Morton et al. 1972b: 279).

European contact was established within two generations after the great typhoon. With regard to actual European discovery of the atoll, there is uncertainty. Hurd (1977: 13) thinks that the first actual sighting may have been as early as 1527 with deSaavedra's search for the members of the Magellan company on his return from the Mollucas to Mexico. Certainly, it is probably true that during the latter part of the sixteenth century a sighting could have occurred when the station at Guam was incorporated into the return galleon route from Acapulco to Manila (Hezel 1983: 32; Hurd 1977: 14).

The Nineteenth Century

Whether or not Pingelap had been among the atolls sighted during the early Spanish penetration of the western Pacific, there is more substantial evidence to assign sighting, if not discovery, to Musgrave in 1793 (Eilers 1934: 409; Hurd 1977: 14) and the atoll was named McAskill after the next captain who sighted Pingelap in 1809 (Eilers 1934: 400). First actual contact with the Pingelapese that is recorded occurred during Duperrey's visit in 1824 though it does not appear that any of the party went ashore. From that date onward there are available dual accounts of the history of Pingelap: a continuing oral history, and records of ships who visited the atoll. In this regard it is interesting to note that there is very little mention of European contacts or residences in the oral history until the very end of the period of whaler trading-ship contacts and immediately before the establishment of a mission on Pingelap in 1873 (Morton et al. 1973: 327).

Undoubtedly, the most significant Pingelapese figure and the one who is featured in greatest detail in the oral history of the atoll is Okonomwaun, born probably just before the beginning of the nineteenth century; whose reign as *nahnmariki*, estimated by Morton et al. (ibid.: 321) as 1822-70, spanned the period of early contact. He appears to represent a picture of the most complete autocrat depicted in the oral history of the atoll. While it seems clear that the man possessed unusual human qualities, it is thought that his supernatural gifts were even more responsible for the power that he held. This power appears to have shown its first impact when the rightful heir to the title of paramount chief was passed over in Okonomwaun's favour because of convincing the people of Pingelap that the spirit of Isoahpahu was personified in him. This spirit existed first in the form of a human who bore that name. The earth is said to have shaken at his death. He reappeared in spirit form to inhabit the bodies of a number of prominent Pingelapese through the years, including that of Okonomwaun. Hurd (1977: 60) writes of him as representing "a rationalization of dissonant behaviour" and, indeed, in the case of Okonomwaun's possession he was able to "attract and impregnate as many women as he chose" with impunity because it was thought to be the spirit, not Okonomwaun, who was so acting. That chief was believed as well to have had the power to heal vested in him by his god and is said to have received gifts of land for healing acts and for otherwise influencing the spirit of Isoahpahu.

While in a later chapter I shall try to demonstrate that chiefly status did not always imply large land holdings, the paramount chief (*nahnmariki*) always seemed to have had substantial holdings, some of which may have been due to such accretions as those attributed to Okonomwaun. Another aspect of land tenure that will be examined later is the assertion by Pingelapese oral historians that it was during this time that grants of land were first given to women as dowries.

Two noteworthy episodes are referred to in the oral history of the reign of Okonomwaun. It is said that a seven-year famine occurred, though we are given no reason for this. While no typhoon of catastrophic proportions is reported in the legendary history for this period, it is possible that a prolonged drought could have been the cause of food shortages, as might have been the case if the generalized Pacific drought of 1983 had continued, but no such occurrence is remembered by my informants. This period of famine must not have been too severe, since the population of the atoll continued to expand throughout the nineteenth century.

The other event of note, and one which is strongly supported by historical researchers, was the visit of Marshallese about 1856 (Eilers 1934: 415; Morton et al. 1973c: 321; Hezel 1983: 222; Riesenberg 1965: 155, 161, 163). A large party from Ebon atoll was blown off course en route to Jaluit and reached Pingelap, spending about three months living on Sukoru during that time. A fight is said to have broken out, but eventually the Marshallese left. There are a couple of accounts which detail this episode, but the novelist Becke (1894) in his *Ninia* developed these accounts into a fictional tale, some details of which were unfortunately accepted as fact by Eilers (1934: 415) who is our chief source for the early history of Pingelap. While this visit of Marshallese is supposed to have resulted from an accidental off course, there is an account related in Weckler (1949: 68) of "a combination exploring plundering expedition from Kwajalein to attack the island of Pingelap." This visit is variously dated at 1820-25 or much later in the century (Riesenberg 1965: 161,163).

About two years before the end of Okonomwaun's reign missionaries tried to establish themselves on the atoll, but perhaps due to the influence of freebooter Bully Hayes, the chief forbade their activities. The reign of his successor, beginning in 1870, marks the advent of missionization, for by 1873 the American Board of Commissioners for Foreign Missions (ABCFM) had established themselves on Pingelap (Morton et al. 1973: 327).

The account of Pingelapese history which parallels and supplements, rather than duplicates, the events throughout most of the nineteenth century is drawn from the logs of ships who visited the atoll. Hurd (1977: 11-36) has summarized this material, much of which is also well represented in Eilers (1934: 409-21) whose account stems from the researches of the Thilenius Expedition which under Krämer visited the atoll in 1910.

The European accounts of Pingelap begin with that of Lesson (ibid.: 410-12) who described Duperrey's visit of 1824. The natives showed no fear in their encounter with the French and that fact, together with their obvious appreciation of iron objects, may indicate that this ship was not the first visitor. If that was the case such earlier encounters must have been friendly in nature. This easy commerce did not characterize relations between the Pingelapese and ships which visited the island subsequently. In view of Duperrey's report of initial great friendliness, and because of the widespread practice of blackbirding and commandeering women by whalers throughout the Pacific, it is most probable that the cases of violence which followed that first recorded visit were brought on by abuses inflicted by the European visitors.

Lesson's account (ibid.) of the 1824 visit describes the heavy vegetation covering the islands of the atoll and houses visible here and there from the sea which were said to have been in poor repair. The Pingelapese who came aboard were fearless and friendly, and brought gifts of taro, mature coconuts, and a particularly sweet variety of bananas. They highly prized iron tools given in return for the food gifts. The men who visited the ship bore axes made of shell or coral. The French visitors were especially impressed with the finely shaped canoes which, though they had neither masts nor sail, were large enough to carry seven or eight people. The Pingelapese themselves were described as being of "reasonable stoutness" though some were "buried in thick layers of fat" (ibid.: 41). They were also described as being light in complexion, resembling Japanese in their features, and with the men having only light facial growth. The people showed a fondness for decorating themselves with flowers. Lesson provides a vocabulary of nine Pingelapese words which describe parts of a ship (ibid.: 4), another indication that Duperrey was probably not the first European to visit the atoll.

We get very little in the way of description of the atoll or its inhabitants in the next reference to Pingelap, the visit of the *Nimrod* in 1832, when the master and a passenger were killed and three officers wounded as they went ashore "to obtain produce" (Hurd 1977: 16). Five natives were also reported killed in the skirmish. The next account is that of Hammet, who visited the atoll in 1853. It is clear from the latter's description that the landing area and the village were located then, as now, along the leeward shore of the largest of the three islands of the atoll. The sailors heard that fowl were numerous and they secured about a dozen of them as well as some coconuts. Hammet also reported that rain was the only source of water on the atoll. The natives were extremely wary of the firearms of the sailors. Hammet and his men had heard of the murder of a Captain Lewis (ibid.: 18-19), 18 months before, and Hammet assumed that the incident had to do with the Pingelapese coveting the ship's boat which brought the sailors ashore. Another version of motives has it that the murders occurred due to the prolonged absence from the island of two beachcombers as well as natives, when they visited the ship. These men had been presumed killed (ibid.: 15-16).

The presence of white residents on the atoll and Hammet's report that some broken English was spoken by the natives begs examination of the possible role of beachcombers in Pingelap history. Hurd (ibid.: 16) cites an early source which reported "two runaway sailors on Ponape" about 1828, and "between 1833 and 1840 some forty-seven American and English whalers and other vessels visited there, probably plying past Pingelap on their runs to and from the whaling line." Captain White of the *Nimrod* rescued no fewer than *nine* whites from the atoll in 1832 after the fight described above, according to his report (ibid.: 12; Hezel 1983: 112). It is, of course, almost impossible to judge the effects of either the visits of ships or the residences of beachcombers on the local culture, but it is perhaps significant that the legendary history is devoid of mention of white contacts during this same era. This omission is notable in that accounts of other conditions and happenings during the nineteenth century are given in fairly complete detail, albeit laced with supernatural ingredients.

The visit of Hammet in 1853 also provides the first population estimate of 400-500 for the atoll.[4] This range would represent an annual increase of about three percent a year following the typhoon of the 1770s, if one assumes a surviving population of about 40, a figure which is roughly in keeping with information gleaned from genealogies. Beyond this estimate there are only a few fragments of ethnographic information that can be derived from the accounts of this period. Ship captains were interested mainly in weather conditions, landing conditions, physical descriptions of the natives, and items of trade. The reputation that Pingelap had acquired for being notorious as the scene of murders undoubtedly accounts for the paucity of accounts for the early and middle years of the nineteenth century, but Hezel (ibid.: 140) notes that "by the late fifties however, all this had changed, and Pingelap along with Mokil and Ngatik, became a regular stop for whaleships."

The next account comes from Captain Moore (Eilers 1934: 414) of the mission vessel "Morning Star" (first of a number of mission vessels which bore that name) in 1857, though missionaries appear to have visited the atoll the year before as well (Hezel 1983: 151). This account describes the paramount chief, Okonomwaun, who is depicted as being about sixty years of age and "exceedingly voluble." He offered fruit, chickens, and pigs in exchange for hatchets, tobacco, and files. One of the missionaries, Mr. Doane, was able to communicate in the Pohnpeian language. Most interesting in view of the chief's later resistance, was the desire to have a missionary come to the island. Okonomwaun promised land to any missionary of that profession who would settle there (Eilers 1934: 414).

Although Moore's account does not mention white residents on the atoll, it was about this time that two whites entered the scene. One, a Portuguese named Perez, was said to have acted as middleman in trade, which at this period dealt in the local products of fruit, pigs, chickens, and especially the trepang (*bêche-de-mer*), which was so highly valued in China. Perez fled the atoll by swimming to a passing ship after having been accused of cheating the natives. A second individual, John Higgins, who is more famous for a five-year stay on Mwaekil (Weckler 1949: 76), came to the island shortly afterwards and apparently served in the same capacity as Perez. He was reportedly killed by a Pingelapese, also having been considered a cheater in his dealings.

In contrast to the situation on Mwaekil (ibid.: 71-80), the beachcombers on Pingelap appear to have had little influence in political life there. More influential was the notorious freebooter, Bully Hayes, who is remembered with some warmth by the oral historians of Pingelap. It appears that several years before the death of Okonomwaun Hayes persuaded the chief to sign a 10-year agreement to exclude missionaries from Pingelap (Lubbock 1931: 248-52) and that in 1868, and again in 1871, attempts to establish a mission there had been repulsed. Shortly thereafter another violent incident occurred, the last to be reported. While crew members were trading for food, several young men swam to the ship and were attacked, with one being hacked to death and the others badly wounded (Hezel 1983: 237). Hayes had left his trader Restieaux on Pingelap in 1871,[5] who established very good relations with the people. Not only did he, for instance, dress the wounds of the boys mentioned above, but he is also credited with warning the people to avoid blackbirding ships that called during his ten-month stay on the atoll. Restieaux was provided with food and with a native "wife," while refusing the gift of two adolescent girls (ibid.: 250). The next trader placed on the island by Hayes, Sam Biggs, described as "a weak-kneed, gin drinking Cockney," incurred the wrath of both the Pingelapese and Hayes himself (Lubbock 1931: 248-49). The latter was particularly incensed when he returned to the atoll in 1873 to find that Biggs had been unable to forestall the establishment of the ABCFM mission. Okonomwaun'successor, Ierininger, had allowed two Pohnpeians trained by the church to begin activities.

Morton et al. (1973a: 329) have described the captivity of the chief by Hayes, who demanded a ransom from the Pingelapese of two girls and 7 000 coconuts, later reduced to one girl and 5 000 of the nuts, but neither this incident, if it happened, nor the thrashing of his trader by the freebooter, is part of Pingelapese oral history.

Hayes's biographer, Lubbock (1931: 244), quotes him regarding a typhoon which is attributed to a time some years previous to Hayes's 1873 visit, as follows:

> [Y]ears ago when the hurricane came and destroyed their houses and plantations—when their little ones were crying with hunger—that brought them to his ship and [he] fed them. Have they forgotten who it was that carried them to Ponape and there let them live on his land and fed them on his food until they grew tired of the strange land, and then brought them back to their homes again? Did not the men of Pingelap say then that no man should be more to them than him?

Apparently this speech to the atoll dwellers had an immediate effect, for afterwards even the two missionaries joined in the wild dancing which ensued. It is noteworthy that neither this reputed typhoon nor the removal to Pohnpei is part of the remembered history of the atoll. If indeed such an occurrence did take place at about this time, the typhoon could not have resulted in any marked depopulation, for the numbers on the atoll continued to grow steadily during the latter half of the nineteenth century. It does seem likely, on the basis of the frequency of typhoons in the present century, that there must have been others during the post-1770 period. They could not have been of the magnitude of either that great disaster nor that of the major twentieth-century storms, or they certainly would have left their impact on the legendary history of Pingelap as well as restricting population expansion.

However inaccurate the above account may be, the eventual triumph of puritanical Christianity over the loose ways of the traders and such occasional visitors as Hayes was established, at least on the surface, during the 1870s. The missionary Doane reports in 1874 as follows:

> Good news comes from Pingelap. Hayes of infamous notoriety called there a few days since—on the Sabbath—and as the boat went ashore not one called to visit it—but passed by on the other side of the church—God can draw where a boat crew can't. And, yes, but recently the reverse would have been the case, as a boat is usually to these islanders on its arrival a great event. Lots to see and trade. But the Pingelapese cared less for trade that day than to hear the story of the cross. And yet, perhaps I am putting this too strongly (Hurd 1977: 25).

Perhaps he was. We do not know the source of Doane's information, and one wonders as to its strict accuracy. In another letter that year Doane displays what must be considered an un-Christian competitiveness with the supposedly evil influence of the copra trade. After recounting a report from the atoll which indicated that on the visit of a ship there were no coconuts to sell, he rejoiced as follows:

> Revenge is sweet—you know 'tis said. Well I do feel like clapping a little when one of these beachcombers and wicked sailors of high sea robbery—the natives of the island can themselves come down and meet with the spirit and implements of Christ's welfare—I like such revenge as that (ibid.: 26).

But the trade in coconut oil or copra did flourish when resident traders lived on the island. Unfortunately, their accounts, in the few lines that are available, suffer in the extreme from exaggeration, as for instance, that of Westbrook (Dana 1935), who claims to have lived for a year on the atoll about 1875. This source describes the chief as being 6′4″ tall and carrying a pouch of tobacco in one ear lobe and his clay pipe in the other. He also gives 1 500 as the population of Pingelap and reports, among other exaggerations, that the "king" (paramount chief) had 20 wives. The accounts of the missionaries who visited the island in the late nineteenth century were too preoccupied with the details of conversion and "civilizing" the natives to note much about their culture. Between these two sets of scanty data we do get a picture of intense competition. In the end both Christianity and the copra trade were served and they eventually became the two greatest forces in acculturation.

From the legendary history for the early period of mission activity there are accounts of the struggles between the Christian God and the pagan gods, especially with Isoahpahu, who it is said, was eventually exiled (Hurd 1977: 213). Conversion of Iengiringit, the successor to Okonomwaun in 1870, came about with a faith-healing episode, and soon afterwards the ABCFM triumphed with mass conversion of the population.

The advent of the coconut oil-copra trade, virtually simultaneously with the coming of the cross, deserves special attention in this study of Pingelapese land tenure. In the case of the neighbouring atoll, Mwaekil, Weckler (1949: 86) thought that the practice of dividing the land on that atoll into multiple plots stemmed from the inception of the copra trade due to the greater importance being placed on the coconut palm than had been the case formerly. Having this information at my disposal before coming to Pingelap, I expected to find the same historical assocation. But in exploring land tenure histories, I was able to determine that division of the land area of Pingelap predated the copra trade by a good many years.

The disappointment which the researcher finds in the accounts of this period does not preclude appearance of a few pieces of information which help shed light on this crucial phase of Pingelapese history. A church was built about 1881 and a school was established shortly thereafter (Hurd 1977: 22), and mission reports tell how the people continued to embrace Christianity. Significant is mention of another typhoon in 1885 by Doane (ibid.: 23-24). There is little information regarding this incident, and since the peak populations occurred perhaps a decade later, it must be assumed that little or no loss of life resulted. There is no mention of outside aid being offered, and recovery must have been rapid and managed internally.

While Spanish ships probably discovered most of the islands of the Carolines during the sixteenth and seventeenth centuries, Spain began to show an interest in the eastern Carolines only after the Germans under the Capelle Gesellschaft established a copra trade which operated out of the Marshalls. The Spanish acceded to the German takeover of the Marshalls, which was achieved in 1885 through the use of warships, but won the case for the Carolines which had been submitted to Pope Leo XIII for arbitration (Fischer and Fischer 1957: 36-37).

The Spanish period (1885-99) was a difficult time for the Protestant missions in the area, and indeed, their chief missionary, Doane, was actually arrested and deported for a time (ibid.: 37). During that period ties with

Pohnpei which had flourished in the period after 1870 were less intense due to the decline of ABCFM operations. But there is no record of any attempt by Catholic missionaries to convert the Pingelapese to their faith in either the legendary history or in the documents to which I have had access. It was well within the Spanish period when the gunboat *Quiros* visited the atoll in 1895, apparently to establish sovereignty. The account of this visit given by Moya as cited by Eilers (1934: 418-20) allows a brief glimpse of the Pingelap of that period.

A description of the landing area, the reef, and the location of the village on the west shore of the largest of the three islands confirms earlier reports. We learn that the paramount chief's house was built largely of wood while the others were made of "cane," with all dwellings having thatch roofs. This report states that there were about 300 dwellings and 100 canoe houses and the population was estimated at 1 000. These figures do not quite jibe, as this would mean only about three persons per dwelling place. It seems, rather that, if the total population figure was accurate, cooking houses may have been counted as dwellings, if indeed any actual count was made. A visit was made to the school, which was attended by about 200 students. The only book mentioned was the Protestant Bible translated into "Kanaka" (Pohnpeian). While most of the men are said to have worn European suits at times, they usually went about in loin clouts of native materials while the women wore skirts. We have a description of the "king" as tall, and corpulent, dressed in European clothes except for being bare footed, and having pierced ears in which he carried flowers (ibid.: 420).

A letter from the paramount chief addressed to the Spanish governor in Pohnpei is quoted (both in Spanish and German) by Eilers from this account. The chief begins by telling him what obedient and well behaved people there are on the atoll, principally because they follow his (the chief's) dictates. He ends the letter by requesting gifts of a boat valued at 50 dollars, a sack of flour, and a bottle of wine (ibid.: 420-21). In view of the strong stand against alcoholic beverages taken by the Protestant missionaries in the area, the last item requested is quite remarkable.

Another brief account of this period comes from the traveller and popular writer, F. W. Christian (1899: 46-50). Christian's account (from 1896) is somewhat coloured by his notions of native mentality and his theories of far-flung Asiatic relationships in language and culture. There appears to have been no resident trader on the island at that time and European goods were especially sought after. Christian (ibid.: 147) describes the natives as employing "coaxing, pleading, wheedling accents, wherewith the native so often reaches the soft spot in the white trader's heart." He refers to Tomas, the Pohnpeian teacher and describes a conversation with the reigning *nahnmariki*. On his sojourn ashore he notes an abundance of taro, large breadfruit trees, bananas, pigs, fowls, and arrowroot, and the healthy appearance of the children. He says that "a little over 1000 lived on the atoll" (ibid.: 51), but it is difficult to know the basis of his estimate. A hat and mat industry is mentioned, as well as a huge feast being laid before the visitors (ibid.: 149).

The next report of the atoll comes from the renowned scientist, Alexander Agassiz, who visited Pingelap in 1899 and who gave a good description of the physical appearance of the atoll. Agassiz's remarks on the crowded conditions on the atoll again gives the figure of 1 000 inhabitants (Eilers 1934: 420-21).

Thus, three estimates in the period 1895-99 gave the same number of inhabitants (1 000), though the origin of this figure is not clear. It is possible that Christian and Agassiz may have relied on the earlier estimate by Moya. Such a number as 1 000 appears to be consistent with a levelling of the population for the period spanning the end of the nineteenth century and the beginning of the twentieth, and would imply an annual increase of about 2 percent after the visit of Captain Moore in 1853, if the estimate of 400 to 500 based on that source is reasonably accurate. Agassiz (ibid.: 421) reports that the last ship called at the atoll eight months earlier, an observation which supports my view that the Spanish period was one of decreased contacts.

There are two population estimates given for the first decade of the twentieth century which imply contradiction. Eilers (ibid.: 424) cites the figure of "870 from the data of the Reichsmarine authority" for the period before the "dreadful typhoon of 20 April 1905." She (ibid.) also refers to an estimate of Findlay of 900 for 1908. The former figure, at least, must be doubted since Eilers (ibid.: 425) also states that 70 people died from beriberi after the storm and that 67 emigrated shortly afterwards to Saipan. If Findlay's figure is approximately correct this would mean a population somewhat over 1 000 for the period immediately preceding the typhoon of 1905, which estimate jibes well with the figure given above for the last years of the nineteenth century.

The German Period

It is the account (ibid.) of the Thilenius expedition[6] visit to Pingelap under the leadership of Krämer in 1910 which provides our next picture of that atoll. The first part of the report comprises an annotated summary of reports of earlier visitors to the atoll which I have already drawn upon. The remainder describes the material culture, including houses, canoes, clothing, and basketry; tattooing, the effects of contact; character of the people; etc. It also provides a partial census and correctly identifies the four clans represented on Pingelap. This compilation, together with other writings by N. E. Morton and his colleagues (Morton et al. 1971; Morton et al. 1972a, 1972b; Morton and Greene 1972; Morton 1972; Morton and Yammamoto 1973; Morton and Lalouel 1973), while focusing on physical anthropology, also provide demographic, historical, and linguistic information. Among the contributions of Morton and associates is a review of contacts with other Micronesians (Morton et al. 1973: 326-30). This survey includes legendary accounts of precontact as well as nineteenth-century voyaging, of which some of the latter have both documentary and oral traditional accounts. While this compilation is impressive, it does not give a picture of the sort of intentional and regularized inter-island communication as found in the Western Carolines (Alkire 1965; 1978). Elsewhere I (Damas 1979: 192) have attributed the decline in matrilineal emphasis on Pingelap to the failure of the clan system to establish or maintain its role as a basis for communication among the atolls and islands of the Eastern Carolines, as is the case further west. At least part of the reason for the irregularity of inter-island contacts in the eastern part of the archipelago may be found in the following quotation from Morton (Morton et al. 1973: 318, 322).

> In the centuries after the islands of Ponape District were colonized from the West, there was a marked decline in navigational skill, especially on the high islands of Kusaie and Ponape, where the seagoing outrigger canoe was gradually modified into a shallow-draft vessel suitable for the sheltered waters of the reef. Loss of navigational skills in high islands probably accounts for the infrequent mention of Ponape in the ethnohistory, when all other evidence indicates the closest ties to Pingelap.

I might add that there is very little evidence of long-range intentional voyaging emanating from Pingelap itself in the oral history of the atoll or in the documented post-contact history.

The material provided by Eilers (1934) from the Thilenius expedition and by Morton and his associates has been of inestimable value to my own work. With regard to my own interests, I have tried to focus on aspects of culture and society that have had minimal treatment by the above sources. Returning to my original project, that of studying double descent on the atoll, I (Damas 1979, 1981) have described the *sou* as the matrilineal clan which today serves only to regulate marriage, though in the past may have been also a feuding unit. The *keinek* has been the subject of discussion and debate (Damas 1979; Schneider 1980; Damas 1981). My understanding of the structure of the *keinek* is that it has a patrilineal core similar to a classic patrilineage but that membership can be achieved in the case of women through marriage, and in the case of members of either sex, through adoption. The *keinek* channels succession to titles and, as suggested in the previous discussion, may have been formerly involved in land tenure. Building on my study of the *keinek*, I have examined the process of title succession through using actual genealogies going back to the time of the great typhoon of the 1770s and putative genealogies for earlier periods (Damas 1983a). A study of adoption practices on Pingelap (Damas 1983b) also grew out of my study of these genealogies. My conclusion was that although much of the adoption on Pingelap can be understood in demographic terms, the claims of kinship are also crucial in shifting children from one nuclear family to another. Residential practices on Pingelap were the subject of another study (Damas 1986) in which I tried to show the operation of a principle of virilocality, which, however, was much affected by emigration and cyclic demographic factors. Another study was devoted to the impact of the emergence of the Compact of Free Association (Damas 1985) where I point out that the Pingelapese of the 1980s sought to maintain and to enhance ties with the United States. Exploration of problems of descent, of adoption, and of residential practices through their relationship to genealogies brought me face to face with questions of land tenure. Later chapters will deal in detail with how these studies are all intimately involved in land inheritance, ownership, and use.

Apart from Eilers's account, other glimpses of life during the German period come from one informant who was born in 1898, which are partly from remembrances of his youth and partly information he got from now-deceased elders. From his testimony it appears that a trading vessel visited the atoll at intervals varying from three to six months, indicating that trade that had been irregular earlier was now regularized. My informant also reported that nominal taxes were paid the Germans and that there were no medical services. There were no normal grades for students, but children would attend school for about four years, and the subjects taught were German, arithmetic, and reading. The *nahnmariki* was allowed the power of enforcing native customary law. According to Morton et al. (1973: 327) export labour was instituted in 1907. My informant stated that men signed for service in the phosphate mines of Nauru for terms of three years, which terms could be renewed. This informant said that he had himself worked on Nauru for the period 1914-23, where there were "about 5 000 Chinese and 1 000 Micronesians" in residence. With regard to the typhoon of 1905, my informant indicated that contrasting to the level of aid given typhoon relief during the American period, the Germans provided only "some rice and biscuits." This order of dietary supply would be consistent with the occurrence of beriberi as reported by Eilers. My informant thought that these supplies were inadequate, and he related emigration directly to food shortages in the aftermath of the storm. There was a store which sold essentially the same goods as today, with some exceptions, but in much smaller quantities.

The accounts of German residence on the atoll are somewhat conflicting among the sources. Morton et al. (ibid.: 321) report that a German named Perman had a family on Pingelap. The name Hammond is also mentioned by a chief informant as being that of a trader who came from Kosrae but left after a year, having found trading on Pingelap unprofitable. There may be confusion between the names. Perman and Hammond may have been the same person. Only the name of Perman appears in genealogies. Hammond is described alternately as being a teacher or a trader.

The story of the relocation of people from Pingelap in connection with the famine following the 1905 typhoon will be treated later. A second migration to Sokehs Island near Pohnpei in 1911-12 was another event of import during the German period. It is generally felt by my informants that this further emigration can be attributed to the availability of space on Sokehs Island after the removal of natives engaged in the Sokehs Rebellion,[7] and to overcrowding on the atoll itself. I will examine the events surrounding this latter relocation in a later chapter.

Returning to the practice of employing Micronesians, including Pingelapese, in the phosphate mines of Nauru, it is evident that large numbers of the men were absent for considerable periods while they were engaged in this employ. Stewart Firth (1978: 50) cites correspondence between officials of the Deutsche Südsee-Phosphate Company indicating that, in 1913, there had been recruited no less than 72 labourers from Pingelap atoll. It is interesting to note that an original policy of restricting labour recruitment to 16 percent of the working population of any given island was being flagrantly violated (ibid.: 49). Sixteen percent of the male labour force on Pingelap at that time would have been about 26 men. If the above-cited figure for Pingelapese labour on Nauru is to be relied upon, it must suggest that a considerable economic strain must have been put on the men and women who remained on the island. Stewart Firth (ibid.: 50-51) states that after the Allied takeover of Germany's Pacific possessions in 1914 the Australian administration of the Nauru phosphate industry employed only Chinese and New Guineans. But this information is contradicted by the direct evidence of my informant from that period and by indirect information from descendants of others who worked on Nauru until sometime in the 1920s.

Hurd (1977: 31) mentions a nine-year contract (1911-20) with the German Liebenzeller mission, during which time Pingelapese sailed back and forth to Pohnpei to visit the mission there. However, there is no indication of any serious break in dogma or affiliation throughout the period from the first coming of the ABCFM missionaries until the present, so it is unlikely that many actual conversions to the German faith took place.

While strenuous and apparently largely successful efforts were made to alter the traditional land tenure system on Pohnpei, German land reforms appear to have had little impact on Pingelap. Apparently German officials visited the atoll and, observing that the local customs were close enough to the "normal" patrilineal emphasis they espoused, they decided not to interfere with local custom in this regard. On the other hand, the system of Seven Men was instituted. The Seven Men were a body of men selected by the Germans to settle land disputes informally so that they did not have to be taken to court.[8]

With the establishment of the colony on Sokehs Island, the immigrants became subject to the German laws, and two major aspects of the laws did affect elements of the Pingelapese populations, specifically those who emigrated to Sokehs at Pohnpei. These disallowed deviations from strictly patrilineal inheritance and the division of properties among various heirs. A later chapter will treat the attempts to put these strictures into practice at the Sokehs colony. Movement of people from the atoll could be seen as relieving overall pressures on land, though later discussion will show that the picture is uneven with regard to equity in ownership and use privileges on the atoll. The move to Sokehs also brought on a system of stewardship for absentee owners which will be seen to have introduced definite complications in the land tenure system of the Pingelapese.

The Japanese Period

Autonomy in internal political organization, religion, and largely for atoll inhabitants, in land tenure arrangements which had characterized earlier periods, continued throughout the next major period in Pingelapese contact history, the Japanese period of 1914-45. The Japanese wasted no time in moving into Micronesia when World War I began in August 1914, for they seized the islands by October of that year. Indeed, Purcell (1976: 190) notes that Japanese writers had cited the economic and immigration possibilities of the area since the 1870s, and Japanese traders had been established throughout much of Micronesia during the Spanish period, though there is no indication that their influence reached Pingelap during either the Spanish or German periods. Japanese eagerness to establish apparently long-dreamed-of hegemony in the area could be easily accomplished at this juncture in history, for Germany's island empire was poorly defended (ibid.: 189). By this time as well, the Japanese had developed clear-cut objectives regarding their interests in Micronesia, categorized as mining phosphates, management and acquisition of land and development of agriculture, ocean resources, and commerce (ibid.: 190; Peattie 1988: 121-22). The Japanese period in Micronesia can be divided into three chief phases: the period of military administration during World War I, the period between the wars, beginning under their League of Nations Mandate, and the World War II phase.

During the first phase there was little impact on such outpost islands as Pingelap. The German Liebenzeller missionaries continued to operate out of Pohnpei, but were replaced by Japanese protestants in 1920 (Fischer and Fischer 1957: 60). Immigrant labour continued on Nauru, though now managed by the Australians. The copra trade was taken over, with ships continuing to visit the island about three times a year.[9] We also know that by 1915 the South Seas Trading Company, operating under the Navy Ministry, had begun scheduled sailings between Japan and the islands (Purcell 1976: 208; Peattie 1988: 121-23). Resident Japanese traders begun to work on Pingelap during this first phase. Four traders are remembered by my informants, and with some warmth, though their individuality seems to fade in the memory of my informants. It is said that they treated the natives fairly in trade and in their social contacts as well.

On Pingelap, land use and inheritance continued along traditional lines, with, however, the stewardship which had its advent at the very end of the German period. In the area of internal political life there is little evidence of interference before World War II. Indeed, the Japanese accepted the legitimacy of the traditional title system by naming the reigning *nahnmariki* Island Magistrate sometime after 1924 (Morton et al. 1973a: 321). On the other hand, the role of traditional title holders was beginning to weaken by this time, for it was during the reign of Sapwenpar (1881-1924) that church elders were given larger shares in the food-distribution events (Hurd 1977: 64), a privilege formerly accorded only the title holders. The growth of the church in Pingelap politics was due to internal developments, since by this time all island church officials were native Pingelapese. Two Japanese missionaries, Tamera and Asina, are remembered, both of whom are said to have visited the atoll for only short periods. They belonged to the Japanese Protestant Church, which was regarded as being allied to the ABCFM group out of Hawaii and none of my informants was aware of any doctrinal differences nor of any external religious pressures being brought to bear on the islanders, except for an apparent increased concern with adultery.

A tax of one yen a year (later increased to two yen) was assessed for each man. The copra ship offered passage to Pohnpei at about $2.00 U.S. a person, and it appears that during the Japanese period more or less regular movement between Pingelap and the high island was established, mainly with the colony on Sokehs Island. Five years of schooling were required from about age 8 to 14-15 (Yanaihara 1976: 23). The Japanese also instituted the practice of taking island chiefs to Japan, and the *nahnmariki* for the period 1924-64, as well as his son and successor visited the home islands. The latter was also trained in carpentry and used his skill widely in subsequent building operations on the atoll.

Export labour to Nauru appears to have ceased some time before 1930, but beginning at about that time a number of Pingelap men became involved in agricultural labour on Pohnpei under the Japanese. Later, when Japanese relations with the United States worsened, some of the labourers worked on military installations on that high island. The Japanese paid workers the equivalent of $0.75 a day from which they had to buy their own food. Yet these labourers were often able to return to the atoll with small savings. Recruitment for labour on Pohnpei differed from earlier work on Nauru in two important respects. Work was contracted for shorter periods, three months as compared to three years, and families often accompanied men going to Pohnpei.

Meanwhile on the atoll itself, there were certain results of the Japanese influence which could be felt into the 1980s. The *riaka* or two-wheeled hand-pulled cart, most useful in collecting coconuts and other produce, is said to have been introduced early in the Japanese period. The *zori*, or sandal which is gripped between the toes, also became established as the chief footwear. A number of new food items began to have roles in the diet. Among these were canned sardines, mackerel, and vegetables, but most important was rice, which became a highly prized food despite the already high starch content of the native diet. Such commodities as sugar, white flour, and coffee which are prominent on the shelves of Pingelap stores today were probably present before the Japanese period. While kerosene was available for use in lamps, there were no outboard motors or supplies of gasoline during those times.

Japanese excursions into crop experimentation were highly developed on islands with greater land area, but the only experiment attempted on Pingelap appears to have been a program of trying to prevent damage to breadfruit by rats through the use of poison. This procedure, unfortunately, caused the death of some of the larger trees on the atoll. The lack of large canoes in later years for use in deep sea fishing and in travel is said to have stemmed from this destruction of canoe-building material.

While the period of civilian Japanese contact is one of largely pleasant memories, the period of wartime military occupation recalls more negative ones, though some of the stories related to me undoubtedly exaggerate conditions, and accounts of this occupation on Pingelap are sometimes contradictory. My understanding of this period yields the following picture. One informant stated that seven Japanese arrived as early as 1939. These men appear to have been weather-reporting personnel. Another group arrived, probably in the summer of 1942, and estimates of the total number on the island then run as high as 35. These latter men were military personnel who built cement structures near the bottom of the main island. These structures included quarters and baths, ruins of which are still visible today. There was also a lookout tower which is said to have been raised above the level of the trees. The detachment built a road (actually a broad path) leading from the village to the south end of the island, passing close by the Japanese buildings. The supplies from surface ships, and later from submarines, were hauled from the unloading place opposite the Pingelapese village along that road. After American troops occupied key islands in the Marshalls in February 1944, a series of raids were launched on Truk and Pohnpei (Fischer and Fischer 1957: 63) from the newly won bases. On several occasions excess bombs were dropped on Pingelap by planes returning from such raids. The accounts of these raids have reached somewhat legendary proportions, and there are inconsistencies in the statements of informants when taken together. It is clear that the church was bombed out (St. John 1948). Craters can still be seen on the main island. Only one casualty is reported to have occurred among the Pingelapese.

The period from the beginning of the bombing in early 1944 to the end of the war, some 18 months later, was one of some hardship. The Japanese could no longer be supplied from the sea and took to growing their own crops which, according to informants, included beans, corn, potatoes, and onions. These crops were fertilized with human excrement, a practice deplored by the Pingelapese as was that of corporal punishment which is said to have been used on adults as well as children in school. After several unsuccessful attempts the Japanese were evacuated by submarine sometime in the summer of 1944. The village site was abandoned, or largely so, after the church had been bombed, and the islanders sought refuge on the long peninsula jutting northward from the main island, and on Daekae.

It is not clear as to when shipments of copra ceased to be sent from the island, but it was probably prior to 1944, at a time when American naval forces began to restrict shipping in the area. My information is that the last group of labourers sent to Pohnpei stayed there at least two years instead of the previously normal period of three months. It is not clear how many workers from the usual atoll population typically lived on Pohnpei. The first post-war account of a visit to Pingelap (St. John 1948: 97) mentions the return of 75 people at the end of World War II in 1945. It appears that these workers were usually counted in the censuses of the atoll by the Japanese, for the number of 190 Pingelapese residents on Pohnpei given for 1946 by Bascom (1965: 6) corresponds to the more permanent residents of the Sokehs colony, according to my own data. The censuses taken by the Japanese for the atoll are as follows: 1920-601; 1925-601; 1930-638; 1935-694, and for the first census in the American period taken in 1946, 639 (ibid.: 10). If 190 is, as I suspect, the typical number for the colony, then it can be seen that a stable total Pingelapese population of 800-900 was maintained throughout most of the Japanese period, a range which is, however, below the apparent peak of about 1 000 reported for the turn of the twentieth century. In another place, I (Damas 1983b: 6) have attributed this stagnation in numbers to the effects of introduced disease, more specifically to venereal diseases, which I think to be responsible for sterile matings. This position is supported by the report of Yanaihara (1976: 23) who states that on his visit to Pohnpei in 1940 natives there "think of gonorrhea as a disease inevitable for every human being, and called it the 'disease of men' or the 'disease of women.' " While venereal disease probably was frequent on Pingelap as well, and seems the most likely cause of limited births, a high death rate can be attributed to a variety of other introduced diseases. According to Yanaihara (ibid.: 249) tuberculosis caused 48.2 percent of deaths in Micronesia in 1931, but health measures had reduced that percentage to 19.8 percent by 1934. Amoebic dysentery and various intestinal parasites were also common to the native population during the Japanese period (Purcell 1976: 101-102).

St. John visited Pingelap atoll on December 27, 1945, and reported conditions of impoverishment. In referring to the return of the labourers to the atoll he observes "they returned in want of new clothing and goods to find their families and neighbours in similar need" (St. John 1948: 91). His photographs show that the natives of the atoll had been reduced to rags and scraps of European clothing. The interruption of the copra trade and, indeed, apparently almost all contact with the outside world including Pohnpei during the latter part of the war meant that the atoll experienced a period of reversion to a subsistence economy. For those left behind it was a period of deprivation from the trappings of a foreign economy, which had already for over half a century increased appetites for goods and services.

In summing up the influence of the Japanese, it is likely that on Pingelap, as in Micronesia as a whole, the copra industry grew considerably in the period between the two world wars. Purcell (1976: 203) reports that between 1922 and 1935 for the Mandate as a whole, copra production rose from 4 373 tons annually to 13 770. The Japanese are said to have forbade canoe or boat travel in Micronesia. Most or all travel between Pohnpei and Pingelap appears to have been accommodated by the copra carrying vessels. These vessels provided transportation not only for the short-term employment on the high island but also kept alive important contacts with the colony at Mwalok on Sokehs Island. Such contacts implied not only periodic renewal of kinship ties but also kept the colonists within the traditional political system of Pingelap and ultimately the purview of the paramount chief of the atoll. Two of the court of chiefs eventually took up residence and a third adopted shifting residence between these two centres of Pingelapese population to insure continuity and communication within the total political system. Implications of this contact, especially as it concerned land tenure practices, will be considered in later chapters.

Developments in the American Period

In turning to the American period of administration in Micronesia, the anthropologist who hopes to document happenings or to conduct field research in that area quickly realizes as I did, the great debt owed to preceding colleagues. Micronesia proved to be an excellent training ground in applied anthropology. Anthropologists served as producers of basic ethnographic information which was oriented toward providing recommendations for administrators, and some worked as administrators themselves. For the Eastern Carolines, in particular, I am especially grateful to be following after the work of Oliver, Bascom, Fischer, and Riesenberg who were employed there under government contract during the early years of American trusteeship. Bascom's report, though not published until 1965, became a government document in 1946 and was based on field work from April to August of that year, or dating from the first year of American occupation in Pohnpei. Some of his comments are relevant to the situation on Pingelap at that time. He (Bascom 1965: 118) writes of the mood of Pohnpeian disillusionment and even hostility toward the Japanese and their military occupation of Pohnpei and of the hopeful expectation for improved conditions under American administration, together with great forbearance shown for the lack of tangible improvement during that first year. With regard to the initial lack of progress "or even return to prewar conditions" which Bascom noted for Pohnpei, Pingelap felt the effects in several ways. I have remarked on the ragged condition of the atoll dwellers at the end of 1945 and, indeed, the flow of goods to the outer islands had not resumed one year later. Bascom (ibid.: 15) also indicates that while all Japanese currency had been collected from the outer islands in the district by the time of his visit, that currency had not been replaced by dollars. The same author (ibid.) reports a boat journey to Pohnpei made by Mwaekilese in order to collect the exchange currency. More important than the restitution of funds, which I understand was accomplished shortly after Bascom's departure, was the lag in establishing the copra trade which had been interrupted since some time before 1944. On Pohnpei this meant a return to a subsistence that which had not been followed since some time in the nineteenth century. For Pingelap it meant continuance of such an economy from wartime conditions.

Bascom's study of Pohnpei was part of a larger survey made during 1946 under the direction of Douglas Oliver (1971) and which submitted a number of recommendations to Washington. These dealt with housing, establishment of native-operated private businesses; education, with special emphasis on vocational training and training of native teachers; fishing programs; and agricultural development. It was recommended that four commissions be established, one for land questions, one for wages, a third for conservation, and a fourth to handle war claims (ibid.: 12-13). One of the recommendations that was to most strongly affect Pingelap was that of restoring and developing further the copra industry and the associated transportation services which had lapsed during World War II. With regard to the potential for agricultural development of atolls, Oliver's report was not optimistic since he found that they displayed "an exaggerated appearance of fertility and vegetative well-being" when they were favoured like Pingelap with ample rainfall, for Oliver felt that even under such conditions "possible improvement was definitely limited by soil and water deficiencies" (ibid.: 12).

It was recommended that the establishment of a land office and regulations regarding land tenure be handled with caution and, "native concepts about land tenure must be regarded with respect," with the "guiding principle to safeguard native rights." Especially germane to the Pingelap situation was the statement that "no attempt should be made to create uniformity of land tenure concepts in Micronesia for the sake of convenience on the part of the administrators" and that "communities should be encouraged to iron out difficulties among themselves." Where disputes cannot thus be settled, "administrators familiar with the local land-tenure concepts should act as arbiters, paying due respect to local traditions and equity" (ibid.).

Also pertinent to the problems of outer islands like Pingelap was communication, especially with regard to health and other emergencies. The recommendation was that while a long-term plan to install low-power radio stations should be entertained, it was not expected that such a plan would be put into effect immediately on all atolls. On the other hand, all of the outpost islands should be visited regularly "and their populations should be especially assisted to become more self-sufficient because of their greater isolation" (ibid.: 82). Writing in 1952, Oliver (ibid.: xii) rejoiced that it was a "rare and exhilarating experience" that many of these recommendations were being carried out, but this was to prove to be a somewhat optimistic appraisal of developments during the decade of the 1950s.

In the political realm, the U.S. Navy, which administered the Trust Territory from 1945 to 1951, was quick to encourage elective local government and very early the institution of an elected Ten Man Council was adopted in such places as Mwaekil (Weckler 1949: 29) to replace the lingering remains of a native title system. There is no evidence that such a body was instituted on Pingelap, however, with the title system continuing to exist. Later an elective system grew up side by side with this title system which gradually relinquished some of its political powers (Damas 1983a: 10-12; 1985).

With regard to recovery of commerce, the Island Trading Company (ITC) which had been operated by the navy and which had begun restoration of the copra trade was quickly replaced by the U.S. Commercial Company (USCC) in 1947. While the ITC had no profit-making plans, the USCC was aimed toward such an objective in its transportation and copra ventures (Fischer and Fischer 1957: 65).

Some remarks are in order regarding the period of Navy administration. Nevin (1977: 82) assesses the economic philosophy of the Navy as follows, "the islands cannot be expected to be self-supporting [and] are a liability and an inevitable drain on the public purse." In this respect it should be noted that for those Pingelapese who have remained on the atoll, expectations of improvements and benefits from whatever administrations which were in power have always been modest and tempered by a conception of the limited potential of their tiny universe. But one area which might have been more highly developed during the American period was that of commercial offshore fishing, an activity which has been in the hands of the Japanese since a brief period subsequent to the end of World War II (Nufer 1978: 117). Under both German and Japanese rule, Pingelapese, along with other Micronesians, were subject to small head taxes. In the eyes of the Navy such taxation was seen as "symbols of oppression" and thus not reinstituted (ibid.: 118).

One of the early programs implemented during the period of Navy administration was improved medical treatments. The use of penicillin and other antibiotics had especially dramatic effects on the health of Micronesians. In this regard the phenomenon of uneven but significant sterility (Damas 1983a) in the population of Pingelap quickly disappeared, due no doubt to the effects of penicillin treatment on venereal disease. Such treatment was to have a drastic effect on birth and death rates, resulting in a great expansion in numbers in the American period for a population which had remained virtually static for nearly half a century.

With the transferral of the Territory from the Navy to the U.S. Department of the Interior in 1951 there was little change in economic policy for a number of years. Indeed, the period 1951-61 has been referred to as that of the "Rust Territory" (Nufer 1978: 12) where policies are characterized by Nufer as "retrogressive" as compared to the Navy period (ibid.: 121). The annual total budget for the area was held at about $7 000 000 during that time, an amount which was regarded as less than that spent annually by the naval administration, though it is difficult to arrive at an estimate of Navy expenditures because of peculiarities of accounting (ibid.: 122).

By the beginning of the period of Department of Interior administration the copra trade was flourishing through its outlets in the United States. Nevin (1977: 82) reports that 12 000 tons of copra were marketed by a San Francisco firm in 1952, and that in 1955 a stabilization fund was established to "set aside income when the price was high in order to maintain payments of about $100 a ton to producers when the world price was low" (ibid.). This meant that harvesters of copra like the Pingelapese could expect to earn five dollars per 100-pound bag, at a minimum.

On the other hand, most observers of this period were critical of policy and pessimistic regarding improvement (cf. Fischer and Fischer 1957: 67). On Pingelap, culture change related to Americanization moved slowly but steadily during the 1950s. By that time the church had gained further dominance over the title system. Part of the decline in the traditional chiefly roles had to do with emigration of title bearers to the colony at Sokehs and to the frequent absences of others in their visiting that colony. Another factor leading to the weakening of the traditional title system was a reorganization of local politics and administration according to American models of democratic elections. Roles of several title holders were taken over by newly elected members of the community although in the beginning, through the force of tradition, title holders were themselves elected to these posts, and gradually, popularity rather than hereditary considerations began to dominate. All of these are now elected positions or appointments made through the Trust Territory administration.

Another change during the American period was the abandonment of the *katella*(s) or bachelor houses about 1955. One reason given for this sloughing off of an ancient institution was that since so many of the young men were already leaving the islands for long periods for education and employment, the houses were too poorly patronized to be kept in repair.

The most important event of the 1950s, aside perhaps from the disastrous typhoon of 1957, was establishment of a second Pingelapese colony on Pohnpei in the district of Mand, at one of the former Japanese plantation locales. While I will treat the planning and actual movement of people to that colony in 1954-55 in another chapter, it is appropriate to cite the report of Coulter (1957) who went to the atoll in 1954 in order to make known to the islanders plans for such relocation.

Coulter stayed on Pingelap for five days in July 1954 for the purpose of observing and enquiring about the perceived problem of overpopulation and to consult with the Pingelapese regarding the relocation plans. While his report suffers from certain ethnocentric evaluations and some inaccurate attempts to portray Pingelap as a "typical atoll," or presenting conditions there as typical for United States' possessions in the Pacific, it does reveal good powers of observation and provides us with the first documented glimpse of life on the atoll since that of the Thilenius expedition visit in 1910. It is also interesting to compare this description with that of 20 years later which I sketched in Chapter 1.

We learn that there is yet no radio on the atoll (ibid.: 323). The field trip vessel visited the island every two or three months, twice within five days, as she went to Kosrae after stopping at Mwaekil and Pingelap, and then returned to pick up copra en route to Pohnpei again. This compares to scheduled monthly visits for the 1970s and 1980s. By this time as well, almost all houses were framed structures with corrugated iron roofs. Apparently the cement block industry had not yet commenced. The iron roofs were used for catchment in outdoor cisterns, but Coulter (ibid.: 325) also reports scoring of coconut trees still being used as catchment basins, a practice not in evidence in 1975. Whaleboats as well as canoes were in general use. In fact, 14 of the former crafts met the field trip ship. Coulter (ibid.: 323) describes the diet and indicates that rice is valued above all food, as witnessed by the theft of his own 100-pound bag of that grain which was to extend his visit on the atoll (ibid.: viii). We have a description of copra preparation which indicates that it was still being largely sun dried with no mention of screens for fire drying. There is indication of a reliance on the copra trade for most outside derived commodities. We get vignettes of daily routine around the village and a fairly good description of the islands themselves, including the boundaries between land plots (ibid.: 329-31, 340-41). In keeping with his interest in the problem of overcrowding, Coulter provides information on the primary concern here, that of land tenure. The taro patch is described and Coulter makes an attempt to assess the extent of holdings of certain individuals in the taro patch as well as on the land, though his sample is very limited. He describes the character of disputes over boundary trees and plants, and mentions the problem of absentee ownership without referring directly to the colony on Sokehs Island (ibid.: 333). Planning for the relocation to Mand, however, was already well advanced in the summer of 1954 when Coulter visited Pingelap, and when implemented within the next year, made possible pioneering for the second time in the century.

Most of the commentators of this early American period criticized the slow rate at which education was introduced and what has been described as a "philosophy of restraint" (Nevin 1977: 85) based on the notion that education would awaken expectations beyond those which realities could provide. But Pingelapese had already become involved in off-island education in the 1950s. Indeed, my chief informant was the first to leave the island for schooling when he went to Pohnpei in 1946. Later, during the fifties, he went on to college in Hawaii and eventually received a B.A. degree from a mainland American college. His comments regarding the demise of the men's houses (above) are particulary interesting in this regard.

Nevin (ibid.: 97), in comparing philosophies of administrations in Washington regarding the Trust Territory, characterizes the end of the Eisenhower period as being one of holding down the budget. Under Kennedy's administration, beginning in 1961, the Trust Territory was conceived of as "just the place to demonstrate the New Frontier manner" (ibid.: 98). A report of a United Nations Visiting Commission in 1961 criticized United States management of the Territory in several areas, including lack of indigenous economic development, lack of recruitment of native leaders to important administrative posts, failure to revive island industries of the Japanese pre-war period, and, what was probably most devastating to the new administration, the assessment that "considerable dissatisfaction and discontent" was found among the islanders (ibid.: 103). It took some time for response to this negative report to be realized, for the budget for the 1962 fiscal year had already been set; but that for 1963 was doubled (from $7 900 000 to $16 000 000) (ibid.: 136). While the 1961 U.N. report was largely negative, the commission did praise the strong beginnings to education, especially with regard to the universality of elementary schooling. This emphasis has continued to be important in later administration of the Territory. It was during this period that the new elementary school was built on Pingelap.

In 1962 President Kennedy sent the Solomon Commission to investigate conditions in the Territory after one of his aides, Michael Forrestal, had returned with shocked reactions to existing circumstances there (ibid.: 123). The Solomon Commission found the Territory in a state of deterioration and economic dormancy, and warned that "the time could come, and shortly, when the pressures on the U.N. for a settlement of the status of Micronesia could become more than embarrassing" (McHenry 1975: 231). Recommendations of the Commission included the eventual goal of "movement of Micronesia into a permanent relationship with the U.S. within our political framework" (ibid.: 232). Accordingly, a "favourable" plebiscite was to be prepared and capital improvement programs were to be instituted which would be aimed toward improving education, public health, and raising cash income (ibid.). Plebiscites did not materialize until late in the 1970s, but the flow of U.S. capital into the Trust Territory did accelerate, along with continuing educational and medical programs.

With regard to the majority of the Pingelapese, it was chiefly in the late 1960s when Peace Corps volunteers began to live on the atoll that significant face-to-face contact with Americans began. Most of the comments that I received regarding Peace Corps workers on the atoll were positive, though there is one report that a worker was asked to leave because of his bad temper. Peace Corps workers on Pingelap have served as teachers, storekeepers, and paramedics. My impression of those I met is that while their training for the tasks performed was far from adequate, in most cases good general educations and some little imagination allowed them to function fairly well in their assigned roles.

At about the same time (the late 1960s) as the Peace Corps began work on the atoll, a small group of U.S. Air Force missile watchers established themselves at a station at the extreme northeast corner of the main island. They were supplied by helicopter from their base at Kwajelein in the Marshalls. They were visited frequently by the Pingelap people. The visits were remembered as times of good-natured relations. Helicopter rides broke the routine of island living, but most important was a large shipment of food which was brought in from Kwajalein when island supplies of what had become important commodities began to fail due to a long absence of the field trip vessel, apparently during one of her numerous trips to Japan for repairs.

By 1970 a major construction project financed by American funds had been implemented. This was a cement pier which stretched from the beach in front of the village to the edge of the reef so that the field trip vessel could unload and load directly there, without the need for many trips by small boats to carry cargo to and from the beach piecemeal. Unfortunately this pier was destroyed by the typhoon of 1972 and had not been restored at the time of my last visit to the atoll in the spring of 1983.

The same disaster also demonstrated to the Pingelapese, perhaps more forcibly than ever before, that the flow of U.S. government funds and goods into the atoll was necessary to their continued survival and well-being. This storm is reported to have been the worst in memory and resulted in flooding of the village area as well as the taro patch, bringing on major destruction of the taro crop and of breadfruit and coconut trees. As with the apparently somewhat less severe, but still highly destructive storm of 1957, large amounts of food and other supplies were furnished by the United States while replanting and maturing of crops proceeded.

More permanent help was evidenced by the provision of funds to build two retaining walls, one along the front of the village, and a second, higher one, across the lagoon shore facing the north end of the taro patch. Other important projects and benefits which were realized on Pingelap have been financed by the budget of the Trust Territory which had expanded to an annual $80 000 000 by 1974 (Nevin 1977: 136). Ongoing benefits include provision of radio services, medical aid, and educational services. During my 1975-76 stay on the atoll, funds were obtained for fencing material and an enclosure built around the taro patch to keep pigs from damaging that crop. Pigs had been a source of crop destruction, especially in the patch, ever since their introduction to Pingelap over 100 years before. By 1980 a newer, more modern vessel with more adequate passenger quarters had replaced the ancient field trip ship whose visits had become increasingly irregular due to periodic engine breakdowns. In 1976 I helped survey an area at the north end of the village and extending into the lagoon for a proposed landing strip. This was begun in 1978, but funds ran out in 1980. Subsequently, additional funding made possible completion by the fall of 1982. When I reached the atoll by plane in the spring of 1983 scheduled flights of three planes a week had been organized by the Liebenzeller missionaries, who had re-established themselves in Pohnpei. At the time of my visit in 1980 a solar radiation unit had been installed to power the radio set on the island, and by 1983 provision of new wooden houses by the U.S. Federal Housing Commission was being implemented from a budget which lay outside of the normal Trust Territory monies.

There were several island events or processes which affected the lives of the islanders significantly during the years 1975-83 that spanned my visits. In 1978-79 a religious crisis stirred conflict. This was brought on by the advent of a Seventh Day Adventist mission on Pingelap. I have described the details of this perceived intrusion elsewhere (Damas 1985). Here I will only briefly summarize the outcome. The triumph of the established church in overruling the new mission's desire to work Sundays, objection to which practice was backed by both local and territorial courts, reinforced the ABCFM mission's position of power in the community. I noted a quieter more devout and somber Pingelap on my visit of 1980 and the power of the then-reigning *nahnmariki* who had been accused of being too lenient toward the new mission appeared to be somewhat weakened as a result. More importantly, the support of the ABCFM by the High Court of the Trust Territory headed by an American judge, and the failure of the Senator to the Congress of Micronesia, police, and District Administrator to interfere, demonstrated that Pingelap remained largely insulated in its local political management despite some reshaping according to the American model.

Certain demographic changes were taking place during these years as well. Hurd (1977: 2) reports a 1970 population of 800 on the atoll, but by the time of my visit this number had declined, since my June 1976 census showed 676, including school children just returned from Pohnpei and teachers who had departed for that place for their summer training. The decline may have been in part due to some emigration after the storm of 1972, but probably more to the absence of youth for both schooling and employment. My census of June 1978 showed a slight increase to 742, but an apparent levelling was occurring by May 1983, when 753 were counted. The most significant aspect of this latter census was the larger number of males in the 18-23 age group than in the two previous censuses (Damas 1985). This trend clearly indicated the shrinkage of the job market in the civil service of the Trust Territory (by then the Federated States of Micronesia) government which had been previously available to a number of Pingelapese, especially males of high-school-level education or beyond. This youthful element posed a problem with its usual detachment from the social and economic life of the atoll. Boredom brought on by exposure to the excitement of urban or quasi-urban living off the atoll led them to seek the distraction of home brew and many were involved in violence, theft, and other drunken misbehaviour. They tended to drift back and forth between Pingelap and Pohnpei, an expedient made possible by the still inexpensive deck passage available on the field trip vessels. It is true, as well, that some appeared to be making a readjustment to atoll living, marrying and becoming involved in subsistence activities and the still important copra economy. Indeed, that economy was going through one of its periodic peaks due to a rise in the price of copra, though, as always, one could not predict the duration of such a boom.

American administrations continued to be criticized by observers, including anthropologists, for creating a "pseudo welfare state" (Peoples 1978) of heavy subsidization, rising expectations, and channelling employment services largely into the ever-expanding civil service, at the expense of industrial development and with the end result of continued and, perhaps steadily increasing, dependency. With regard to Pingelap, I (Damas 1985) have argued that the islanders do not conceive of American subsidies negatively but rather, welcome them and consider them to be the only realistic source of improvements and services on the atoll.

Throughout the American period in Micronesia there have been few attempts to develop local industries, and the outer islands like Pingelap appear to have little potential for them. On the other hand, there has been some improvement of horticultural and arboricultural pursuits. Several quick-growing species of aroids have been introduced to Pingelap and have aided recovery from the 1957 and 1972 typhoons. Since several native species of taro are said to take 5-10 years to mature, these introduced species were most important at such times. Other agricultural innovations made by American scientists were not so readily accepted, as for instance, the proposed use of the sea cucumber (trepang) for fertilizing banana plants. The coconut crop undoubtedly has been improved by periodic thinning of trees beyond their productive years from the forests of the atoll's islands. I witnessed such a project in 1976 when a young man from Pohnpei operating with a chain saw, cut down several hundred coconut trees in order to make room for replanting.

The most important event during the period of my field studies was the emergence of new nation states in Micronesia. A preliminary plebiscite was held in 1978 in order to sound out Micronesian opinions of restructuring of U.S.-Micronesian relations as an alternative to the Trust Territory arrangement.

I have no reliable figures regarding the results of the vote taken on Pingelap, but already at that time Pingelapese were expressing concern over the possibility of loosening ties with the United States.

In 1983 a Plebiscite Commission was formed in order to inform Micronesian voters of the options which were being offered to replace the Trust Territory administration (Damas 1985). These were Free Association, Commonwealth status, Territory, Independence, and State. My assessment of the activities of that Commission was that they were actually stumping for the Free Association Option. This option implied 15 years during which definite sums of money would be allocated, full sovereignty in internal and international matters, and delegation of defence responsibilities to the United States. The Pingelapese reacted with considerable distress to the prospect of termination implied by the 15-year limitation, and when the vote of June 1983 was counted the Free Association option was rejected by greater than a two-to-one margin (ibid.: 51). Instead, the islanders chose the option of Commonwealth status, which I have interpreted to be their conception of the closest sort of relationship with the United States that was being offered among the options. This local vote was, however, overridden by Pohnpeian representatives to the Congress of Micronesia (The National Union 1983).

The chief concerns of the people of Pingelap atoll during the 1980s have been, on the one hand, the desire to maintain as close ties with the United States as possible and anxiety that, with the new focus of power within the State of Pohnpei government, the special interests of their remote atoll may not be served.

CHAPTER 3

Habitat and Economy

The soils of coral atolls are poor compared to those of volcanic islands. Nevertheless, under certain conditions they can sprout forth surprisingly lush covers of vegetation, including food plants for the support of human populations. Indeed, some atolls exhibit concentrations of people highly unusual among pre-industrial societies. Pingelap is one of those atolls which is truly remarkable in this respect.

Models of Atoll Habitability

In seeking to understand the physical conditions which make possible the bounty of Pingelap, two schemes which outline conditions favouring human habitation of atolls can be cited. Mason (1968) lists the variables of amount of rainfall, land area, occurrences of drought, and of typhoons, as well as lagoon size, as crucial. Alkire (1978) excludes lagoon size but adds island height, while incorporating the others of Mason's variables, though modifying that of land area to individual island size. Alkire applies quantified criteria in his scheme, and I will employ it here, though later reference will be made to Mason's formula as well.

Four of Alkire's variables concern presence and retention of adequate fresh water for plant growth. The obvious factor of actual amount of rainfall must be fortified by conditions of islands which help to form a layer of relatively fresh water (the Ghyben-Hertzberg lens) lying on top of more saline water in the porous interior of the islands of coral atolls. Alkire sees these conditions as being the following: (1) height of islands above sea level, with a height of over 20 feet being considered too great for the roots of food plants and trees to reach the Ghyben-Hertzberg lens; (2) island size, with dimensions of less than 350 by 350 feet being too small to support a lens free enough from saline tidal seepage from the perimetres; (3) frequency of droughts, with droughts occurring as often as once in four or five years seriously affecting maturation of food plants.

Notes to Chapter 3 are on pp. 247-48.

With regard to Alkire's final variable, (4) frequency of typhoons and assumed destruction of trees and other vegetable sources; he considers that typhoons coming more frequently than once in four or five years inhibit recovery of chief crops from damage (ibid.: 14-18).

Turning first to the most essential of these variables, Table 3.1 gives rainfall statistics collected on Pingelap for the period October 1969 through March 1974, or a time just prior to my first visit to the atoll, with data for 15 of the months missing.

Table 3.1
Precipitation Records from Pingelap Atoll (in inches)

Year	Oct.	Nov.	Dec.	Jan.	Feb.	Mar.
1969	8.96	5.14	10.96	—	5.75	14.36
1970	16.34	9.85	8.58	5.86	3.05	1.88
1971	11.52	8.55	5.14	12.54	24.77	11.73
1972	12.11	2.67	2.33	17.34	13.31	18.96
1973	11.60	19.06	14.55	1.03	2.70	2.92
1974	—	—	—	5.01	12.60	21.52
Average	12.11	9.05	8.31	8.36	10.36	11.90
Year	**Apr.**	**May**	**June**	**July**	**Aug.**	**Sept.**
1969	22.63	11.23	—	18.43	9.60	15.81
1970	—	—	—	4.94	17.17	12.81
1971	18.28	25.78	11.25	—	16.96	14.31
1972	20.46	28.41	5.75	40.99	30.24	23.96
1973	18.42	5.17	11.39	4.58	5.93	9.19
1974	—	—	—	—	—	—
Average	19.95	17.65	9.46	17.24	15.98	15.22

The total average of about 156 inches annual rainfall is consistent with the thesis that the zone between five and ten degrees north latitude in this part of the Pacific is one of substantial precipitation (Alkire 1978: 12). Remarkable is the rainfall for 1972 of 215 inches. The other extreme is represented by 1973, when 106 inches of rain fell on the atoll. These years might well span the normal range, with the median of 160 inches closely approximating the sample mean. As is common in regions visited by trade winds only seasonally, rainfall is not distributed evenly over the year. Table 3.1 is arranged to show this seasonality. During the period of the northeast trades, from October through March the average monthly rainfall is 9.65 inches. During the season of variable winds, April through September, the average is 15.72 inches. However this latter figure is distorted somewhat by the small sample for the month of June (for only three of the years). Discounting that anomalous month, the average would have been nearly 17 inches, or about double the monthly average for the months of the trades. Even considering this seasonal variation, these figures place Pingelap among the most moist of the low islands in the Pacific, sharing that distinction with the southern Marshall atolls (Wiens 1962: 360; Alkire 1978:132). With regard to height above sea level, I estimate the maximum height of the main island at less than 15 feet, an elevation which is not reached on the other two islands. All of the three islands of Pingelap are greater in size than the minimum suggested by Alkire, with the smallest, Sukoru, being 1500 feet in its longest dimension with a maximum breadth of 600 feet and, an average breadth of about 450 feet. The lack of taro pits and the existence of but one breadfruit tree stump on Sukoru might argue that Alkire's minimum dimensions are on the small side. However, my informants state that formerly both of these crops were grown there. The present situation of Sukuro reflects the great vulnerability of that island to the tsunamis which have accompanied recent typhoons.

Pingelap is well situated with regard to low frequency of droughts. The general Pacific drought of 1983 is the only such occurrence in the memory of any of my informants. Indeed, with the possible exception of a similar drought which I have conjectured for the nineteenth century, there are none mentioned in either the written or the oral history of the atoll.

Alkire's final variable, occurrence of typhoons, requires some examination in the case of Pingelap. In the preceding chapter I emphasized the long-term effects of a typhoon of the 1770s and also postulated that, indeed, the atoll may have been completely depopulated as a consequence of such events at various times. I also cited the calamitous nature of the 1905 typhoon and suggested that those of 1957 and 1972 might have resulted in similar disaster had sufficient supplies not been provided from outside. Thus, although the frequency of typhoons is well below an interval posited by Alkire as being highly disadvantageous to habitability, they have had substantial impact on the history of habitation on Pingelap. However, since Alkire's formulation aims toward defining *potential* support of human populations rather than actual curves of population decline or extinction, and expansion, the possibility of recolonization can be allowed for.

In summarizing the conditions for habitation against the scale posed by Alkire, Pingelap must be rated as "exceptional" (ibid.: 18). Of course, this conclusion only confirms the highly evident facts that Pingelap supports lush vegetation and has sustained heavy population concentrations of up to 1 500 persons per square mile at times when the economy was overwhelmingly internally generated.

The Plant Life of Pingelap

The conditions discussed above pertain to the success of horticulture and arboriculture. In view of the traditional and current importance of these occupations on Pingelap it is not surprising that knowledge of species and varieties of plants is considerable. Indeed knowledge of subtle differences in varieties goes beyond the level of the amateur naturalist or concerned anthropologist, to that of a professional botanist. The information provided in the Appendix illustrates how the degree of differentiation of Pingelapese terms for plants is seldom less detailed than that of the scientific designations.

Agricultural Techniques

The extensive inventory of plant varieties recognized by the Pingelapese (Appendix)[1] reveals broad utilization of plant resources when lumber uses, and the use of grasses and leaves for fertilizer, are added to sources of food. Vegetable consumption is concentrated in the two major crops, aroids (especially Cyrtosperma) and breadfruit.

Turning first to the aroids, two planting or rather, replanting techniques are practised. The most common method is to remove from the top of the root a thin cap with a stem attached. This is buried below the surface of the mud. The second method is to use a subsidiary stem which contains rootlets. In either case the cutting is buried deep, since the root grows upwards and absorbs the stem into itself. The main aroid patch, developed through centuries of adding compost, is said to be up to four feet deep of soft mud. I have seen men immersed to their groins while working there. The vast majority of plants in the patch are Cyrtosperma or *maeyung* in Pingelapese. Methods of planting this aroid are described above. The true taro (Colocasia) or *sawa* is planted around the edges of the main patch or in minor rows in the otherwise empty spaces between the major divisions of the patch. Dry taro grows at various places on the main island and on Daekae but must be considered a very minor source of food, in view of the small numbers observed. It is fertilized by coconut husks, which are seen lying on the surface at the base of these plants, a fertilizing medium not considered suitable for most wet taros, where the mulching is done with various grasses and leaves. Most of the varieties of dry taro require special preparation before they can be eaten. The skin must be removed, the root sliced and dried in the sun and then cooked in earth ovens. These processes are designed to prevent itching in the mouth when eating. In the case of wet taro, the skin can be removed after cooking, but should be done then or itching will also occur. Dry taro, especially, is often ground into a coarse flour which is then formed into a cone mixed with sugar or into cakes flavoured at times with bananas.

The large leaves of Cyrtosperma are used as umbrellas during showers when people are dressed in their finer garments as when en route to church services. In these cases the lower leaves only are used, since cutting them is said to be not fatal to the plants. One of my informants stated that an average value for a corm was about $5.00 U.S. on the atoll (1975). These corms may reach two metres in length and 6 decimetres in diametre (St. John 1948: 108).

With regard to the life cycle of these aroids, the *maeyung* is harvested after longer or shorter periods, depending on the variety. Many corms are left in the ground for up to 10 years, while five years is perhaps a general average for harvesting when all species are considered. The faster growing plants like the *sounpwong walnu* or "six-month" variety, and *sawa*, or true taro, are most important in the periods of recovery after greater or lesser flooding of the main patch. My informants also indicate that as plants mature the greater part of nourishment is absorbed by the roots so that after peak growth is attained the leaves, branches, and stems actually *shrink* in size. Therefore, one expects larger root growth after this process is observed. Fertilizer is applied when rain water is high in the patch so that the grass and leaves strewn on the surface will deteriorate in the water and then sink to the bottom where the resultant product will then work effectively.

In addition to the major typhoons of prehistory and those of the present century in 1905, 1957, and 1972 when nearly all of the aroid plantings were said to have been affected and famine occurred or threatened, my informants revealed that every few years minor floodings occurred as well. These minor incidents came when especially high seas from westerly quadrants invaded the lagoon. Flooding is said always to come from the direction of the lagoon, for the highest point on Pingelap is a ridge running along the west side of the patch, sheltering it from the westerly seas which accompany high winds from that direction. Indeed, the sea wall constructed in 1973 was built along the north side of the patch, or that side adjacent to the lagoon, in order to prevent such floodings as had occurred previously from that direction.

After the major 1957 flooding, an attempt was made to drain into the lagoon the salt water which has a lethal effect on the aroids. It was found that the water would not flow northward through the channel that had been dug to connect with the lagoon. Gravity worked against such a flow. Next, the Pingelapese dug a ditch extending from the narrow south end of the patch, and this ditch was widened into two depressions. In the second of these depressions they dug a drainage hole or well, which was then blocked during the period of waiting for the rains to raise the water level. The rain water then flowed into the depressions, forming ponds. When sufficient water from the rains had accumulated the hole was unblocked and the now considerably less but still saline fluid drained into the porous understructure of the island. After that the *inepwuel* was not invaded by the men for over a month so that the rootlets that might still be growing from the severely damaged corms could develop. When the rootlets were assumed to have grown beyond a very fragile state, the men dug up the corms, repaired and replanted them. In the event of replanting of *maeyung*, there often remained parts of the original plants in good enough condition to supply the basis for regrowth. Segments of corms rotted by the salt water were cut away and the holes from which the roots were drawn also carefully cleansed of rotten matter. The healthy part of a corm was then put back in such a hole and fertilizer applied. This procedure applied to the *maeyung* is similar to the normal replanting method except that often a substantial part of the corm was intact. In the case of *sawa*, the Pingelapese applied the normal and much less elaborate method, that of planting the stalk alone after discarding what remained of the corm. A significant number of *sawa* roots were mature enough for eating three months after the patch had been drained. Most *maeyung* required over a year and, as suggested above, some varieties took several years before they could be harvested. Apart from these occasional disasters to the *inepwuel*, the aroids can be harvested at all seasons. However, in past times the taro patch was not used for about four months of the year, from the end of April until about the beginning of September. During the later three months of this period, after late May, came the season for ripe breadfruit, the second major crop of Pingelap.

Breadfruit trees reach great ages and sizes and, as the above outline indicated, provide important building material, especially for canoes, in addition to their fruit for human consumption. During the period of my visits to the atoll I saw very few young trees, and informants reported that the islands of the atoll have lost quite a number of the older trees due to recent historical events. It is said that during Japanese times a rat poison was introduced that appeared to kill breadfruit trees. Secondly, there was a breadfruit blight reported which was killing trees at the time of Coulter's visit in 1954, as mentioned earlier. Finally, flooding of the islands during the typhoons of 1957 and 1972 killed a number of trees, especially on Daekae, where their stark trunks stood out on my arrival in 1975, though most were sawn down during the next year.

Breadfruit trees are concentrated in the interior areas of the main island and on Daekae, though as noted above, their number on the latter island has markedly decreased during recent years. There is also a significant number growing in the village amongst the houses on the landward side of the main road, but actually within a few yards of the beach. This latter location is remarkable and attests to a very extensive Ghyben-Hertzberg lens, though as well these trees are protected from the salt spray by a thick growth of coconut and pandanus trees between the beach and the road.

I saw little evidence of attempts to restore the declined growth of breadfruit trees during my visits to Pingelap from 1975-83, but the method of replanting was described to me by informants. One of the roots which spread from the trunk well above ground is cut. From this cut a shoot usually sprouts. When the shoot reaches a height of three or four feet it is planted in a hole fertilized with grasses together with a section of the root to which it is attached. It takes seven to ten years after planting for the trees to bear fruit.

Fresh breadfruit is cooked by baking it in the earth ovens as well as by frying it as crescent shaped "chips" in coconut oil. The Pingelapese also preserve by a method known throughout Oceania, that of burying the fruit in the ground, where it ferments. In this process Pingelapese soak the fruit in salt water for at least 24 hours and then it is peeled before being placed in pits about three feet in depth and of about that diametre. The now softened fruit is wrapped in leaves and covered with them as well as with dirt. In time the fruit assumes a thick, moist consistency, dark orange in colour, and appears at feasts in sheets of about 2 inches in thickness, resembling the slabs of young cheese which I have seen in cheesemakers' vats. My informants told me that this *mar* is still edible after a year or more in the ground if the leaves are renewed periodically (about once a week). Nowadays plastic garbage bags are used more frequently than leaves to contain the fermenting fruit in the pits.

The coconut is the third important crop for food, and of primary importance for providing a natural beverage, as well being the only cash crop. The Appendix lists nine stages of the nut and tree and the uses which accompany several of the stages. With regard to planting techniques, I had sometimes noticed fallen brown coconuts lying in neat rows of eight or ten, in groups of 70 or 80, with roots anchoring them to the ground, and with shoots beginning to sprout from the nuts. I had thought that these represented cases where a number of nuts had been counted out for bagging, and for some reason or other, had been forgotten or abandoned. I learned later that, instead, I had witnessed a stage in the standard planting practice. After germination, with the new plants feeding on the embryo within the mature nuts, and with roots then beginning to provide nourishment from the ground, the nuts are replanted at various places on the islands. Since World War II the Pingelapese have been influenced in their planting of coconuts by American agriculturalists, who recommended digging holes. They then plant the germinated nuts together with leaves and grass for fertilizer in these holes. Coconuts grown near the shores are planted with the emerging stems pointed toward the sea so that as they grow they will bend first in that direction and then, influenced by the winds, bend upwards. This gives the characteristic curvature of coconut trees seen in photographs of tropical shorelines.

Coconut trees are normally said to bear copra nuts after about five years. It is also said that with special care they can bear earlier, when the branching occurs about eight feet from ground level. Good copra crops come from trees less than 50 or 60 years old. After that it becomes necessary to thin the forest of old trees. Coconuts formed a significant part of the diet in earlier times, but by the time of my visits to the atoll, store-bought foods and beverages had to a large extent replaced them. The major food use of coconuts was then as a cream sweetened with sugar, which is applied to a number of recipes involving taro, breadfruit, or bananas. Though replaced to some extent by coffee, tea, sweetened canned or powdered milk, and soft drinks, the green nut is still important as a beverage. The latter use is especially important when people are working at some distance from the village, at which times the drinking nut supplies the chief source of fluid and the jelly of the green nut provides a daytime food ration. Drinking nuts are also in evidence at food-distribution ceremonies. Pingelap is endowed with a seemingly limitless number of coconut palms. Together with the pandanus trees, which also are salt resistant, they grow right up to the beach line, and the coconut tree can also be found almost anywhere on the islands of the atoll.

Although a number of varieties of pandanus are present they do not form a very important part of the diet, the fruit usually being eaten raw and serving as something of a confection. The sweet flavour is enjoyable but the stringy fibres clog the spaces between one's teeth, thus making pandanus a questionable treat to outsiders. As noted in Chapter 1, the female, or fruit-bearing, pandanus trees occur mainly along the shorelines of the three islands, while the male, or staminate, form is found in the interior. Of the lesser foods, the banana plant is planted as a shoot cut from the tree after the fruit is picked, each plant bearing one large bunch which is harvested after about six months. There is an area beginning about 150 yards south of the taro patch designated as "the banana plantation" where large numbers were formerly grown. However at the time of my visits, bananas, papayas, and the one mango tree grew only in close proximity to dwellings, where they are said to be less immune to theft by children, adolescents, and young men. Papayas seem to thrive especially well on Pingelap and the fruit often reach the length of 18 inches or more. This fruit is usually saved for presentation at feasts. Sugar cane grows interspersed with the aroids in the *inepwuel* for the most part. It is eaten at any time, but especially when the supplies of refined sweets decline at the local stores.

These vegetable products serve to provide the bulk of food for the population, though the amount of store-bought food used can be considerable at times when the stores are well stocked, and when copra returns or other sources of cash are significant. Flour, rice, and sugar are the chief foods bought, and they, of course, only serve to augment the already ample carbohydrate portion of the local diet. The amount of store-bought food that is eaten also varies considerably from household to household.

The only protein products sold in the stores are canned mackerel, sardines, and corned beef, and the amounts available can in no way be considered adequate to supply the needs of the 600-700 people who lived on the atoll in recent years.

Marine Sources of Food

The chief source of protein food came from the sea and the reefs surrounding the islands of the atoll. The largest fish caught with any regularity is the yellow fin tuna (*Thunnus albacares*) which reaches well in excess of 100 pounds and is caught in the deep waters just outside the reefs. This quarry is caught by a method called *selong*, or long-lining. The fishermen use either a lead sinker or tie rocks into the stout lines in order to sink the baited hook to depths of 60-70 fathoms where the large tuna usually feed. The favourite bait used in *selong* is the flesh of the flying fish. I was told that the yellow fin seldom have much fight in them when they reach the surface from such depths and are usually easily dispatched with a stick or the handle of a machete. The returns from this method of fishing show marked variation over time. At times I have counted over 30 small canoes floating off the reef facing the village engaged in *selong*. When the catches fall off, so does enthusiasm and participation, but during most of the year one sees two or three of the one-man outrigger canoes, with fishermen shaded under pandanus straw hats, when the sea is calm. Whenever any of these dedicated and determined fishermen begin to have success, they are quickly joined by a fleet of the less committed. The *selong* method is also used at night with the quarry then being the large oilfish (*Ruvettuf pretiofuf*).

Of great importance today is trolling, which is carried out from open, planked boats powered with outboard motors. Even though the fish caught by this method are smaller than those caught by long-lining, the larger numbers make for a total bulk of meat which is said to exceed *selong* catches over the year's time. Success, however, is often limited by gasoline shortages and engine breakdowns. Before the advent of motors, this method, called *ilarak*, was carried out in canoes, either with men paddling rapidly or with the use of sails. I have seen these latter methods used during the frequent times of gasoline shortage. I was told that in former times canoes under sail ranged far from the atoll, so far in fact that the fishermen could at times sight Mwaekil atoll, about 60 sea miles away. The chief species of fish caught by trolling are the bonita (*Katsuwonus pelanis*), dolphin fish (*Coryphaena hippurus*), and sometimes, smaller yellow fin tuna, usually ranging up to 10 pounds.

The most popular method of fishing is torch fishing at night. This method, called *kahlek* or "dancing," is named for the skilled movements of fishermen required to keep balance while swinging the net in the air to intercept flying fish (*Cypselvrus poecilopterus*) in flight (Morton et al. 1973: 317). Much of the canoe-building activity, which appeared to be a continuous industry on the island during my stays, was directed toward fashioning the graceful, slim, paint-decorated outrigger canoes of about 20 feet in length used in this pursuit. It is important that the hunt be carried out after the moon sets in order to avoid its light which would distract the fish from the torches held in the canoes. On the nights when a hunt proceeds, the canoes and the torches made from palm fronds wrapped around sticks, about 10 feet each in length, are arranged on the beach, and most of the men retire, leaving behind a couple of watchmen. When the moon has set they raise a hullabaloo which wakens the other fishermen wherever they may be sleeping in the village.

When the men are assembled at their canoes they load the torches, about four to a boat, and paddle out to deep water, forming a fleet as they do so. The hunt is usually carried out between a quarter- and a half-mile from the reef which connects Sukoru with the main island. There the canoes form a concave line. With torches lighted they present a striking sight. Flying fish attracted by the torchlight leave the surface for flights of 50 yards or so at a height at which the netmen can intercept them. Usually there is a crew of four, with one man steering the canoe and holding it in its position in the line, one man lighting and holding the torches, and the other two wielding the nets, which are about 18 inches in diametre on the ends of short poles. This method carries with it danger from needle fish (*Belonidae*), which leap from the water in pursuit of the flying fish and sometimes pierce the arms or bodies of fishermen. Several of the men bear the scars of such accidents. Another imminent danger is falling overboard when sharks are present.

Flying fish may supply an important source of meat during the season from January to the end of June or early July, when *kahlek* is practised, but I have seen periods when the hunt brought poor returns but was still patronized by a number of the young men. On the other hand catches of several hundred of these fish averaging one to two pounds in weight were sometimes made in the course of a night's hunt. It appeared to me that the recreational aspect of the pursuit was every bit as important an incentive as subsistence.

While the three methods described above together produce the greatest bulk of fish over the year, there is also considerable activity devoted to catching the smaller fish found on the reefs of the atoll. One of the methods of catching reef fish in the daylight hours is to use a pole and line in high tide. A feather and float are worked on the surface in such a way as to create erratic movements on the surface through action of the end of the pole, something in the manner of a spinning rod. This movement is said to attract the fish, which will bite the hook submerged just a few inches below the surface. This method, *eketar*, is said to be most successful in catching flagtails (*Kuhlia mugil*), some small groupers (*Serandae*), trevellay (*Garangidae*), as well as various lizard fishes (*Synodontidae*), squirrel fishes (*Holocentridae*), and soldier fishes (*Myripristis benndit* and *Myripristis kuntae*).

Another method, called *pongolikilik*, is followed by groups of men, women, and children fishing together after nightfall. Pieces of hermit crab or fish are strewn on the surface for bait. *Pongolikilik* is practised with pole and hook but without a sinker and especially on nights with a full moon. Small groupers and goatfish (*Mulidae*) are caught by this method.

Yet another method practised largely by women on the reefs surrounding the islands, including the broad windward reef and the reefs bordering the lagoon, is called *weteke* "piece of wood." Two pieces of wood (apparently of balsa brought from Pohnpei) are strung on a line, and the second, nearest the end of the line, is attached to the hook. Fish, coconut meat, or chunks of breadfruit are used as bait. When the fish bites, it drags the piece of wood nearest the hook under the water while the other acts as a float marking the spot and also as an additional drag. The women then can pull the line and catch to the surface.

Another method bears the loan word *perumw* (broom) which describes the sweeping process used. This method employs up to 50 or 60 men standing on the reef, usually the men of one of the four sections of the village. Here two of the men hold the extreme ends of a large net, 50 or 60 feet long, while a group of beaters drive the fish toward the open net. When the net is closed around the fish, spearsmen dispatch them.

Still another technique for catching small reef fish, *uhkesik*, employs a hand net somewhat larger than that used for flying fish. This net is larger and has a heavier handle to offset the resistance provided by the water when in use. Men using this method work in pairs. One man wearing goggles puts his head under water in order to locate the schools of fish. The second man then dips the seine when fish are attracted by spreading bait on the surface. The baits normally used are either softer fish flesh, dried fish, or fish cooked in the earth oven and broken into small pieces, all of which will sink below the surface.

Lobster fishing is carried out in the third quarter of the moon, at times when the tide has receded, so that about a foot of water remains on the reefs. When located, the lobsters are pinned down with a forked stick and then collected with the same hand nets used for catching flying fish. Nowadays men also hunt the lobster with a flashlight and a rubber tube. The fisherman blows into the tube in order to dislodge the animal from its hold on the coral.

Spear guns are used with face masks today in order to catch several varieties of fish, particularly the poisonous scorpionfish (*Scorponidae*). Bows and arrows were used formerly to hunt lizard-fish (*Sauride gracilis* and *Synodus engleman*), and gobies (*Gobidae*), but today slingshots made of rubber are employed. The giant grouper (*Promicrips lanceolutus*), which lurks in ledges among the shadows of the reefs was hunted with a harpoon as were the now protected turtles. A heavy metal point is needed in order to pierce the thick shell of the latter animal. Formerly the turtle provided the important lagoon quarry, and it usually lived in about four to seven feet of water. When dolphins appeared close to the atoll they, too, were hunted with harpoons, although this weapon is no longer used. One more method of fishing was described to me, though I did not see it practised: that is a method of slow trolling, *seilululak*, where the line is dragged somewhat deeper in the water than in the case of *ilarak*. Other methods were used but they appear to have been relatively minor in importance. It can be seen that not only do the species fished form an extensive list, but also that a wide range of techniques are or have been employed in catching them.

The amount of time devoted to fishing and the amount of protein food procured from fish varies widely today from one household to another. Some households have the reputation for neglecting both native vegetable foods and fish out of laziness, preferring store-bought rice, flour, and canned meats. As for the fish that are caught, one can see people gathered at the beach to receive them from men returning after successful *ilarak*, *selong*, or *kahlek* excursions. While kinship networks do allow for the dispersal of such catches without recompense, others outside the networks purchase them from the successful fishermen. School teachers and those employed at the cooperative store have daytime activities which interfere with their ability to practise some of the fishing methods. Other methods such as *ilarak*, best carried out at dawn, and *kahlek*, and some forms of reef fishing which are practised during the night, make it possible for these men to succeed in getting a fair amount of fresh fish for their families if they are willing to put forth the effort.

Preservation of fish is rare today, but I have seen salted tuna drying in the sun on roofs of village houses. I am told that flying fish, when caught in great numbers, are smoked. However, such practices are not common, and fish are eaten either raw or cooked within a day or two after the catch, a circumstance which is not surprising when one considers the large population and conditions which limit the maritime phase of the economy. Individual ambition and participation are variables in the protein-provision equation, but certain features of the atoll itself as well as periodic unfavourable weather and other factors hamper fishing as well.

Earlier, I cited Mason as including lagoon size among "factors influencing economic potential" of atolls. Actually, Mason expands his consideration of maritime conditions which affect subsistence, as follows:

> Variability in marine resources is another critical factor in our assessment of economic potentialities. Size of lagoon, extent of reefs, access by canoe to the open sea, and seasonal variation of wind and wave patterns combine in different ways to define the relative availability of this essential source of protein (Mason 1968: 323).

Looking first at the factor to which Mason seems to have given priority, lagoon size, Pingelap is obviously one of the most disadvantaged of atolls.

While a number of species of fish inhabit the lagoon, they are almost all also found on the reefs, where they are more easily caught. Indeed, I have seldom seen men fishing from canoes in the small lagoon itself. Rather, the reef bordering the southern end of the lagoon was the most frequent place where fishing could be said to have been carried out within its confines.

With regard to the extent of reefs, the actual dimensions of an atoll is the chief variable of importance in this regard. For instance, with a maximum diametre of only two-and-one-half miles, Pingelap could not approach having the area of reef of Kwajalein with its maximum diametre of about 66 miles.[2] One compensating factor on a small atoll like Pingelap is that all of the reef area is within easy reach of fishermen. Most of the reef fishing is carried out to the west of the lagoon and of the main island, during the northeast trade wind period from October through March, but so is nearly all of the deep-sea fishing, including long-lining, trolling, and torch-fishing. The unusual, for an atoll, location of the village on an ocean shore rather than along a lagoon shore appears in part to be related to neglect of the lagoon as a fishing site. Probably more important in determining this location is accessibility to calmer seas there for much of the year. The shape of the main island of Pingelap (see frontispiece map) produces this lee, for its main axis extends well south of the lagoon, jutting well into the ocean. This leeward side also has a narrower reef than the windward side and a natural channel leading to the village site. Thus, Mason's third factor relating to maritime exploitation, "access by canoe to the sea," is nicely met.

A closer look at Mason's fourth variable "seasonal variation of wind and wave patterns," and other possible factors influencing fishing can be had by consulting my notes regarding the cycle of marine exploitation from early August 1975 to early July 1976, as well as notes from the period June to August 1978.

The Cycle of Marine Exploitation

August 1975 was a period of intense activity, both social and economic, on Pingelap atoll. A choir from the colony on Sokehs, including many members with their families, was entertained, bringing a total of over 100 visitors to the atoll. These visitors, together with the usual presence in summer of high school students, had swelled the population to about 800 people. A great deal of food was required because each day's routine of entertainment included three large meals for all of these people. The situation was aggravated by the delay in the return of the field trip vessel, a circumstance that extended the period of swelled population to three weeks. Several measures were taken to meet this greatly increased strain on local resources. First, virtually all the domesticated animals, except for a few breeders, were slaughtered. I was told that about 50 pigs and 75 dogs were killed during this period. Only a few of the men could escape from the heavy schedule of daytime activities associated with the visit of the choir. This limited *selong* fishing, but the products of morning trolling and the frequent night-long reef-fishing expeditions, supplemented by flour and rice from the store, helped meet these extra demands. After the departure of the choir and students in September a certain success was experienced in *selong* fishing, and fish combined with the *mar* or fermented breadfruit which was now stored in the ground from the summer's breadfruit harvest enhanced conditions of subsistence.

I had been told that after about the beginning of October enough fish would be caught so that most families could eat them daily. Such did not seem to be the normal situation throughout the entire period of the months to follow. With the coming of the trades in early October, weather conditions were good for a period, but for some reason or other *selong* fishing was not highly successful. Reef fishing accounted for most of the haul because already a gasoline shortage was hampering *ilarak*, though a few crews tried trolling with paddled or sailed canoes, with indifferent results. However, on October 24 an *ilarak* competition was held, with 11 boats taking part, using carefully hoarded gasoline supplies. Catches of 3-27 fish per boat were made, with an average weight of perhaps four pounds per fish, amounting to over 700 pounds in two hours of one morning.

During the first half of November there was reasonably successful *selong* fishing, but for five days beginning on the 15th, heavy surf from the southwest caused by a passing typhoon brought all deep-sea fishing to a halt. After that, long-lining and other fishing methods were particularly unsuccessful and nightly flashlight hunts for coconut crabs were undertaken in order to add variety to the predominately vegetable diet. On December 1, it was reported to me that 24 women gathered over 1 200 coconut crabs in several rainy morning hours. This was to be the only time in the period witnessed that coconut crabs added measurably to the diet. A few days later another *ilarak* competition, using the little remaining gasoline, produced about 1 000 pounds of fish. The period of December and much of January was an indifferent time for fishing. Winds in the autumn had often been at variance in direction from the expected northeast trades, but even with full establishment of the trades during the winter, conditions were not always favourable for *selong* fishing. Even in the lee of the main island, when the trades blew stronger than was normal, the waves impeded the fishermen in their attempts to hold their light canoes steady over their lines. *Ilarak* was now hampered by many engine breakdowns, a serious occurrence since there was not a skilled mechanic on the atoll. Men again tried trolling with canoes powered with paddles or sail but generally had poor success. As ever, at such times when these two chief fishing methods were not bringing good results, the main source of fish was the smaller species taken from the reefs.

On January 5, 1976, an elderly man returned from an all-night offshore *selong* session with four large oilfish. For a few days afterwards several other men were inspired to seek this quarry and were rewarded with about 25 of the fish, averaging perhaps 50 pounds each, before interest or success fell off.

On the night of January 19-20 the first torch-fishing expedition took place but with disappointing results, an experience which was typical until sometime in the later part of February when large catches of up to 100 fish to a canoe were experienced. It was at that time that *kahlek* provided the main source of protein from the waters. However, on March 9 a record yellow fin tuna was taken, and after that, through the remainder of March and most of April, *selong* fishing was highly rewarding. Commonly, fleets of 30 or more canoes could be seen lying off the reefs to the west and northwest (off Sukoru) in this period, and many large fish were caught, with a record for the season being nine in one day for one lucky fisherman.

From April 24 to 28 deep-sea fishing was suspended due to strong southwest and west winds and high seas. Even reef fishing had to be stopped but was resumed afterwards as the most successful source of fish during early May. Again, in mid-May heavy seas from the west, said to be caused by another distant typhoon, brought all fishing to a halt. After that, although *selong* was practised assiduously in late May and early June, the method met with only indifferent success. By mid-June my notes carry concern about the absence of meat or fish from my diet. While several methods of fishing, including *kahlek*, were pursued up to the time of my departure on July 3, the season was mainly devoted to harvesting the now ripened breadfruit and no notable luck was experienced by those fishing.

Having missed most of the month of July and the early part of August in my previous visit, I was anxious to observe summer economic activities on my return to the atoll in June 1978. I noted that this year *selong* fishing was carried out with reasonable success, north and northeast of Daekae, since the winds in June, July, and August come most frequently out of the west or northwest. *Kahlek* fishing continued but with diminished participation until July 8 that year. Again there was a gasoline shortage so that *ilarak* fishing was rarely practised. While reef fishing continued throughout the period of my stay in the summer of 1978, the period itself was one of a general shortage of fish in many families. My enquiries confirmed that fish intake was highly variable from day to day and from household to household, though reasonable amounts were visible at most "feasts" or prestation events at this time.

The above account of my observations regarding the maritime phases of the Pingelapese economy suggests several variables which influence success. First, returning to Mason's factor of "seasonal variation of wind and wave patterns" there are expectable patterns at certain seasons. During the trade wind season most activity is carried out on the leeward side of the main island, whereas at other seasons certain fishing activities can be practised all around the island or in lees created by various other wind directions. High seas can curtail fishing at any season, though it is during the seasons of typhoons in this part of the Pacific that one would expect such disturbances more often. The seasonality of torch-fishing however, is not determined by wind and wave patterns alone and it is indeed poorly understood by the Pingelapese themselves as to why this hunt is reasonably successful only during the half year when it has been practised.

Clearly, other factors influence fishing success. Even though calm weather may prevail, success in *selong* cannot be predicted for much of the year regardless of seemingly favourable weather and wave conditions. In this regard, however, there are two native theories regarding occurrence of the yellow fin tuna which should be mentioned. Most success in *selong* is expected during March, which month is named after torch-fishing (*kahlek*). As noted above that fish is regarded as providing the best bait for catching yellow fin tuna. In the second period of expected better catches of tuna, June and July, the presence of a sea perch, which is another favourite food for the large fish, is said to draw them closer to the surface where they can be caught more easily. In March and April of 1976 both *kahlek* and *selong* fishing of tuna peaked, supporting that association, but the case for sea perch was less clear. As noted above, in June of 1976 most labour went into harvesting the ample crop of breadfruit, whereas more time was spent fishing in June and July of 1978 with *selong* showing reasonable success. This contrast appeared to be related as well to the unusually poor crop of breadfruit in 1978. Other native explanations for the rise and fall of fish catches belong to the realm of observances and precautions, which will be dealt with later in this chapter.

With regard to trolling, or *ilarak*, the above account indicates the chief limitations as being lack of gasoline or operative outboard engines. On the basis of my observations I can say that trolling would produce considerably more fish if these two problems were solved, but by all accounts these problems have been chronic since the introduction of motorized boats. It should be noted that while trolling with paddled or sailed canoes did not produce good results, in former times Pingelapese fishermen ranged much more widely over the ocean in large canoes while trolling. The practices of building the larger canoes as well as distant offshore trolling were discontinued by about 1958 or 1959 due to heavy competition by Japanese fishing vessels in offshore waters. As well, the dangers involved in off shore fishing are considerable. One boat with two fishermen disappeared in 1979, and there were anxious times brought on by long absences of other fishermen during my stays on the atoll.[3]

Animal Husbandry

In addition to occasional crabbing expeditions and, of course, fishing, slaughter of domesticated animals provides substantial amounts of protein food, but only on special occasions. The introduction of these animals and fowl cannot be traced with certainty, though tradition attributes them to post-contact times. The first visit of which we have an account, that of Duperrey (Eilers 1934: 410-12) does not mention any such animals for 1824. While, apparently, none of Duperrey's men ventured ashore, it is significant that animal products were not among the food gifts brought aboard the ship by the Pingelapese. Eilers (ibid.: 413) noted that large numbers of fowls were already present on the atoll by 1853, and that pigs were first reported by Moore in 1857 (ibid.: 414). While it is most probable that these animals and fowl were introduced by passing ships, tradition has it that they were brought from Mwaekil. It is said that the beachcomber, John Higgins,[4] who appears to have been on Pingelap in 1858-60, brought the chickens. The introduction of pigs is attributed to a visit of Pingelapese to Mwaekil during the 1860s, when the chief of the latter atoll held a feast where pigs were killed. The term *koso*, which has come to mean "pig" is also said to be the word for "cut" in Mwaekilese that was used during the butchery and division on that occasion, and as the story goes, mistakenly now applies to the animal itself.

Pigs are not surrounded with the mystique and sacred associations found in Melanesia, nor is their accumulation directly related to measuring wealth on the atoll, but they are indispensable to many major prestation events. Funerals and land-division occasions must especially be represented by considerable numbers of pigs, and often, the latter event is delayed for up to a year before sufficient numbers of pigs can be produced. But there are also a number of other events that require distribution of pigs. In order to meet this substantial demand it is necessary to fatten the pigs as rapidly as possible, so that they are killed usually by the time they are six months old, excepting a few breeders. Accordingly, many animals when slaughtered are essentially obese adolescents. Slabs of skin and fat abound at the major events with little actual pork being attached, due to this rapid fattening process. Such portions are highly regarded by the Pingelapese and may well represent a craving for the fat which, with the exception of coconut products and some of the fish, is largely absent from the diet.

While pigs have an important place, and perhaps an honoured one, in the ceremonial life of Pingelap, dogs are regarded with ambivalence. Informants think that the practice of using dogs as feast animals came from Pohnpei during German times, though Eilers (ibid.: 414) does not mention their presence for 1910. Informants also report that dogs were exterminated periodically on the island not only through being killed for prestation occasions but also because they were considered to be general nuisances, with their droppings littering the villages, their barking, and their tendency to bite people. They are also thought to serve no useful purpose other than consumption at certain feasts.

Pigs are tied, and their escape often means destruction of crops, especially in the taro patch. Dogs and chickens run loose. Both these animals are left to scavenge for much of their food, and one of the favourite items in the diet of dogs is chicken eggs. The latter are usually undersized when they are retrieved, and the chickens themselves are scrawny and tough in the eating. A few ducks which are much tormented by the dogs are also present at times on Pingelap. Cats were introduced probably during the whaling period. They are mainly useful for keeping the omnipresent coconut rats from the houses.

Ritual and the Yearly Cycle

I have noted seasonality in fishing activities. There are also similar peaks and slumps in taro and arboricultural production. Together these seasonal changes have been marked by a definite round of yearly ceremonials, some of which could still be witnessed during the 1970s and early 1980s. Figure 3.1 indicates the traditional yearly cycle of Pingelapese economics and economically related ceremonial events.

If we start description of this cycle with the beginning of the calendar year, the first event *kohta mweniap* marks the advent of the *kahlek* season sometime in January. The word *mweniap* refers to the section of the village where the paramount chief lives. When the ceremony was in full flower this chief received one string of perhaps eight or ten fish from each of the canoes participating in the season's first *kahlek* venture. These he divided among the other title holders. Each title holder, in turn provided a basket of vegetable foods including, if possible, preserved breadfruit, taro, bananas, and pandanus which was presented to the fishermen and eaten at their homes. There is no gathering of people associated with this event. Due probably to the absence of the paramount chief and many of the title holders, the event was much attenuated in 1976 to a gift of a number of fish to the wife of the *nahnmariki*.

The next ceremonial associated with economic seasonality was *umwanpahdah* which marked the closing of the taro patch. Here the act of *kousahkis* or "putting up a piece of wood" was practised. A board is placed against two upright stakes to serve as support for the corms of *maeyung* which are entered in a contest to compare lengths. Each man, including the title bearers, brings his largest corm. The owner of the longest is given a prize of several of the other corms. The remainder are distributed among the men of the village with the title holders getting the largest shares (later the church elders were also so honoured). None of the taro is cooked or eaten at that spot. This ceremony takes place at the end of April and for the next month not only is taro not eaten, but since the new crop of breadfruit is not yet ripe, the chief items of diet are fish, preserved breadfruit, bananas, papayas, and coconuts.

The next seasonal ceremony, *mwungamwung*, is a true "first fruits" event that marks the advent of the ripe breadfruit season on Pingelap. I witnessed one of these ceremonies in 1976 and another in 1978. The 1976 event occurred on schedule on May 30th and was held in front of the church. About 30 or 40 men had gathered and brought planks which had been covered with leaves and then with newly ripe breadfruit cooked in the earth ovens and flavoured with the white cream of coconut sauce. There was also the meat of tuna and the oilfish. After a short speech and a prayer by one of the leading churchmen, several of the men divided a large portion of the breadfruit. They gave each of the four title holders who at that time were residents on the island the breadfruit, which covered about half of an eight-foot plank, while the church officials each received an entire plankful. Those of us present ate of the remaining fruit and the fish, but after our repast much food remained and was carried home by donors. I was told that women and children were simultaneously enjoying such

Figure 3.1
Yearly Economic Cycle and Associated Rituals

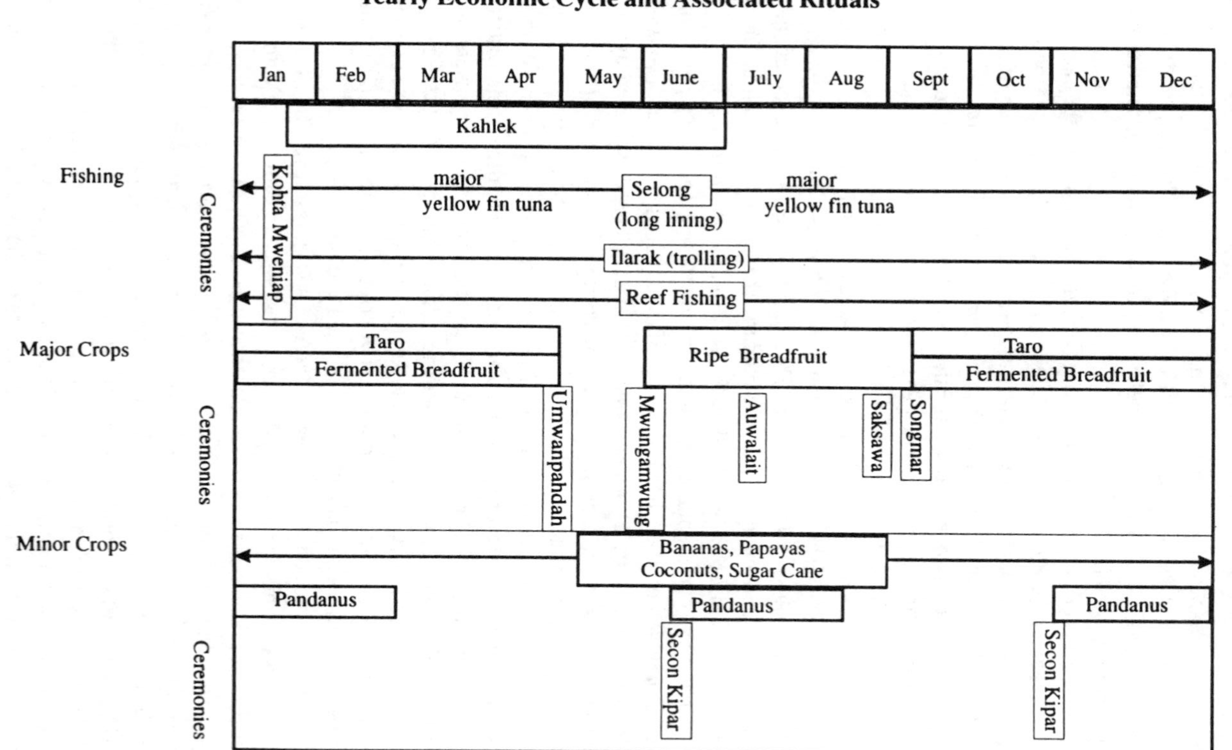

repasts in their homes. The location of the ceremony at the church, the largest shares being given to the church elders, and direction of the event by the senior churchmen, all attest to a Christian overlay to what had been a pagan ceremony formerly honouring the titled persons on the atoll. My information is that church elders were drawn into the ceremony at about the end of the German period.

In the summer of 1978 not one but two *mwungamwung* rituals were held, one at about the normal time, early in June, and the other, which I witnessed, on the aberrantly late date of July 29. The reason stated for this duplication was that 1978 was an unusually poor breadfruit year with not only a much smaller but also late ripening crop. It was felt that the first ceremony had been rather a failure because of the poor state of the product that had been presented. Even in the later ceremony some of the fruit was regarded as being still too green. After this event the season for ripe breadfruit is at hand. The Pingelapese acknowledge a certain conservationism implied by the *umwanpahdah*, marking the closing of the taro patch, but spoke of the *mwungamwung* as setting off the season when they "want to eat all the fresh breadfruit we can while it is here." Actually the custom of closing the taro patch had been abandoned by the time of my visits to the atoll. The reason given for no longer observing this practice was that after the typhoon of 1957 the Pingelapese had the unpleasant experience of having to wait some time for a new crop to mature and were now reluctant to give up their taro during this period of the year.

A short time after the first breadfruit ceremony takes place, the semi-annual ripening of pandanus is celebrated, usually about the middle of June, with the *secon kipar* ritual. Here each man presents several fruit to the gathering of his *pwekil* or village section from which five of the prize specimens are chosen (a total of 20 for the village) and presented to the paramount chief. The remainder of the assembled fruit is divided among the households of each of the four donor *pwekil(s)*.

Another ceremony, the *auwalait*, celebrated usually in July when the yellow fin tuna are plentiful and ripe breadfruit abound, appears to be a sort of "harvest home" celebration of a time of unusual bounty with pigs, fish, ripe breadfruit, and raw pandanus much in evidence. Much of the food is eaten at the gathering of men, women, and children but greater portions are brought home and leftovers fed as usual to the pigs and dogs or tossed away among the debris which help form the boundary markers near the village. The term *auwalait* refers to "waiting for the fishermen." This ceremony was not held in 1978, probably due to the absence of the heavy surpluses which are normally expected at this time of the year.

In late August the Pingelapese hold the *saksawa* event which focuses on the true taro or *sawa*. Each man displays his largest corm in a manner similar to the spring ceremony featuring *maeyung* and the winner is given a similar prize and again the title holders and (today) the church elders bring their shares and take away the largest portions. This observance is associated with the reopening of the taro patch. About a week later, in early September, the first *mar*, or fermented breadfruit, of the year is dug up and distributed as at the *mwungamwung* with parts of the fruit eaten with fish on the spot and other parts taken home. This ceremony, *songmar*, coincides closely with the end of the ripe breadfruit season, for I noted that in 1975 about 90 percent of the crop had been harvested by that time. The remaining customary seasonal ceremony is another *secon kipar* event which coincides with the second semi-annual pandanus crop, about the beginning of November.

It should be noted that among these rituals, women were not permitted at *mwungamwung*, *saksawa*, and *songmar* for it has been believed that otherwise "the old gods will punish the men by taking away their strength" that the food eaten at these ceremonies, or taken home from them, would ordinarily give. I could not attest to the continuing belief in the power of pagan gods in these cases, only that the rituals which among the above I attended were assemblies of men only.

The social anthropologist intent upon understanding the integration of traditional religion with the social order will be frustrated today in studying these rituals on Pingelap. I have noted the overlay of Christian elements in extant events. Such elements eclipse the former roles of the *nanapas* or "priest of the land" and of *nahlaimw* or "priest of the sea" who in pre-mission times presided over the foods of their respective domains at ceremonies. In these and other aspects of ceremonial we are removed from any analysis of pagan elements for the most part, though they may be present in elusive form. On the other hand, there would appear to be a secularization and rationalization in practical terms of customs which may have had traditional religious elements in earlier times. For instance, I have noted that in the *mwungamwung* and *songmar* feasts, fish, and not pig or dog, was eaten with the harvested or preserved breadfruit, but my chief informant insisted that this was because pork and breadfruit "just don't agree in the stomach."

In considering this cycle of ceremonies or rituals, the terms "ceremonious" or "ritualistic" do not seem accurately descriptive for the recent period, for these events are not marked by significant formalized, sacred, or emotive elements. While I have described Christian prayer and supervision of some of the events by church elders, the liturgical elements in the final analysis are minor. Rather, the chief emphasis rests on economic matters, particularly the careful distribution of food. These distributions are carried out with seriousness and with discussion regarding correct procedures, but are otherwise devoid of emotion or formality. While it is possible that I missed some of the events which could have been held during the period of my stays on Pingelap, it is clear that very few were extant by that time. The essential survival of the traditional system of land tenure, as will be described in the following pages, despite the sloughing off of associated ceremonials, strengthens my conviction that the system can be largely understood today in economic terms. Of course, these practices continue to be enmeshed in social relations and social action.

Observances and Precautions

While I heard repeatedly that since the "Good News," or arrival of Christianity in the 1870s, "the old gods are dead," economic activities can still be surrounded by a complex set of avoidances or precautions. These are no longer considered to be in the realm of divine sanctions by the gods, nor are they seen as incompatible with Christian beliefs and observances. Rather, they are considered in terms of their power to produce "good luck" or to avoid "bad luck." Today they are by no means believed in or practised by all Pingelapese. In some cases where they are followed, the practices are complemented by Christian usages. An example can be seen in the observances and avoidances surrounding *kahlek* fishing. While the men pray on the beach before embarking, the expeditions have also been preceded by traditional practices which in large measure are still observed. Formerly, men taking part in *kahlek* slept in the men's houses (*kateri*) on the night of the hunt before being called out and refrained from eating during the day before. I am told that today they still refrain from taking food and from sexual relations preceding the expeditions, even though they sleep in the same houses as their wives, but use separate sleeping mats. Torch-fishing implies not only success or failure in the hunt but also special dangers. As noted above the possibility of being impaled by needlefish is ever present and there is also the danger to the netmen of falling into the sea during their acrobatic actions, with the presence of man-eating sharks always a possibility.

Other fishing methods are considered less dangerous, but they are thought to require certain avoidances to insure "good luck." Women are not allowed on any deep-sea fishing canoe or boat. The use of the *kateri* before days in which *selong* and *ilarak* were practised has been modified as in the case of *kahlek* to avoiding sexual intercourse and using a separate sleeping mat. The *selong* fisherman should not eat breakfast before fishing, but rather carry a lunch which can be eaten only after the first sinker is dropped. Men should not go fishing during their wife's menstruation or for the period after the birth of a child while she continues to bleed. Fishing gear is removed from one's house at such times as well. It is believed that the penalty for failing to observe these precautions is bad luck in the catch.

In the case of *ilarak*, the fisherman should not walk in the dark in order to avoid bumping into people. It is thought that sharks will eat the bait if this happens. No meals are to be eaten until returning from *ilarak*, but this imposes no special difficulty because trolling is usually practised in the early morning hours. In *perumw* fishing everyone taking part must enter the water simultaneously, and return to land afterwards must be made in a group. Otherwise the fish will not enter the net. The *uhkesik* method requires much care in practise since fish will come into the nets only when the moon is one-quarter full and then sometimes only once or twice a year. The uncertainty of this method again requires that a man sleep apart from his wife the night before. In *ilarak*, *perumw*, and *uhkesik*, as in *kahlek* and *selong*, menstrual and childbirth regulations are to be rigidly enforced. It is believed that violations of these prescriptions will cause fish to dive deeper.

There are, as well, certain precautions to be observed in farming, though they are not as extensive as those which accompany maritime activities. When salt water has entered the main taro patch and the new crop is being restored, the planter cannot sleep with his family, and coconut oil is rubbed on the body. These precautions are said to reduce the number of worms and insects which infest the plants at such times. Restriction involving menstruation and the period surrounding it also apply during such times of crop recovery. Particularly important at other times is total avoidance of the *inepwuel* by men whose wives are menstruating. All planting should occur only at special times, including various phases of the moon according to the crop; but harvesting can take place whenever fruit is ripe.

Another set of precautions surround eating practices. Several of these relate again to conditions of female physiology. A woman cannot eat tuna or other deep-sea fish before delivery. If she violates this regulation it is thought that diarrhea will occur and/or that the mother will produce poor milk. Also during pregnancy women cannot eat octopus or clams, for this would cause a difficult delivery. Another eating regulation involves both men and women. During a meal when both reef- and deep-water fish are eaten, once having sampled one or the other of these products, and then moving to the second, one should never return to the first. Violation will cause strife with others and indecision in the day's activities.

These practices in the main can be understood in terms of widely accepted anthropological theory (e.g., Malinowski 1929). A large part of them refer to female physiology and associated notions of ritual uncleanliness. Others appear to relate to notions of intimacy with females weakening virility or in some other way bringing bad luck in uncertain or dangerous occupations. In the case of Pingelap it is not surprising that the greatest number of precautions are related to fishing, especially deep-sea fishing. Not only do these occupations sometimes involve danger, but as the above description of fishing activities indicates, the fickleness of returns from that phase of the economy appears also to contribute to that emphasis. Many of these practices have parallels within Micronesia. In this regard, interesting similarities as well as contrasts can be seen in the example of Woleai as provided by Alkire (1968). On that western Carolinian atoll there are sharp separations of male and female realms not only in occupations but also in regions of identification; for examples, canoe houses — men, dwelling places — women. On Woleai women work the taro patches while men, as on Pingelap, fish in the lagoon and sea. But while in the former place it is the women who must avoid the taro patch during menstruation and after childbirth, on Pingelap it is also the men whose wives are undergoing these physiological phases who must remain away from the taro patch. It may be suggested that this latter practice could have some evolutionary significance in the possible shifting of taro cultivation from women to men in the history of Pingelap. Indeed, I have elsewhere (Damas 1979) posited a shift from the predominately matrilineal emphasis of the Carolines toward a stronger patrilineal bias on Pingelap. This shift could be conceived of as having had a change in the division of labour at its base. However, there is nothing in the legendary history of the atoll to support such a change, and both on Pohnpei (Bascom 1965: 105) and on Kosrae (Wilson 1968: 72), the most likely places of Pingelapese origin, men carry out the work of Cyrtosperma cultivation.

The Division of Labour

While dissociation with women preceding uncertain or dangerous occupations is a strong theme in the belief and *tabu* system of Pingelap, there are less stringent rules or possibilities of supernatural sanctions regarding the division of labour by sex. The accompanying chart (Table 3.2) shows customary male-female and age-youth division of occupations. While exclusion of women from deep-sea fishing, and possibly from planting and harvesting yams[5] are examples of *tabus*, the distinctions more often follow lines of practicality, or simply the force of tradition, without having any known or suspected bad and good luck associations. The information has been elicited from informants, but I have observed nearly all of the practices to be in agreement with the stated ideals as depicted here.

Practical considerations include cases like boys not being allowed to participate in fishing until they are good swimmers, nor being allowed to gather coconuts from trees until they can demonstrate that they can climb the trees with skill and in safety. Carrying bags of coconuts is considered men's work because few women are strong enough to carry the 100-pound loads. It is also felt that planting and fertilizing taro should not be the work of the boys because the delicacy of the rootlets requires more careful movements than expected of the young.

Other customary divisions of economic tasks reflect a certain rather chivalrous attitude toward women. For instance, while I have seen only men climbing coconut trees, I was told that widows or otherwise single women can and do climb them with impunity, but if a man's wife is seen in that act, the husband is liable to criticism or ridicule. Likewise, if any man of the atoll sees a woman climbing a tree, he feels an obligation to help and would be similarly ridiculed if it became known that he failed to do so. While most often I saw women carrying the bundles of grass and leaves used for mulching taro, I was informed that a man must not neglect his share in this work or he will be accused of "treating his wife like a slave." On the other hand, men are not ridiculed when they cook or carry out other domestic chores in the absence of female household members.

Table 3.2
Customary Allotment of Occupations on Pingelap

Men	Women	Men and Women	Children
Deep-sea fishing	Drying and cooking fish	Fishing on reefs	Fishing on reefs
Hunting turtles and crabs; gathering eggs of turtles. Shell fishing	Cooking turtles, eggs shellfish and crabs	Gathering crabs	Gathering eggs, shell-fish and crabs
Planting and fertilizing breadfruit tress. Climbing the trees for fruit and gathering fruit on the ground	Storing breadfruit in ground. Cooking breadfruit	Gathering bread-fruit on ground	Gathering bread-fruit on ground. Picking up bread-fruit leaves
Planting banana plants	Cooking bananas	Fertilizing banana plants	Fertilizing banana plants
Planting and fertilizing coconut trees. Climbing trees. Husking coconuts. Making copra and sennet.	Preparing and cooking recipes with coconuts. Gathering fertilizer for taro. Cooking taro.	Gathering nuts on ground. Making copra. Pulling wagons (riakas) loaded with copra nuts	Gathering nuts on ground. Boys climb coconut trees
Planting and fertilizing taro		Digging up and planting taro	
Making lumber. Building houses and canoes	Making thatch roofs. Gathering gravel for floors		Gathering firewood
	Care of children. Laundry. Making clothes. Gathering firewood.		

The Nutritional Status of Pingelapese

Ecologically oriented anthropologists often attempt calorific studies, seeking to understand through input-output analyses measures of energy expenditures and replenishment, and to gauge the nutritional status of populations. At any place such studies, if conscientiously pursued, require prodigious and meticulous measurements of food procured, food intake, activity patterns, and estimates of basal metabolism rates. Usually such studies depend on samples of households, which are then projected to larger populations. There are estimates of calorific contributions through animal and vegetable sources, and sometimes estimates of protein, fat, and carbohydrate requirements, and of ingredients, in actual diets. In the case of Pingelap the problems of carrying out such studies with any degree of accuracy seemed to me to be overwhelming. A team of observers would be needed to follow the procurement phase of such studies, gathering of plants and capture of fish, and weighing and calculating energy and protein components of these sources. One of the variables which would have to be taken into account is the tendency for many, if not most, Pingelapese to show a gradual gain in weight over time. There is also a great deal of variation in the individual expenditures of energy as well as the tendency for this expenditure to decline with age. Dietary habits show considerable variation from one household to another. Some rely overwhelmingly on vegetable foods. Others show a better balance between seafood and the land products. Still others rely very heavily on store-bought foods such as rice, flour, and sugar. Then there are the seasonal as well as year-to-year fluctuations in supplies of these various food sources. A large sample of households would have to be taken over a considerable period in order to attempt to control these variables.

But even if these variables could be controlled, the great extent of food wastage would be a most difficult matter to handle in any formula seeking to balance energy output with food consumption. With the constant round of food prestation ceremonies, only a few of which have been treated in this chapter, such leaks of produced commodities would confound any attempts to balance both sides of the input-output ledger. It is significant, I think, that the word for these feasts or prestation occasions, is *kamadipw* which translates "to kill" and "to waste." In other words, the ceremonial events of Pingelapese are predicated on the wastage of at least temporarily surplus foods. Of course, a good deal of this wastage is absorbed by animal feeding, and one would have to take into account estimates of the extent of this recovery by carefully accounting for the consumption of widely fluctuating populations of pigs and dogs.[6]

It should be clear that Pingelap, even in the days before store-bought foods, should not be considered as strictly speaking a subsistence economy, but rather one in which periodic surpluses are required by the redistribution practices of the culture. Although there are also periodic or seasonal shortages of certain food sources, the continuous productivity of coconut trees, of taro, and to a lesser extent, stored breadfruit assure ample supplies of vegetables and fruit year-round. While I have indicated periodic slumps in supplies of certain fish species, reef fishing could probably help alleviate such lack if persistently carried out. Accordingly, a period of shortages as conceived by the Pingelapese might mean one in which there was not so much danger of starvation but rather, one in which there was not enough productivity to sustain these periodic and frequent "feasts."[7]

While the Pingelapese, with their tendency toward corpulency in later years, cannot be said to be an underfed population, neither can they be said to be a particulary healthy people. Careful documentation of the incidence of specific physical disorders and of the possible relationship of some of them to dietary practices would constitute useful studies. For instance, I have presumed a protein shortage in the diets of some households at least. The problem of whether such shortages would account for lowered resistance to some diseases could be explored. The possible relationship of the use of such store-bought foods as white rice, white flour, sugar, and soft drinks to nutritional deficiencies and/or excesses leading to some diseases might also be one of the other sorts of rewarding studies which I cannot attempt here. Ultimately such problems do relate to the broader picture of Pingelapese economy and subsistence.

CHAPTER 4

Boundaries, Norms, and Laws in Pingelapese Land Tenure

A useful perspective from which the study of land tenure can be approached is provided by Crocombe (1974: 7-8). He writes of four basic dimensions of land rights: (1) an area dimension, or concern with the boundaries within which rights are exercised; (2) a time dimension which outlines the period over which "the right or other relationship has force"; (3) a population dimension which "enumerates the persons and groups involved and classifies them in relevant categories, statuses, and social classes, each different category having specific rights"; (4) "a complex of legal and customary criteria" which condition rights. The second and third of these dimensions will be dealt with in later sections, while I shall treat the others in this chapter.

The Area Dimension

Any study of land tenure must be concerned with spatial dimensions and spatial designations, the manner in which the actors in local land tenure systems divide their universe of ownership and utilization. There are various orders of spatial divisions on Pingelap, some of which are largely irrelevant to land tenure considerations, some of which bear some possible historical relationship to them, and some which are demonstrably intrinsic to them today. To begin with a brief treatment of the first of these orders, the atoll itself as well as the individual islands are called *daekae*. The reef or *pereu* is distinguished from the lagoon or *lam*, and from the deep sea, *medau*. Then there are directional designations such as *lepous* or inland, and *ilik* or the windward shore of the islands. The village is *kahnihmw*, while the shore facing it is *maesdah*, and the forest is called *wael*. The islands themselves are named (as indicated on Map 1 in a clockwise direction beginning in the south) Pingelap, Sukoru, and Daekae (or Daekaelu).

Notes to Chapter 4 are on pp. 248-49.

However, even in this basic terminology there is disagreement among my informants. Some use no special designation for the main island itself but rather divide it into its main body, or Meseirung, and Likin Epin, the long peninsula, which juts from it and which curves northeast, north, and then west.

The next smaller divisions within the islands are called *kousapw*(s) a term used to designate political divisions on Pohnpei (Bascom 1965: 27). In the case of the main island, but more specifically the village itself, northern and southern sections are called Lepung and Lepier respectively, and these designations have had political importance, with the paramount chief being considered head of Lepier, and the second-ranking chief head of Lepung. Further political divisions within the village are the four *pwekil*(s), Serkerakapw and Mweniap in Lepier; and Kahkahlia and Nahmahl in Lepung. Each of the *pwekil*(s) was represented by a minor chief, and more recently each has its elected officials. The island of Daekae is divided into two major sections called Lopeti or "the left," and Lopeta or "the right," which are classed as *kousapw*(s), but this term appears to be analagous rather than precise for I could determine no political significance for these latter divisions on Daekae.

The islands, including the village and its *pwekil*(s) are further divided into no less than 100 locales called *lepinsapw*(s) (see Maps 2 and 3). In Chapter 2 I indicated the possibility of these divisions once representing land-holding units. If this was the case in the past, it is no longer true today. They now serve mainly as convenient place names for describing points of reference for departure or anticipated arrival, and for designating sites of specific activities. One is constantly being asked when encountered in the forest "where are you going?" or, "where do you come from?" Reference to one or the other of the *lepinsapw*(s) provides the appropriate answer.

The *lepinsapw*(s) are honoured in the song recorded by Hurd (1977) which describes a trip around the islands of the atoll with the distinguishing features or associations of each being noted. References include legendary events, the dwelling place of a ghost or a spirit, location of a well or a species of tree, etc. There does remain some linkage with the land tenure system in that, when speaking of an owned plot, an informant will specify by *lepinsapw* where he holds the land. However, it was evident that the boundaries are not as well established in the minds of some informants as our apparently meticulous survey had mapped them, and often my assistant and I had to search on our maps in *lepinsapw*(s) adjacent to the one named in order to locate the plot in question.

The divisions of the land area of the islands which provide the precise plots of individual ownership are the *peliensapw*(s) that are indicated on the maps of the islands. This term refers to "farmsteads" on Pohnpei (Bascom 1965: 27).[1] On that high island they are much larger and are designated by name. On Pingelap the *peliensapw*(s) are not named but they are designated by precise boundaries which I have described as being rows of piled palm fronds, other arboreal matter and waste material of various sorts. These rows are called *pulliculliculli*(s) and they divide the islands of the atoll into approximately 1 100 separate holdings. Later analysis will indicate how the plots have been divided

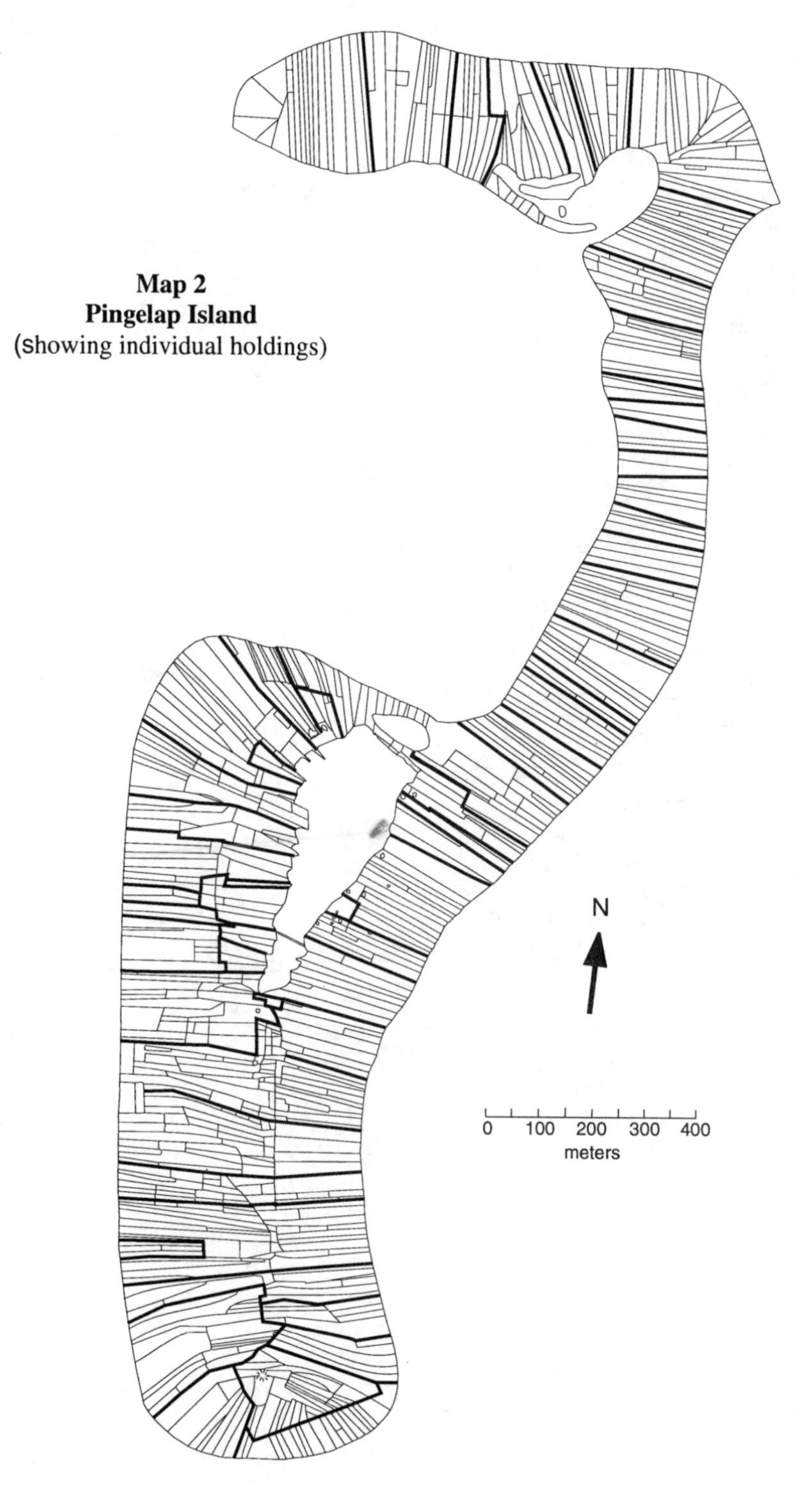

Map 2
Pingelap Island
(showing individual holdings)

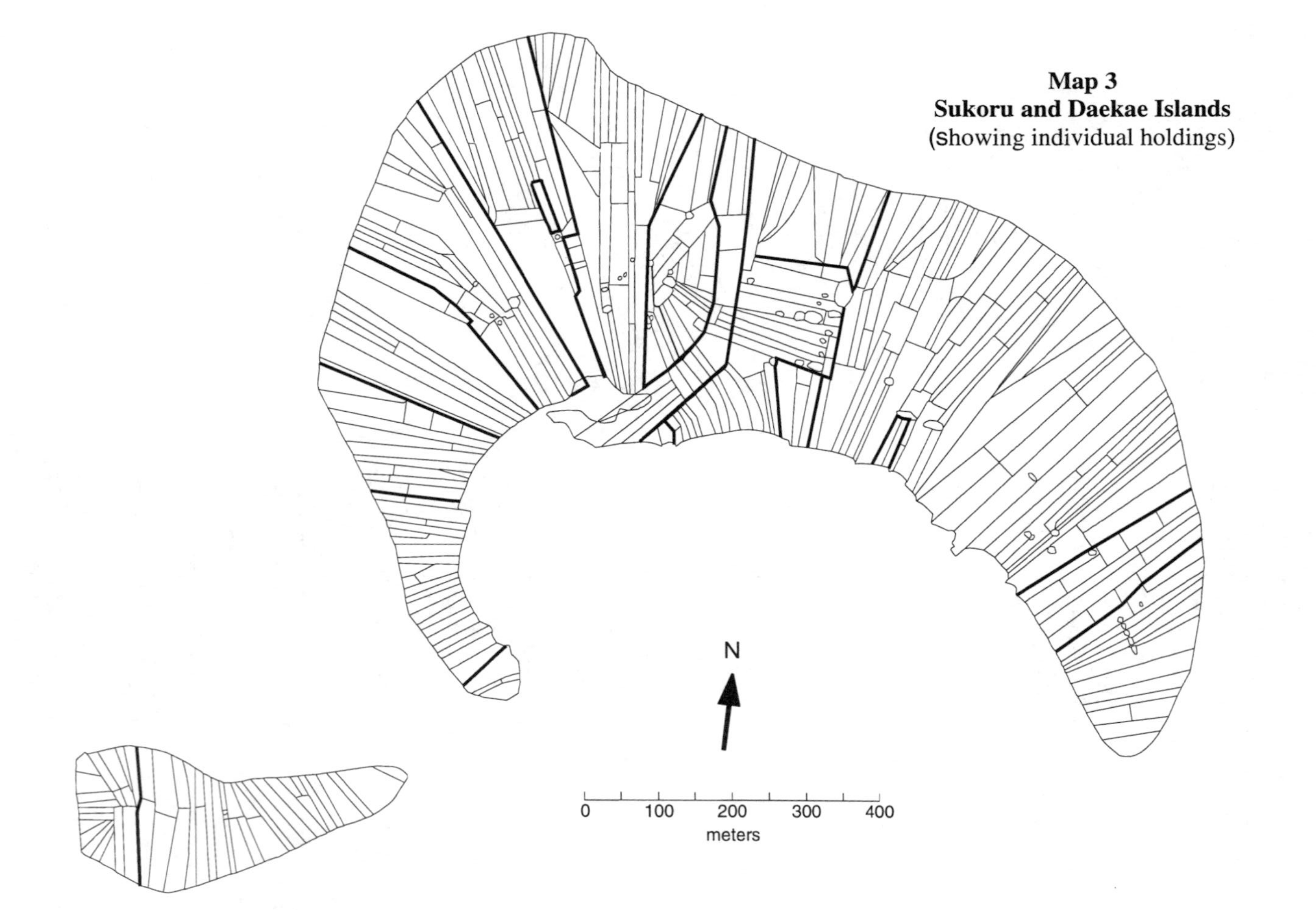
Map 3
Sukoru and Daekae Islands
(Showing individual holdings)
N
0
100
200
300
400
meters

and redivided, and in some cases combined, according to the vagaries of demography. From place to place one will observe both traces of boundaries which have been recently removed as well as freshly placed rows of fronds and husks. Together, these signs represent both processes.

The main taro patch or *inepwuel* is also divided into sections and further subdivided. The most obvious divisions can be observed if one follows the path which encircles the patch. These are the muddy spaces about three feet wide that transect the patch at right angles to its main axis and which are called *sukor*(s). Here and there *sawa* (true taro) is planted in these spaces which serve to segment the patch into its main sections called *maekah*(s). Like the *lepinsapw*(s), the *maekah*(s) are named, some after historical or legendary personages, others for obvious characteristics such as "the great *maekah*" or "the small *maekah*." The origins of other names are obscure. As with the *lepinsapw*(s) each of these segments may have in the past represented private ownership parcels. Today they serve only to locate bundles of rows referred to as *manime*(s) which are individually owned. The ownership parcels are represented on the map of the taro patch (Map 4) by cross-striping. The ownership sections range from 1 to nearly 30 rows each. Most individuals own sections of several *maekah*(s) and each *maekah* contains many *manime*(s) as shown on the map. It is difficult for the outside observer to recognize boundaries between *manime*(s). Spaces between rows can be seen clearly from the causeway which divides the patch near its lower end, but only the concerned and experienced observer can designate which of these is relevant to the separation of *manime*(s). I was told that at times the boundaries are marked by slightly wider spacing between rows, and in other cases double rows of Cyrtosperma mark the borders of individual parcels. The placing of boundaries is sometimes the basis for dispute. More often, disputes arise over the ownership of entire *manime*(s) and especially the use of products from the holdings of others.

At the ends of many of the *maekah*(s) are areas in which the plants, either Colocascia or Cyrtosperma, are planted in irregular or roughly circular fashion rather than in rows. These sections of the patch are called *pong*(s) and are owned by single individuals. The same term is applied to minor excavations in which taro is planted at various places on the main island and on Daekae.

Not only do the widths and numbers of rows in each *manime* vary widely, but the lengths of rows do as well. Phrased in another way, as the map shows, there is considerable variation in the widths of the *maekah*(s) or main horizontal divisions of the patch. Also, some rows of taro are composed of single plants, while others have double rows, with the Cyrtosperma planted so close together that their stems and leaves intertwine. Accordingly, it is all but impossible to estimate not only the total number of plants in the patch but also the number of plants in the holdings of each individual.

In addition to the divisions within the taro patch and the primary divisions of the forest, other such *peliensapw*(s) include house sites in the village. For those plots which border the main road no markers are evident, but some distance back from the road, the familiar rows of fronds and husks commence.

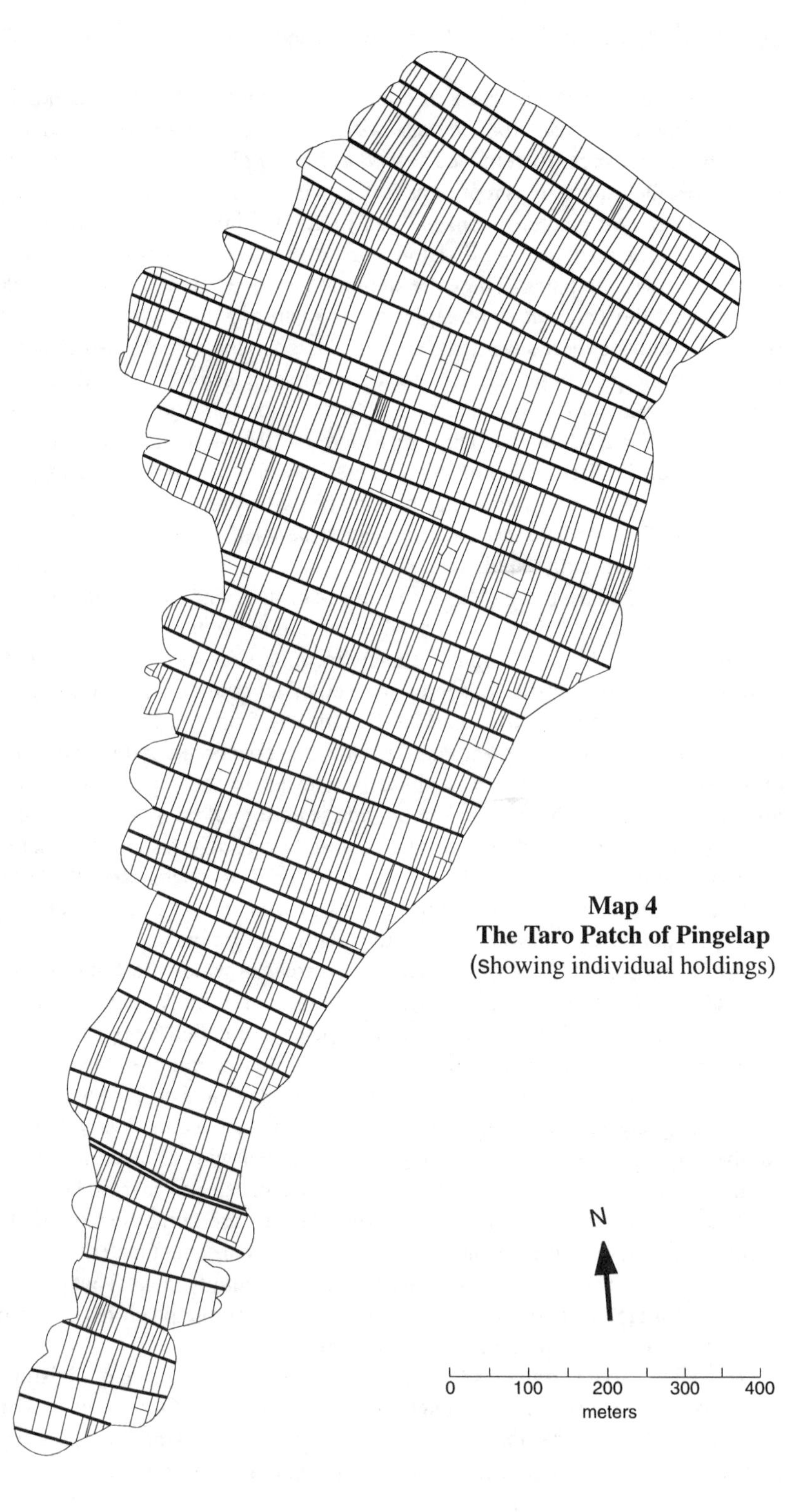

Map 4
The Taro Patch of Pingelap
(showing individual holdings)

While the divisions of the taro patch, house plots, and plots in the forest have precise boundaries for ownership and use of property, there are other places where the possibility of ambiguity may arise regarding boundaries. Tidal areas present such ambiguity. On Pingelap, land under water traditionally has been considered to be communal property for purposes of fishing. At low tide, however, the tidal area is considered to be the property of the owner of the individual plot from which it extends. There is little evidence for problems of ownership on the ocean sides of the islands, for the beaches that separate the forest from the reef are never crossed by markers of any kind. On the lagoon side one can see in low tide rows of rocks here and there extending outward from the ends of landward boundary markers for some distance over the tidal flats. Some of these are closed at their lagoon end by more rocks. Such concern for claiming ownership for tidal areas is, however, rarely evidenced.

Another type of ownership situation which is not marked, but only understood by the principals, occurs in cases of ownership of trees, usually breadfruit trees, which are less plentiful than the ubiquitous coconut palm. In the examples that I have found individuals granted full-use privileges of trees growing on their land, usually to close relatives who had fewer breadfruit trees, or none at all. In my treatment of the history of Pingelap (chap. 2) I mentioned traditions which suggest shifts in land and taro-holding ownership and use rights, and I will examine later in greater detail the probable course of these changes. But a word regarding the nature of land ownership as I observed it on the atoll is, perhaps, appropriate here. Each of the individual plots of land and minor divisions of the taro patch is identified by names of individual Pingelapese and not by any larger unit. Such indicators, together with the testimony of all informants, which points to the right of disposal of such properties by individuals, clearly signifies the degree to which individual ownership has developed on the atoll. On the other hand, use privileges generally operate within the extended family of father and adult sons and their wives when such units are in full operation, even though assignments of land and taro sections may have been made previously. The chief way in which use privileges are extended in the contemporary land tenure situation on Pingelap is through a system of stewardship of land owned by Pingelapese not resident on the atoll. I will discuss the operation of that system in later chapters.

Customary Norms of Pingelapese Land Inheritance

Given these physical dimensions of land tenure, I move now to another basic set of Pingelapese land tenure dimensions, those regarding customary understandings which reveal notions of rightness or the realm of norms. For some anthropologists the idea of seeking or enlisting norms constitutes pursuit of entities which are too vague or elusive to warrant consideration. In many cases the concept of a "pragmatic design" (Nadel 1957: 139-52) may be so remote from the actualities of field situations as to warrant suspicions that when employed they consist of abstractions conceived in the ordering mind of the anthropologist. Such a design might be regarded as being enlisted in order to facilitate presentation of data in an artificially neat manner, rather than reflecting either the conceptions of the subjects of study, or plausible representations of the empirical reality.

In the case of Pingelapese land tenure, notions of normativeness arise at times from implicit or unacknowledged guides which operate without the threat of sanctions and which are subject to the constant flux brought on by practice. Then there are those which appear to have roots in tradition, and may in some cases carry with them the memory, at least, of traditional sanctions. Finally, in recent years codification has entered the scene and implies legal settlements. The plan to use native conceptions of norms (either elicited or inferred) to form a map or guide for analysis of land tenure may not be acceptable to all anthropologists concerned with land tenure, but it is my conviction that not only does such an approach provide a convenient framework for study, I cannot conceive of the development or operation of the main features of the Pingelapese land tenure system without enlisting what appear to be its underlying principles.

Having said that, however, I want to avoid the trap of reification of such principles as may be said to exist. The conditions of gathering data in the field are still too fresh in my mind to dismiss them easily, and the chapters that follow will be in large part an exercise in testing the efficacy of such norms as are posed here. The conditions of field work also do not permit in most cases a neatly ordered sequence of understandings such as is possible to present in a written work. In that sense my presentation is artificial. The anthropologist working in the field who tries to organize his material in terms of both the dimensions of norms elicited from informants or inferred, and of empirical data, must often proceed on these two fronts simultaneously. I think that it is a rare field situation that provides anthropologists with a consistent version of such norms as those sought here in a study of land tenure before they have already embarked on gathering empirically verifiable data. In my own experience on Pingelap, I was able to derive some guides to understanding principles of Pingelapese land tenure from initial interviews directed toward that end. Some of these initial guides proved to be misleading, and, by and large, expressions of normativeness emerged during interviews conducted in the period when I was surveying the islands, and especially afterwards during the collection of life history material. While the frame of norms was derived in part from the interviews which produced the material that forms the empirical base of this study, these very interviews also revealed departures from the norms. For the remainder of my field work on Pingelap and during my work with Pingelapese on Pohnpei I continued to move among these levels. Questions of norms came to mind in the intervals between field sessions and were tested out on my return trips. Appraisal of their efficacy continued through my examination of the corpus of life history and cartographical material after returning from my last trip to the area. In my review of Pingelap history I cited various native versions of the evolution of the current system of land tenure. I shall return to a consideration of the possible credibility of the various versions later. In this chapter I am more concerned with what appears to be the existing norms themselves, whose origins may have been spread over considerable periods of time.

Chief among those norms which receive general acknowledgement is that of a patrilineal bias in land inheritance. It is considered normal that the bulk of the land and taro to be inherited will pass from father to children, and correlatively, it is expected that the sons will be given larger shares than the daughters. A second principle points to the eldest son being awarded a significantly larger share than succeeding sons, and shares definitely larger than any of the daughters, though no precise scaling downward according to age or sex could be revealed in my inquiries.

While the shares of the father will be expected to provide the largest source of land and taro, some or all, of a couple's offspring may expect to receive land from the mother as well, especially if her holdings are substantial. A woman is said to have the right of disposal of her dowry[2] or any other land which she may have acquired. Ideally, at least, she can also take her property with her in the event of divorce or remarriage after being widowed. A woman may also give back land to her natal *peyneyney* (extended family) at any time. Normally, disposal of a woman's property is decided during her lifetime, but if, in the event of sudden death, or for some other reason, this has not been arranged, her father or older brother (if the father is deceased) has the right of disposal. In spite of her basic right to sell or give land as she pleases, convention supports the practice of the largest part of it passing to her children. The extent to which women do indeed influence or control distribution of property considered to be their own must vary. One of my informants noted that he had quarrelled with his father for taking too active a role in the distribution of his mother's property. There may be other cases where women not only controlled their own property but also had considerable influence in settling the husband's estate as well.

With regard to the actual decision-making in the dispersal of properties, the testator himself is expected to be the chief designator with this exception of consultation with his wife. Usually decisions as to how an estate is to be divided are made well before actual disposal is made. If a man dies intestate, the eldest son, either natural or adopted, if adult, will make the division of the estate. Pingelapese take special care to provide heirs for their property and I know of no example where lack of heirs has occurred, at least in the present century. On the basis of informant statements it would appear that if such a situation should occur the division decisions revert to the level of the *keinek* with the senior male or *mesieni en keinek* apportioning the property. While examples cited later will show that the process of land inheritance is bilateral and regulated largely within the extended family, these exceptions when the *keinek* is said to have been involved reinforce my supposition that this latter unit did indeed have a stronger role in Pingelapse land tenure in former times.

Another set of norms concerns adoption.[3] An adopted child should be provided with a piece of land and some taro rows by both the donor and recipient parents. Ideally the adopted child carries land from the natal family and is eventually given property from the estate of the adoptive parents as well. During the adoptee's childhood the land that is brought along from the natal family will be worked by the members of the adoptive extended or nuclear family, but in theory, remains the child's to dispose of. With regard to the fate of such property in the event of such children returning to their natal family, I encountered contradictory information from my sources. Some said that the land should go back with him. Others deny that this is an approved procedure. It appears that this circumstance presents one of the soft spots in the rationale of ideal land tenure procedures and implies the basis for dispute. Adoptive children will also expect equal treatment with natural children in the adoptive family, if such children exist, when estates are redistributed.

In addition to recognizing the assignment of land by both donor and recipient families to children, another time-honoured mode of transferral is from grandparents to grandchildren. Assignment of nominal ownership of property to small children raises the question of distinguishing between practical control and putative control. In these cases, while such children will be the actual beneficiaries in that they are fed from the products of these holdings (along with the products of other land held by the adopting family, or that of the father), the labour of production is done by others and the products, whether for subsistence, or in the case of copra, for cash returns, are not held in trust for their maturity. They are consumed or converted to cash for the discretionary use of the head of the family with which the inheriting child lives. Immigrants traditionally have been absorbed into extended families, matriclans, and *keinek*(s) and eventually acquire land rights, which are willed, along with other adoptive and or natural children in the extended families to which they are attached. This adoption of adults is otherwise a highly unusual, but not unheard of, practice.

It is widely agreed that property given in estate settlements can be reassigned or redistributed by the senior male heir. Such cases occur when there is perceived to be an unfortunate distribution of land and taro rows so that one or the other of a sibling groups is disadvantaged to the point of hardship. Redistribution among siblings may also occur when certain members of the group acquire large windfalls, as for instance, through marriage into a land-affluent family, especially one with few offspring.

In addition to getting land through these close sorts of natal or adoptive relatives, land can be acquired through gifts by distantly related or unrelated people. One of the most frequent circumstances under which such gifts are given is when the beneficiary has helped the donor in subsistence or other matters, usually in the old age or sickness of the donor.

The Usufruct System

All of the above statements refer to the conventions or norms of transferring true ownership, including rights of disposal. Conventions of use privileges are also important and can be best understood in the context of the cycle of domestic units. My chief informant recognized four main stages as they relate to land use, as well as ownership, as follows:

(1) When the father is living, all married sons normally live together with him in a compound sharing a cooking house and meals. All are expected to use land in common and share in its subsistence, and in the case of copra, cash proceeds.
(2) With the father still living but with land divided either at the marriages of the sons, or in case of assignation of parts of estate in old age, the traditional norm was for the sons to continue to live together in a compound with the father, and ideally at least, the father would continue management of the land. Even though the land is divided and the men worked separately, the products should continue to be pooled.
(3) After the death of the father the sons will be expected to set up separate residences and to work and use the products of the land separately.
(4) In time when the sons reach middle age they will head extended families as in stage (1), and the same practices are re-established as in that stage.

One departure from the traditional picture is also recognized in stage (1). This has to do with the emigration which has characterized the present century. Under these circumstances the stated norm was for one son to remain with the father forming a minimal use and sharing unit, whereas other sons in the colonies acquire new lands there and work them separately and use their products independently. Another contemporary situation diverges somewhat from this model. This concerns long-term absences of young men for employment or higher education. When the young man is a member of an operating extended family, the land continues to be used by other members of such family units. If married, his wife and children (if there are such) remain in close residence with other members, cooperating in harvesting and sharing in consumption of the property claimed by such units. There have been other cases where the young man will turn over temporary use of his properties to other relatives or friends if he is not a member of an operational extended family group. But sometimes, as well, the property remains unused or is used by the wife herself under conditions where the isolated nuclear family has become the land-owning unit. The wife in such cases may also enlist the help of her siblings or parents in harvesting the products of her husband's land and taro holdings.

In connection with this cycle and regarding the use of an in-marrying woman's land, the husband, and later the sons, should carry out the main agricultural work except for certain tasks which are occupations shared with women. The raw products of this land are expectably to be pooled within the extended family of the husband, but ideally at least, this pooling of products of the woman's land is regarded as being voluntary on her part.

The Occasions of Land Division

Another important aspect of Pingelapese land tenure regards the occasion at which division of the land occurs. Some division takes place on a very informal level at times but is often reaffirmed later in ritual. There appeared to me to have been a degree of flexibility as to what is considered proper in this matter at the times of my studies on Pingelap. Transferral of land is expected both at the time when a child is adopted and when a woman marries, and coincidentally, assumes the normal practice of virilocal residence when she leaves the natal household. It might be well to add a note regarding the concept of dowry at this point. The term for dowry, *pelienenmwar*, actually refers to a reciprocal practice, since it derives from the expression which is used when a man presents a gift of food to the father-in-law at such times when the wife has returned because of a quarrel. The sons-in-law are also expected to present such gifts weekly through the life time of the wife's father. Thus, the system of dowry on Pingelap not only provides the insurance, or seed, estate function outlined above, but is also enmeshed in a system of what amounts to long-term bride price.

The division of lands for male offspring can occur at any one of three occasions. The occasion which is regarded as most appropriate is that of the *derak mour*.[4] In this instance an aged man, or one suffering from chronic debilitating disease which renders him incapable of contributing significantly to the family economy, will declare a ceremony to formally assign division of the estate. This act of formalizing land division theoretically implies full ownership, with rights of disposal included, but sons are expected to consult with the father in cases of sale or gift awarding of this property.

The *derak mour* ceremony proceeds with each member of the recipient party bringing gifts of pigs and taro in proportion to their share of the estate, as has been determined beforehand. This ceremony allows for least dispute, since the donor is present to regulate the division of the gifts which follows, thus affirming the appropriate exchanges.

A variant occasion, which seems in actuality to occur about as frequently as the above-described event, is the *derak mehla*, which takes place after the death of the donor male. In some cases this adjustment is made because of the sudden death of the donor. At such times final assignment may not have been made and some dispute may arise and must be resolved by the heir-apparent to family headship, usually the eldest surviving son. In many cases there is already such an understanding, and division usually proceeds smoothly. In some cases a delay of about one year will ensue after the death of the estate holder before the *derak mehla* is celebrated. This arrangement is often necessary in order that enough taro and pigs (especially) can be accumulated. It is clear that not only considerations of internal kin group reciprocity must be served by this accumulation, but family prestige must be upheld as well, as the *derak* ceremonies are attended by a large part of the community. Normally women do not receive lands at either of the *derak* cermonies but almost always at the times of their marriages. Those latter acquisitions are celebrated or "paid for" at such occasions.[5]

The other occasion at which land is awarded to males occurs at marriage. As in the case of dowry awards there is no special ceremony at such times. Even though rights of disposal are in theory, at least, granted at such times, though subject to consultation with the father, the final affirmation of such awards must be made at one of the *derak* occasions. My chief informant indicates that the practice of awarding land at the marriage of sons sometimes occurred in traditional times as an insurance measure against sudden death such as loss at sea or from the effects or after-effects of typhoons.

Other Forms of Land Disposal and Use

The sale of land is generally agreed upon as having been a product of the recent cash-income phase of Pingelap history, and it appears to be more frequently practised with each passing decade during the American period. On the other hand, instances of exchange of properties appear to have preceded the advent of land sales. Cases cited to me are of the nature of oral history regarding people long dead and thus may be apocryphal, but perhaps one is worthy of mention. In this case one of the title holders who flourished about the middle of the nineteenth century had been ridiculed for not having bananas on his land. In response, he traded a large *peliensapw* for a smaller one in a locale where bananas grow in profusion to counter this ridicule.

One other situation of gift giving of land was mentioned by informants and presumably refers to the period before the present century. This was said to have occurred in cases where casting men adrift as punishment for serious breaches of customary law had been threatened. In such cases the offender might offer a large prestation to the *nahnmariki* in order to get his sentence revoked. If he succeeded, he would in cases where another individual was considered to have been offended, also give such an individual a section of land and rows in the taro patch "in gratitude."

The phenomenon of absentee ownership and stewardship by residents on the atoll, or *kohwa*, appears to be a twentieth-century practice following upon the establishment of colonies on Pohnpei. It is possible, though I have no evidence to support the notion, that something similar may have transpired earlier when men were absent from the atoll working aboard ships. Although the practice of stewardship probably has a short history, a definite convention of use and recompense has been established. The absentee owners on Pohnpei when interviewed declared that the property on the atoll is owned by them in perpetuity. In the abstract at least, this condition was conceded by residents on Pingelap as well, and affirmation of this absentee ownership comes in the form of periodic sending of products of such land by the steward at intervals which are not specified, but generally coincided with the visits of the field trip vessel to the atoll. In practice, this obligation has been often neglected as the years and generations pass. At the same time non-resident claims to lands have been weakened to the extent that by 1980 the stewards were already awarding their own heirs land thus held in trust. In a later chapter there will be examples presented of how this system of *kohwa* has become the most critical basis for land disputes at the present time.

Sanctions and Pingelapese Land Tenure

The above discussion of normative dimensions of Pingelapese land tenure is based on a number of interviews conducted over an eight-year period. To be sure there was disagreement on some points among informants, as well as substantial agreement on others. There were even some apparent contradictions in the testimonies of single informants. Judgments had to be made regarding both of these orders of disagreement. In dealing with the area of idealized behaviour, anthropologists have at times applied the concept of *rule*. Here, I have avoided that usage, preferring instead the terms "norms," "principles," or "conventions." As indicted above, there is a sliding scale involved, with some of the norms or conventions having only implicit backing, others having apparently general verbal acknowledgement, and still others being more rigidly defined precepts.

The Webster definitions of *rule* cover a range of meanings, from "an established guide or regulation for action, conduct, methods, arrangement, etc." to at another pole "a fixed principle which determines conduct, habit, custom." It is fitting to separate usage of "norm," "principle," or "convention" from the idea of a more firmly fixed notion of "rule" as described in this second definition in terms of the concept of *sanction*. In several of the above examples the first of these definitions is most fitting, especially regarding the norms or conventions of land distribution. These received general support but, on the basis of my interviews, they operated or were departed from on the basis of decisions made within extended family units and must be relegated, for the main, to the realm of conventions which are not subject to sanction.

The idea of sanction in Pingelapese land tenure is most strongly associated with the concept of *pirap*, that is theft, or trespassing. Sanctions which relate to *pirap* find their roots deep in the traditional history of the atoll. One of the important duties of the court of chiefs was to rule on property disputes and to assign penalties and awards which were to be enforced by the village police. In cases of thefts of plant products from the *peliensapw*(s) the entire court convened at the point of the the alleged infraction to consider the evidence. After discussion with the principals, they made a decision and the immediate sanction of a public scolding was administered, since usually a number of bystanders were present at this scene. Afterwards the court assessed fines. It was reported to me that a typical fine was 100 coconuts for the convicted in cases of use of products of another's trees. The plaintiff was also levied a smaller fine, with 50 coconuts being cited as typical. This latter assessment apparently was designed to discourage questionable cases from being brought before the court of chiefs and to encourage informal settlement between principals.

In cases of taro patch disputes the court of chiefs also convened at the site of alleged infraction. After a decision was made as to the worthiness of the case of the plaintiff, the chiefs could rearrange ownership of rows as they saw fit. Again, a public scolding session ensued, after which the convicted had to dig up three of his largest corms of Cyrtosperma to give to the court as a fine. Such a fine was severe since as has been stated above, in traditional times the species of taro then known on the atoll took five to ten years to reach a size large enough for harvesting.

A form of destruction, rather than theft, which had a long history on Pingelap until a fence was built around the taro patch in 1976, was that caused by loose pigs entering the *inepwuel* and destroying crops. In those cases it is said that the plaintiff could kill the offending pig, but must return the carcass to the owner.

As far as I am able to determine, trials and consequent fines and scoldings or other penalties obtained between members of different recognized *keinek*(s). Matters of offences committed within these patrilineally oriented kin units were ideally, at least, regarded as being internal matters and were expected to be settled on that level. Later examples will show that illegitimacy, step-siblingships, adoption, divorce, and other bases for shifting *keinek* membership were at the roots of many of the disputes that arose and which sometimes festered over several generations.

Transitional to the system of court trials which was introduced during the American period was the institution of the Seven Men. The Germans introduced this system first to Pohnpei. It was an appointed body which served to settle land disputes in an informal manner. At some point during the German period the system was introduced to Pingelap as well. It continued in force throughout the Japanese period and was said to be still in operation as a first line of settlement procedure even at the time of my visits to the atoll. By the time of my study, however, the body had been expanded to ten men in order to achieve balanced representation. That is, there are now two members selected from each of the *pwekil*(s) and two members at large. Some, but not all, of the present roster are titled persons and all are appointed for life by the *nahnmariki*. I was told that, usually, rather than acting as a body, the appropriate member quietly approaches the plaintiff and defendant in disputed cases in order to persuade them to settle their differences amicably. It is difficult to assess the efficacy of this procedure because of the confidential way in which it is conducted, but judging from the importance of land ownership on the atoll, and taking into account the few cases actually brought to court during my years of contact with the Pingelapese, some degree of effectiveness must be granted.

The Effects of Codification

After such attempts at "friendly persuasion" fail, the disputes move to the local court, whose jurisdiction has been outlined in the *Trust Territory Code* (Steincipher 1970a, 1970b). My notes for 1975-76 show several cases being brought before the local court which concerned land tenure disputes. One elderly man was the most frequent offender over a period of years, according to my informants, and he was brought to court twice during the 11-month span of my first visit to the atoll. He was regarded as being peculiar, for he had plenty of land and taro for his own subsistence and copra production, and it was thought that he was merely trying "to put one over" on others. On one occasion he even resorted to the obvious expedient of shifting the boundary marker separating one of his plots from an adjoining one. This was done while the copra ship was being loaded and most of the men, including the owner of the encroached upon plot, were occupied in the operation. The shifting incorporated about a half-dozen bearing coconut trees that previously had been located outside the old man's land. In this case the obvious infraction was not brought to court since the offended landowner was informed of the encroachment and quickly paddled his canoe across the lagoon to the site on Daekae and restored the boundary to its former position. The same elderly man became involved one morning in a loud and heated argument with a man who claimed theft from a section in the taro patch. This case was later brought to trial and the old man judged guilty. The court fined the offender $5.00 for each stolen corm of Cyrtosperma for a total of $35.00, half of which amount was given to the rightful owner and half kept by the court for costs.

A second case was tried the same day. This concerned theft of pandanus fruit, breadfruit, and coconuts from a neighbouring plot. The offender, of course, claimed that the land from which these products were taken was rightfully his own. However, the plaintiff won his case and the offender was fined $20.00. The reason for the smaller fine in this case was not so much the possible lesser value of the stolen property, but because the convicted was a first offender in contrast to the more heavily fined old man who was a habitual transgressor. These fines are significant when one considers that both men had cash income only from the widely fluctuating copra prices. The severity of punishment can be especially appreciated when it is noted that each of the offenders in these cases was also sentenced to 30 days labour on public projects from 7:30 a.m to 2 p.m. daily, except for Sundays.

With definite sanctions being administered in both the quasi-legal framework of traditional custom and with the advent of the municipal court in American times, the examples of theft and encroachment cited above could be regarded as violating *rules* in terms of the definition of that term which I have adopted here. Today if cases are not settled on the atoll to the satisfaction of the plaintiff, he may appeal to the District Court in Pohnpei. As subsequent case studies will show, even such cases that normally were supposed to have been settled on the level of the extended family or the "lineage" were brought to the attention of the court in Pohnpei during the American period.

Certain of the regulations of the *Trust Territory Code* (ibid.) have little application to an atoll situation like that of Pingelap. For instance, Section 11101 entitled "Restriction Upon Land Ownership," which states that "only citizens of the Trust Territory may hold titles to land in the Trust Territory" has no present applicability, since Americans or other nationals have not attempted to buy land on the atoll. To my knowledge the stricture that the metric system be used in measuring as specified in Section 11151 (Steincipher 1970b: 544-50) has been applied only in cases of land sale, not in cases of inheritance. Section 11152 (ibid.: 550) requires payment for land markers to the District Land Title Officer, but on Pingelap only natural materials having no monetary value are used as markers.

Other regulations imposed by the *Code* do have application on Pingelap, for instance Section 11153 reads as follows:

> Any person who willfully and maliciously defaces, alters, or removes any marker erected for the purpose of designating any point in the boundary of any lot or tract of land shall, upon conviction, be imprisoned for a period of not more than one year, or fined not more than one hundred dollars, or both (ibid.: 550-51).

Thus if the injured party in the case of the shifted boundary mentioned above had brought his case to court this regulation could have been enforced with an indeed severe penalty liable to have been imposed.

Regarding another regulation of the *Code*, it is clear that not all records of land transfers are kept on the atoll, as specified under Section 111201 (ibid.: 551), or that notice has been taken of failure to comply as indicated in Section 111202 (ibid.) in cases of transferrals within families as are organized in the *derak* ceremonies or other less formal divisions.

Later legislation as presented in the 1975 *Cumulative Supplement* of the Code (Steincipher 1975) refers to the *Land Planning Act* of April 14, 1972. This act states that "to regulate the use of lands in the Trust Territory and to regulate the quality and type of structures placed thereon is the prerogative of the Congress of Micronesia" (ibid.: 250). Thus there has clearly been an attempt to impose a higher degree of order and standardization on land tenure practices during the Trust Territory period of American influence. Such attempts at standardization run counter to the proposal of Douglas Oliver and his associates in 1951 regarding such policies of the Trust Territory government (chap. 2). I have observed that some or most of the regulations of the *Land Planning Act* were being applied on Pohnpei in the early 1980s, but they were slow to diffuse to the outer islands at that time. The Act appeared to place a great deal of decision-making power in the hands of the Planning Commission on Pohnpei. If these policies continue into the Free Association phase of Micronesian history, judging by my observations regarding another attempt to impose outside legal strictures on Pingelap (Damas 1985), such attempts will have a rocky road ahead if they are perceived as running counter to Pingelapese conceptions of land tenure.

At the time of my last visit to Pingelap in 1983, traditional norms of land tenure continued in force to a large extent. However, the ambiguities apparent in that system, and which are perhaps inherent in all similar systems not strictly regulated by codification, continued to provide contention. With the establishment of court hearings many cases which could not be resolved, and perhaps of a type which had never been resolved by traditional means, were being settled. It appears that, more and more, court decisions will be resorted to on the atoll and in the District Court in Pohnpei. While Pingelap remained to no small extent a locally autonomous political and legal entity, the tendency to appeal to the High Court appeared to be entering a new, more active phase. Such recourse appeared to be especially on the horizon in cases of disputes over *kohwa* lands and taro holdings, an aspect of Pingelap land tenure that will be addressed in detail later.

While appeal to codified bases for decisions in land tenure disputes may be on the increase, the process of codification is far from complete in terms of dealing with some of the special problems of the Pingelapese. There is clearly a trend on the part of the emerging nations of Micronesia to develop legislation aimed toward uniformity or standardization of land laws, at least on the state level. Ultimately such uniformity, if achieved through codification, poses the danger of lacking flexibility to deal with the sorts of disputes arising under conditions of specific traditional systems of land tenure. This is especially true in the Pingelap case where the traditional means of conveyance through oral arrangements still pertains. Indeed, the Pingelapese may have to go over to the practice of registering wills. Meanwhile, the resistance which they have shown toward outside pressures suggests that there will be a conflict before more highly developed codification, or even effective application of existing laws, will be completely accepted.

Summary

Following upon my stated objectives for this chapter I first examined the various divisions of the land areas and of the taro patch of the atoll. This survey revealed several levels of land division, of which some have political significance, others are intimately involved in ownership and use practices, and at least one, the *lepinsapw*, has survived mainly for purposes of orientation. The taro patch was also seen to have major and minor divisions, with the latter being composed of individually owned parcels or rows of plants.

I then moved to the level of the norms of Pingelapese land tenure practices which included considerations of patrilineal and primogenitive biases in land inheritance; and rights of disposal of properties, including those acquired by women in dowry. A usufruct system was revealed which involves a series of norms that relates to the "developmental cycle of the domestic group" (Goody 1958). The phenomena of sale and gifts of land and the concept of stewardship were also introduced. Consideration of norms drew me into questions of sanctions, beginning with traditional sanctions brought to bear against violations of some customary norms. Ultimately, the effects of codification on Pingelapese land tenure practices had to be considered.

The outline of the area dimension of Pingelapese land tenure will help provide a frame within which to consider the parcelling and transferral of lands, and recognition of elicited or inferred norms provides a template of expectations regarding the practices themselves. In the following chapters I will consider fidelity to or divergence from such norms and assess their efficacy in structuring the land tenure system of the Pingelapese.

CHAPTER 5

Patterns of Pingelapese Land Inheritance

In exploring actual land tenure practices on Pingelap against the backdrop of norms discussed in the previous chapter, it is necessary to summarize the procedures followed in the field. Once having become committed to devoting a substantial part of my time in 1975-76 to the study of land tenure, the obvious first step was to survey the three islands of the atoll in order to mark off the boundaries of individual holdings. Maps 2, 3, and 4 represent the results of this survey. On the maps of the land areas (Maps 2 and 3) the finer lines indicate the boundaries of the *peliensapw*(s), or individual plots, while the heavier lines indicate the approximate boundaries of the *lepinsapw*(s) or orientational districts. On the map of the taro patch (Map 4) the heavier lines mark the *maekah*(s) or major patch divisions, and the finer lines the *manime*(s) or individual parcels of rows.

While I measured the plots,[1] my field assistant gathered information from a large number of people which served to identify ownership of holdings. When this survey was completed, I interviewed selected informants regarding the sources of their lands. My methods of selecting informants leaves something to be desired in terms of producing a model statistical study, but I had to yield to the limitations of the field situation. With the great elaboration of land division on the islands of the atoll, it appeared that it would be an impossible task to achieve a total coverage of the atoll in the time available. While my assistant and I succeeded in identifying ownership of each of the segments of the land area and of the taro patch, it proved to be all but impossible to work from the scattered holdings of individuals to produce complete histories of transferrals of ownership for all of them. The absences of a large number of plot owners from the atoll made for further limitations. Preliminary inspection of the data gathered indicated that there would be a wide range in the extent of individual holdings, and if we devoted much time to interviewing small landowners, our efforts would be poorly rewarded in the time available. Since I could not conceive of any approach that would produce a random sample, I decided to pro-

Notes to Chapter 5 are on pp. 250-51.

ceed by first interviewing those individuals who were acknowledged as the largest landholders, so that the interviews could proceed with maximum efficiency. We also tried to interview informants who belonged to family groups to which large holdings were attributed for several generations. After these persons were interviewed we planned to work through a roster of people who held less and less land until the time that could be devoted to the study was exhausted. We hoped that by following this plan we could produce as large as possible sampling of the entire land and taro areas.

In practice this procedure could not be followed precisely, for the extent of the knowledge of the holdings of individuals is limited even for such well-informed persons as my field assistant. The sample which was produced did, however, show a wide disparity in the amounts of land and taro owned, even though we did not reach most of the putative small landowners. Proceeding along these lines, I was able to interview and gather life histories of land transferrals from 13 informants in the late spring and early summer of 1976, and from 19 others in the summer of 1978. In that same summer I also made corrections to maps occasioned by later (subsequent to 1976) transferrals, and again, during a short visit in 1980. With this updating the maps used in this book should be accurate to the latter date.

The Sources of Inherited Property

A basic approach to the study of land transferrals is to examine material on the sources of land acquired by individuals in local schemes of land tenure. For Pingelap I have such information available from two recipient population samples. One of these samples represents mainly individuals actually interviewed, together with their spouses. This was a living population at the time of my inquiries and their properties had not yet been completely dispersed. But some had made assignments of eventual disposal, and married daughters and some married sons had already been awarded property. This population sample includes the holdings of 36 males and 36 females born between 1898-1932, with the largest number of people having been in their 50s at the beginning of my study in 1975-76. This gives a mean birth date of about 1920. As a consequence of the spread in ages, the sample does not represent a single generational span, but I elected to use all individuals thus covered in order to gain as expansive a sample as was possible.

The other population sample treated here represents largely the biological and adoptive parents of the informant-oriented sample. Members of this "parental" sample were all deceased and their holdings completely dispersed. It was possible to get a nearly complete record of the sources of their holdings. It was not possible to get birth dates, but I inferred from genealogies that a small minority were born after 1900 and even fewer before 1870, with a probable mean birth date of 1890. My sample of this population covers 39 females and 38 males. In some cases it was possible to retrieve histories of transactions going back one or two generations further, that is, parental and grandparental to this latter sample, but for purposes of the analysis attempted here those in the 1890 sample will have to serve as the closest approach to a traditional base line for land tenure on the atoll.

For convenience, and in keeping with the sequence of analysis, I shall hereafter refer to the earlier recipient group as Pingelap Sample A, and the informant-oriented recipient group as Pingelap Sample B. But before discussion proceeds it will be well to note that all holdings were expressed by informants in terms of nominal individual ownership for both population samples, even though usufruct privileges almost always extended beyond those individuals. It is clear that, consistent with the versions of Pingelap land tenure given in oral tradition, the concept of individual ownership was well established before the advent of the Sample A group.

Table 5.1
Sources of Inherited Property for Pingelap Sample A

Relationship to recipient	F	AF	Other males	M	AM	Other females	Total
I. *Male Recipients*							
Number of transactions	236	28	22	17	13	4	320
m² of land inherited	276 281	45 162	25 530	26 019	6 803	1 497	381 292
No. of rows in taro patch inherited	842	113	70	48	31	4	1 108
II. *Female Recipients*							
Number of transactions	94	21	20	20	5	5	165
m² of land inherited	77 413	18 819	15 358	29 105	2 676	7 496	150 867
No. of rows in taro patch inherited	255	54	41	50	7	4	411

Key: F = father, AF = adoptive father, M = mother, AM = adoptive mother.
Sample: 38 males and 39 females.

Table 5.1 shows the sources of acquisition of land for Sample A people. The table shows some important characteristics of land inheritance as it applied to Pingelap at the turn of the present century and continuing to about 1950. First, it must be noted that land inheritance for this sample was regulated almost entirely within the context of kinship relations. Of 320 individual transactions received by males, there were six for whom information regarding kinship connection was lacking and only two cases where donors were declared by informants as being unrelated to recipients. In the case of females, of 165 individual transactions only one was of unknown kinship connection, and three were instances where lack of relationship was declared. It is evident that any understanding of land tenure on Pingelap involves essentially an exploration of kinship relationships.[2]

What, then, are the specific sets of relatives which are most important in the transferral of property on Pingelap? The table shows that, consistent with the norm expounded in the previous chapter, the most important source of land and taro rows for both males and females in Sample A was the father (F) of the recipient. This occurrence would also be consistent with the norm of patrilineal inheritance in the cases of the males of this sample. Establishment of the dowry system, which is attributed in the oral history to the reign of Okonomwaun (ca. 1822-70) might lead one to expect a possible matrilineal convention in land inheritance, from mother to daughter, paralleling the patrilineal pattern for men. The figures in Table 5.1 reveal that there was indeed some tendency for daughters to inherit (very slightly) more from their mothers than did sons, but for both male and female recipients, the largest amount of land derived from fathers. The second most prominent source of property for males was an adoptive father (AF). Adoption had already become a part of Pingelapese society at the period during which Sample A people were being born, and 12 males and 13 females in this sample were inheriting land and taro from adoptive fathers, although the amount that was being transferred from adoptive fathers was still well below that which came from natural parents. The other significant source of land and taro for this sample was from adoptive mothers (AM). A breakdown of the remaining categories shows a wide and thin scattering, with few transactions involving any other particular class of relatives or the slim minority of sources unrelated to recipients.

Consistent also with the norm of expecting greater shares for males than for females, Sample A males inherited an average of 10 315 square metres of land and 29.8 rows of taro, while females acquired an average of 3 785 square metres and 10.4 rows, figures which represent almost 3 to 1 ratios favouring males.

Table 5.2 shows figures for Sample B which can be compared with Table 5.1 for Sample A. A pronounced shift is evident in that adoptive parents have taken on a much more important role in the inheritance picture. Clearly this shift results from both a historical change in Pingelapese populations and, secondly, represents an artifact of my sampling method. In an earlier paper (Damas 1983b), I indicated that adoption rates burgeoned at about the end of the nineteenth century and continued high throughout the German and Japanese periods. I related this rise in adoption to an increase in sterile matings, undoubtedly a contact phenomenon, and a corollary move toward expanding family size by adopting children, usually those of close relatives. The highest rates of adoption and of childlessness occurred in the time span of those women born between 1870 and 1919 when the rate of childlessness averaged about 25 percent and that of crude adoption rate[3] about 15 percent. Thus, while some of the mothers of sample A were born during this period, a far greater number of the mothers of sample B people were so represented, which accounts for the greater number of adoptive relationships being expressed in Table 5.2 than in

Table 5.1. But the rate of adoption found in the Sample B group is several times the expected rate, with 24 of the 36 males and 19 of the sample's 36 females having been adopted. All of those adopted also gained property from one or both adopting parents. These findings are clearly affected by the sample bias. Since, as stated, my sampling method is slanted toward the larger landholders and representatives of the histories of largest family holdings, and since both natural and adoptive parents are expected ideally to contribute to the estate of the children in question, it is not surprising that these recipients of multiple sources should be overrepresented in a sample so constructed. That a larger number of males than females is represented is consistent with a preference for males in adoption that is clearly evident in my earlier study (ibid.). That the total of lands and taro rows transferred from adopting father to adopted son exceeds those from natural father to son despite the absence of this second source in one-third of the cases, is readily explicable as well. As case histories to be explored later in this chapter will show, often the factor of how well the child adopted out will be looked after in terms of a potential estate plays a part in selection of adopting parents. Then, too, adoptive parents have usually been those without prospect of progeny after several years of marriage and the division of estates is restricted to fewer heirs in these cases. Often the adopted child received the full family estate or shared it with one other adopted sibling. Conversely, parents who give up children in adoption may be childless at times of such adoptions, usually other children enter the inheritance picture because donor parents are generally those of matings which continue to be fertile (ibid.).

Table 5.2
Sources of Inherited Property for Pingelap Sample B

Relationship to recipient	F	AF	Other males	M	AM	Other females	Total
I. *Male Recipients*							
Number of transactions	106	111	18	45	49	9	338
m² of land inherited	121 718	128 432	11 705	42 357	44 868	9 009	358 089
No. of rows in taro patch inherited	369.5	333	47	80	163	35	1 027.5
II. *Female Recipients*							
Number of transactions	58	46	23	29	15	5	176
m² of land inherited	48 561	37 046	20 139	26 515	17 314	1 756	151 331
No. of rows in taro patch inherited	149	123	55	61	31	17	436

Key: F = father; AF = adoptive father; M = mother; AM = adoptive mother.
Sample: 36 males and 36 females.

Table 5.2 also shows that although the amount of land and taro inherited from the adoptive father by females does not exceed or approach that from father, as in the case of males, that source is a strong second and exceeds land inherited from mother, the next most prominent source for Sample A females.

There is a second major feature in the inheritance picture for Sample B that differs from that of Sample A. Table 5.2 shows that the inheritance of property from mother to son has increased dramatically. Table 5.4 reveals more of the corollary shift regarding sex linkages in transferrals for Sample B that can be compared to similar figures for Sample A in Table 5.3.

Table 5.3
Transferrals to Pingelap Sample A by Sex of Donor and Recipient

	Transactions		m^2		Taro rows	
Donor/recipient	No.	%	No.	%	No.	%
Male to male	286	59.0	346 873	65.2	1 026	67.5
Female to male	34	7.0	34 319	6.4	83	5.5
Male to female	135	27.8	111 590	20.9	350	23.0
Female to female	30	6.2	39 277	7.4	61	4.0
	485	100.0	532 059	100.1	1 520	100.0

Table 5.4
Transferrals to Pingelap Sample B by Sex of Donor and Recipient

	Transactions		m^2		Taro rows	
Donor/recipient	No.	%	No.	%	No.	%
Male to male	235	45.7	261 855	51.4	749	51.2
Female to male	103	20.0	96 234	18.9	278	19.0
Male to female	127	24.7	105 746	20.8	327	22.3
Female to female	49	9.5	45 585	8.9	109	7.4
	514	99.9	509 420	100.0	1 463	99.9

These tables represent lumping all male sources including father, adoptive father, and other male relatives; and mother, adoptive mother, and other female relatives in the donor categories as, respectively, "male" and "female." The total proportion of land and taro rows received by males as compared to females remain little changed when acquisitions by Sample A people are compared with those of Sample B people, with 71.6 percent of square metres of land being acquired by Sample A males from all sources, and 70.3 percent by Sample B males; and 73 percent of taro rows being received by A males and 70.2 percent for Sample B males from all sources. The proportion of these transactions remained practically identical, with males getting about 66 percent as compared to 34 percent for females in each sample. On the other hand, there was a rise in contributions by females, mainly mothers, and a consequent drop in the proportion of lands received from males as revealed in comparisons of

Tables 5.3 and 5.4. Male contributions to Sample A in numbers of transactions were 86.8 percent and in Sample B 70.4 percent; in square metres of land the drop was from 86.1 percent to 72.2 percent, and in rows of taro, from 90.5 percent to 73.5 percent. Clearly the women of Sample A, who were donors to Sample B people, had more property to dispose of than had their mothers. This comparison, while agreeing with the legendary establishment of the dowry system during the mid-nineteenth century, indicates that the system reached full flower only after the beginning of the twentieth century.

The Dispersal of Inherited Property

So far I have considered the sources of property holdings by sample recipient populations, but the other face to land inheritance practices, that from the standpoint of the donors, must also be considered in order to round out this study. It should be clear that most Pingelapese are at one time or another both a recipient and a donor. My information, unfortunately, is incomplete regarding the dispersal of property by donors to the Sample A group. But I do have the complete record of dispersals of land and taro by that group. The individuals included in that sample population are not only all of the Sample B group but also all other heirs. The advantages of using this latter enlarged sample over Samples A and B are as follows: (1) it is not biased toward the larger landholders; (2) a much larger corpus of individuals is represented; (3) it also represents over 40 percent of the land area of Pingelap and a similar portion of the taro patch and thus gives a more comprehensive coverage of the picture of land tenure for the entire atoll. This sample is broken down in Tables 5.5 and 5.6 where averages of property dispersal by Sample A individuals are given.

The symbols used require some explanation. Siblings are numbered according to the sequence in which they were brought into the families, either through birth or adoption. Thus, if the firstborn son is adopted out he will be labelled SAO^1. If the second son enters the family through birth he is labelled S^2, and if the second son is an adoptee he is designated as AS^2; subsequent sons are labelled S^3, S^4, S^5. The same scheme is used in the tables for daughters, as DAO^1, D^2, D^3, D^4, D^5, etc. Grandchildren are indicated as GS = grandson and GD = granddaughter.

It can be seen that first sons, whether natural or adopted, received by far the largest average shares from male donors. It would appear that though the total share of eldest son or eldest son adopted was considerably larger, the bulk of his property came from the father, with other sons having their shares evened out somewhat by acquisitions from the mother. With this qualification, therefore, the norm of eldest sons receiving the largest shares is supported in Table 5.5 and, when information from both tables are combined, his share is considerably larger than that of other sons or daughters. In this regard it would be well to mention that both Sample A and Sample B are biased in their overrepresentation of eldest sons, with 24 of 38 males in the earlier sample being first sons, and 18 of 36 in the more recent sample. By contrast this sampling circumvents that bias.

Table 5.5
Recipients of Principal Male Donors of Pingelap Sample A

Relationship to donor	No. of recipients	Average m²	Av. no. of taro rows
S^1	26	5 195	14.5
AS^1	12	7 180	11.6
S^2	16	3 004	8.7
AS^2	8	1 542	7.0
S^3	15	1 287	5.0
S^4	16	1 167	4.3
S^5	4	226	3.8
SAO	33	1 407	5.1
D^1	32	695	2.4
AD^1	3	2 885	3.3
D^2	26	550	2.4
D^3	16	572	0.8
D^4	11	605	1.1
D^5	1	543	0.0
GS	4	490	5.5
GD	3	1 881	3.5
Other	10	920	2.4

Note: Tables 5.5 and 5.6 deal with recipients and are not to be compared to Tables 5.1, 5.2, and 5.3, and 5.4 which indicate transactions of separate pieces of property. Since in a number of cases donors bequeathed more than one such segment, there are more of these than recipients. The figure of 632 transactions to this larger sample should be used in comparing the number of transactions indicated in previous tables in this chapter.

Of interest, also, is the disclosure that adopted first sons averaged more land acquired from fathers (but not taro) than did natural first sons. This is not altogether surprising when, as noted earlier, one considers that adoption usually takes place when a couple has despaired of having children and, consequently, the adopted son will normally be the eldest in a small sibling group and will be in line to be the chief, and perhaps the only, heir.

Table 5.5 shows a progressive scaling down of amounts of land and rows of taro acquired from male donors according to relative age of recipients. For natural sons and if first sons adopted out are excluded, second sons received 50 percent of the land and 60 percent of the taro of the holdings of first sons; third sons 24 percent of land and 25 percent of taro of first sons. This is an essentially smooth cline that suggests the existence of a principle governing such a pattern of dispersal, even though I could not elicit an ideal for such an arrangement from informants (see chap. 4).

Table 5.6
Recipients of Principal Female Donors of Pingelap Sample A

Relationship to donor	No. of recipients	Average m^2	Av. no. of taro rows
S^1	24	1 188	4.2
AS^1	8	1 086	5.6
S^2	19	1 135	1.9
AS^2	9	1 555	4.0
S^3	14	464	0.6
S^4	10	204	1.4
S^5	5	575	1.4
SAO	18	608	1.0
D^1	24	972	2.4
AD^1	7	1 329	3.3
D^{2a}	20	541	2.4
D^3	12	338	0.8
D^{4b}	16	386	0.8
D^5	4	1 025	0.0
AGS	2	0	5.5
GD	2	0	3.5
Other	5	832	2.4

a Includes 3 AD^3.
b Includes 4 AD^4.

While informants did indicate that children being adopted out should take portions of land with them, these shares are normally smaller than either of those of adopted sons or natural sons; and for the four cases of fourth sons, and one case of fifth son adopted out, such shares were not existent. There was, again, a scaling downward according to age. It is not surprising that shares of children adopted out should be small, since one loses a source of family labour, without taking into account severance of emotional ties when giving children in adoption.

Amounts given to daughters by male donors were consistently and considerably smaller than shares of first four sons. The eldest daughter received somewhat more land than second daughter. In the three cases of AD^1 an apparently anomalously large share was awarded, but the sample is very small. This source of skewing notwithstanding, such an occurrence is consistent with the fact that as in the case of first sons who are adopted out, adopted daughters move to families with fewer heirs to share among. There are not examples of third and fourth adoptive daughters in Table 5.5 which is consistent with the small sibling groups in families formed through adoption and the preference for adopting males (ibid.).

There is a scattering of small shares given out to a number of categories by both male and female donors in this sample, but I could find only one case of land and taro being given to an individual for whom a consanguineal, affinal, or adoptive relationship could not be traced. This circumstance reinforces my observation made earlier that transactions in land tenure on Pingelap are also clearly transactions in kinship. Some anthropologists might object to classing adoptive relationships as kindred but even such skeptics might be impressed to learn that 75 percent of children given in adoption already had some sort of other kinship tie, usually consanguineal, with the adopting parent (ibid.). It is also true that adopted children are absorbed into the nuclear and extended family of the adopting parents and these are the units within which inheritance of land occurs.

Turning to Table 5.6, in noting the distribution of average shares of land and taro by female donors it is clear that the areas of plots and the numbers of taro rows are smaller than in the preceding table, which is consistent with the expectation that females will own less property than males. There is a more even spread in property dispersal across the scope of relatives than in distribution of the estates of males. The total of land and taro given to males by these female donors was somewhat larger than the total given to daughters which is, again, consistent with the patterns revealed in Tables 5.3 and 5.4. First and second sons, both natural and adopted, received more property than did first natural daughters. Second, third, and fourth daughters gained less land than that received by the first daughters. The single fifth daughter got an anomalously large amount of land (but no taro). This occurrence is the product of one large land award and, of course, would tend to skew the results. Almost all daughters did receive a token parcel of land, at least, with the exception of daughters adopted out. Although awards to individuals adopted out were about 50 percent larger than those given for dowry (assuming that awards to females were given at marriage — see below) the totals for dowry awards were about double the properties lost through adoptions. Slightly over 57 000 square metres and 143 taro rows were given persons adopted out and more than 119 000 square metres and 315 rows given to women as dowries. The apparent discrepancy is due to the much larger number of persons receiving dowry shares. While nearly all men adopted out got shares and some received them from two sources, only a small minority of females were awarded land when they were adopted. Only five such cases were noted in the record of receipts in this sample. It would appear that the expectation of women getting dowry properties from adopting parents made the practice of giving land to those adopted out not of great urgency.

Norms of Land Inheritance and Practice

In summarizing the results of the analysis of the tables so far presented in this chapter, it can be seen that some of the norms which were treated in the preceding chapter find expression in the empirical data. The norm of a patrilineal bias in land inheritance pervades the statistics given here. All samples revealed that father-to-son, and overall male-male transfers were more frequent and involved more property than mother-to-daughter or general female to female transfers.

But the latter transactions were far from being insignificant and were not unexpected considering the long period over which women's rights in land have been acknowledged on Pingelap. The increase in women's holdings between the 1890 sample and the sample of those people whose average birth date was 1920 was striking and pointed to confirmation that the practice of dowry had begun sometime in the nineteenth century as depicted in the oral history of the island, but that it reached its fullest development sometime afterwards.

While conventions specifying grants of land to adoptees by both donor and recipient families was elicited from informants, there was no suggestion of the proportions contributed by each of these sources and especially of the large acquisitions from adoptive parents in most cases. The high rate of adoption found in the population in the first half of the present century was revealed in my earlier study of adoption (ibid.) so that its impact on the picture of land tenure for that period was not unexpected.

The practice of granting progressively smaller shares to younger male siblings was not suggested by interviewed informants and emerged only from the analysis of the tables. But the tables did not in themselves reveal anything about the times, or stages in life cycles, when land and taro rows were granted. I did make the assumption that, based on oral history, women's shares were given as dowry. I also assumed, on the basis of informant's statements, that the shares of children adopted out had been given at the times of adoption, but neither of these patterns could be discerned from the statistics. There were a few examples of gifts to unrelated people, and of the sale of land, but most of these latter were secondary transactions which did not figure prominently into my analysis of land inheritance practices. The preceding discussion does not give insight into special problems of contention, for instance, those brought on by the institution of stewardship on the atoll, but these problems will be dealt with later.

Case Histories of Land Inheritance

The above statistical treatment of land-inheritance procedures on Pingelap does provide the outlines of averages or tendencies in land distribution as well as providing some notion of adherence to or departure from norms or principles. It also suggests some principles which did not emerge from interviews. But one needs to look further in order to expand understanding of the realms of variability and of practice which remain obscured by such averages. Any land tenure study worth its salt must make an attempt to explore the processes of decision-making which are involved in actual transfers. In this study there is the need to explore the contingencies which arise in the operation of the complex and fascinating drama of Pingelapese land tenure. Fortunately, case history material gathered from Pingelapese informants provides some insight into these areas of concern.

The first example gives indication of possible trends toward lineality in transferrals, in that it was possible in this instance to trace genealogies to greater depth than in most other cases.

Case 1

A female informant age 58 traced acquisition of one *peliensapw* through her mother to her mother's father. Another plot was traced through her mother to the step-father of her mother. It is obvious from these examples that acquisition of land by a female through her mother did not display the depth that could be regarded as being truly matrilineal. Another plot acquired by this woman derived from her father, who had received the segment from his father, who in turn got the land from his father. This series of transferrals shows a clear patrilineal bias except in the final transaction when land was given to a daughter. The possibility of unilineal transference of property raises the question of the existence of "lineage lands" on Pingelap. The concept of lineage land appears to be appropriate in other parts of the Pacific where lands are often either (1) transferred solely within a lineage, (2) used mainly or exclusively by lineage members, or (3) both of the preceding. Inquiries regarding these possibilities revealed, first, that on Pingelap land use is regulated within a much smaller unit — the extended family. With regard to the concept of the lineage or *keinek* ownership, I did not elicit support for such ownership on Pingelap, at least during a period within the memory of my informants. Land transactions were spoken of in terms of transferrals between one individual and another, despite some case histories like the above which are examples of serially unilineal transfers over two or three generations in cases of males.

The conventional expectation that female shares will be smaller than the shares of males can be confounded by certain demographic situations, as seen in the following case.

Case 2

In this example the male donor to the focal individual did not have a son, but his wife did bear him two daughters. At that time adoption had not yet been practised to the extent that it normally served to adjust such demographic imbalance as seen here in the lack of a male heir. The total estate, accordingly, was divided between the two daughters. In this case the senior daughter, who is the focal individual, brought to her marriage a dowry totalling 10 000 square metres. This inheritance exceeded the land acquisitions of her husband, who eventually got 8 000 square metres. The husband did acquire 45 rows of taro, an anomalously large number for either males or females, and compared to 11 rows of the wife, our focal person. This couple had three natural sons and one daughter, and later adopted a grandson. All four sons inherited land and taro rows from the father, with the oldest getting the largest share, according to custom, including 25 of the taro rows. The land of the wife was divided among the two older sons, who also received all of the wife's taro holdings. The daughter did get a larger share from her mother, 3 100 square metres, in a single *peliensapw*, while the younger two sons' total acquisitions from both parents were smaller than her share. In this case it might well be that the convenience of awarding whole plots rather than subdividing them could have been a factor in giving a daughter a larger share. On the other hand, further inquiry showed that in some cases extra allotments to favourite children can confound any systematic attempt to make logic out of all transactions. It is not clear as to which of these two factors, or possibly a slight matrilineal bias, was ascendent in this instance.

The next example shows how a combination of special circumstances can result in an individual becoming a benefactor of a multiplicity of land sources, as well as considerable holdings, while not being an heir to a substantial estate passed on through parents.

Case 3

The focal individual was the third son in an offspring group of four children of a man with very modest holdings. In this case the land ownership situation was so bad, that, according to my informant, the eldest son was adopted out in order to improve his potential landholding status. The total small estate of the father and mother was divided between the second son and the dowry of the sole daughter except for the small (500 square metres and 3 taro rows) portion given the focal individual on his being adopted out. From his adoptive father he eventually received 1 200 square metres of land and 6 rows of taro, but from his adoptive mother he got 5 000 square metres of land and 10 rows of taro. In this case there were also two less usual sources of land. The focal individual had worked for the island paramount chief who had adopted the practice of contracting men to work his extensive holdings. The man in focus was rewarded with a small parcel of 550 square metres for such labour. His largest holding came from his first wife who had brought a dowry of 6 000 square metres and 14 rows of taro. While none of the various sources provided exceptional amounts of land and taro, together they provided the holder a substantial estate.

While in the above discussed cases land reverted to husbands when wives died, in the following instance another arrangement was made.

Case 4

In this case the husband and wife, a childless couple, died a very short time apart. Here the land of the deceased woman reverted to her own extended family, an arrangement which, according to my chief informant, was supported by convention (chap. 4). The property went specifically to her sister who had lived with the couple for a time before her marriage. This transaction was affirmed as being normative, especially in cases of childlessness of the recipient, the circumstance of that sister.

The following example shows another situation under which a woman can acquire an abnormally large holding through a fortuitous life-cycle situation.

Case 5

A woman had become widowed while her children were still young, the husband dying suddenly without leaving a will. According to custom, the disposal of this estate, and at least temporary nominal ownership, was invested in the widow. Under these circumstances she controlled 10 300 square metres of land and 36 rows of taro, or nearly three times the land and taro owned by the average of other women on the atoll, and indeed, more than the average owned by men. This circumstance was in part attributable to her husband having been the only son of a reasonably well-endowed landowner. In 1980 this estate was partially divided, one son being awarded about one-third of the holdings on his marriage, one daughter a small dowry on hers, and a third yet-unmarried daughter, her share. This latter transaction appears to represent a situation where eligibility for marriage was being enhanced by this award which could serve as a dowry for this daughter, already in her mid-20s and a mother, circumstance is considered to be a definite handicap in the marriage market on Pingelap. She married later and left her child with the mother, a common pattern in such cases.

In most of the above examples the recipients of land were well-endowed in their eventual receipts of land and taro. In the following cases a more common, and the most crucial, problem throughout much of the recent history of the atoll of Pingelapese land tenure is addressed. This is an unfortunate lack of balance between family numbers and availability of land and taro. In the first of these examples an adequate solution of the problem was in fact delayed for some time.

Case 6

The father in this family and his wife bore seven sons and two daughters among whom they had available for distribution an estate of 12 310 square metres of land and 52 rows in the main taro patch. While this is a moderately large holding by Pingelap standards, the expansive progeny limited individual shares drastically. In the event of disposal of this estate, the sixth son did not receive property, but later on, with the death of second son and first daughter, he got their shares. Even so, the shares given to the others were much smaller than the average holdings among Pingelapese, so that when opportunities for emigration became available, the obvious solution was to move. One son left the island shortly after the typhoon of 1905, moving to Saipan, where he died. Two others took land on Sokehs Island when that colony was established in 1911-12. The sixth son moved to Mand when that colony was founded in 1954-55. Offspring of the entire sibling group now live in these colonies with my informant residing only temporarily on the atoll and with the family's holdings there being entrusted to stewards.

In this case one cannot attribute the wholesale emigration solely to the fractionalization of holdings, for any one member of the sibling group could have stayed on the atoll and enjoyed substantial usufruct property. Only one son among the offspring was adopted out, an expedient which if more widely practised might have relieved the pressures on land distribution. It would appear that, consistent with one of the above cases, since all the members of the inheriting sibling group were born between 1880 and 1905, they had not yet moved into the period when infant adoption had become a general solution to demographic imbalances. In the following case which concerns a sibling group all of whose members were born since the turn of the century, this practice was widely employed.

Case 7

There was available for distribution among six sons and two daughters only 5 185 square metres of land and 20 rows in the taro patch. This property was distributed as follows; first son 750 square metres and 3 rows; second son 565 square metres and 3 rows; third son 335 square metres and 4 rows; fourth son 565 metres and 4 rows; first daughter 1 670 square metres and 3 rows; second daughter 735 square metres and 3 rows. Neither the fifth nor the sixth son received any property, though a nephew got 565 square metres of land.

While the estate was thus spread very thinly among the children of the estate holder, two of the sons who were adopted out, the first and the second, took small shares with them, observing a custom which resulted in the remaining heirs getting smaller shares than if it had been ignored. The fifth and sixth sons had to rely on the usufruct privileges of their wives' property for land to work. But the first, second, and third sons, all of whom were adopted out, also all benefitted from the substantial estates of their adoptive parents.

Case 8

The focal individual, now in his 70s, had earlier given out shares at marriage, not only to the two daughters but also to each of three sons (one adopted) at such times. Another son, the second, had been adopted out in infancy and had been awarded a small plot of land and some taro rows at that time. In the case of the eldest son, the nature of the division was qualified, for after his mother's death the father shared quarters with him, and throughout his marriage, copra and other cash sources (this son drew a teacher's salary) were merged within the extended family.

In this instance the eldest son who also had acquired by far the largest share of the estate at marriage had worked for a man lacking sons and had been awarded land for this service. The next case illustrates another variation in land-dispersal customs based on early residential separation of father and son.

Case 9

A man in his late 70s lived apart from his only natural son while an adopted son-grandson lived with him. The natural son was said to keep his own cash income while the adopted son contributed to the support of the old man. A large part of the father's estate was still undivided, even though the natural son was approaching 50. The latter had been given 1 670 square metres of land and 11 rows in the taro patch at his marriage, but these shares comprised only about one-eighth of the estate. It was told to me, however, that this son could use the proceeds of the father's property if he needed them and that he could be called upon by the father to help harvest food and copra from that land. While at first sight the arrangements made in this case appear to be rather different from those in the preceding one, in actual practice the difference might not have been so great.

While the normal use and ownership unit has been the virilocal extended family throughout the remembered history of Pingelap, the next case represents a variation from that pattern.

Case 10

The focal individual's father (number 2 in Figure 5.1) represented one of the rare instances of uxorilocal residence. He had not inherited property from his natal parents and only small holdings from his adoptive father and mother. A shift in residential and economic alignment brought him into the estate of the father-in-law, which had to be shared with a much younger adopted son of that man (number 4 in Figure 5.1). The focal individual's father sired seven sons and a daughter and thus his total holdings of only 2 500 square metres and 28 taro rows from natural and adoptive parents would have been spread thinly had not the lands gained through his wife's inheritance been available to pass on. Even so the average inheritance was meagre and the solution was to give four of the sons in adoption, including the focal individual (1), as well as the daughter, while awarding each a small "seed" share. In the case of the focal individual, he was later adopted by his mother's adoptive father (3), and in effect, became his mother's adoptive brother. This arrangement was said to have come about due to his becoming a replacement for the first adoptive son (4) of this grandfather who had been killed in an American air raid during World War II. Later, on the death of the old man, the title held by that man was passed to the focal individual rather than to his father. This occurrence illustrates the principle that adoption can be a route to succession through an alternative possibility of using an affinal tie such as son-in-law. As the accompanying figure shows, the route of estate transmission was somewhat different. In this case all land and taro rows went to the adopted daughter, with our focal individual not acquiring land until his mother's death, though, of course, use privileges had been available before that time. This arrangement in fact put him in the position of senior male in his natural sibling group rather than as adopted son-grandson in the inheritance picture. Another unusual feature of this set of land tenure arrangements was that land was passed to all children of the woman heir even though five of the eight had been given in adoption. The amounts distributed were small, and in the case of the focal individual, even though he received allotments from both father and mother, they totalled only modest holdings as a consequence of this widely spread dispersal of the estates.

Figure 5.1
Case History 10

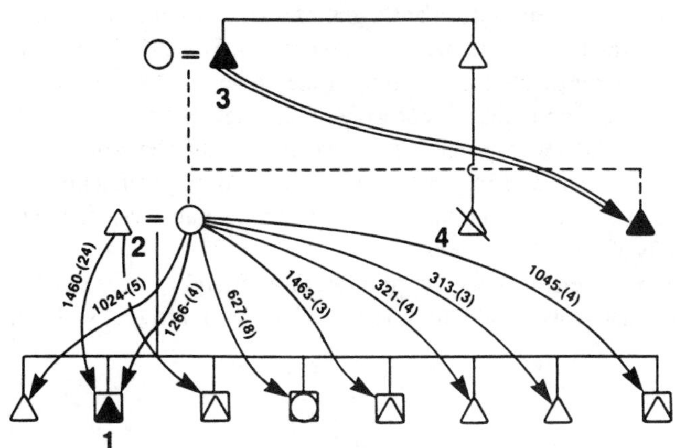

1. Focal individual
2. Father of focal individual
3. Focal individual's adoptive father
4. Deceased son of 3

→ Routes of property transferrals m² and (rows of taro)
⇒ Route of title succession
☐ Individual adopted out

Succeeding case histories illustrate various other combinations of adjustments from the normative principles outlined in the previous chapter.

Case 11

The normal distribution pattern obtained for the estates of father and mother among their children: the eldest son got the largest share, and the third son also got a significant share, while the second son (adopted out) and six daughters received significantly smaller portions of the estates. In this case, despite the large number of heirs there was sufficient land and taro rows to go around so that some, though not always large, shares could be apportioned among the offspring. Somewhat anomalous in this case was the acquisition of land by the eldest son from his sister's husband. Upon the death of the woman in question the former got land and taro from the widowed husband, a grant which was conceived of as being payment for having had the services of the sister during her lifetime. This occurrence is especially interesting in that it complements the emphasis on dowry and suggests an example of a form of bride-price augmenting or replacing periodic gifts to the wife's consanguines a practice mentioned in the preceding chapter.

Another unusual feature of land tenure practice in this case (although such a practice was not rare in the past, according to my information) was exchange of land in the forest for a house plot in the village.

Case 12

Here, at the time of my informant's grandfather's death, two of his sons were married and the two other sons were adolescents. The eldest son was entrusted with the property of the latter two until they reached maturity, thus being an example where land management worked on a horizontal plane. In the case of the informant, land was granted not at marriage or the death of the testator, but when the informant was 54, married with two children. At that point in time his father was quite elderly and largely confined to bed and wished control to rest in the hands of his only son.

The next case shows a great proliferation of land sources due to the combined circumstances of adoption, return adoption, marriage, widowhood, and remarriage.

Case 13

The focal individual (number 2 in Figure 5.2) was a second adopted son. Having previously taken the genealogy of his adoptive parental group, it came as a surprise to me to learn that, apparently, the first adopted son (number 1) had received no property from the foster parents. Then I learned that even though land had been given at marriage, (1) had rejoined his natal father's extended family group as well as *keinek*. In the preceding chapter I noted that there was ambiguity in the statements of informants regarding the fate of land from adoptive relatives in such cases as these.

Here the land was returned to the adopting parents. This occurrence put the focal individual in a very favourable position. Not only had he eventually acquired the second adoptive son's share, but he also got the returned share of the first, formerly adopted, son. These properties were added to the somewhat smaller shares that he had brought from his natural parents at the time of his adoption. The combined acquisition totalled 12 000 square metres of land and 31 rows of taro. He was also fortunate in adding as usufruct holdings the dowries of his first wife (whose property was absorbed completely into his estate at her death), and of his second wife. This additional land amounted to a further 3 500 square metres and 10 rows.

While this case showed some complications, they were relatively straightforward as compared to the complexities of the following case.

Figure 5.2
Case History 13

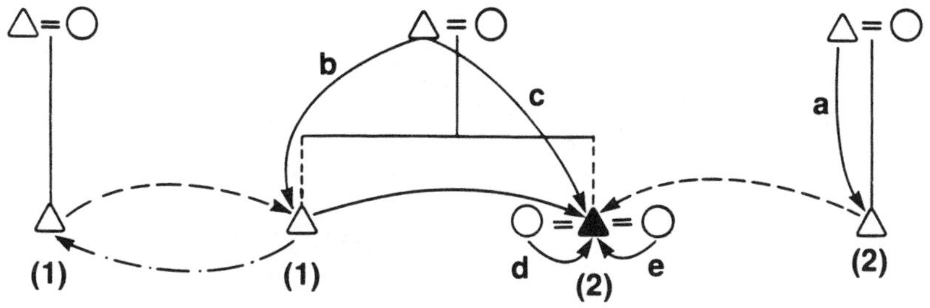

Routes of Adoptions
Route of Returned Adoption
Routes of Land Acquisitions of (2)

a F → S
b AF → AS[1] → AS[2]
c AF → AS[2]
d W[1] → H
e W[2] → H

Case 14

To begin with the first of a series of unusual transactions, the accompanying diagram (Figure 5.3) shows movement of land in the third ascending generation above that of the focal individual.

Transaction (1) moved the property in question from a sister's husband to his wife's brother. The rationale for this transferral was that the donor couple did not bear children and, in keeping with the weak development of the practice of adoption in their generation, did not adopt any either. One might expect that, given the patrilineal emphasis in the land tenure system, such land would have reverted to the man's side, but my genealogy of that man is incomplete.

Transferrals (2) and (3) in this case are not unusual, that is, moving from father to son and from man to grandson-adopted son. Even though this latter movement of property was on the maternal side which would not be as frequent a sort of transferral as from paternal grandfather, the addition of an adoption link cemented a strong claim. The amounts of property that were transferred to the central figure of the case were, however, quite unusual. In transaction (2), even though he was the second son and got only one-third of the land of eldest sons, a not unusual proportion, this award amounted to 4 630 square metres of land and 6 rows in the taro patch. His position with regard to his maternal grandfather-adoptive father was particularly favourable since he was the single adopted son, and the only other offspring of the senior man in transaction (3) was a natal daughter with whom to share an estate. This inheritance amounted to a total of 12 230 square metres of land and 25 rows in the taro patch (four of which rows were later given to the adoptive sister).

Figure 5.3
Case History 14

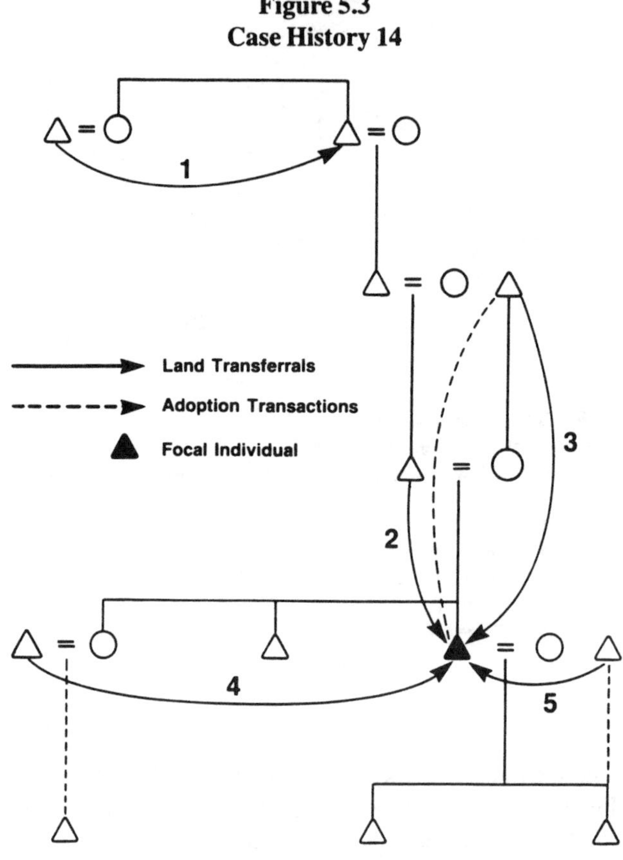

An unusual movement of land in this case was a plot of land and some taro rows from the husband of his oldest sister (transferral number 4). This type of transaction, from sister's husband to wife's brother, which though unusual was the second of such for this group (transaction number 1 being the other) as well as appearing in case 11 (above). Such transactions are called *kasapwasapw en peyneyney* and is said by the informant in this case to have been an ancient practice. This movement of property is interesting in that it is another example (as in case 11) of an apparent reversal of dowry, or a form of bride-payment or, perhaps, reciprocal swapping, since it appears to have occurred at the focal individual's marriage.

Another aberrant transferral in this case was the acquisition of land by the focal individual from the adoptive father of his second son, transferral (5). As discussed in the preceding chapter, some property is usually given with a son who is adopted out in order to start a "seed" estate. But the reverse situation, as is evident here, was encountered only in this case among my sample. In this circumstance the informant made it clear that a definite "deal" was involved in this adoption, specifically, that the son adopted out by the focal individual was not given the usual accompanying property because he was moving to Sokehs on his adoption, and under such circumstances "seed" awards were not normally given. Another card was dealt in that in the event of death of the adoptive father, the son would also return to his natal father's household. This latter event actually occurred in 1977.

Adopting out one of the oldest sons to a sister is a very common arrangement (Damas 1983b) in Pingelapese adoption, but a further arrangement was not so common. That was an agreement that when the brother-in-law died, all of the latter's land would revert to the central figure in this case, paralleling his arrangement with the adoptive father of another son as indicated above.

In this case the engineering of adoption agreements bore direct relationships to the land tenure system. These transactions occurred during the 1940s, when adoption was still practised widely. While it is not unusual for a man to adopt out the first son to an older sister, as in this case, the practice of adopting out a second son not only from the immediate family but also from the *keinek* is, indeed unusual. These instances point to the expectation that further children would come to the couple, and, indeed, this man and wife eventually produced a progeny of six sons and five daughters.

In addition to the holdings directly acquired and provisions made for expanding his estate further through provisions made that involved children adopted out, the same informant had assumed stewardship for extensive segments of the islands of the atoll and of the taro patch. These included the substantial holdings of his older brother who had emigrated to Mand, a younger brother who had moved to Sokehs, as well as the atoll holdings of the father-in-law of the son who had been adopted out to Sokehs. The total of these transactions comprised an intricate combination of fortuitous factors, including demography, the large increments from maternal grandfather, unusually large increments from the natal family, emigration, and some very shrewd manoeuvers related to affinal and adoptive ties which all combined to produce the largest individual landholdings on the atoll.

This case shows how an extremely astute manipulator of property operated in achieving rights to a sizeable portion of the resources of the atoll. Such cases of success in the game of manipulating land on Pingelap highlight an important shortcoming in the system itself, which places a great strain on the bounty which is Pingelap. What is particularly remarkable in this case, and which would be disturbing to one concerned with the possibility of inequity in landholding, is that the progeny of this focal individual was scattered. Most of them lived off the island and were not participating in the use of these, by Pingelapese standards, vast resources. In my 1976 and 1978 censuses this man headed a household made up of young sons and daughters and two adult daughters, one widowed and the other a spinster. This unit thus lacked resident male producers, except for the focal individual, a man of 60. By 1983 the man himself began spending increasingly long periods on Pohnpei living in the households of the sons referred to above in the Pingelapese colonies. One can only conjecture in this case as to how much of the acquisition of property was accumulated through the manoeuvering noted above for insurance purposes rather than for foreseeable practical needs.

A Special Case Study

I shall devote substantial space to discussion of the final case to be considered here because it traces disposal of an originally large estate through several generations, while at the same time providing insight into the process of fractionalization of the islands and main taro patch of Pingelap. This case also illustrates how lines of major land inheritance and title succession can diverge.

Case 15

Figure 5.4 shows the history of transferrals of land[4] from the original landholder, born ca. 1820, through four (and in a couple of cases five) generations. Those individuals who shared in the original estate and all others who received portions of it are numbered. This presentation reinforces some of my speculations and the accounts of the oral history of the land tenure system on Pingelap previously presented. The original landholder, individual (1), held a substantial estate, approximately five hectares, which was acquired by (1) about the middle of the nineteenth century. These acquisitions did not constitute a block but were scattered so that they included holdings on all three islands of the atoll, with several disconnected plots on the main island and in the taro patch noted. This means that if, indeed, each surviving male of the typhoon of the 1770s was given a plot of contiguous land, by the 1850s or 1860s, during which time the population had expanded tenfold from its lowpoint after that disaster, the mixing of plots was already well advanced. Just as the population of the atoll grew geometrically throughout the nineteenth century, so had the progeny of the focal individual (1) expanded at the same time. The central figure in this case had a large number of offspring (a child by a third wife who died about age 10 or 12 is not shown in this figure), so that in the next generation the estate had to be divided among seven recipients. Heirs numbered 15 in the generation that followed. These two generations, which include people born between about 1840 and 1900, also represent a period of continued population growth on the atoll which contributed substantially to the fragmentation of plots and taro sections. During the next generation (essentially the third down from number 1), there was only a modest increase in the heirs, from 15 to 18 as is consistent with the demographic history of the island, since this generational span was made up of people born after 1900 and before about 1935, or the period in which the total Pingelapese population remained static. During that period the on-island numbers actually declined from a high of about 1 000 at the turn of the century to a number ranging between 600-700 throughout the Japanese period. During that time as well the division of land and taro rows on the islands of the atoll appears to have remained at about a stable level until the population boom which followed World War II. It should be noted once more that the total on-island population never again reached the 1890-1905 levels, as emigration has become widespread in recent years.

Since the total property of the original estate can be accounted for in each generation on the chart, another conclusion of the earlier discussion can be

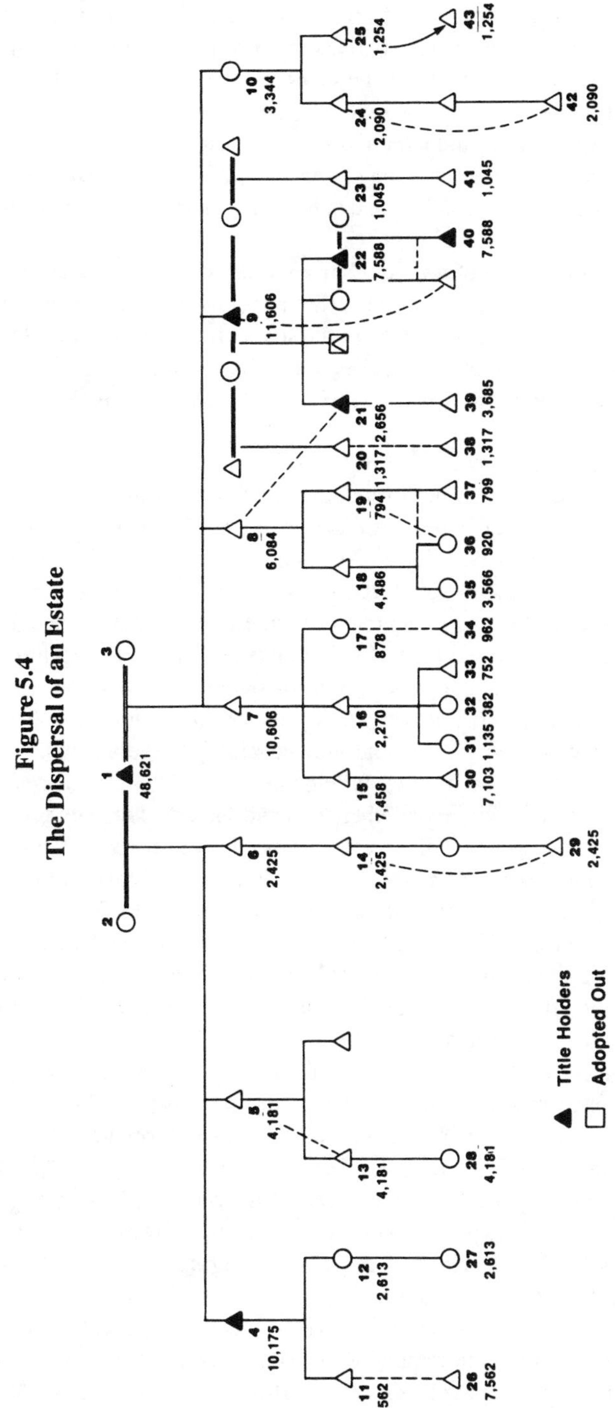

Figure 5.4
The Dispersal of an Estate

substantiated here; that is, land transactions on Pingelap have been almost exclusively regulated within the bounds of kinship ties. Only one of the numerous transactions represented on the chart involved a person who showed no relationship to the donor, individual (43). So, despite a time-honoured practice of making gifts of land, and later, payment for services, transfers which ideally at least, did not have to obtain only between kin, the bulk of transferrals are in fact controlled within a unit which can be considered to be the extended family of the donor.

The predominance of males, 32 of 45 individuals on the chart involved in land transactions, also supports an earlier conclusion. In the cases of individuals (29), (35), and (36), women were the sole heirs to the shares of the original estate passed on by donors since they were the sole offspring of those donors. There is, again, no indication of a chain of inheritance of female shares along matrilineal lines.

One is able, also, to test out the stated principle of primogeniture in land inheritance. There are some difficulties of resolution in this area. A special complication arises as a result of the practice of polygyny which has not entered my previous discussion of Pingelapese land tenure. My chief informant stated that, ideally, the eldest son of the wife considered to be the senior wife had first priority in the apportionment of the estate. After that the eldest son of each succeeding wife should receive holdings in order of the seniority of their mothers. Then, second and succeeding sons would get property according to the same general order, following this principle of seniority. In the example illustrated here this sequence is not followed strictly in every detail.

The first sons of each wife, individuals (2) and (3) of (1), were granted almost equal shares, with most other sons and the one daughter getting somewhat smaller shares conforming to the pattern derived from the tables. The one truly anomalous transaction was that which gave the third son of the second wife the largest share of all from the original estate of (1). The favoured position of (9) is further emphasized by the knowledge that the entire holdings of the mother (3) were divided between him and the daughter (10). Subsequent discussion of title succession in this group will reinforce this impression of favouritism being shown individual (9).

In the next generation of transferrals more information is available and a couple of departures from the principle of primogeniture can be resolved. Individuals (11), (13), (15), (18), and (24) all show receipt of larger portions of the father's share of the original estate if eldest of two or more siblings; or inheritance of the entire share derived from the founder if a single offspring. Number (21) appears to be highly anomalous in this regard, however. The chart shows receipt of only 2 656 square metres from the original estate of (1) with a third son (22), getting nearly three times that much. Of this area of land, about 800 square metres, came from individual (8)'s share as payment for agricultural help, while the larger and remaining portion derived from his father as a normally inherited share of the latter's estate. But colonization enters into the landholding of the individuals concerned here as well. Individual (9) was appointed leader of the colonization party to Sokehs in 1911-12 and, along with all other males, he and his sons each received plots on Sokehs Island. When (9) died his holdings there were divided among (20), (21) and (23) and a *mwol,* or grand-parent-grandchild gift to the half-brother (unnumbered) of (40) with (22) being omitted from that part of the will. The final divisions gave individual (21) 21 530 square metres of total holdings, on and off Pingelap, and (22) 14 580 square metres. The omission of the second brother (unnumbered) in either of these dispersals is worthy of comment. This individual was adopted out to a Pohnpeian in infancy, being one of the cases where a "seed" estate was not provided. He thereby moved out of the sphere of Pingelapese land tenure.

A problem arises with regard to the offspring of individual (15). The genealogy shows a son adopted previous to the birth of (30), but the entire portion of the estate of (1) acquired by (15) was moved to his natural son (30). I do not have the inventory of this adoptive son's acquisitions from other sources, but unless he got an unusually large "seed" grant, and such cases have been rare, his position as an adoptive son did not bring with it the usual enhancement of acquisitions. It should be noted also that in this case the individual in question (15) was one of the Sokehs immigrants and he was given a plot of 5 000 square metres upon getting established there. While it is appropriate to mention that arrangements for division of the lands on Sokehs Island were engineered by the German administration, it is also noteworthy that such allotments did ultimately affect land divisions on the atoll itself.

The chart also reveals other aspects of the effects of adoption on the system of Pingelapese land tenure. I have mentioned one instance of *mwol* where a grandfather (9) willed land to a grandson (unnumbered) and adoption figured into other land transferral as follows: (5) to (13); (14) to (29); (17) to (34); and (8) to (21). There are also two step-relationships which involved land grants, individual (9) to (20), and to (23).

Another interesting and anomalous instance is seen in the lack of involvement of the (unnumbered) older half-brother of (40) in the original estate of (1). Such a line of inheritance would have transmitted to him property through his father (22). Indeed, he did get land from (9) in Sokehs. In spite of this award his total acquisitions were still far smaller than those of his younger half-brother (40) who eventually also got a share of land in Sokehs even larger than that of his older half-brother. It seems clear from additional information to be discussed below with respect to succession to a title that the older son was regarded as being something of a black sheep in the family.

Title Succession and Land Inheritance

The disposal of the original estate of individual (1) also raises the question of the possible confluence of title succession and primogeniture in land inheritance. The darkened triangles on the chart indicate the successors to the title held by individual (1). The first transference of title followed the normal route in going from father to eldest son (4) of the senior wife (2). An adjustment from the norm of primogeniture in succession that involves a consideration of land tenure practices occurred in the next title transference indicated on the chart. Individual (4), while holding substantial land by Pingelapese standards, was considered to be not energetic enough in his exploitation of that property and often had to rely on the help of his half-brother (9) in making his contributions at the numerous prestation events. These events especially require sizeable contributions of products of the land from titled persons. When the typhoon of 1905 struck, property of (4) was especially hard hit by the storm and, as a result, he became to a considerable degree dependent on the support of close relatives. Again (9) was the chief contributor. At about this time the title was transferred horizontally but apparently voluntarily, to (9) by (4). Other survivors among the offspring of (1) could have been considered for succession but they had not helped (4) by making contributions to him. The case of individual (5) was mentioned especially in this regard. There is also, as mentioned above, a suggestion of favouritism on the part of (1) in that individual (9) actually got the largest share of those given to the numerous sons and daughters of (1), though again I do not have complete data on the acquisitions of all of these offspring. Certainly, such acquisitions, normally made either through the other main sources of mother, and wives at marriage, do indeed constitute consideration when the final allotment of lands is made by estate holders. The transferral of the title from (4) to (9) was thus strongly affected by elements of competency and of reciprocity. Another horizontal transferral occurred during the lifetime of the ceding title holder (21) when it was passed to his younger brother (22). Individual (21) had gotten the title through the normal route of patrilineality and primogeniture, being the eldest son of (9). This occurred in 1937, and the title carried with it the function of being a minister or intermediary between the atoll and the colony on Sokehs Island. By 1946 the *nahnmariki* of Pingelap had decided that (21) had failed to carry out his responsibility of looking after Pingelapese visitors at that colony and removed his title. It was transferred to (22) the next oldest of the sons of (9) who had not been adopted out. The latter had sizeable holdings on both Pingelap and Sokehs Island with which to fulfill his ceremonial obligations in either place, when as part of his duties he moved between the two centres of Pingelapese population.

The next transferral of the title ran contrary to the rule of primogeniture as well, but did coincide with the eventual inheritance of the largest segment of the title holder's (22) land to his second son (40). In this case the older son had been adopted out to his paternal grandfather (9) and had gotten land from that man in Sokehs. Later, after the death of (9), incumbent (22) made the decision to pass it to (40), though the older brother (unnumbered) would have been eligible despite having been adopted out within this close family unit, and also passed the bulk of his estate to (40). The reason for these departures from primogeniture in both succession and land inheritance was said to be because this oldest son of (22) had not fully met obligations for caring for first his grandfather-adoptive father, and after the death of that man, for his true father (22).

It can be seen from this discussion that some provision is made for meeting the heavy ceremonial gift obligations of title holders through the land-inheritance network, and I have cited an example of a man renouncing his title in his lifetime due to his failure to meet these obligations. One can trace the retention of the largest shares of the original estate along the movement of the title to some degree in that title holders (9), (22), and (40) all held the largest part of the estate of (1) in each of their respective generations. But two other holders of the title, (4) and (21), did not enjoy such favourable positions with regard to inheritance from that estate. Individuals (11) and (26) closely rivalled the shares of title holders in their generations. There is, then, no clear accompaniment of largest share of original title holder for the successors to his title over a series of generations, but it should be noted again that the chart does not show total holdings of most individuals, and especially those acquired from mothers and wives among other chief sources.

This history of transferrals of land and of titles thus suggests a general, but by no means invariable, association of the two, even though there is the need for titled persons to draw on substantial resources to fulfill their ceremonial obligations. In order to explore such possible associations further it would be instructive to compare the holdings of current title holders on the background of our survey of Sample B landholders as given in Tables 5.2 and 5.4. By the time of the great typhoon of the 1770s a system of nine title holders had evolved (Damas 1983a). The *muten kas piete* or "upper house" was composed of the *nahnmariki* or paramount chief, his heir in succession to that title, the *wasahi*, the *nahlaimw* or "priest of the sea," the *nanapas* or "priest of the land," and the *nahneken* or "talking chief." The *muten kas pa* or "lower house" consisted of the *nahlik*, *souwel*, *lompwei* and *nahno* who represented each of the four *pwekil*(s) or political divisions of the village. In addition to forming a judicial council for such matters as land disputes and other trials, various other individual responsibilities are associated with some of the titles. While the paramount chief had ultimate decision-making powers, he was expected to consult with the others, and his decisions were announced by the *nahneken* after private consultation between the two. The "priest of the land" and "priest of the sea" carried out special propitiation observances at all feasts over the products of their respective domains. The four representatives of the *pwekil*(s) or lower house members operated as enforcement agents in their sections. While all the chiefs were expected to make large contributions to all feasts or prestation events; they were most importantly involved in the proceedings surrounding the *pwakamwar*, or ceremony where normal father-to-son transmission of title occurred, and at the *waliempo* where titles shifted between lines within major *keinek*(s). Wives of the male title holders also had titles and these women were charged mainly with organizing the work of women. During the nineteenth century the original nine titles, some of which had been vacated due to deaths during the disaster of the 1770s, were restored and the roster expanded upon. One important change was altering of the title of the heir-apparent from *wasahi* to *nahpwusak*, and later, the replacement of that title holder in the "upper house" by a new titled post of *nahnawa* who was thereafter (about 1870) regarded as the second leading title holder. After the introduction of Christianity in the 1870s the priests of land and sea gradually lost their ceremonial roles, but later, after the establishment of the Sokehs colony in 1912-13, they were given supervisory roles there. After that time as well the *nahneken* took over as go-between, travelling frequently between the atoll and the colony, carrying directives from the paramount chief to the colonists.

During the Japanese period the influence of the council of chiefs became eroded by the growing strength of the church elders (though some individuals occupied positions in both systems). The Japanese awarded the title of Chief Magistrate to the *nahnmariki* who reigned from 1924-64. The American administration instituted a political-judicial system in Micronesia during the 1950s which affected the political strength of the council of chiefs. During that period the office of Chief Magistrate was affirmed and a Chief Justice, Associate Justice, and Public Defender appointed. While the formal judicial powers of the chiefs was thus supplanted, the old chief continued as Chief Magistrate, to be followed in that post by his son and successor, so that important continuity between traditional and introduced systems was achieved for a time on that level. Most of the titles, which were added in the twentieth century to fill out the roster of chiefs to 15, had no special portfolios. The *nansaho* had been designated as "chief of police." This post and that of the four *pwekil* representatives who had served in the capacity were now replaced by an elected police force (Damas 1983a).

The paramount chief who reigned from 1964-82 moved up in the new political hierarchy of the Trust Territory holding successively posts of district legislator and member of the General Assembly of the Congress of Micronesia. Later, in 1983, with the formation of a bicameral Legislature of the State of Pohnpei, the new *nahnmariki* and the *nahnawa* joined the *Mwoalen Wahu* or Council of High Chiefs. While this reorganization enhanced the power of two traditional chiefs, especially in external affairs, the remainder of the council had by the 1980s at the latest suffered a marked decline in their powers.[5] But at the same time whenever the chiefs were present on the atoll they were still expected to contribute large shares at most of the prestation occasions, and correlatively took away larger shares than those not holding titles or high positions in the church. The holdings of nine of the 15 hereditary chiefs of 1980 are shown in Table 5.7.

The chiefs are ranked according to an accepted hierarchy, with the first three members of the *muten kas piete* or "upper house" of traditional title holders; and numbers four, five, six, and seven constituting the *muten kas pa* or traditional "lower house." The remaining two titles were established in the present century (ibid.).

If comparisons are restricted, first within the roster of chiefs represented in the table, a certain rough correlation can be perceived between rank of chiefs and rank in landholding. The first or paramount chief holds substantially more land on Pingelap itself and, with the exception of title holder number four, more

Table 5.7
Nominal and Usufruct Properties of Nine Pingelapese Title Holders

Title	Total nominal holdings		From father		Usufruct property	
	m^2	Rows	m^2	Rows	m^2	Rows
1. Nahnmariki	22 750	51.5	22 750	42.5	23 180	111
2. Nahnawa	11 580	28	4 682	10	12 416	32
3. Nahneken	24 326[a]	13	19 079[a]	3	0	0
4. Nahlik	13 633[a]	52	750	3	8 858	77
5. Souwel	7 511	42	1 252	18	8 348	47
6. Lompwei	5 330	16	3 344	7	0	0
7. Nahno	3 418	19	2 979	10	5 508	27
8. Nahnit	2 730	28	1 463	24	0	0
9. Nanpei	13 754	34	6 271	23	7 274	54

a Includes holdings of 10 000 square metres of property on Sokehs Island in each case.

taro rows than the others. Two chiefs from the "upper house," the first and the third, have shares of land significantly larger than those of all other chiefs, except for the holder of the most recently established number nine title. This case, of course is the most anomalous in this respect, but the extent of holdings by that individual is not unusual in the total Sample B. The total holdings of chiefs numbers three and four includes 10 000 square metres of land in the Sokehs colony. Even discounting that property, however, the third chief ranks second behind the paramount chief in land owned on the atoll. Turning then to a broader comparison, that between the title holders represented in Table 5.7 and their largely contemporary Sample B recipients as given in Table 5.2, the average holding of the chiefs was 9 448 square metres of land on the atoll and 11 670, including Sokehs Island holdings, and 31.5 rows in the taro patch, while the average for the remainder of Sample B men, excluding the title holders, was 10 090 square metres and 28 rows. We would expect that, ordinarily, most of the land or other property inherited by chiefs as well as other males derives from fathers. In this regard the preponderance of donations by fathers in the cases of chiefs as compared to others of Sample B is clear. Chiefs inherited on the average 6 952 square metres in total, and 5 841 on the atoll and 15.6 rows from fathers as compared to 2 740 and 9.6 for the rest of Sample B males from their fathers. This finding is consistent with an expectation that there would be a correlation between primogeniture in land and title inheritance, and with a supposition that there would be, in addition to observance of that stated norm, special care taken to provide an especially large legacy to successors to titles, in keeping with increased demands on their resources for ritual occasions. But, since primogeniture does indeed prevail in land tenure as well as title succession, a better comparison would be one between the title bearers and first sons or, more precisely, between first son title bearers and other first sons in population Sample B. When this comparison is made the difference is less pronounced. Among the eight title bearers given in Table 5.7 who are first sons, the chiefs averaged 5 440 square metres on the atoll and 6 551 in total, as well as 14.6 rows acquired from fathers, while other first sons in Sample B averaged 5 090 square metres and 14.5 rows. The consideration of greater demands made on chiefs as reflected in their getting larger shares is not strongly supported by these figures. The limiting factor, is, of course, availability of property as provided by donors to the chiefs.

It becomes clear in examining the life history data on land inheritance that the main factor leading toward expansion of individual holdings in the phase of Pingelap history represented by Sample B has been the practice of adoption. In this regard four of the nine title holders of the sample got land from adoptive fathers, and in addition, three received allotments from adoptive mothers. In Sample B, excluding the incorporated title holders, 21 of 24 benefitted from land inherited from adoptive parents, and 15 of 24 of these people got land from adoptive mothers. While chiefs, therefore, benefitted less from acquisitions from adoptive parents, it is noteworthy that those chiefs who did so benefit were able to build substantial parts of their estates through that medium. In each of these four cases acquisitions from adoptive parents were markedly greater than those from natal parents.

The circumstance of heirs to titles being adopted out needs to be examined more closely. Adoptive children do not return to their natal family with great frequency, as appears to be the case in other Micronesian societies, particularly for example as described for Kosrae by Wilson (1976). In fact, on Pingelap, it is mainly those heirs to titles who eventually come back in their adult years when such titles become vacant. In this circumstance, then, these heirs are able to enjoy the best parts of the dimensions of both land tenure and succession. One of the chiefs did acquire his title through an adoptive relationship, but this is not common, as counterclaims within *keinek*(s) usually take priority in such cases.

Returning to the comparison of the landholding status of the title bearers as compared to others in Sample B, we find the former to be spread along virtually the whole range, holding 2 730-22 750 square metres of land and 13-52 rows of taro. Only three from this list of title holders are represented among the ten largest landholders on Pingelap. Indeed, four of the nine rank well below the average of all males in population Sample B. That sample is admittedly biased in favour of first sons, but then so is the chiefly group.

One does not normally rise to chiefly prominence on Pingelap through providing large offerings at ceremonial events, as is the case is other Pacific societies where achievement may provide equal or even preferential bases for such promotion. Based on the foregoing discussion, there does not seem to be a great deal of special advantage in holding or being heir to a title in the game of increasing one's real estate holdings. At this point it seems that the disadvantages of having to provide large shares at food prestation occasions outweigh whatever honourific or power concomitants might be resident in the titles. The history of Pingelap notes at least two cases where titles were yielded because of this economic strain. On the other hand, there is recourse for obtaining the extra supply of food needed for such occasions.

In another place (Damas 1986) I have dealt with residential patterns on Pingelap and stressed the importance of a virilocal extended family unit as a productive and resource-sharing, as well as residential and commensal, unit. In Chapter 4 I reviewed the nature of the domestic cycle, which indicated that at some stages in an individual's life history he or she will be part of such a unit. On Pingelap the extended family household is identified with either a house occupied by two or more nuclear families linked by parent-child and spousal ties, or by a cluster of houses domiciling such persons occupying a single lot and sharing a cooking hut. Ideally, all members of such units pool the products of arboriculture, the taro patch, marine resources, and cash income from copra and other sources. If the title holder is head of such a group, the labour potential of such a close circle of relatives is also important in producing the wherewithal for prestation occasions as well as for subsistence. Even though the resource base of this essential landholding and using unit may not be great in some cases, a wider scope of kindred can also be enlisted to aid in the necessary production. Some examples may serve to illustrate this potential.

The highest ranking chief has the burden of providing the largest shares at many major redistribution occasions. The incumbent for that title at the beginning of my research on the atoll held one of the largest estates, 22 750 square metres and 42.5 rows from his father, 9 rows from his mother, and usufruct privileges of the dowry of his wife for another 5 535 square metres and 24 rows. Dowries of wives of married sons brought another 6 555 square metres and 18 rows into the usufruct network of his extended family. To work this land, four of his eight sons whose residences were supposed to be on the atoll would normally be available, but there was a considerable degree of travel between Pohnpei and Pingelap by all of the sons. Through the system of *kohwa* or stewardship of lands owned by Pingelapese living off the atoll, the paramount chief had additional access to over 11 290 square metres of land and another 69 rows in the taro patch as well as land in the colony of Mand held by his eldest son. Without counting the last holding, the total resource base on the atoll was 45 930 square metres of land and 162.5 rows in the main taro patch. Of this total, 70 percent of the taro holdings and more than half the land area came from sources other than direct inheritance.

Such a large access base suggests that there would be no difficulty in supplying the vegetal products sufficient for subsistence as well as for the substantial ceremonial demands that the paramount chief's position requires. There was, indeed, more of a problem recruiting labour to harvest products of the land as well as maritime resources. He and four of his sons (some of whom were adopted out but still contributed to him) lived off the island most of the time and, as indicated above, the other four sons were also absent for periods. This imbalance between land and effective labour resources has been filled to some extent by hired labour. The cash income base for this extended family was considerable and made it possible to hire men for pay. Indeed, with the family's large holdings, the chief was able to make a grant of land to one of these workers (Case 3 above). In other cases the actual lack of land was the chief obstacle for getting together enough produce for the frequent prestation occasions, if they had to rely only on inherited land. But chief number four in Table 5.7 who had inherited only 3 633 square metres of land but a substantial 52 rows in the taro patch, had more than double that amount of land for use through property owned by his wife to make up a fairly sizeable estate, especially taro holdings. In addition, he acquired both small properites on the atoll and an additional 10 000 square metres on Sokehs Island from his adoptive father.

Another less well-endowed chief, number seven in Table 5.7, also inherited little land but increased his estate for use purposes by nearly 50 percent through his wife's contributions, though the total was still not impressive. This man was also handicapped by not having grown sons to help with the work, but he was able to get labour and product contributions from a younger brother.

With the exception of the paramount chief, the titled men in the above examples appear to have barely met the demands of their stations. The acculturation factors of the rise in prominence of church officials and the absence of some chiefs from the atoll for long periods confused the picture regarding the apparent failure of the land tenure system to support the roles of chiefs in ceremonial events. That is, I have indicated above that the title holders occupy a somewhat lesser role than formerly in the first fruits ceremonies. But it is not clear to me whether the effects of a breakdown in the land tenure system also contributed to the disqualification of certain of the title holders from being principal contributors to several of the prestation events.

Social Status and Land Ownership

I have argued that the position of head of an extended family is the chief situation under which obligations of sharing land, labour, and produce operates. The foregoing discussion suggests that the material benefits of holding title are questionable. While it is true that the title holders, and today the higher church officials, carry away the largest shares at each prestation occasion, this gain is largely symbolic, for those proceeds must in turn be redistributed among those who helped in the production and preparation of the products thus acquired. Also, the proceeds from these occasions cannot last for more than a day or two, in view of the climatic conditions and the lack of effective preservation facilities.

With regard to the possibility of prestige accruing from ownership of large land and taro holdings, I must cite some cases which would tend to confound such speculation. In going over my land tenure data with my chief informant, I noted two individuals as being among the leading landowners. At first he expressed disbelief and doubted my figures. After reflecting he suggested that I had probably included the *kohwa* holdings which, in fact, I had not. It is not surprising that exact knowledge of the holdings of others is not well known, considering the previous lack of maps showing accurately measured plots or numbered taro rows. Under those conditions there is only some general notion of who are the largest holders and who are the land-poor people.

The two men in question are among the least conspicuous members of the Pingelap community. Neither is in line for succession to any of the titles of Pingelap, nor are they important in church activities, nor has either held any of the numerous elected posts on the atoll. One is deformed, and I got the impression that neither is considered to be very bright. On another occasion, without special reference to these men, I expressed the view to the chief informant that owning large shares of property on Pingelap does not in itself provide much respect or status in the community. He agreed and remarked that such people were acknowledged as being "rich" but really nothing beyond that. He also indicated that often such land-rich but otherwise insignificant people came from families that had experienced a great deal of sickness. From these remarks and those of other informants, it became clear to me that the Pingelapese are aware of some of the chief factors that lead to substantial inequalities in individual holdings. Demographic imbalances are chief among the recognized factors that influence creation of such inequalities. There are several components involved. One is the simple people-to-land ratios in extended families. The number of offspring inheriting land from estates will vary inversely with the shares of the estate available. Sex ratio is another factor. If a man has more sons than daughters, little land will be lost from the unit through dowries, and at the same time dowry shares are added to the unit through marriage under the prevailing virilocal residence practices (ibid.). With daughters a man will lose land at their marriages without gaining a working man. On the other hand, another aspect of sex ratios figuring into land distributions is that a man with few sons will inevitably create larger dowries for his daughters. There is no doubt that such considerations entered into arrangements of marriage when such arrangements were common in former years.

Adoption has been the most important factor in regulating family size and balancing the people-to-land ratios in the period 1900-45, when these imbalances were most prominent due to a high frequency of sterile matings (Damas 1983b). The introduction of improved medical care during the American period has ameliorated the problem of unevenness in family size. At the same time these improved health conditions have resulted in a rate of population growth unprecedented in the history of Pingelap, even given the remarkable expansion of the nineteenth century. Increased pressures on the land of the atoll would have accompanied this recent expansion had not emigration also increased.

The Variant Value of Individual Holdings

At this point it is important to address a matter which has been only touched upon so far. Both in analyzing tables and in discussing case histories in this chapter, I have relied almost exclusively on quantitative evaluations of estates: their division into shares which are expressed in terms of the numbers of square metres and of taro rows. Such an approach is deficient in its failure to take into account more precise differences in the value of specific holdings. I have already referred to the difficulty of classing taro holdings in the main patch only by rows, due to the existence of some double rows, and the variations in length of rows. With regard to taro affecting the value of *peliensapw*(s), the presence of the small pits in which taro grows may seem significant, but these pits can be dug anywhere (though with some little labour). While taro continued as the staff of life on Pingelap during the period of my study, it cannot be said to be a favourite food. I heard complaints about tiring of its prominent place in diets when other sources of food fail. Such products as bananas, papayas, mangoes, sugar cane, and pandanus appeal to the sweet tooth which appears to be a universal Pingelapese failing. Earlier I pointed out that bananas, papayas, and the one mango tree grew close to the houses today in order to prevent theft. Such was not always the case with regard to bananas, and in earlier times, as one reference in this chapter shows, conditions which promote growth of bananas on land actually enhanced its value to the point of encouraging the exchange of lots. Sugar cane grows best in the moist soils of the taro patch, but it is a short-lived plant that can be planted anywhere in that patch and thus does not present a long-term asset. Pandanus, though not a staple food, may somewhat enhance the value of a plot, especially if both the pistillate and staminate forms are found there, because of the value of its lumber and leaves.

Coconuts formerly provided a more important source of food and are today the chief source of a commercial product, copra. The current value of any plot could greatly depend on the number of good bearing trees. The care with which previous plot owners have assured the supply of such bearing trees by continuous replanting is very important, while the potential for growing the trees is widespread, with only a few very rocky places and some mangrove swamps not providing adequate soils for their growth. In general, the gross size of plots and the current condition of bearing trees are the most important factors in relating the value of land to coconut trees, though destruction through the typhoons that periodically hit the atoll is also a factor.

Undoubtedly the crop which most greatly enhances the value of land is breadfruit. Valuable both for its lumber and as a highly prized food (especially in the fermented state), the trees grow in places of least salinity of the lens and which are well protected from salt spray.[6] Thus the best areas are around houses in the village and sections of the island in the interior well away from the windward side. Even then, periodic floodings may reach some distance inland, as was the case of the high water of the 1972 typhoon, which destroyed many breadfruit trees on Daekae. It takes many years to grow a tree which will be useful in canoe-making, and the loss of any breadfruit tree is a serious tragedy to any landowner. A completely thorough assessment of the relative worth of land plots on Pingelap would have to take into account the current state of mature trunks of this tree.

The relatively minor attributes of presence or absence of several varieties of crops, the greater importance of bearing coconut trees, and the greatest quality-enhancing feature—the presence of breadfruit trees, taken together probably account for some of the apparent discrepancies in granting land according to the principles laid forth here. Indeed, such bases for discrepancies, when combined with a large number of situational factors presented in this chapter, might well lead the reader to assume that the anomalies, the adjustments, the variances, and the imponderables of land tenure on Pingelap produce a state of randomness which defies understanding in terms of form or regularities. Regardless of whatever weight these factors can be given, I hope that the foregoing presentation, which is based on levelling values of rows of taro and reducing landholdings to a simple quantitative treatment, has served to explicate general tendencies in Pingelapese land inheritance. Flexibility is necessary in any set of land tenure practices that operate in societies like Pingelap, where pressures on land are great. But this is not to say that such flexibility is not bounded within limits. It is hoped that the case-by-case treatment used here which dealt with specific situational adjustments, and which as an artifact of procedure, overstressed them, does not obscure the degree of regularity which I see in Pingelapese land tenure. For while each reader may have an individual rule-of-thumb standard for assigning the term to any such set of practices, I have tried to argue for the concept of *system* as applied to Pingelapese land tenure.

CHAPTER 6

Confirming the Division of Estates: The *Derak* Ceremony

The most important life-cycle events for any Pingelapese man are those which surround his death or the imminence of death. One of these is the *mwurilik*, or true funeral. In cases of the death of title holders there will be also the *pwakamar* which marks the transferral of the title to a successor. In Chapter 4 I indicated that the most frequent times for dispersal of properties were either at a period very late in the life of the testator, or after his death. In either instance, the *derak* ceremony is held in order to validate passing of property to one's heirs.[1] This ceremony also includes confirmation of assignments of parts of estates made at earlier times, as at marriages or through out-, or in-, adoptions. At times, all three, or two of the three ceremonies surrounding death are held simultaneously. In these cases it is particularly difficult to sort out contributions that relate to one part or the other elements of the joint occasion. A limitation to my study regarding *derak* is that I was able to actually observe only one of these events and had to rely on informant recall for other examples. While there was a range in recall of exact donations and receipts by my informants, a sufficiently large corpus of information was available to justify the following examination of case histories of *derak*(s).

The *Derak* Ceremony: Case Histories

The purpose of the following discussion of case histories is to explore the network of relationships among participants in *derak*, or the system of arrangements which are made to formally recognize or in Pingelapese terms, "pay for" the receipt of land. In Chapter 4 I noted that the chief principle upon which *derak* is based is that pigs and taro (actually Cyrtosperma) corms are presented in proportion to the amount of land that is awarded from the estate being

---

The note to Chapter 6 is on p. 251.

honoured. At this point it would be well to elaborate on this basic norm as it applies to the event. By extension from the norms that apply to land inheritance, corollary principles could be expected to follow in the *derak* ceremony. Since, according to the principle stated above, the larger landholders would be expected to contribute the larger shares at *derak*, it would follow that the principles of seniority and of male predominance or patrilineal preference would be expressed also in prestation of local products at *derak* events. Accordingly, since the eldest son normally gets the most land in estate settlements, one would expect him to be the largest donor of pigs and taro corms. There has been seen to be a descending order of land receipts in sibling groups according to age. One would also expect such a pattern to occur in donations at *derak* events. Women would be expected to contribute less at these events than men because normally they would be ceded less property. Heirs adopted into families would get shares of land and taro equivalent to similarly placed natal children, and would be expected to make equivalent *derak* donations. Persons adopted out would not be major donors, since their shares of estates would be usually small.

Thus a set of expectations regarding donors to *derak* can be derived from preliminary statements and logically formulated from a generalized pattern of land-inheritance conventions. It was not possible to derive a guide to the expectations of the recipients of prestations at such events other than statements that "those who contributed to the estate would be paid." In retrospect, I realize that my method of inquiry could have been improved, and if I had persisted I would have achieved a more complete picture of the network of recipients at *derak* than I did. In actual practice I derived my understanding of this network from examining case histories and from inquiring of informants regarding understood conventions as this examination proceeded. With this consideration in mind, and in order to explore both the patterns of prestation and receipt in *derak*, it seems appropriate to move now to the case histories themselves. My corpus includes accounts of 10 cases, eight of which occurred on Pingelap, with the others involving Pingelapese who lived much of their lives and died, on Pohnpei.

Case 1

This case illustrates a range of transactions and serves to document both adherence to norms as well as departures from or accommodations to norms. The chart of relationships between testator and donors and recipients and amounts given and received are recorded on Figure 6.1 for this case. This *derak* took place in 1956, about a year before the death of the central figure or testator and thus is referred to as *derak mour* (see discussion in Chapter 4). In this and succeeding cases donors to *derak* are indicated by number and recipients by letter, and the honoured testators by darkened triangles. My informant in this case, individual (3), said that the estate had been divided earlier, with the informant, his adopted brother (4), and adopted sister (2) all getting their shares at the times of their marriages. As is usual in such cases, the extended family, consisting of the central figure (B) (darkened triangle), his wife, and the two adoptive

Figure 6.1
Derak Case 1

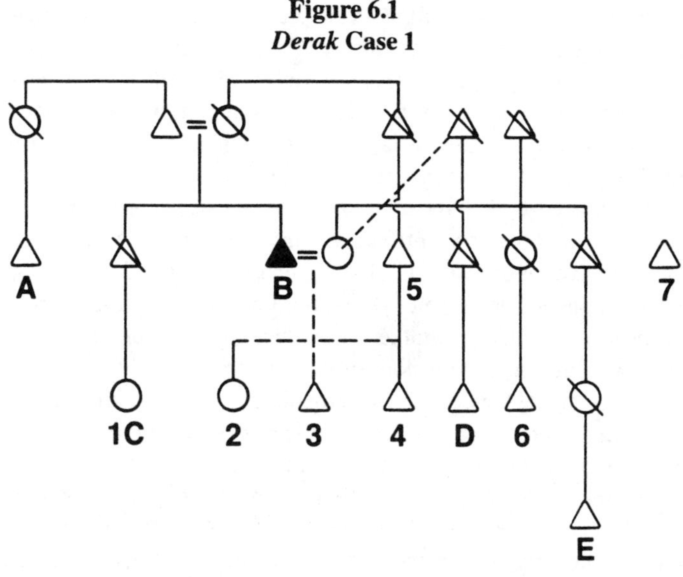

I.	*Donors*			
Relationship to testator	Goods donated: Pigs	Goods donated: Corms	Property received: m^2	Property received: Rows
1) BD	1	10	?	?
2) AD	1	30	1 045	8
3) AS[1]	2	60	21 550	45
4) AS[2]	1	20	3 553	6
5) MBS	1	10	?	?
6) WZS	1	5	1 942	4
7) Unrelated	1	6	2 822	9
Total	8	141		

II.	*Recipients*		*Putative Donors*		
Relationship to testator	Goods received: Pigs	Goods received: Corms	Relationship to testator	Property attributed: m^2	Property attributed: Rows
A) FZS	1	20	F2	2 691	4
B) Testator	1	10	B	⟩ 22 957	35
C) BD	1.5	40	B		
D) WAFSS	1.5	25	WAF	?	?
E) WBDS	1	20	WB	?	?
Total	6	115			

sons (3) and (4), and their nuclear families, continued to cooperate in joint use of the total property and its products until the actual death of the central figure. According to the practice of virilocal residence, the daughter had transferred her share to the household of her husband. Adopted son (3) received the largest share of the estate and, accordingly, in keeping with the principle stated above, contributed the largest share at the *derak*. The expectable pattern of matching land shares received with contributions at this event was departed from to some extent for the other two adopted children of the central figure. The second adopted son (4) had received a larger share of land (but not taro) than his adopted sister (2), but he contributed less than did his sister. According to my informant in this case, this apparent anomaly was occasioned by this brother living on Pohnpei at the time of the *derak*. Individual (3) served as steward for this brother's land on the atoll, but having had the chore of harvesting for his own contributions to the ceremony, had not had time to gather taro from the patch sections owned by his brother to produce the appropriate contributions. In keeping with the smaller portions of the estate received by (1), (5), (6), and (7), these recipients of land gave much smaller donations of taro corms, and the number of pigs was reduced from two for the principal land recipient and product donor (3) to one each for the others. The routes through which these individuals got land from the estate of (B) were somewhat involved. In the case of (1), she had received considerable property from the father of the central figure since she was the only child of the older brother of (B) who had been the original principal heir of their father. Later, on the death of the older brother, (B) received a substantial part (excluding only that given to this daughter) of the older brother's share, though I do not have figures for these shares.

With regard to (5), a rare WBS-FZH transferral had taken place. Individual (7) contributed to the *derak* because his father (deceased at this time) had lived his later years with (B) and had gotten land from him despite there being no traceable kinship link between the two. In the case of (6) land had been transferred from MZH to WZS, an unusual but not unique occurrence.

The recipients at this distributional ceremony followed the conventional pattern of their being considered to have been contributors to the estate honoured at the *derak* or their representing direct descent from those who were so considered. At this stage in my examination of case histories it had not yet become clear that the central figure or testator, if living, is seldom honoured by direct receipt of gifts at his own *derak*. The rationalization of his receipt of a small portion in this case was that the testator had been a secondary heir to his father's estate, as it had originally been largely assigned to his older brother. Since that man had no sons (B) as next senior (and in this case only) brother had assumed the role of conduit of the estate derived from their parents to his own adopted offspring and other recipients of parts of the estate which he passed on. An especially interesting aspect of this *derak* is that the daughter of the deceased brother of (B) was not only a recipient, as individual (C), but also a donor, as individual (1). Her role as recipient at the *derak* was by virtue of her being the sole direct descendant of the older brother, also a contributor to the estate. As a donor she had been recipient of land from the same individual.

Transferral of claim to WBDS(E) was somewhat anomalous if dominance of patrilineal inheritance of land is expected. My information is that, in this case, this wife's brother had borne no male offspring so that his direct descendancy was measured through a daughter. This claim was solidified by the condition that his wife's brother had lived with the central figure and had given to (B) all of his land before his death and had thus materially contributed to the estate whose division was being validated at this *derak*.

Recipient (D) got his shares of taro and pigs through his being the direct living descendant of the adoptive father of (B)'s wife who had provided a dowry share to the estate of (B). Another dowry share had been contributed to the estate by the natal father of (B)'s wife so that individual (E), as grandson of that man, representing his daughter, now deceased was considered his representative and, accordingly, had another justification (see above) for receiving a pig and some taro at this *derak*.

This *derak* illustrates some of the circumstances under which departure from a dominant patrilineal theme in land inheritance is evident. Exceptions to the preference for male-to-male transferrals can be seen in the examples of individuals (C) and the mother of (E), since these women got larger than normal shares from their parents than if they had male siblings who would have received the lion's share of the estates involved. These transferrals, and their celebration by prestations and receipt of taro and pigs, highlight the principle that property can pass outside the *keinek* or patrilineally oriented kin unit. This finding reinforces my previous statements on the matter, that property is not conceived of as passing through *keinek*(s), at least during the time period covered in my genealogies.

With regard to the event itself, I queried the informant closely and it appears that it was very much an informal affair, with the emphasis being placed on the actual distribution of the products brought to the *derak* event. There were no prayers, or speeches, and no religious ingredients, either Christian or pagan, reported. Food was not consumed at the site of distribution. Rather, all received products were carried from the scene, with some being further redivided. Figure 6.1 shows that more pigs and corms were brought than actually given to the designated recipients. The difference of 2 pigs and 26 corms of taro was reportedly divided among the donors, though I could get no exact accounting of the portions given to each.

Case 2

This *derak* was part of a simultaneous two-phase ceremony. The other element was the transfer of the paramount chief's title, *nahnmariki*, in the *pwakamar* since individual (1) in the table was both the recipient of the largest share of the estate of the deceased central figure as well as the successor to his title. The gifts he donated were divided equally in amounts for the two parts of the ceremony, but the accompanying diagram in Figure 6.2 shows only the portions considered to have been associated with the *derak*.

In comparing donations with the proportions of land received, the estate shares of this primary recipient (1) clearly predominate over those of all other heirs, as does his contribution to the ceremony. Clearly the disproportions in both receipts of land in compensatory contributions to the *derak* are linked to

Figure 6.2
***Derak* Case 2**

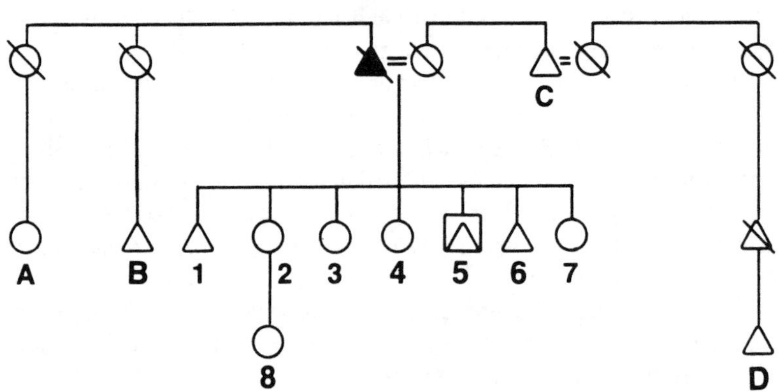

I. *Donors*			Property received	
Relationship to testator	Goods donated Pigs	Corms	m^2	Rows
1) S[1]	2.5	150	22 750	51.5
2) D[1]	1	10	1 338	3
3) D[3]	1	10	4 389	5
4) D[4]	1	10	1 045	5
5) S[2]AO	2	50	3 637	122
6) D[5]	1	10	1 505	0
7) D[1]D	1	10	1 338	0
Total	12.5	290		

II. *Recipients*			*Putative donors of property*	Property attributed	
Relationship to testator	Goods received Pigs	Corms	Relationship to testator	m^2	Rows
A) ZD	1	20	Z	36 262	80.5
B) ZS	1	20	Z		
C) WB	1	10	W	2 282	4
D) WBWZSS	1	10	WBW	732	9
Total	4	60			

the special circumstances of office carried by this primary title on Pingelap. As related in the preceding chapter, this title was one of those for which the consideration of special shares to meet the demand of office was observed. The very large donation of 2.5 pigs and 150 corms of Cyrtosperma (which as noted above, constituted only half of [1]'s total contributions) is truly remarkable, since the entire combined *pwakamar-derak* occurred on one day while the body lay in state. Often a period of up to a year would have been set aside to collect a quantity of produce and perhaps to raise a sufficient number of pigs before a *derak mehla* would have been staged. That such a collection could be produced in short order in this case attests to the ample holdings, but more specifically, to the large workforce which included both those from a circle of relatives as well as others who were enlisted in this case.

The amounts contributed by the other donors to the *derak* represent more closely male orientation and relative age than they reflect proportionate acquisitions from the estate. The sisters received varying portions of land and numbers of taro rows from the testator, but all four sisters contributed the same portions, one pig and 10 corms, to the *derak*. The shares of land given the second (5) and third (6) sons were substantially smaller than those normally given such siblings. This division, again, reflects the great concern for providing large property holdings for the successor to the paramount chief's title. The contributions of the sons (5) and (6) were substantially greater, and larger in proportion to land acquired, than those of the four daughters of the testator, that is, a correspondence between land received and donations at this event was only a rough one, except in the case of the eldest son, and male heirs brought more to the *derak* than did females, regardless of portions of estate received. As well in this case, the small number of recipients of pigs and taro corms as compared to donors reflects a demographic circumstance, in that the testator had but two siblings, both sisters, and his two wives had only one sibling each. All members of these sibling groups would be normally considered to be putative donors to the estate and correlatively, recipients at this *derak*. Only one individual (C) in that generation was still living at this time and thus, as in the previous case, the principles of representation by descendants, with male preference, are applied. The exception to the latter norm is found in recipient (A) who was the only offspring of the senior sister of the central figure. Again, this sort of identification serves to emphasize that land tenure, and its celebration in *derak*, is focused on the extended family notwithstanding a patrilineal preference, and not on the *keinek*. If the *keinek* were the crucial unit, land would pass only through males or from in-marrying females. The putative rather than actual status of several recipients of gifts at this *derak* again should be noted in that although some shared in the estates of the mother and father of the central figure, they did not actually contribute to them. In comparing the contributions of donors with the shares distributed, a large surplus can be seen in Table 6.2. This was pooled with the substantial contribution of the new title holder to the *pwakamar* phase of the occasion and dispersed throughout the village. My informant in this matter recalled that day in 1964 vividly when the new chief and his wife marched the length of the village accompanied by a chorus of hooting sea shells.

Case 3

In sharp contrast to the preceding case, the estate in this example was very small, and by comparison as well, so were the donations to the *derak* event. Turning first to the donors at the event, the four daughters and one son (adopted out) contributed the same amounts—one pig and 30 corms of taro each. Only the informant in this case, individual (6), contributed significantly more, despite his getting a share in the estate which was only marginally greater than that of the son adopted out. To be sure, this individual was the senior male in the actual extended family household unit after the adoption out of his elder brother. In this position he would normally be expected to contribute the greatest amount to the *derak*. That he was able to do so despite his small inheritance from the testator in this estate was due to the significant properties brought in through his wife's dowry. These generalizations apply mainly to the taro presented at the *derak*. Other arrangements would have to have been made regarding pigs which, of course, have too short a life span, given the ceremonial demands of the culture, to be considered to be permanent sources of produce to be tapped at such occasions as the *derak*.

With regard to the recipients of taro and pigs, the normal apportionment of donations at the ceremony to the siblings of the testator, or their representatives, was followed. But adoptive relationships appear to have carried more weight than natal ties in two instances. In the first instance, the central figure himself inherited all of his property from his adoptive father with there being no evidence of receipts from either his adoptive mother or either of his natural parents. In a second instance, the son (A) of an elder adopted brother, as his representative, got the largest share of the donations of pigs and corms. On the other hand, this transaction also involves the preference of males over females in the redistributions since all other recipients were descended from sisters of the testator, with the exception of (D), who descended from and represented the brother of the testators' second wife. As in Case No. 2, we have two examples of a third generational representative among the recipients at the *derak*, individuals (B) and (C). That these latter individuals were quite advanced in years at this time attests to the longevity of the central figure in this case. It also attests to the degree of extension of receipt privileges at *derak* occasions.

In this case the degree of imbalance between donations at the *derak* and redistribution to indicated recipients was considerable. Aside from the numbers of corms and pigs or parts of pigs shown on the table accompanying Figure 6.3 the testator willed 50 corms and two pigs to the church in light of his having been the first deacon of the mission on Pingelap. Even so, there remained 150 corms and 5 pigs and a substantial portion of a sixth after these above transactions had taken place. This large share of donations was divided among the people who had helped prepare the contributions, and also, I was told, among others who attended the *derak*. These later prestations point to the significance of the ceremony extending beyond the land tenure realm itself to the realm of cementing social relations, whether or not they are circumscribed by kinship, since I was told that among those attending were neighbours to whom kinship ties were denied.

Another important point illustrated in this case is that, with the example of individual (6), a contribution to a *derak* can be based not entirely on the actual share of the estate received but rather on the ability to muster adequate resources to present at such occasions in order to uphold the position of male seniority in the sibling group who shared the estate of the testator.

Figure 6.3
***Derak* Case 3**

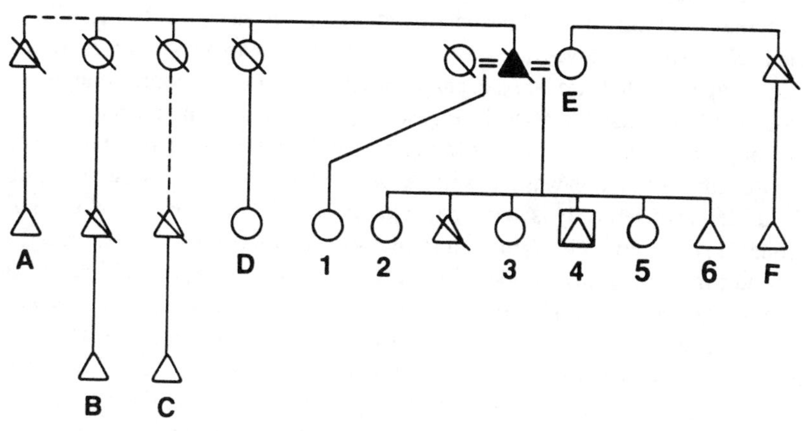

I.	*Donors*			
Relationship to testator	Goods donated		Property received	
	Pigs	Corms	m^2	Rows
1) D^1	1	30	502	6
2) D^2	1	30	535	5
3) D^3	1	30	489	0
4) S^2AO	1	30	1 873	2.5
5) D^4	1	30	0	0
6) S^3	5	100	2 299	5
Total	10	250		

II.	*Recipients*		*Putative donors of property*		
Relationship to testator	Goods received		Relationship to testator	Property attributed	
	Pigs	Corms		m^2	Rows
A) ABS	1	20	AB	5 163	11.5
B) Z^1SS	1 leg	—	Z^1		
C) Z^2ASS	1 leg	5	Z^2		
D) Z^3D	1 leg	5	Z^3		
E) W^2	.5	10	W^2	535	
F) WBS	.5	10	WB		
Total	2 +3 legs	50			

Case 4

Both the central figure and his wife were honoured in this *derak* because, it was said, they died only a few days apart, and because of her great contribution to the family estate. She was the elder of two daughters with no brothers in the sibling group (refer to Case No. 2 in chap. 5). The land of the honoured couple was passed to the management of the eldest son, individual (1) in the chart of relationships on Figure 6.4, in the old age of the couple to be redistributed after their deaths. Thus, this was an example of *derak mehla*. In this case fidelity to the principle of seniority is dominant in influencing shares donated. While individual (1) retained for himself a somewhat smaller area of land than he ceded to second brother (3), in consideration of the reservations expressed in the preceding chapter regarding relative worth of land, it is not clear that his was not a more valuable plot. He did retain more rows in the taro patch, assets which are in the long run more valuable. This is especially the case with regard to contributions to *derak*, since taro is the vegetal product presented. Thus his greater donated share can be seen to conform to the principle of seniority, but also to possession of a somewhat superior base from which to extract the necessary prestation. The daughter (2) got a smaller section of land and no taro rows and she contributed the same amounts as (3), while an adopted son (5) contributed somewhat less taro. The third natural son (4) was considered too young to contribute to this *derak*. This would mean that he was younger than age 15, which I was told was the minimum age at which prestations to *derak* were expected.

With regard to the recipients at this *derak*, they were persons of the generation of the testator or above (in one case), which marks a contrast to earlier cases where descendants were the usual recipients. This occurrence coincides with the young age at death of the chief testator and his wife. Recipient (A) was considered to be eligible because he had used land in common with the central figure, being a rare case of cousins forming a productive and sharing unit. The sister (B) was, of course, an appropriate recipient according to the rationale of the *derak* as developed above. Since the wife of the central figure who also figured in this *derak* brought large holdings to the extended family of the testator, her step-father (C) as surviving member of the conjugal triad was considered the representative of that side of the family. The table accompanying Figure 6.4 shows that only half of the taro corms were apportioned to these three recipients. In this case, I am told that the remainder was redivided among the donors themselves. Thus the prestations of food represented not only "payment" for the land received but also, with this large surplus, the act of redistribution appears in this case to have been concerned with reinforcing already existing close kinship ties within an extended family, rather than expanding such a network to include a wider circle of kin and nonkin. Taken together Cases 3 and 4 show the degree of flexibility which is inherent in the *derak* in these matters.

Figure 6.4
***Derak* Case 4**

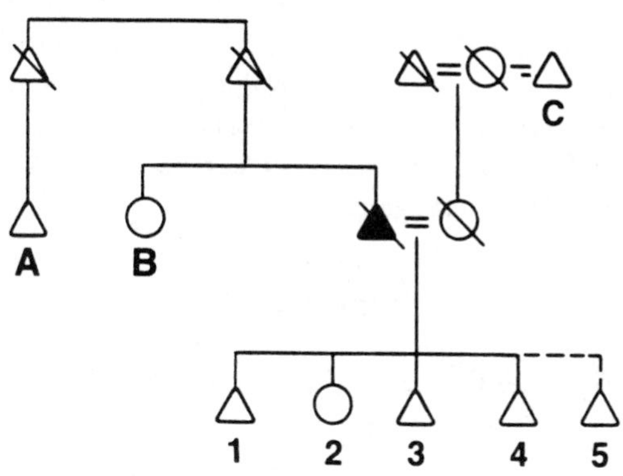

I.	*Donors*			
	Goods donated		Property received	
Relationship to testator	Pigs	Corms	m^2	Rows
1) S^1	1	50	5 853	30
2) D^1	1	15	3 135	0
3) S^2	1	15	6 877	17
4) S^3	0	0	1 045	8
5) AS^4	1	10	1 568	0
Total	4	90		

II.	*Recipients*		*Putative donors of property*		
	Goods received			Property attributed	
Relationship to testator	Pigs	Corms	Relationship to testator	m^2	Rows
A) FBS	1	10	FB	⟩ 8 466	44
B) Z^1SS	1	25	Z		
C) WSTF	1	10	W	10 012	11
Total	3	45		18 478	55

Case 5

Here minimal detail was available, with only the number of pigs given at the *derak* being remembered. Note that the informant, individual (1), gave two pigs as compared to one each by the other donors. The larger number is in keeping with his being the oldest male in the sibling group and also because of his having received 3.5 times the land and more than 3 times the number of taro rows of any of the others in that group who made up the roster of heirs in this case. Since the testator (C) in this case and his wife were still living, this event was a *derak mour*. As is sometimes the practice at such times, they received contributions, but these shares were said by my informant to have been much smaller both in land and in parts of pigs than the shares of the other recipients. One apparent anomaly was that it was reported that the children of the step-father of the central figure, individuals (A) and (B), got the largest portions of land and pigs. But this was because the step-father had been the largest contributor to the estate of (C) since the latter's father had been an immigrant Gilbertese with no land. It is particularly unfortunate that there is little detail regarding the amount of taro contributed to the *derak* and how it was redistributed, since the informant, individual (1), was the largest landholder on Pingelap (see Case 14 in chap. 5) at the time of my investigations.

Figure 6.5
***Derak* Case 5**

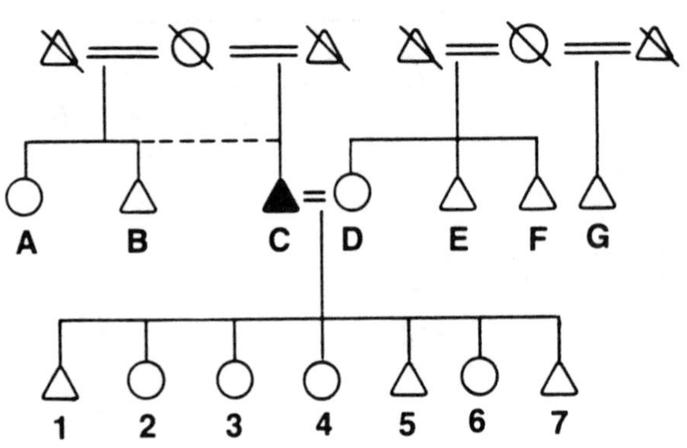

I.	*Donors*				
	Goods donated			Property received	
Relationship to testator	Pigs	Corms		m^2	Rows
1) S^1	2	?		11 208	31
2) D^1	1	?		2 090	5
3) S^2	1	?		1 463	10
4) S^3	1	?		1 463	7
5) D^2	1	?		2 090	6
Total	8	?			

II.	*Recipients*		*Putative donors of property*		
	Goods received			Property attributed	
Relationship to testator	Pigs	Corms	Relationship to testator	m^2	Rows
A) HZ	?	?	HZ	} 2 429	3
B) HZ	?	?	HZ		
C) Testator	?	?	Testator	13 377	53
D) W	?	?	W	} 4 390	11
E) WB	?	?	WB		
F) WB	?	?	WB		
G) WHB	?	?	WHB		
Total	?	?			

Figure 6.6
***Derak* Case 6**

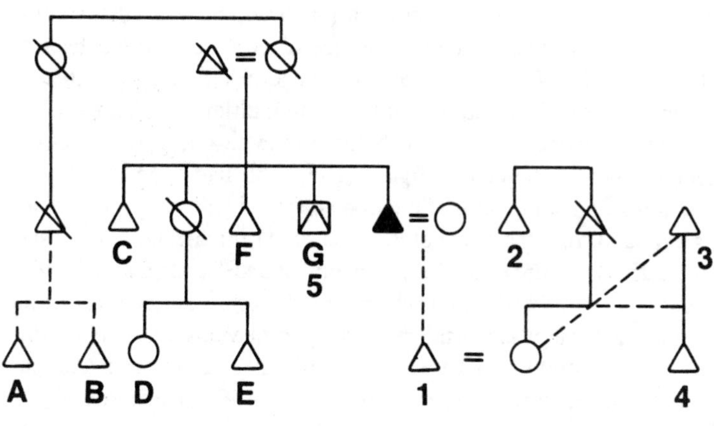

I.	*Donors*			
	Goods donated		Property received	
Relationship to testator	Pigs	Corms	m^2	Rows
1) AS	4	70	5 276	35
2) ASWFB	1	10		
3) ASWAF	1	15	5 226	35
4) ASWAB	1	10		
5) B^{3}AO	1	10		
Total	8	115		

II.	*Recipients*		*Putative donors of property*		
	Goods received			Property attributed	
Relationship to testator	Pigs	Corms	Relationship to testator	m^2	Rows
A) MBSAS^1	.5	2	M	0	0
B) MSSAS^2			M		
C) B^1			B^1		
D) ZS^1			Z		
E) ZS^2	4	54	Z	5 266	35
F) B^2			B^2		
G) B^{3}AO			B^{3}AO		
Total	4.5	56			

* Not part of Estate of Testator (see discussion in text).

Case 6

This was a *derak mour* with the testator being present about five days before he died at age 72. He was not alloted a share himself. Due to the special circumstance of the central figure having no offspring other than (1), an adopted son, some adjustments were made regarding the individuals who donated pigs and taro to this *derak*. While the principal heir to land and taro rows, individual (1), contributed the largest share at this occasion, it will be noted that all other contributors were his affines, with the exception of a brother who had been adopted out. These individuals were conceived as benefitting from the estate through their relative, the wife of the central figure and, ultimately, her children. They thus formed a second line of contributors in the absence of siblings of (1). A younger brother of the central figure (G-5) who had been adopted out also donated a pig and some taro. The rationale for this prestation was that he had been given land from the estate of the testator at his marriage. That testator had been awarded the entire estate for management and redistribution by his father. Consequently, individual (G-5) was both a donor and a recipient of taro and pigs in this case. He was considered a recipient because, as is normative, as a brother of the central figure he was considered a donor to the estate according to the principle which has emerged in this analysis of case histories.

While there is a precise recording of gifts brought to this *derak* by contributors, the shares of the recipients are lumped together, except for these given individuals (A) and (B). The situations of (A) and (B) are interesting because of their genealogical remoteness from the testator. Their inclusion was justified by my informant on the basis that their father (deceased) had contributed to the *derak* of the father of the honoured individual of the present *derak* ceremony.

After the designated shares had been distributed there remained 61 corms and 3.5 pigs for redistribution. These were then divided among those who had helped in the preparations for the ceremony, and to neighbours who attended the event.

Case 7

In this case there were only two donors of goods at the *derak* as compared to seven recipients of their prestations. My informant, individual (2), contributed significantly more than did his adopted sister (1), in keeping with the larger share of the estate received, and in keeping with the principle of patrilineality. It is noteworthy that this individual was one of the largest landholders on Pingelap, but that his contribution here was not as great as some of the other primary heirs considered in previous cases, and these gifts had to be spread thinly among the several recipients at the *derak*. There may be two reasons for this situation. One would be that a substantial part of his holdings came from each of his two wives, whose relatives were not honoured at this occasion. The other perhaps more compelling reason would be that while he did have significant holdings in the main taro patch, he did not head an extended family of adult producers in residence on Pingelap. Therefore, the labour of production was not augmented beyond his own efforts. As in most of the other cases cited, the recipients were siblings of the testator and of his wife.

Figure 6.7
***Derak* Case 7**

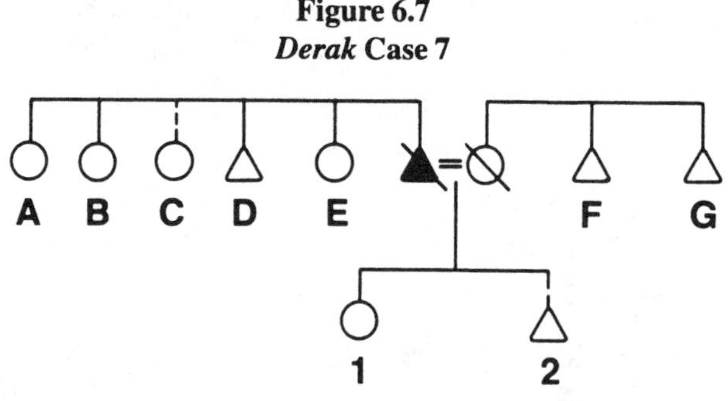

I.	*Donors*		Property received	
	Goods donated			
Relationship to testator	Pigs	Corms	m^2	Rows
1) D	1	20	552	3
2) AS	2	50	2 249	13
Total	3	70		

II.	*Recipients*		*Putative donors of property*		
	Goods received			Property attributed	
Relationship to testator	Pigs	Corms	Relationship to testator	m^2	Rows
A) Z[1]	?	?	Z[1]	1 748	6
B) Z[2]	?	?	Z[2]		
C) AZ[3]	?	?	AZ[2]		
D) B	?	?	B		
E) Z[4]	?	?	Z[2]		
F) WB[1]	?	?	WB[1]	1 053	13
G) WB[2]	?	?	WB[2]		
Total	?	?			

Case 8

My informant, individual (2), could not remember the amounts of food exchanged but did remember the donors and recipients at his father's *derak*. Only he, and a sister (1), and brother (3), contributed and, as in the above case, the number of recipients was greater. It is interesting to note that even though all siblings of the testator's wife were included in the distribution of pigs and taro (amounts unknown), the wife had brought only a modest dowry to the usufruct estate of the testator. Again, there is one individual (C-1), who was both donor and recipient at this *derak*. As adopted daughter of the central figure's father, she is considered a sibling and, thus, in keeping with the logic of *derak*, eligible for receipt of goods. As natal daughter of the testator she was also called upon to donate such goods. This is another indicator that adoptive statuses are additive rather than replacive with regard to Pingelapese land tenure. That is, an individual never completely surrenders natal ties in favour of adoptive ones in the universe that involves granting of land and the system of reciprocal exchanges that confirms land awards.

Figure 6.8
***Derak* Case 8**

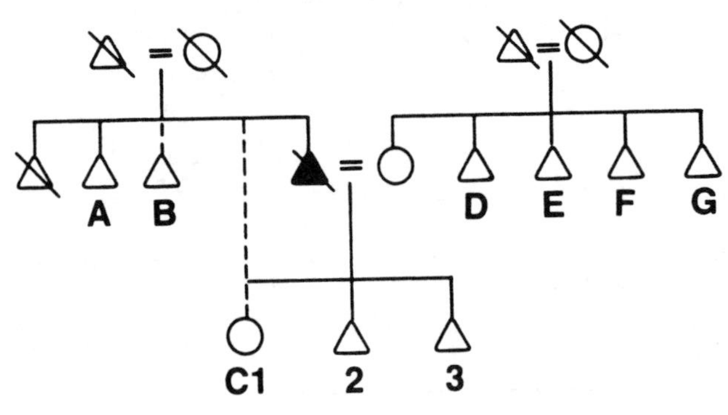

I. h	*Donors*				
	Goods donated			Property received	
Relationship to testator	Pigs	Corms		m²	Rows
1) D(AZ)	?	?		1 347	11
2) S¹	?	?		6 016	16
3) S²	?	?		940	5
Total	?	?			

II.	*Recipients*		*Putative donors of property*		
	Goods received			Property attributed	
Relationship to testator	Pigs	Corms	Relationship to testator	m²	Rows
A) B²	?	?	B²	5 900	27
B) AB³	?	?	AB³		
C) AZ(D)	?	?	AZ		
D) WB¹	?	?	WB¹	2 403	5
E) WB²	?	?	WB²		
F) WB³	?	?	WB³		
G) WB⁴	?	?	WB⁴		
Total	?	?			

Case 9

This *derak* was part of a three-phase ceremony observed immediately after the death of the *nahneken*, or the title holder who acted as intermediary between the atoll and the colonists on Pohnpei. According to the testimony of the testator's son, my chief informant, it was held in the community house at the Sokehs colony of Mwalok on April 25, 1972. The title succession ceremony or *pwakamar*, the funeral or *mwurilik*, and a "little *derak*" were held simultaneously. The designation, "little *derak*," is occasioned by the previous occurrence of a *derak mour*, celebrating division of the central figure's land sometime previously. The amount of both country products and store-bought foods that was brought to this triple ceremony was prodigious, and it is said to have been the largest such event in the history of Pingelap. Because of the scope of the joint ceremonies, the large number of contributors and donors, and the complexity of exchanges thereby included, it was not possible for my informant to give a complete accounting of all of the individual contributions or receipts. Nevertheless, the information which I did get, much of which is contained in Figure 6.9, does give insight into some of the special circumstances of this particular *derak*. In this case the bulk of prestations came from the relatives of the wife of the honoured deceased figure. One reason for the absence of the children of the testator from the transactions represented in Figure 6.9 is that they had previously contributed substantial goods to the *derak mour* and thus had confirmed their receipt of land from the central figure during his lifetime. With regard to the triple ceremony as a whole, they had also made major contributions to the *mwurilik* phase. The rationale for the largest portions being given by the relatives of the wife of the deceased was that the offspring of their sister or aunt would be benefitting from the estate of the deceased.

With regard to recipients, my informant indicated that there were several portions given to the descendants of the father of the honoured deceased, that is, of the siblings of the deceased. None of the siblings were living, but their offspring drew from a pool of gifts. The only one of these shares remembered in detail was that of individual (B) whose receipts are listed in Figure 6.9. This was the largest share carried away from the event. Other remembered shares were those of (A) and (G), which were smaller, as indicated on the chart. With regard to the justification for the share given (A), it is said that his father had contributed land to the central figure some time previously. In the case of (G) his grandfather had given land to a grandson of the testator and thus was a qualified recipient at this *derak*. Especially remarkable in this *derak* is that all of the gifts listed in Figure 6.9, except for one-and-one-half pigs, were store-bought products. Most of the remainder of donations to the *derak* and also to the total for the triple ceremony were of such commodities, though some taro and breadfruit and a number of pigs as well as one dog helped make up the total prestation for the entire occasion. At first sight the use of commercial products appears to have occurred because of practical considerations. While the ceremony was held on Pohnpei much of the material had to be sent to Pingelap where a number of recipients lived. Since shipping between the two places was irregular and the preservation of native foods difficult, it would be more practical to use products like rice and canned goods. Another factor was that several of the donors were only marginally engaged in agriculture or animal husbandry on Pohnpei and that with cash income, contributions of store products may have been more easily managed. Notwithstanding these considerations, it is also apparent from discussions with Pingelapese on the high island that the ability to produce and present Australian-, American-, or

Figure 6.9
***Derak* Case 9**

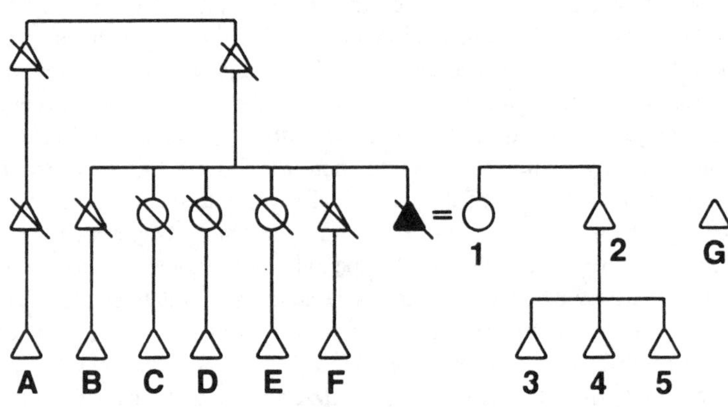

I. *Donors*	Goods donated		Property received	
Relationship to testator	Pigs	Corms	m²	Rows
1) W	Unknown		6 750	7
2) WB				
3) WBS				
4) WBS				
5) WBS				

II. *Recipients*		*Putative donors of property*	Property attributed	
Relationship to testator	Goods received	Relationship to testator	m²	Rows
A)	5 sacks rice 3 cases canned fish 1 case sugar 5 yards cloth	FB	225	0
B)	20 sacks rice 15 cases canned fish 10 cases sugar 50 yards cloth 1.5 pigs	B^1 B^3		
C)	Unknown	Z^1	8 750	7
D)		Z^2		
E)		Z^3		
F)		B^2		
G)	3 sacks rice 2 cases canned fish 1 case sugar	unrelated	225	0

Japanese-derived goods had a definite prestige value. Indeed, the circle of relatives represented in this triple ceremony was well represented among the wage or salary earners on Pohnpei.

Such radical departures from use of traditional products did not characterize two other ceremonies for which I have information and which occurred on Sokehs Island among the Pingelapese there. One informant was not able to provide sufficient data to be included among the case histories here, but he did offer useful information regarding items contributed to a *derak* being held for a titled person dying in Mwalok. The Pingelapese, in order to prevent spoilage of shares, sent to Pingelap unprepared taro, some coconuts and preserved breadfruit, as well as sun-dried fish rather than dead pigs and dogs or the certain amount of prepared taro which sometimes is part of this ceremony. Yams were also included among the gifts sent to the atoll, a product which is the most important vegetable food on Sokehs Island as well as Pohnpei itself.

Derak Observed

Case 10

The final case represents the only *derak* which I personally witnessed during my four trips to Micronesia. At first I had no awareness that such ceremonies were taking place on the atoll or of the significance of the event itself. Later, after observing a pig being gently prodded down a path on Pingelap, I inquired about it and heard something about a ceremony being held a year after a man's death. Only several months later did I realize the significance of this incident to the land tenure study in which I was then becoming involved. Subsequently, it seemed that whenever a man died on the atoll or on Pohnpei, if I happened to be living there, the *derak* was either delayed to a time beyond the length of my stay in the area, or I was not informed of the happening. In tragic irony it was in the last month of my final trip to Micronesia that my chief informant died on Pohnpei and made it possible for me to observe a *derak*. My friend thus served me in death as in life.

He died in the hospital in Kolonia at about 4 p.m., May 9, 1983 and his body lay in state at his home throughout the next day until about 5:30 p.m. when a long procession of pickup trucks, one carrying the casket, proceeded to the village on Sokehs Island. The burial took place in the graveyard behind the church in Mwalok, while the combined *mwurilik* and *derak* was carried out in a small vacant lot across the road which fronts the church. Women sat on the church steps or in trucks parked along the road or stood nearby with their children. Men stood in clusters on both sides of the road, a number of them ready to receive their portions from the men actively sorting out the baskets of breadfruit and taro or chopping up and slicing the pigs. The principal figure in the proceedings directed the division of pigs and sorting of taro and shouted out names of recipients while his assistants passed the goods to individual men who broke briefly from the small aggregations near the road. But his shouting barely rose above the general din that prevailed. The shouting and talking of the crowd, the squalling of babies, the barking of dogs, and the honking of small trucks as they worked their way along the crowded road provided what seemed to me to be formidable distractions. But the sorting and chopping went on through the dusk until only a small light from a chapel nearby gave a minimal break from total darkness. The division had been preceded by a brief prayer, but otherwise I could find no religious elements in the proceedings.

Although the man who had promised to act as interpreter stood by my side, I was able to gain only a disjointed impression of the activities, such as noting that first shares were taken by the principal figure of the divisions and his brothers, a man standing near him taking down figures on a pad, and the fast-paced action of men chopping up carcasses of pigs with bush knives. I guessed that during a 45-minute period a couple of hundred corms of taro, and perhaps 20 pigs, were distributed in addition to a few breadfruit. No one received a whole pig, since all of them were dismembered, and most of the larger taro corms were also cut into pieces. I did not see in evidence any of the giant yams which I had been told were part of *derak*(s) held on Pohnpei Island. Some of us bystanders were given foil packages which contained balls of cooked rice and boiled chicken.

Considering the speed of distribution and the general chaos, together with the loss of daylight, I could not see how anybody could keep accurate count of shares given out. I was told that some of the goods passed out were part of the *mwurilik* ceremony and some belonged to the *derak*, with the two sets of distributions progressing simultaneously. My interpreter received a *keliek* or pandanus leaf basket of food gifts which he told me was his share of the *mwurilik* because of his being a minister in the church, and in part, because he was considered to be head of one of the *pwekil*(s) in the village of Mwalok.

The above was all I could derive from being present at the only *derak* which I was able to attend, and which I had waited eight years to witness. The picture which follows was based mainly on a series of conversations with a field assistant and the central figure of the distribution procedure over a period of about two and one half weeks following the occasion. Even then the account must remain incomplete in several rather important respects.

The chart shows individuals involved in the occasion who either contributed or received shares of food. This *derak* was complicated by the facts of demography which decreed that there would be more recipients than donors, for 56 individuals received portions of what were supposed to have been 41 pigs (or equivalent in dogs), while the 11 actual donors brought only 18 pigs and a few dogs which are prorated as portions of pigs in Figure 6.10. Adjustments were made so that those on the chart who are featured as having received one pig may have gotten about half a pig. The chief distributor at the event could not remember, and apparently no written account was taken of the taro corms and other vegetable products (principally breadfruit) that were distributed. But on the basis of the material at hand it is apparent that at least a rough apportionment was made according to the principles that usually govern such prestation events.

Figure 6.10
Derak Case 10

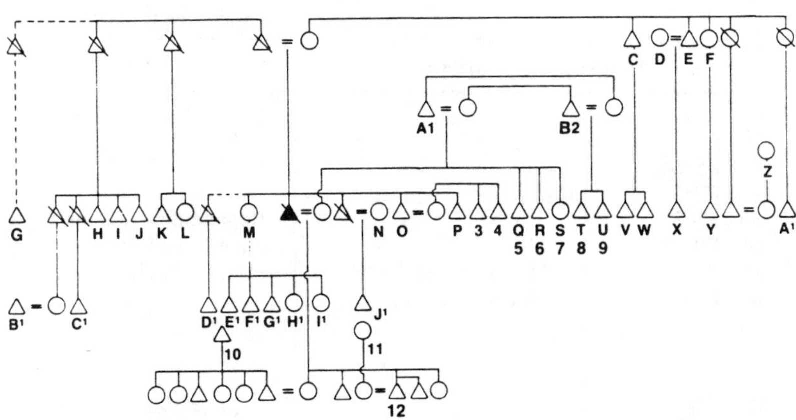

I. *Donors*

Relationship to testator	Goods donated: Pigs	Goods donated: Corms	Property received: m²	Property received: Rows
1) WF	4		See discussion in text.	
2) WFZH	3			
3) B^2WB^1	1			
4) B^2WB^2	1			
5) WB	1			
6) WZ^1	1			
7) WZ^2	1			
8) $WFZHS^1$	.5			
9) $WFZHS^2$	.5			
10) D^1HF	6			
11) S^2WM	1			
12) S^2	2			
Total	22			

II. *Recipients* — *Putative donors of property*

Relationship to testator	Pigs rec'd	Relationship to testator	Attributed property: m²	Attributed property: Rows
A) WF	4		Representing total estate	
B) WFZH	3		(24 320	13)
C) MB^1	5	MB^1	Representing testator's mother's donation	
D) MB^2	2	MB^2		
E) MB^2W	1	MB^2		
F) MZ	1	MZ	(5 251	10)

Figure 6.10 *(continued)*

II. *Recipients*		*Putative donors of property*		
			Attributed property	
Relationship to testator	Pigs rec'd	Relationship to testator	m^2	Rows
G) FABAS	1			
H) FB^2S^3	1			
I) FB^2S^4	1			
J) FB^2S^5	1			
K) FB^3S^1	1		Representing testator's	
L) FB^3S^2	1		father's donation	
M) Z	5	(divided with D^1+OH^1)	(19 075	10)
N) B^2W	3	(shared with J^1)		
O) B^3	3			
P) B^4	2			
Q) WB^1	1			
R) WZ^1	1		Representing	
S) WZ^2	1		total estate	
T) $WFZS^1$	1		(24 326	13)
U) $WFZS^2$	1			
V) MB^1S^1	1	(shared with I)		
W) MB^1S^2	1	(shared with I)		
X) MB^2S	1		Representing testator's	
Y) MZ^1S	1		father's donation	
Z) MZ^2SWM	1		(19 075	3)
A^1) MZ^3S	1			
B^1) FB^2S^1D	1			
C^1) FB^2S^1S	2			
D^1) $(h)B^1S$	3			
E^1) ZS^1			Representing testator's	
F^1) ZS^2			mother's donation	
G^1) ZS^3		(shared 5 with M)	(5 251	10)
H^1) ZD^1				
I^1) ZD^2				
J^1) B^2S	3	(shared with N)	Representing total estate	
			(24 320	13)

While in the previous cases discussed here one or two individuals had been both donors and recipients, in this case a larger number, specifically the relatives of the widow of the testator, had such dual roles. These were (A^1), (B^2), (Q^5), (R^6), (S^7), (T^8) and (U^9) in Figure 6.10. They qualified as receivers because one of the important pieces of land divided among the children of the deceased testator came from that family group. The reason for them being donors is less normal, though the above cases also yield precedents. The rationale given was that the younger children of the deceased could not make their appropriate contribution, being too young or absent in Hawaii or the mainland U.S., so that this group which was affinally linked to the testator agreed to help. If this provision had not been made, these heirs would have stood in danger of having their shares of the estate usurped by the siblings who did make such contributions on this occasion, or so I was told. This circumstance was brought on by certain atypicalities in the life cycle of the deceased. He had married about 10 years later than the average age for Pingelapese males. This delay had been occasioned by long years of absence in Hawaii and in the mainland U.S. for higher education. That circumstance, and his early death at age 52, meant that several of his children were not adult at this time.

The relationship between the *mwurilik* and the *derak*, which were being simultaneously celebrated, involved special arrangements regarding the brothers and sisters of the deceased and their offspring, in that the amounts they received in *derak* were said to be directly determined by the relative amounts they contributed to the *mwurilik*. The contributions of the widow's siblings and (S^7) and father (A^1) and her mother's brother (B^2) which were so crucial to the status of the younger children of the deceased would expect to be compensated for at later occasions sponsored by these offspring, though not necessarily at another *derak*. With respect to the shares received by the siblings of the deceased mother of the testator [(C),(E), and (F), and (E)'s wife (D)] or their living children [(V),(W),(X),(Y),(A^1)], they were regarded as being ultimate providers of the land of the testator. The same rationale was cited for a mother-in-law, that is (Z), though here the connection was rather more remote.

In this case as in others discussed in this chapter, the deceased testator's father and the father's siblings, who are also regarded as the ultimate sources of the estate, would have been important recipients of the prestations offered at the *derak*. But since all of these persons were deceased in this case, the actual recipients were necessarily descendants of those persons, that is individuals (G), (H), (I), (J), (K), (L), (B^1), and (C^1). Eight pigs were distributed among these descendants. The son of deceased elder half-brother of the testator (D^1) got two pigs while the sister (M) received five, which were shared with her children (E^1)-(H^2). This division showed a departure from primogeniture and the usual predominance of males in land division and confirms the outcast status of the elder brother (see discussion accompanying Figure 5.3 regarding elder brother of individual 40). The testator's next younger brother was also deceased, but son (J^1) received with his mother what would have been his share, that is three pigs. The final two brothers in the sibling group of the central (O) and (P) figure received three and two pigs respectively as ultimate contributors to the estate of the testator's children. Thus one sister, two brothers, and seven children of siblings received a substantial share of the distributions for a total of 15 pigs, or what passed for that many.

Of special interest is the situation of individual (B^1-10) who appears in two places on the chart. He was married to the daughter of the eldest brother of the testator's father, and through his wife received one pig. Because his son was married to the testator's daughter he contributed six pigs, for his children were expected to gain property from the testator's estate.

In summary, the contributors to this *derak* were the following: (1) the mother of the married son of the deceased testator; (2) the father-in-law of the testator's married daughter; (3) relatives of the widow of the central figure, who included her father, father's sister's husband (also her mother's brother) and their offspring. As noted above this latter group constitutes a special category, which in this case was substituting for the shares normally contributed by the children of the testator who were unadult at the time of the *derak*.

Recipients were the following: (1) the family of the widow, who were regarded as having brought land into the estate of the deceased central figure; (2) the offspring of the brothers of the father of the deceased testator, because through their fathers they were regarded as having contributed to the estate through the testator's father; (3) the siblings, or their descendants, of the mother of the deceased. They were considered to have brought land through the dowry of the latter; (4) the siblings and/or their offspring of the testator because they too were regarded as having through their father contributed to the estate.

Derak and Reciprocity

At the outset of this discussion of the *derak* ceremony I stated that my informants conceived of this ritual as payment for the land granted and that those who had received land from the person being honoured were called upon to bring gifts of pigs and taro to those regarded as being responsible for contributing to the estate of that honoured individual. In representing *derak* in those terms the case histories which I have reviewed here reveal salient features of reciprocal exchange. It is clear that the payments, or rather presents, approached only rough equivalency to the portions of land and other property granted to the donors at the ceremony. The symbolic value of such awards must be appreciated, as there is no exact equivalence or precise value involved in these *derak* transactions, as, for instance, number of taro corms given to rows in the patch or pigs to areas of land holdings. It is true that the eldest son, who is also considered to be the chief beneficiary of the estate in question, contributed more than succeeding siblings, but the amounts given by succeeding siblings or other givers at the ceremonies varied from any precise equivalence of their estate shares. Pigs are valuable property and they are slaughtered, divided, and consumed only in connection with such events as *derak*. Taro, or more properly speaking Cyrtosperma, is the most important commodity in the diet of the Pingelapese so that occurrence of these two items in *derak* is not surprising, though I have noted elsewhere the possibility of substitutes for both products. With regard to assessing any proration of land received to contributions made at *derak*(s) there is also the problem of qualitative differences of plots. As indicated in Chapter 5 these vary according to resources such as (formerly) bananas, and (always) breadfruit trees. In addition, land inherited as contrasted to land sold has not been precisely measured. It should be noted, however, that some examples have shown that it was kinship position rather than actual awards of land which most strongly influenced amounts to be contributed at *derak*(s). In sum, each of the cases examined above had a principal donor at *derak* events. He was usually the eldest of the sibling group (including adoptees). The shares contributed by the other heirs was usually smaller but not finely prorated to the extent of inherited holdings. The principle of substitutability, or proxy donations and receipts, at *derak* occasions figured very strongly, and, indeed, a number of those who gave or received in each of the cases examined were often quite remote from involvement in actual land transactions.

One factor which affected the actual quantity of donation to the ceremony was, of course, the amount of produce and pigs which an individual could realistically contribute. There were several factors influencing these amounts. One was the actual number of pigs and taro rows that the individual owned. Another was his ability to harvest enough taro in the time available, regardless of the number of corms he had in the ground. My information indicates that individuals often augmented their production by the contributions of various relatives. The burden of accumulation of taro and pigs is cited above as the chief reason for delaying the *derak* ceremony for periods of up to a year. But in the sample presented here, most often the *derak* was held either before the death of the honoured figure or a few days afterwards. This fact highlights the degree of cooperation among donors to the events in the harvesting, slaughtering, and sharing of goods to be distributed in the cases considered here. Such a degree of cooperation provides a strong element of generality to the concept of reciprocity in the ceremony in other ways. With regard to those honoured as recipients of goods in the ceremony, often they did not serve as direct conduits of goods to the central figure of the *derak*. They were, instead, individuals who had certain usufruct privileges to parts of the estate in question. In this sense it was often membership in a kin group, usually on the extended family level, that influenced contributions at these events. It was also indicated that "payment for lands received" by nephews or grandchildren was affected through affinal links, and implied vicarious rather than actual benefit from the dispersal of estates.

Derak and the Ties of Kinship

In another place I (Damas 1986) have argued that the virilocally oriented extended family constitutes the residential, sharing, and cooperative unit of Pingelap. In this study I have argued as well that the extended family also constitutes the unit within which land was held, used, and divided, even though, ultimately, shares devolved to individuals in terms of nominal ownership, including right of disposal. In the *derak* ceremony the transactions also appear to pertain within and between such units as they are commonly conceived. But in the course of time such units bud and multiply. While sibling groups have been shown to be important kinship units in *derak*, in time they represent clusters of extended family households, thus expanding the network of kin involved in this ceremony. This extension is further expressed in the subsidiary distributions which take place after *derak* participants carry their products from the scene of the event. My information does not include detailed coverage of such subsequent distributions, but it is clear that they pertain among a body of kindred well beyond what can be considered to be extended families.

Another realm of kinship which is involved in land transferrals and their celebration in *derak* is the dimension of adoption. The dual role of adoption in the land tenure system was considered earlier when it was noted that the child adopted out will almost always carry with him a piece of property, and that the child adopted into a nuclear or extended family will often benefit greatly through multiple sources of land. In the *derak* ceremony he or she is often the donor of substantial portions as well as recipient. The child adopted out will have to contribute equally with the natural child who stays at home to "pay for" receipt of land he takes with him. He is thus not completely separated from his natal family any more in terms of obligation than in award. The additive aspect of adoption as opposed to the concepts of replacement and cancellation is thus emphasized in the study of the *derak* ceremony. All in all, considering that the placement of individuals within circles of kin is perhaps as important as their actual or even putative contributions to or receipts of portions of estates, the *derak* ritual can be seen to be as much an expression of kinship ties as it is one of reciprocal dealings in the transferrals of estates.

While the majority of individuals taking part in the ceremony are those between whom kinship ties can be recognized, there are others who figure at least indirectly in the *derak* events. Land given for services and shared economic relations between individuals who are unrelated provide circumstances which have been cited in the sample given above. It is clear, however, that purchased land is not honoured in the *derak* ceremonies. In addition to straightforward allotment of land at marriage or death, according to prearrangement within extended families, it was reported to me that there are also gifts to illegitimate children by assumed fathers, even though they were sociologically identified with other fathers. These cases would lie at the margins of kinship but would imply repayment of the donor at the *derak*.

Kinship relationships have as usual concomitants socializing functions. Indeed, the gathering of kin at the *derak* can be viewed as an important occasion for reinforcing ties. In the case of Pingelap, the entire on-island population lives within easy communication of one another. Even though the Pingelapese population has been dispersed through emigration, reinforcement of kinship ties within the total population is also possible, though usually not through such aggregates as occur at *derak*.

Beyond the scope of kinship relations, other ties are established or reinforced through such occasions as *derak*. The gatherings which occur in connection with this event usually include unrelated persons, both as participants and as spectators. In some of the examples cited above, those invited to the *derak* rituals include non-kindred. Sometimes the term used to designate these were "those who helped" or "neighbours." In some cases significant portions of the products brought to the *derak*(s) that have been examined here were redistributed among the spectators rather than wholly among the direct participants of the ceremony. Many of these individuals did not demonstrate kinship ties to the central figure of the event. A number of people included among recipients in *derak* occasions, who are often distant kin or who bear no kinship relationship to the central figure of the ceremony, become involved in the exchange system of that ceremony on the basis of past contributions to other *derak*(s) or to ceremonies entirely unrelated to land tenure. An example of how *derak* prestations may extend to other types of celebrations comes to mind. While analyzing the network of exchange related to a first-birthday event, I learned that some of the recipients of food gifts had contributed or would contribute to *derak*(s). Reciprocally, some of the case histories presented in this chapter, and especially the last, exhibited instances where distributions secondary to the ones recorded here were made on such bases. Those primary kin who are the chief donors and recipients in *derak* (as well as in other ceremonies) are called *siwih perian*, while the secondary participants or donors are referred to as *kumangen um*.

The reinforcement of social ties extending beyond the circle of kindred, which is widespread throughout the world, may be supplemented by another motive. I conclude on the basis of a number of suggestions by informants and on the basis of observation that family pride is an important element in *derak* and other such occasions which involve distributions and in some cases definite displays of valued goods. The ability to display and distribute large quantities of taro and pigs (in the case of *derak*) serves to affirm the affluence of given family units. Prestige is an important element in Pingelapese society, and displaying and awarding important food products provides tangible evidence of material eminence. As indicated earlier in this study, the term which refers to distributional events such as *derak* is *kamadipw*, which translates as "to kill" and "to waste." This terminological association is but one of the more overt expressions of the prestige factors involved in such prestation events as *derak*.

CHAPTER 7

Land Tenure in the Pingelapese Colonies

Aside from cases of blackbirding or of voluntary enlistment on passing vessels during the nineteenth century and a couple of cases of elopement which resulted in individual long-term absences or emigration from the atoll, movement off Pingelap has been a twentieth-century phenomenon. Large-scale emigration began with relocation of a number of people after the disastrous typhoon of 1905. As noted earlier, Eilers (1934: 425) placed the number of emigrants then at 67. Most of these people appear to have moved to Saipan. One informant listed 22 adult males in the group that eventually came to Sokehs Island and the village of Mwalok from Saipan after the latter colony was established in 1911-12, but several men and their families are said to have remained in the Marianas for some time afterwards. The Saipan colonists suffered considerable religious persecution on that Catholic island. There is the story of Alik Menite (or "Alik the Mighty") a folk hero of the Mwalok people who was the leader of the group on Saipan. It seems that a local woman stole the shell used to call the Pingelapese to the chapel. The night after the theft a typhoon destroyed all the buildings in the village except for the Protestant chapel and the next day the woman returned the shell trumpet and died a short time afterward. These happenings were attributed to special powers which the Saipanese believed to reside in Alik. Because of this and other events which appeared to prove his powers, he gained the name "Alik the Mighty" and became known by that name thereafter rather than by his Christian name, Alexander.

It seems clear from that episode and from other remembrances conveyed to me that relations with the Chomorros on Saipan were uneasy and that the migrants moved to the newly opened acreage on Sokehs Island without regret. The distance of only 140 sea miles provided proximity to the home atoll, which must have been an important incentive as well for that move, since close contacts with Pingelap have continued throughout the present century, except for

Notes to Chapter 7 are on pp. 251-52.

the period during World War II when contacts with the outer island were cut off due to the American naval presence.

In addition to the people who came from Saipan, I have identified three Pingelapese men who joined the new colony from where they had languished in Truk. As well, there was a Trukese man who married a Pingelapese woman, and a woman from there who married a Pingelapese man, all of whom later moved to Sokehs. There was also one Guamanian man and a Saipanese man who married Pingelapese women who had followed the movement to the Pingelapese colony at Mwalok. According to my informants in these matters, there were others from those points in the Central Carolines and the Marianas who returned directly to Pingelap after an absence of several years during the restoration period following the 1905 disaster on the atoll. The land tenure histories have shown that the majority of men returning from Saipan who joined the Sokehs colony must have done so very shortly after it was established, for they shared in the original apportionment of land there.

Pingelapese Move to Sokehs Island

Two versions of the selection of emigrants were given to me. One, which seems to have had wide support among my informants, and which appears at first sight to be backed by logic, is that those individuals who were land poor on the atoll at the time of the original migration chose to come to the new land. My chief informant, however, argued that this factor was not necessarily the case for a number of the migrants. He described selection as follows: When the Germans came to Pingelap in order to recruit immigrants for the now vacant Sokehs Island, they placed a large mat on the ground and asked those who wanted to move to step onto the mat. When a designated number had stepped forward recruitment was closed. I received the names of 28 adult males who made up the immigrant party, though not all were married in 1911-12 when the move was made. These men and the families of the married were joined a short time afterwards by the men and families from Saipan, and somewhat later, from Truk. In all, some 55 individuals were eventually granted plots at Mwalok on Sokehs Island. As for the actual numbers of immigrants, lacking a complete census, I can only estimate from typical family size at that time that there was a total of approximately 200 in the groups which settled there during the first several years extending into the beginnings of the Japanese period. This number corresponds roughly with the figure of 190 Pingelapese on Pohnpei for 1946 given by Bascom (1965: 60) at the end of the period of stable numbers for both those living on the atoll and the total Pingelapese population. At that time, according to my information, all or nearly all Pingelapese on or near Pohnpei lived in Mwalok.

Returning to the problem of the selection of emigrants one is confronted with a rather complicated picture without precise data being at hand. Few of the landholders in the samples which I used in Chapter 5 are represented among the families who settled on Sokehs Island. But the names of some descendants of the migrants do feature prominently on my maps of the atoll. This occurrence, together with other evidence, confounds the simple hypothesis that only the land poor settled at Mwalok. Two large extended family units moved to the new colony because of the decision to have that group represented by title holders. The extended family of the *nahneken*, who was to act as intermediary between the two centres of Pingalapese population, was represented by the title holder himself and two grown sons, together with all their wives and children. This group owned considerable property on Pingelap as did that of the *nanapas* who was to be the paramount chief for the colony. The displacement of these extended families was thus not based on landholding considerations but rather on political bases. As well, the large extended family of the aforementioned Alik Menite, or Alexander, had considerable holdings on the atoll as evidenced by the prominence of their descendants' names on my maps of Pingelap. In contrast to those who moved to the high island in 1911-12, the first group of emigrants from Pingelap, which included the last-mentioned family, may have moved away because their holdings on the atoll were especially hard hit by the 1905 typhoon. The people who came later would have had a recovery period for their crops.

Another approach to understanding the process of selection of immigrants to Mwalok is to consider the family positions of those who moved since, as earlier analysis has shown, younger sons or brothers would be expected to have inherited, or stood in an eventual position to inherit, less land than their older male siblings, and consequently, might be expected to be overrepresented in the migrant group. But in looking at the list of immigrants, such a picture does not emerge, since I have been able to identify 18 first sons among the 50-odd men who settled on Sokehs Island in the early years of the colony. In fact there is a strong representation of father-son ties, and extended families tended to emigrate in blocks, with 20 of the men showing such involvement.

Sokehs Island

In trying to recreate the impressions of the new settlement site as it appeared to the immigrants, certain features of physiography and botany can be inferred from the current condition of Sokehs Island. The island represents a marked contrast physiographically and ecologically to such atolls as Pingelap. With a north-south axis, the island is connected to the main island of Pohnpei by a causeway built in German times, and thus was a feature of the place when the immigrants landed. A central spine which rises to the height of 267 metres culminates at the northern end in the spectacular cliff which has become a prominent feature of travel folders and postcards of Pohnpei. The map which accompanies this chapter (Map 5), shows that the central portion of the island has not been divided into plots. This circumstance is due to the extreme rockiness of that part of the island, including prominent areas of naked rock in the heights around the centre ridge. The island is very steep, dropping precipitously on both the ocean and lagoon sides with only a narrow strip of mainly artificially

Map 5
Sokehs Island
(shaded area shows holdings of
immigrant Pingelapese)

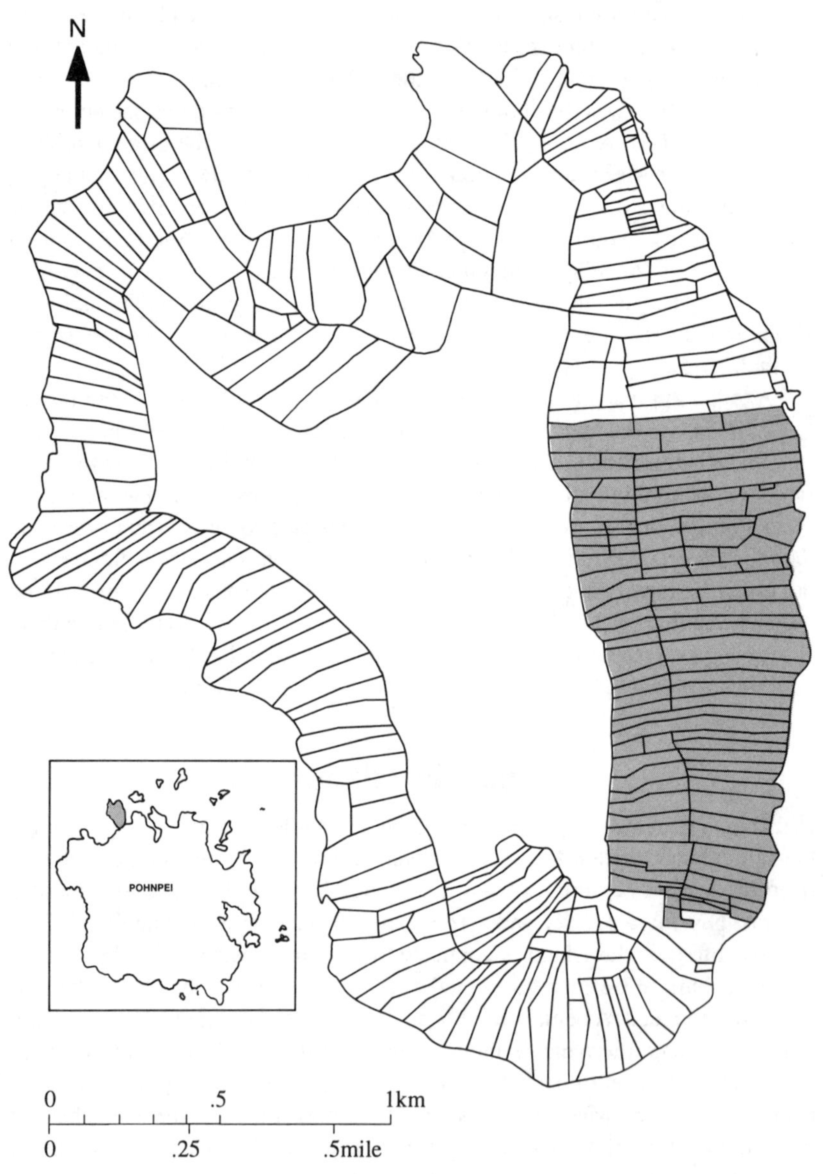

levelled land at the perimetre following the road that at the time of the arrival of the Pingelap migrants circled the entire island. It was the building of this road that lay at the roots of the rebellion that preceded settlement by the outer islanders. Both Ehrlich (1978) and Bascom (1965) attribute cruel treatment by the Germans supervising the road-building natives as the chief precipitating factor. Eventually German warships bombarded the island and forced the Pohnpeians who originally lived there to abandon it, making way for the settlement by out-islanders which followed. Today the road no longer completely encircles Sokehs Island, for a number of large sections of rock have peeled away from the famous cliff and have buried the road in rubble at the north end of the island.

Below the topmost slopes of bare rock, the island viewed from Pohnpei proper appears to be heavily covered with vegetation, but the climber will find much of these lower and middle slopes to be studded with large embedded rocks. While the volcanic soil is undoubtedly much more fertile than the coralline cover of Pingelap, the very rockiness prevents the thick growth found on that atoll. A number of trees and shrubs which do not bear fruit of any kind constitute the chief vegetation on the slopes.

The Pingelapese colony of Mwalok is situated along the eastern shore, with the Mwaekilese village of Danpei almost continuous with it to the north, and with the small contingent from Ngatik atoll living some distance further along, near the north end. Three Mortlockese villages lie along the southern and western shores, each being named for the atoll from which their original inhabitants come. The villages were largely composed of cement-block houses when I visited in the late 1970s and early 1980s. Some of the Mwalok houses in particular are large and attractive in appearance. There is a large hotel near the south end of that village, and while most of the houses fringe the road, several are placed at some distance up the slopes. At the times of my visits there was a water system, and an electrical system which included some street lights along the road, but there had not been installed any sewerage or garbage systems or collections. Refuse was merely thrown down from the houses into the area between the road and the lagoon, or where the road ran close to the water, into the lagoon itself. Rock protrudes at many places in the village.

With regard to the resources of Sokehs Island, contrasts can be seen with the home atoll. Coconut and breadfruit trees, as well as a few pandanus, grow mainly along the road. Wet taro is restricted to some swampy areas adjoining the road with some dry taro found inland up the slopes. The dearth of fruit trees is compensated for to some extent by the giant yam which grows to great size in the rich volcanic soils of the island. Yam growing requires considerable labour in that much rock has to be removed in order to create pits in which the large tubers can expand. Nevertheless, yams have been an important crop in the history of the colony. With regard to sea resources, my informants from Mwalok report that they are at least equal to those of the home atoll. Large reef areas provide areas for fishing on the western shore. I saw no long-lining for tuna, but this activity was practised widely in the past. Today the most popular fishing activity is trolling from open boats provided with outboard motors.

German Land Law and the Sokehs Colony

Turning to the questions of land tenure which are at the heart of the concern here with the Sokehs colony, while German land laws and policies had little impact on Pingelap itself, the situation was otherwise for the colonists. It is therefore necessary to examine the philosophy and the legal strictures instituted by that administration. The Germans were not confronted in their dealings with the Pingelapese colonists with the problem which they saw in trying to convert an essentially matrilineal land tenure system (Fischer 1951: 2, 4-5; 1958: 78, 83-84) for Pohnpei as a whole (though Bascom [1965: iv-v]) disputes this latter characterization). But there were other features of the traditional Pingelap system that ran counter to the policies and eventually the laws of the Germans. Fischer (1951) has presented an analysis of Pohnpeian land tenure which includes translation of both German and native texts of the document on German land deeds for 1912. This code was applied to all Pohnpeian districts, including Sokehs Island. Reference to the particulars of that code are instructive with regard to the modifications made to traditional Pingelapese tenure practices. The main provisions of that code were as follows:

1. This document confirms continuous ownership. Ownership can be lost only if the owner is condemned in exile or death.
2. Upon death of the owner, the property passes *undivided* (my italics) on to a male relative entitled to inheritance. Decision by testament is not allowed. The hereditary succession is as follows:
   (1) Oldest living son
   (2) Oldest living grandson
   (3) Oldest living brother
   (4) Oldest living brother's son.
3. All male relatives who have no property of their own and all unmarried female relatives have the right to live on and use the property along with the owner.
4. Sale, giving away, and rent of property or parts thereof is allowed only with the consent of the Nanmariki and Governor.
5. For official purposes the necessary land is to be given without remuneration.
6. All land for which no title document is issued belongs to the "tribe," also called "state" in Ponape ie. "District"—JIF/within whose boundaries it lies. It may be given away only by the Nanmariki jointly with the Governor.
7. Twice a year, in the Nanmariki's honour feast, each section has to contribute a load of yams. . . .
8. Small services are to be rendered to the Nanmariki without remuneration.
9. The Nanmariki calls his people twice a year for a day's work.
10. The Nanmariki may, after agreement with the Governor, order public works for the good of all. . . .
11. Disobedience against his *just* order is punished by the Nanmariki; first time by five days of forced labour, the second time by ten days of forced labour, and the third time the Nanmariki may suggest to the Governor that the man be exiled . . . (Fischer 1951: 7-8).

The degree to which the traditional paramount chiefs of Pohnpei were granted authority in land tenure by the German code is truly remarkable. There is considerable doubt in my mind as to whether the much more democratically minded Pingelapese actually granted their own paramount chief for the Mwalok colony, their *nanapas*, such rights. Indeed, in discussing land tenure with my informants there I came away with the impression that this chief did not exceed his traditional function of dispute conciliator. There is no evidence to suggest that he was instrumental in the arrangement of the inheritance of land, though the chiefs of Pingelap may have had important input in the original apportionments (see discussion below). In fact Ehrlich (1978: 199) in his review of the German land laws indicates that no *nanmariki* (Pohnpeian usage) was recognized for Sokehs so that the deeds issued under the law of 1912 contained only the signatures of the Germans and the stamp of the district office.

The above-listed strictures were at odds with customary Pingelapese land tenure practices on several other points. First, and foremost, assignments of plots of land and rows in the taro patch of Pingelap are left to the decisions of the family head or estate holder. I have shown these transferrals to have a patrilineal slant which is roughly consistent with the German philosophy of land tenure. Under the 1912 code the choices of heirs would be restricted. The restrictions would prevent not only the granting of dowries and other shares to women, but they precisely outlined a sequence of patrilineal heirs in contrast to a much broader system that operated on Pingelap. The outstanding difference, one that was even more drastic than the strict adherence to patrilineal inheritance, was the indivisibility of estates. The discussion in Chapter 5 showed that in almost all cases examined, estates on Pingelap were split among several heirs with, in many cases as well, multiple sources being available to recipients. Obviously, such a system as that outlined by the Germans would leave out a large number of the adult male population, as well as all females. Both the paramount chief and the German governor had to give consent in cases of land sale, rent, or gift, matters which were handled on an individual basis on Pingelap. In short, a great deal of individual control as well as the flexibility which the traditional Pingelapese land tenure customs allow would not be possible under the strict operation of the German land laws. Let me now examine the situation on Sokehs Island with regard to the actual application of German land policies and land laws.

There appears to have been an attempt to standardize the size of plots (which on Sokehs Island are marked by small cement markers at their corners) as they fall into plots of 5 000 square metres each or some multiple or regular fraction thereof. This division exists despite the roughness and uneven contour of the land, and consequently is reflected in the irregularity of the outline of plots shown on the map. The three largest shares fell to men who were recognized as the leaders of the colony. This occurrence may have been due to either the chiefs themselves participating in the original assignment of lands or to the German notions of control as outlined in their land law making such provisions for rank. The *nanapas* or designated paramount chief in the colony and the *nahneken* or intermediary each got 35 000 square metres of land, made up of several of the measured plots. The third individual receiving a disportionate share, 30 000 square metres from four of the plots, was the above-mentioned leader of the Saipan group. The most typical grants were those of 10 000 and 15 000 square metres. Beyond those usual plots, a minority got larger shares. Discussions with informants leads me to the view that in addition to the chiefs, those receiving larger shares were generally cases of land owned further up the slopes of the island where rockier soil made planting difficult. Such an explanation seems to apply for most of those with apparently anomalously large shares. Those owning plots under 5 000 square metres (there were seven of these) were later immigrants from either Truk or Pingelap itself. There were among the latter group, however, two large holdings of 30 000 and 24 000 square metres. Although one of these plots was indeed associated with the poorer uphill lots, the other stretched from the shore inland. While it is possible to account for the allotment of most shares of land through the above analysis, this last and a few other assignments cannot be explained with the information that is available to me.

There could have been no attempt to prorate grants to the size of nuclear families, nor does one get any indication of honouring the traditional landholding unit of the virilocal extended family-household. Each man considered to have been adult, married, or single was given his separate holding. In a sense this practice would seem to bring pressures toward fractionalization of kinship units as landholding units, but later analysis will show that this was not entirely the case. There appears to have been an attempt to serve the principle of primogeniture which of course was consistent with both Pingelapese and German philosophies of land tenure. In five cases where brother-brother ties pertained among immigrants, the elder brother invariably got the largest land grant. Also, in cases of father-son pairings, the father received significantly larger shares than the sons. Whether these patterns signify a sensitivity to age and generational differences on the part of the German administrators or, rather, some degree of input on the part of the Pingelapese is not known. Such adjustments are consistent both with Pingelapese notions of seniority in land tenure and also with the stated principles of the German code of 1912. I am inclined to believe that there was indeed some important input by the Pingelapese at this stage, since it seems unlikely that the Germans attained any great degree of genealogical knowledge. Otherwise, they probably would not have granted land to adult sons of heads of extended families, since many of the former would have been heirs to their fathers' estates. One thing is clear about the original allotments of land on Sokehs Island: no woman was granted land at that time.

In his analysis of the German code, Fischer (1951) comments that, regarding Pohnpei, while there was an attempt to limit the power of *nanmariki*(s), certain deference had to be given them, a condition which is very evident in the parts of the code cited here. But if Ehrlich's (1978) and my own impressions are correct, this deference was not manifest in the colony of Mwalok. Fischer (1951: 9) also notes some inconsistencies between the Pohnpeian language form and the German version of the code, notably the substitution of "male clanmate" for Pohnpeian version "male relative." This interpretation is a peculiarly Pohnpeian one which does not apply to Pingelap where the clans did not figure in land tenure. Also appearing in the native version but not the German, is the provision that an illegitimate son "shall obtain his father's land just as a true child" (ibid.: 7).

Japanese Land Policies and the Sokehs Colony

It is ironic that the code of the Germans came into effect only at the very end of their hegemony in Micronesia, but that it appears to have had substantial impact throughout the Japanese period. Indeed, the job of implementing the laws fell to the Japanese. But Fisher (ibid.: 10) states that "the Japanese government does not seem to have taken the code very seriously." He indicates, for instance, that the Japanese did not follow the stricture of confiscation of land as provided for in section II cited above. Fischer (ibid.: 11) points to the Pohnpeian practice of adopting sons-in-law in order to disguise the fact that land was actually being passed to daughters, as well as to some other adjustments.[1] The same source indicates that in actuality the Japanese allowed individual landholders to divide land among several heirs, "or otherwise disposing of it" (ibid.: 13). It will be argued that, on the basis of examining the land-inheritance history of the Pingelapese colony on Sokehs Island, this practice was modified during most of the Japanese period. Fischer refers to the survey of land tenure practices being carried out by the Japanese that was curtailed by the onset of World War II and remarks that the Japanese embarked on a program of calling in all German deeds at that time as based on this survey but, again, the war interfered.

Fortunately, there are now available translations of sections of the report of the Japanese anthropologist, Kenichi (1944), who conducted this survey in the Pohnpei (then called "Ponape") district in 1940-41. On the basis of this report it appears that the German code had not been replaced before that time, for that author proceeds to make a point-by-point analysis of the German code of 1912 as if it were still the basic document upon which land tenure was being regulated in the Pohnpei district. On the one hand, this author did not feel that the then-existing system of land tenure was so much at fault that a redivision of land was needed, nor that a major overhaul of the system was necessary (ibid.: 326). He did, in the course of his review of the German code, make certain recommendations for change. He did not advocate a return to the native Pohnpeian system which he (in agreement with Fischer) considered to have been based on matrilineality and, indeed, he felt that at the time of his survey between one-quarter and one-third of the land was still being passed matrilineally (ibid.: 332). He conceived of a more complete adoption of a patrilineal system as being a "civilized" solution and, as a programmatic statement, asserted the following:

> One reaches the unavoidable conclusion that the previous inheritance system is a deterrent to private land division, and that if affairs are handled under the old customs the confusion in land transactions could never be resolved. Thus there is no alternative other than for the present government to guide and implement policies which will gradually lead to a changeover to the patrilineal system (ibid.: 333).

This statement was to a large degree an endorsement of what the German code had provided for, and which in large measure was strongly shaping the system on Pohnpei, and which, as shall become apparent, was in effect during the Japanese period on Sokehs Island. Several modifications to the German laws were suggested in his report. For instance, in cases where there is no male heir available the son-in-law could inherit the land directly, without the artifact of adoption being brought to bear, as he saw to be the existing practice (ibid.: 331). Indeed, he also thought that matrilineal inheritance was necessary in a number of cases where direct patrilineal succession did not permit the transfer of land, but that there was danger that private ownership would collapse if matrilineal inheritance were fully authorized (ibid.: 332-33). It is also noteworthy that he states the following: "the German approach, evident in the foregoing if taking into account only the heir to a title deed is unworkable. Land must be thought of in terms of the overall group unit which used the parcel of land defined by a title deed" (ibid.: 335). This does not mean that he supported the notion of dividing and redividing individual holdings, for he thought that if further divisions beyond those designated by the Germans were to be carried out, the private land-ownership system would disappear (ibid.). He felt that the provision of land being inherited undivided was of great importance. But he did criticize the German code for limiting the sale, lease, or transfer of land as imposing "great limitations upon the natives' rights" (ibid.: 336).

Fischer (1951: 12-13; 1958: 101-102) summarizes a number of Japanese revisions to the German system, some of which appear to have grown out of Kenichi's report. These concern such provisions as: all children of either sex should inherit property before other relatives; all children should be given land if there is any available, with ranking according to sex and other principles being outlined a general placing of use and disposal in the hands of the owner; and, the right of persons who clear and plant land being given the "justification for their continued use of it and even acquiring a part of it" (1951: 13). Fischer (ibid.: 14) also reports that the Japanese were preparing to cancel German land deeds and set up a new system, presumably on the basis of such considerations as those indicated above, but the war apparently brought a suspension of those plans.

While both Fischer and Kenichi state that accommodations were made to the German laws on Pohnpei, the situation may have been different on Sokehs Island. There remains the task of exploring the effects of German-Japanese land policy in the Pingelapese colony there, especially in terms of possible modifications of customary Pingelapese practices. Having previously noted the probable procedures followed by the Germans in assigning original shares of land to the first colonists of Mwalok, it is appropriate to examine next the subsequent history of transferrals of the estates thereby established.

Estate Inheritance in the Japanese Period

Property transmission in the Pingelapese colony on Sokehs Island took place in two major stages, with a third becoming apparent at the time of my visits to the community in the early 1980s. The first stage consisted of transferrals from the original colonists. Since both father and some sons were awarded land at the time of the original assignments, this group was widespread in age. On average it corresponds roughly with Pingelap Sample A as designated in Chapter 5, with a somewhat earlier median birth date, at perhaps 1880. As in the Pingelap Sample A, the transferrals were complete at the times of my visits. This population will be designated as Mwalok Sample A. The second set of transferrals represents a population of donors roughly consonant with my earlier posed Pingelap Sample B, with a mean birth date of about 1920, as in the former case. I will refer to this group as Mwalok Sample B.

Of the total acreage transferred in the first set of transactions, 41.6 percent had changed hands through the second set of transferrals by 1983. The third set of transferrals, those emanating from Sample B, comprised only four at that time. While I do not have precise dates for the transferrals, the bulk of the first set, those from Mwalok Sample A to Mwalok Sample B, took place during the Japanese period, while the second and third sets fell largely within the American period. In looking at the history of land transferrals at Mwalok in the context of possible influence of German land laws and other locally relevant factors, it is instructive to compare them with material abstracted from Tables 5.1 and 5.2 for the atoll in order to match Mwalok practices with Pingelapese usages.

Comparability with the two Pingealpese samples is far from precise since, while I have discussed the limitations of the two atoll samples in terms of their representativeness, the two Mwalok samples include all those individuals who have taken part in land transferrals in the Sokehs colony. Another limitation is imposed by the circumstance that in comparing sources of land in these samples, sources for Mwalok Sample A must be omitted from Table 7.1 since the German administration ceded all land to the original settlers. It should be noted that this comparison is aimed toward contrasting the effects of German land policies in the colony with contemporaneous and more traditional practices on the atoll. That being the case, the figures for Mwalok Sample B do not include land and taro rows acquired on Pingelap by the colonists. I shall discuss the implications of these latter holdings later.

In the table I have simplified the comparison by using only the number of separate transactions of each piece of property transferred from the indicated sources by category. Comparability of total properties transferred poses some difficulty. First, the fractionalization of atoll *peliensapw*(s) implies much smaller individual shares than the lots on Sokehs Island. Also, taro patch holdings are a prominent part of inheritance on the atoll, whereas there is no central patch in the colony, with only a few Cyrtosperma plants growing along the road and probably even fewer dry taro plants being scattered on the hillside. There is also the problem of comparing the volcanic soils of Sokehs Island, with their undoubted greater fertility, except for the rockiness which occurs on that island, with the probably less fertile but also less rocky holdings on the atoll.

Table 7.1
Comparison of Transactions by Donors

Categories of donors	Pingelap A n	Pingelap A %	Pingelap B n	Pingelap B %	Mwalok B n	Mwalok B %
F[a]	330	68.0	164	31.9	68	58.6
AF	49	10.1	157	30.5	15	12.9
M	37	7.6	74	14.4	0	0.0
AM	18	3.7	64	12.5	0	0.0
H	0	0.0	0	0.0	4	3.4
GF	4	0.8	10	1.9	23	19.8
Other	47	9.7	45	8.8	6	5.2
Total	485	99.9	514	100.0	116	99.9

a Includes step-father.

Beginning with the source most highly represented in all three sets of transferrals, that of father (F), the closest correspondence is that between Pingelap Sample A and Mwalok Sample B, despite the dissonance in time, with a decline in that source in the Pingelap Sample B. The second most important source in all three samples is the adoptive father (AF). In the case of Pingelap B the contributions from that source nearly equal that of father, whereas the ratios of father-to-adoptive-father donations of land is about 7:1 in Pingelap A and 3:1 in Mwalok B. In Chapter 5 I indicated that about 15 percent of children born in the period represented by Pingelap A were adopted. This period incorporates the birth dates of most of those in Mwalok B as well. I also noted that there was a much larger representation of adoptees in Pingelap B than was characteristic of its equivalent generation because of a sample bias in favour of large landholders, these individuals often receiving land from both natural and adoptive parents. The smaller percentage of adoptive father donations in Mwalok B than in Pingelap B attests to the more balanced sample that is found in the former group, with a gross adoption rate of 19 percent as compared to the generations represented by Pingelap B of about 60 percent.[2]

It is not surprising that fathers figure most prominently in all three samples as donors because men were the chief landholders according to Pingelapese custom, and of course this practice was in keeping with the German-Japanese bias toward patrilineal inheritance. The rise in the importance of adoption in land tenure has been in the Pingelap case attributed to a frequent occurrence of childlessness (Damas 1983b). In the Mwalok example this was also a factor, since the same sterility problem prevailed in the colony during Japanese times, with a number of childless couples adopting children (note the close correspondence of 15 and 19 percent given above). In those cases an heir or, in a few cases, heirs, were created thereby. This contingency brings us to a consider ation of allowances for such substitutions in the German code and in its application by the Japanese. While there is in the Pohnpeian version of the code provision made for illegitimate sons, nothing is said about adopted children. Since, as Fischer (ibid.: 11) notes, "a number of adoptions were made purely and frankly for the purpose of inheriting land" (during the Japanese period), and since Kenichi (1944: 332) cites the same practice, one of two things must have occurred during that time. Either genealogical accounting was not accurate, or a general equivalence to natal sons was being given adopted sons. Therefore, with the sole heir often being an adopted son, it is not surprising that the status of adoptive father (AF) was represented in the Mwalok sample.

The most marked contrast between the two Pingelap samples and that of Mwalok is that in the former cases, after adoptive father, mother (M) is the next largest source of lands, especially when the significant number of donations by adoptive mothers (AM) in Pineglap B is taken into account. There is a total absence of land received from mother and adoptive mother in the Mwalok sample. This finding supports the German-Japanese strictures against matrilineal inheritance of land and is consistent with the absence of female heirs among those named in the German code. But, in this regard, Table 7.1 includes the category "husband" (H) for the Mwalok sample, a category not represented in the Pingelap samples. These cases represent the four Japanese men who were granted land among the holdings of the Mwalok colony and who were married to Mwalok women. They all left the area either during the later years of the Japanese regime or at the beginning of the American period. Their properties were then transferred to their wives, though the properties were disguised in their ownership in order to be consistent with the strictures against acquisition of land by women.

Another category which assumes importance in the Mwalok sample is that of grandfather (GF), or the transferral of property to an alternate generation. The 23 transactions involved seven grandchildren or the second category of heirs in line for inheritance according to the German code (see above). This rise in percentage of transactions from grandparent to grandchild must surely have reflected the influence of the law of 1912.

This consideration of the sources of land for the first set of transfers effected in Mwalok is suggestive of some patterns in agreement with, and others contrary to, those seen in contemporaneous or more traditional situations on Pingelap. In considering relationships with the German land code and its application by the Japanese, it is appropriate to look at the recipients of transferrals on Mwalok, for the land laws were oriented toward downward transmission of property. Accordingly, Table 7.2 provides figures for the various classes of recipients by kinship category.

I have again provided comparative material from Pingelap, specifically information on the recipients of land from Pingelap A individuals. For convenience I have combined some of the categories used in Tables 5.5 and 5.6 but otherwise they correspond. In the Mwalok sample all recipients are included in Sample B. As indicated in Chapter 5, the recipients of Pingelap A people include a number who are not found in Pingelap B.

Table 7.2
Comparison of Recipients of Pingelap A and Mwalok A

Categories of recipients[a]	Pingelap A n	Pingelap A %	Mwalok A n	Mwalok A %
S[1]	50	11.5	29	38.2
AS[1]	20	4.6	9	11.8
SAO	51	11.7	0	0.0
Other S	116	26.7	14	18.4
D[1]	56	12.9	6	7.9
AD[1]	10	2.3	2	2.6
Other D	106	24.4	1	1.3
W	0	0.0	4	5.3
S	6	1.4	7	9.2
GD	5	1.1	0	0.0
Other	15	3.4	4	5.3
Total	435	100.0	76	100.0

a The actual number of recipients is smaller than these figures indicate since some recipients had multiple sources of land. This is especially the case in the Pingelap sample since recipients of both males and females are combined in this table. There were fewer cases of multiple sources in the Mwalok sample. With regard to number of transactions, there were 632 from Pingelap A and 116 from Mwalok A.

It is not surprising that first sons, either natural or adopted, feature prominently among the recipients in the two samples, given the preference for primogeniture in both the traditional land tenure customs of Pingelap and in the German code. It has been shown that people in that category (when adopted first sons are included) got the largest shares in Pingelap Sample A when son categories were separated as in Tables 5.5 and 5.6. This prominence is obscured in Table 7.2 since all sons except first sons, adopted first sons, and sons adopted are lumped together (other S) for sake of comparison with the Mwalok sample. In doing so, however, it appears that the practice of spreading estates among all offspring, and especially among sons, which was highly developed on the atoll did not reach such prominence among the recipients of Mwalok A. This difference again reflects to some extent the higher rate of adoption in the Pingelap A sample, for a number of "Other Sons" in that sample are actually adopted sons. What is surprising in this regard, in view of German-Japanese stress on non-partible land inheritance and the priority of first sons, is that a number of succeeding sons do occur in the Mwalok sample.

In referring again to the German code of 1912, it states that "upon death of the owner, the property passes *undivided* on to a male entitled to inheritance" (Fischer 1951: 7). I could not reconcile that stricture with a number of the Mwalok estates being divided in inheritance during the Japanese period when the German code was in force. On closer examination it became apparent that the term *property* must have been identified specifically with individual plots or *peliensapw*(s) and apparently not with total estates. Since some of the original landholders were given more than one such plot, either contiguous or spatially separated, it was apparently a relatively easy matter to redistribute land among a group of sons in those cases. Divided *plots* were much rarer during Japanese times, and since 28 of 58 of the landholders had their estates concentrated in single plots, conformity to the German code did indeed make its mark on Mwalok land tenure practices. As noted above, percentagewise there were far fewer succeeding sons among the recipients in the colony than in the Pingelap sample from the same period. After the first set of transferrals at Mwalok was made, 33 of 51 estates remained undivided. This is compared to only one case of a male donor's estate and five cases of female donor's estates being left undivided after the transfers from Pingelap A were completed.

Another feature of the Mwalok sample of recipients is that no fewer than seven daughters (D^1 and Other D) and two adopted daughters (AD^1) received land in this first set of transferrals, despite there being no provision for such transactions in the German code, and despite strong German and Japanese biases against such cquisition. These distributions amounted to about 7 percent of the total land transferred to Mwalok. In examining each of these nine cases I discovered the subterfuge of attributing ownership to male relatives. Confusion over actual ownership of plots could be possible given the rather liberal German policy regarding land *use* as follows: "all male relatives who have no property of their own and all unmarried female relatives have the right to live on and use the property along with the owner" (ibid.). Under these conditions any man seen working on such a plot would not arouse suspicion. Likewise, a woman might have a husband or some other relative working on land which she actually owned, without awakening suspicion regarding true ownership.

It might seem that the younger sons of a man, together with most females, would be landless under a land tenure system directed by the German code, in spite of the subterfuge of dividing estates without dividing plots. In the case of younger sons, in addition to the practice of dividing the larger estates, there were two factors which conspired against such a contingency. While the first sons, either natal or adopted, did get the largest part of the land, there were a significant number of cases where such persons were also only sons, again related to the sterility situation. Beyond that factor, I did find the names of succeeding sons of the Mwalok population on my maps of Pingelap atoll *peliensapw*(s). There were, as well, a number of sibling sets that were split between the atoll and the colony, so that those living on Pingelap were often in charge of sizeable family holdings from which they could extract subsistence and copra. I was able to collect histories of total holdings for some of the Mwalok residents which revealed ownership of land on the atoll that included both first and succeeding sons. On the basis of my survey and the statements of informants, I am able to infer that it is unlikely that there were many of the residents in Mwalok B who did not own a piece of land or stand in line to inherit some land, either on the atoll or on Sokehs Island. The situation is quite otherwise for the females of

Mwalok. It was only when a male heir was lacking that women of that colony were granted land, even surreptitiously, during the Japanese period. The almost universal practice of giving land as dowries to women on Pingelap has not been in evidence in the colony, though a few females from the colony did get such on the atoll. Another group to consider is that made up of sons who were adopted out. The tables show a substantial representation of that element for Pingelap but they are entirely absent in the case of Mwalok recipients. The practice of supplying a seed estate for such children appears to have been one which could not be accommodated within the stricter confines of the land tenure system of Mwalok as influenced by German land laws, and it did not materialize under Japanese hegemony.

Yet another measure of the total effects of German-Japanese pressures on land tenure practices of Mwalok was that for the Pingelap sample recipients had multiple sources of land in a number of cases, and donors also usually split their estates among several heirs, while both of these practices were more rare at Mwalok. This difference points to another aspect of the fractionalization of land. Although the total land area distributed by Pingelap A donors was greater than that given by Mwalok Sample A donors (761 225 to 633 174 square metres, not counting taro holdings) the total number of those in the categories of actual recipients was far smaller with the Pineglap transferrals showing nearly a 5:1 ratio of recipients to donors as compared to a 1:1.5 ratio for Mwalok. This does not, however, indicate any comparative difference in the *potential* recipient pools, if customary Pinelapese practices had prevailed in the colony. Rather, it reflects the greater degree of impartibility on Sokehs Island as influenced by German land law that extended into the Japanese period.

To conclude the appraisal of the possible effects of the German code on Mwalok land practices, it is appropriate to compare the sequence of prescribed inheritors with that revealed in Table 7.2. While the oldest son was the first prescribed, and indeed was the most frequent heir in the Mwalok sample, deviation from the code is evident thereafter. The code specifies as second in line to receive land the oldest grandson of the testator. The seven cases of grandsons do represent a larger proportion of those in that category than shown in the Pingelap sample, but in the picture of actual inheritance in Sokehs the second most frequent category of heirs is that of succeeding sons who were left out completely from the code of 1912. Their number is twice that of grandsons.

With regard to the third heir in line according to the German code, that of oldest living brother, that category is unrepresented. As for the fourth in line, oldest living brother's son, two cases grouped here in the "Other S" category do occur. As discussed above, the only other significantly represented category of heirs is that of daughters who represent, when combined, 11.8 percent of the recipients of the Mwalok sample. Thus, although 50 percent of the recipients fall in the first son (S^1) and first son adopted (AS^1) categories (and with about 65 percent of the land transferred going to them) the sequence outlined in the code of 1912 had limited influence on the distribution of land given to other categories of relatives in the Sokehs colony during the Japanese period.

Land Transferrals in the American Period

The second set of transferrals, those from sample B, are identified here with the American period, though a few could have occurred earlier. One might have expected the land tenure practices of Mwalok colonists to have been freed from the pressures of the German-Japanese strictures with the coming of an American administration, and particularly after 1957 when the Ponape Island Congress created a new code of inheritance regulations which departed considerably from the German code. The new sequence of inheritance went as follows:

1. The eldest son who is either living or has left issue who are living.
2. The oldest daughter who is living or has left issue who are living.
3. The oldest brother who is living or has left issue who are living.
4. The oldest sister who is living or has left issue who are living.
5. In each case, if the relative named has died leaving issue who are living, the issue shall take in place of their parent by right of representation in the succession specified above (Fischer 1958: appendix).

Contained in this list is the implicit assumption that plots will be left undivided and, perhaps as well, estates, with the same ambiguity possible in interpretation as in the case of the German code of 1912.

Table 7.3
Comparison of Recipients of Mwalok A and Mwalok B

Categories of recipients[a]	Mwalok A n	Mwalok A %	Mwalok B n	Mwalok B %
S[1]	29	38.2	15[b]	34.9
AS[1]	9	11.8	5	11.6
Other S	14	18.4	14	32.6
D[1]	6	7.9	5	11.6
AD	2	2.6	0	0.0
Other D	1	1.3	0	0.0
W	4	5.3	0	0.0
GS	7	9.2	0	0.0
Other	4	5.3	4	9.3
Total	76	100.0	43	100.0

a As in Table 7.2 the actual number of recipients was somewhat less as there were cases in each sample where land came from more than one source.

b Includes two step-sons who were primary recipients.

Table 7.3 represents a comparison of the two major phases of transactions in Mwalok. These data present an opportunity to determine, first, whether there have been any significant changes between the distributions of the two phases; and second, whether these changes if present can be attributed to the influence of this second code. In examining the figures in the table there can be seen to be a rise in percentage of those in the category of succeeding sons in the second set of transactions as compared to the first set. This increase in percentages relates to the elimination of recipients in the categories of wife (W) and Grandson (GS). There are also percentage increases in the first daughter (D^1) and grandson (GS) categories.

In assessing these shifts it seems clear that the new land code of 1957 had little to do with them. Given the implicit espousal of non-partible inheritance, the increase in succeeding sons is in contradiction. Indeed, of the 27 estates settled during this phase of transactions, nine were divided, though only one of these represented a divided lot. On the basis of the inclusion of daughters as the second eligible heir in the code of 1957, one would expect that there would be a greater expansion in this category than is indeed evident. One possible correlation with the 1957 code which could be argued is the absence of grandsons among the heirs. I shall return to a consideration of that circumstance below. There is only one occurrence of transfer of land to a brother, the third heir in the new code, and this one was from a woman to a half-brother. There are no instances of transfer to a sister, which is the fourth in the sequence of heirs given in the land code of 1957. It is not surprising to me that this code drawn up by the Fifth Ponape Congress, which was no doubt dominated by Pohnpeians, would be largely ignored. In Chapter 2 I noted how in the religious crisis of 1978-79 on Pingelap the District Administrator from Pohnpei was unable to exert influence on the Pingelapese. I also noted that in the vote regarding new status for Micronesians in 1983, the atoll dwellers voted contrary to the choice being advocated by the representatives of the Plebiscite Commission, a body made up of outsiders. I did not get the vote for the Mwalok colony for it was buried in the Pohnpei Island total, but in my informal enquiries on the matter I found the same sort of resistance to outside influences. These indications, and the low rate of intermarriage between Pohnpeians and Pingelapese, whether on the atoll or Pohnpei, are only some of the more tangible sorts of evidence which express separation of the Pingelapese from other populations in the region, and especially Pohnpeians, who are regarded as being condescending by outer islanders.

If then there has been minimal influence by the 1957 code on the land tenure practices of the Mwalok colony, what is the significance of the changes that are evident in comparing the two phases of transactions as depicted in Table 7.3? The greater tendency to spread estates among sons found in the second phase is, of course, strongly rooted in Pingelapese land tenure customs, and may represent a reversion to them in the face of relaxed external pressures. On the other hand, there has been adoption of lot-splitting in only once case in the second set of transferrals, a practice which would have been in more direct defiance of the German code. As well, many of the recipients of this second set of transferrals still own multiple plots. The only small increase in female holdings (11.1% for A; 11.6% for B) which results from the second phase of land inheritance in the colony is surprising when both tradition and the new land code support such transferrals. It thus appears that the German code must still exert some influence in practice and, however unconsciously, it continues as part of the Mwalok system. More problematical is the elimination of grandson recipients. Here it would appear there has been a relaxation of the German influence, and a greater application of adjacent rather than alternate generation transferrals. Although both sorts can be found in the Pingelap atoll samples, grants to sons, whatever their order in the sibling group, predominate greatly over those to grandchildren in those samples.

With regard to demographic factors which could have affected the more recent series of transactions, it was largely from the older elements of the Mwalok B populations that land transferrals had taken place, that is, the element born before the median date of 1920. The size of offspring groups began to expand only after 1945. While the cases of inheritance by second and succeeding sons probably is influenced by the actual presence of such sons, in a large number of cases there remained only one son or one offspring when the members of that group died. One can probably predict that when the younger elements of Mwalok B die, they will spread their estates among a larger progeny, with the possibility of dividing existing plots becoming a partial solution to supplying more male offspring with land in the colony.

The Colony at Mand

A second colonization scheme, one which was implemented during the U.S. Trust Territory period, drew a sizeable population from the atoll and involved the Pingelapese in another set of land tenure arrangements. This relocation was organized under the U.S. administration's homesteading program on Pohnpei. I have mentioned Coulter's visit to Pingelap in August 1954. This visit was prompted by a concern by the American administration that Pingelap was among the atolls considered to be overcrowded and which, consequently, should be included in the homesteading program which had already begun. The immediate impetus for Coulter's visit was a crisis that had arisen on Pingelap with the death or the dying condition of many of the breadfruit trees. According to Coulter's (1957: 339-40) account of his discussion with the men of Pingelap, they themselves perceived overcrowded situations on the atoll and had been disappointed when a planned relocation for 1947 was abandoned. At that time Ujelang in the Marshall Islands had been inspected for colonization by chiefs from Mwaekil and Pingelap (ibid.). The council with which Coulter met was concerned with the site which would be chosen. They stated as first preference Ujelang, second, Kosrae, and third, Pohnpei. But by this time plans for relocation to Pohnpei were actually advanced (Emerick 1960: 33). The men of Pingelap were also concerned with the manner in which colonists would be chosen. With regard to the economic conditions on the atoll that might support the notion that the atoll was overcrowded, Coulter (1957: 338) comments on the extreme fractionalization of both land areas and the taro patch as a symptom of such a condition. He also gained the impression that the chief concern in life was food, and he noted the great energy with which subsistence activities were carried out. At the same time he commented on the heavy pig population, as well as the variety and quantity of food which was offered him at a feast (ibid.: 325). The question arises as to the actual population which could be considered as the crucial point for the local resources. Coulter gave 500 as the 1945 population, and 639 for 1953, though he provides no sources for that information, and he estimates 700 for the time of his visit in 1954 (ibid.: 339). These figures do not represent a marked increase from the 600-700 who lived on the atoll during the Japanese period. I shall return to the question of the probable saturation point for the atoll's population in a later section.

The site selected for the new colony was in the Madolenihmw district of Pohnpei, near its east coast, in a locale known as Mand. Previously the area selected had been a Japanese coconut plantation, but except for a small section which in 1954 was being devoted to an experimental farm for the entire Trust Territory, it had been allowed to become overgrown. Beginning in 1949 a group of Pis-Losap people from the Mortlock Islands had been moved into a section of the property (Emerick 1960: 62 ff.). In late 1954 the son of the paramount chief of Pingelap, as well as the chief of the Kapingamarangi colony near the capitol town of Kolonia on Pohnpei, came to inspect the land that was to be the homestead area. Accompanying them were members of the American administration. As it turned out, the most desirable part of the area with regard to coconut trees and access to the sea was chosen by the Kapingamarangi chief. But since the Pingelapese moved in first and occupied part of that segment, they actually usurped part of the land originally chosen by the Polynesians.

The Pingelapese homesteaders moved to this Pohnpei site in four waves, the first in November 1954 in a group of 15 men, and about a month later in a group of 16 men. During 1955 two more parties of 12 and 13 men moved to Mand. Some of the men brought their families as they came, others were joined by them later (Emerick 1960: 86). By May 1956, a year-and-a-half after the first settlers arrived, 20 houses had been built, and by October of that year, 30. An assortment of materials, including saw lumber from a mill in Madolenihmw, scrap lumber from old houses and from derelict ships, were used. Harvesting of coconuts for sale began almost immediately as the trees in much of the settled area were in good bearing condition. The colonists also planted subsistence plants, such as taro, bananas, breadfruit and yams, and they found wild yams and wild taro as well. Other sources of local food were wild pigs and chickens. Two water buffalo as well as certain store-bought foods were purchased with the cash proceeds from copra. Together, these various sources of food helped the colonists through the first period during which crops were growing to the bearing stage (ibid.: 41).

The property used by the Pingelapese settlers is bordered by a stream which separates them from the experimental farm. This creek is spanned by a bridge. The area occupied by the Pingelapese is liberally dotted with coconut trees and is well-drained, with a good water supply provided by the stream. When I visited the locale in 1980, I noted that the population was distributed in the central part of the homestead in sort of a loosely aggregated village, whereas Emerick (ibid.: 40-41) reports that settlement was more scattered in 1955-56 because of the practice of people living on their own property which was spread over some distance. There was an open sunny spot in the centre of the settled area where a ramshackle nursing station and the school house stood, but most of the houses were heavily shaded by a low canopy of trees, some of which were breadfruit, but of much smaller stature than those trees found on Pingelap. Houses at the time of my visit were mostly out of sight of one another because of this growth and shading. The steeply falling stream rushed through a gorge. On the upper reaches, in a couple of pools, boys swam in the sunshine. Further down women could be seen pounding their washing on flat stones with boards. Some of the houses were built of wooden material as described by Emerick (ibid.: 90), but others were built of cement block, as is common on Pingelap. The road from the village led first through a forested area and then through open country, passing close to the large buildings of the experimental farm and then curved seaward through a scrub forest to the dockage area at the shore. A walk from the village to the docks takes about an hour, but at the time of my visit most residents rode to the water front in one of the several pickup trucks which the villagers owned. A boat house sheltered some open boats, while several other boats, making a total of about ten, were tied to a dock extending outward from the boathouse.

American Land Policy and the Mand Colony

Turning to land tenure policies which would be expected to affect the granting of subsequent inheritance of homestead land, Emerick wrote the following of the situation which confronted U.S. authorities after World War II:

> By the time the United States became sovereign in Micronesia in 1945, the land tenure situation on Ponape was rather badly muddled. By this time there were natives who owned or held title to land (or believed that they did) in a bewildering array of ways. There were those who held German deeds with no paper work ever having been done, many who held Japanese lease land and some who occupied land under "temporary use permits" issued by the Japanese to individuals who were suddenly displaced by warfare activities in the early forties. This confusion was unfortunately compounded soon after the beginning of the American period when the United States Military Government gave verbal permission to anyone who requested the temporary use of government land (ibid.: 53).

When the civil government took over from the Naval Administration in 1951 only German land was considered to be owned by the resident; other land was considered public domain (ibid.: 54). This meant that the colony on Sokehs Island was unaffected by American land policy for the most part, and the discussion earlier in this chapter appears to confirm the lack of effect of post-Japanese policies and regulation there. Local U.S. administration in Pohnpei directed its attention to the allotment of lands under the new homesteading program in Madolenihmw. In this connection, a Ponape District Land Advisory Board was established in 1953. This board was constituted by eight Americans, including the district administrator and members of his staff, as well as an

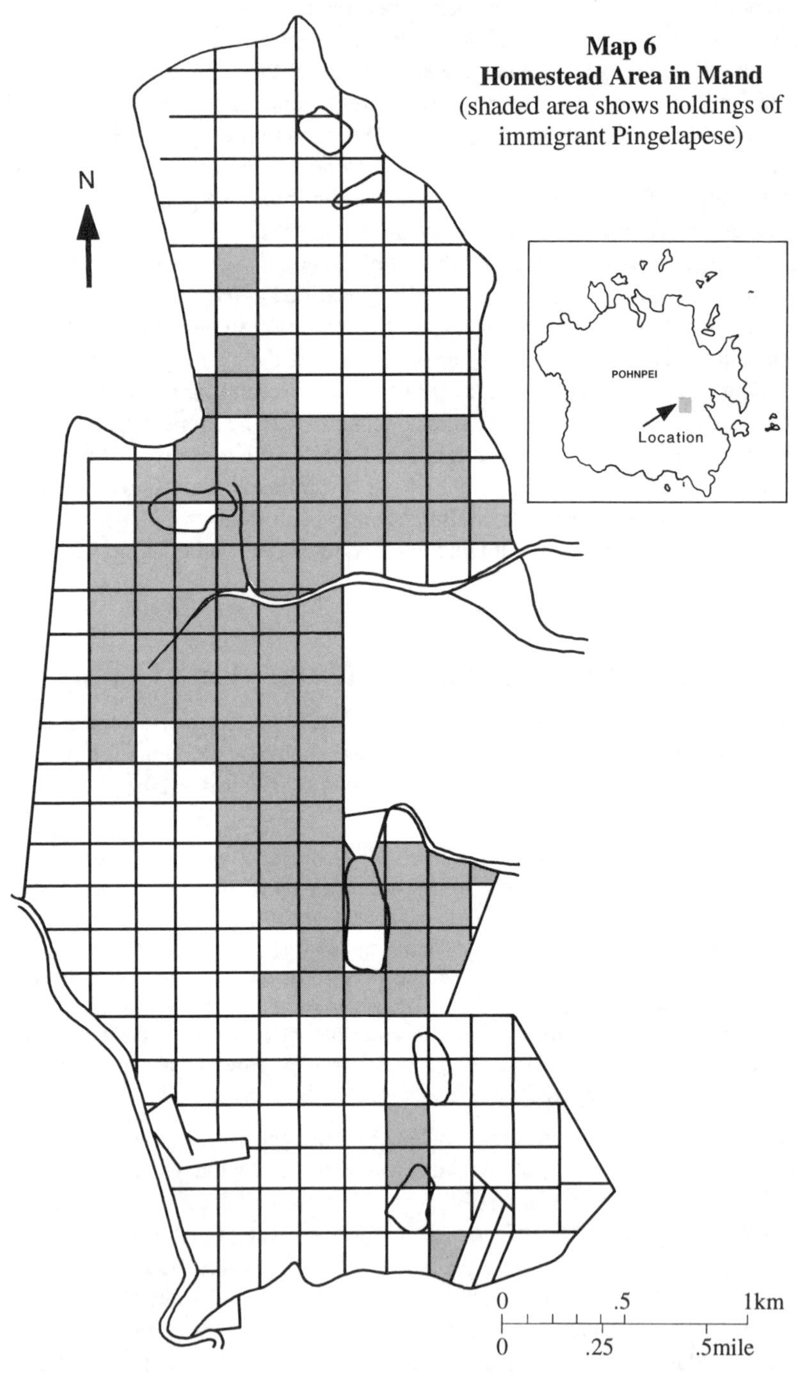

Map 6
Homestead Area in Mand
(shaded area shows holdings of immigrant Pingelapese)

educational advisor, the Madolenihmw plantation manager, surveying and cartographic engineer, and agricultural station manager. In addition, 15 natives, including the main title bearers of the five municipalities of Pohnpei, as well as certain elected officials were also members (ibid.: 54-55). Among the important decisions made by this body was that each homesteader over 18 years of age would be allowed three hectares (30 000 square metres) of land; that the prospective homesteader's application would be formally submitted to the board, as well as to a council of three for each municipality, and to another council of seven, and finally, to the District Lands Office and, for final approval by the district administrator. A five-year proving or trial period was to follow, during which the plot had to be cultivated properly, and if approved by the above chain of boards, the homesteader became owner of the land (ibid.: 56-58). The land code of 1957 followed the settlement of the Mand colony, and I will examine its possible effects on transferrals from the original assignments later in this chapter. At this point it is appropriate to consider the selection of emigrants to Mand and the apportionment of land which transpired on their arrival.

The Assignment of Land in the Mand Colony

During Coulter's visit to Pingelap in 1954, just months before the first wave of migrants moved to Mand, he had heard some concern as to how colonists would be selected (Coulter 1957: 339-40). In the event, from the accounts of my informants, the Pinelapese were given a great deal of freedom to decide among themselves how the selection would be made, with the main stipulation being that 60 men and their families would constitute the total party. Eventually it was decided that each *peyneyney* would provide one member who would be selected by his own kin. (The term *peyneyney* refers to an extended family unit which sometimes has vague limits, but generally is understood to be a patrilateral body of kindred, which is composed of father and married sons, or brothers and their children, even though separated residentially.) When I examined a list supplied to me by Mand residents, I noted that this procedure could not have been followed, for immediately on checking my genealogies, I found a number of father-son and brother-brother pairings. This occurrence was explained to me as representing supplementary recruitment which was employed after appropriate candidates from each *peyneyney* had stepped forward, in order to fill out the quota of 60 men.

In conversation regarding choice of colonists, my main informants offered the view that, as in the case of the Mwalok colony, those men whose landholdings were small were also those who volunteered or were chosen by their close relatives to join the colonizing party. There is of course a definite logic in this means of selection, so that in using that criterion as a guide I examined land tenure histories with it in mind. I made the assumption that if small landholders were to make up the colonizing group, to a large extent that it should be second and succeeding sons, rather than first sons, who would be attracted to the scheme. The genealogical data show that, in disagreement with that proposition, there were 14 first sons in the emigrant group. In addition to those first sons, the men of the colonizing party were represented by position in sibling groups as follows: 7 second sons; 4 third sons; 5 fourth sons; 1 sixth son. There were also 4 adopted first sons, 7 adopted second sons, and 2 adopted fourth sons. The most interesting figure among these is the prominence of second adopted sons. While a first adopted son would normally command some land on Pingelap from his natal father, he would also stand to acquire the largest part of the estate of his adoptive father. A second adopted son would be in a less favourable position with regards to the second of these sources. Their predominance in the party thus appears to lend some support to the notion of the land poor being selected for emigration. It could also be argued that even first sons in families not well endowed with land on the atoll would seek richer holdings in the new colony. Since a number of the Mand settlers are represented in my Pingelap Sample B, it was possible to check out this proposition in several instances. Altogether, I could get information on atoll landholdings for 38 of 59 Pingelap men who made up the colonizing group of the period 1954-55. Of these, five did not hold land on the atoll. The range of holdings ran from these landless men to an estate of about 16 000 square metres and 37 rows of taro. The average property held by the men of this sample was about 5 200 square metres of land and 10.5 rows of taro. This compares to an average of over 10 000 square metres and 28 rows for the total Sample B cohort. These figures tend to support the view that small owners of Pingelap land and taro rows did indeed make up the Mand party. This conclusion should be modified by the realization that, as I stated earlier, the Sample B group were unrepresentative of Pingelap landholding in that they were weighted toward the larger property owners on the atoll. It is not altogether clear that a precise conception of the size of the parcels to be allotted to the men of the Mand party was realized. Nonetheless, the grants of 30 000 square metres of volcanic soil must have been tempting to almost any Pingelap man. One must concede that for a significant number of the emigrant men, disadvantaged estate situations on the atoll must have provided a strong motive for emigration. On the other hand, less disadvantaged men also joined the colonizing party. For them other spurs must have provided motivation. Perhaps we are entering into the realm of imponderables in speculating what these may have been. One might suggest that the pioneering spirit, being a widespread human phenomenon, affected the decisions of some. There might also have been a desire to expand one's holdings well beyond what could be conceivably needed or exploited in a manageable fashion for either subsistence or commercial uses.[3] At least one of the cases discussed in Chapter 5 must be considered in these terms and, indeed, this large landholder, Case 14, who had not only expanded his ownership holdings on the atoll through various manoeuvring, also had use privileges of extensive holdings of a brother who joined the Mand colony. This brother was in his own right already one of the largest landholders on the atoll before his emigration to the colony. Other arrangements between siblings split between Pingelap and Mand have come to light in interviews. One sort of arrangement was for one brother, who could have sizeable holdings on the atoll, to move to Mand and leave behind substantial holdings for a less fortunate sibling to use under the terms of the recognized system of stewardship (*kohwa*).

Two sets of data were given to me by Mand residents regarding land ownership in that colony. One was a list of 60 (including one man from Kosrae) adult males who were said to have been granted the original allotments in Mand. The other was a compilation of ownership by plot current in 1980. I also have available Emerick's (1960: 112) map of the original assignments of plots to the Pingelap homesteaders, as well as an enlarged version of that map with numbered plots extending beyond the limits of these assigned properties supplied by the office of Land Management, Ponape District. In matching the original list of colonists with those holding property there in 1980 it is clear that others later assumed ownership of previously unclaimed land. For while Emerick's map shows 62 plots as the original area allotted to the Pingelapese, the later compilation accounts for no fewer than 83 plots of 30 000 square metres each. These can be located on the map shown here as tracts of land immediately adjacent to the original area on the western border of that assigned area. A section of Emerick's map which, though shown as divided into these plots, was unclaimed or unallotted at the time of original settlement.

In the preceding discussion of Mwalok holdings, I noted that in the original assignment of land there was a degree of inequality, with about half of the original immigrants getting multiple plots, and that total grants were also unequal in size. In three cases I was able to identify abnormally large grants with title holders and an otherwise prominent leader. In other cases I could see that such large allotments included less than desirable plots. In looking at the Mand situation in order to seek possible parallels, I noted that the colony leader, who was also the brother of the man who became *nahnmariki* in 1954, held a plot of land as did the other men of the colonizing party, but that his wife also held an adjacent plot. On closer examination of the map of the area, I noted that the plot of the wife was encroached upon by a section marked "barren," presumably being one of several large rock outcroppings which I noticed in walking about the colony. This part had not been assigned to the colonizing party probably because of this limitation. The nine other cases of women owning land which were revealed in the 1980 compilation were those where expansion had taken place into unclaimed sections of the surveyed area. One case of such joint husband-wife holding occurred within the assigned area and remains problematical. Among the husband-wife plot combinations was that of the eldest son of the then *nahnmariki*, his eventual successor in 1982. Both husband and wife in this case were among latecomers into the colony and took plots from an unassigned section. Since there have been a number of these husband-wife ownership pairings, it is not arguable that the two instances of colony leader and the heir to the paramount chief's title could be said to have been specially favoured. There was only one case in the 1980 compilation where a man was associated with two plots and in this instance the bulk of one of the plots and a smaller portion of the second was encroached upon by a "barren" place as indicated on the map.

It is clear that supervision in assignment was minimal, and that adjustments were made apparently through internal mutual agreement. Emerick's comments regarding these procedures are worthy of note:

> As the four waves of Pingelap settlers arrived on Ponape, homestead and village sites were assigned to them by the process of drawing site numbers out of a hat. This was done to assure the impartiality of land apportionment. In some cases, of course, there was not complete satisfaction with the land which a settler acquired in this way. In fact, in several instances, the homestead sites proved to be unusable. Also not all of the sites were equally well suited for the growing of a variety of subsistence crops. Some entire plots were swampy and suitable for only growing taro, while others were so well-drained or rocky that taro could be produced only with difficulty if at all. In most cases the settlers attempted to work out these problems themselves. A man with an overabundance of good taro ground and a man with high, well-drained land would get together and share homestead sites. This seemed a reasonable thing to do. The administration was frequently opposed to such arrangements, however, largely because of the resulting disarrangement of the official maps of the area and the allocation lists. The settlers, therefore, very quickly stopped attempting to make these land shifts official. Each man assumed official responsibility for the homestead site assigned him, but the internal arrangement continued (ibid.: 87-88).

Emerick's further remarks are also pertinent as we shift to consideration of subsequent land transferral.

> The form of land tenure which was imposed upon the settlers by the terms of the Homestead Agreement was not totally foreign to these people. Individual ownership of land was not uncommon on the home atoll and it had become more common since the period of contact with missionaries and other outside groups had begun. The Pingelap settlers who had been living on Sokehs peninsula for many years had been operating happily and successfully under a system of individual ownership of land (ibid.: 88-89).

Much of the above, of course, agrees with my foregoing analysis, except that my evidence indicates that individual ownerships on Pingelap predated foreign contact.

Land Transferrals in Mand and Mwalok

It was possible to get a complete record of estates of the original settlers which had been transferred to heirs by 1980. There were 21 of these latter, representing 22 plots of land in the colony. Of these estates, 11 were divided among heirs and the other 10 left undivided. This is in contrast to Mwalok where, although estates have been frequently divided, only one plot had been so divided. In the Mand colony division of estates was tantamount to division of lots. These facts lead to a consideration of the circumstances under which estates were divided, or conversely, for whatever reason, some were left undivided. One supposition for the latter condition might be that there were no other direct heirs. But, in looking at the genealogies that are available, a large number of children of the colony have been left unprovided for in these estate settlements. For the 21 estates which have been settled by 1980, there were 51 heirs who did inherit property in Mand, but there were also about 49 children of those 21 testators who received no property in Mand. These were 31 daughters, 1 step-daughter, 15 sons, 1 son adopted, and 1 son adopted out. Some of these people got lands on Pingelap, but not all of them did. Examination of the atoll maps indicate that lands of some of the Mand deceased were still not transferred to new owners. This latter condition could have been due to lack of information on the part of the Pingelap informants. Of the 21 deceased colonists, the names of only five and their heirs failed to appear on the maps of the atoll, while the others held varying amounts, but always much smaller than the three-hectare plots in Mand. Nonetheless, a number of the descendants of those who have transferred land in Mand are without holdings, either there or on Pingelap. It seems clear that the convention of providing land for almost all females as well as all men are falling by the wayside for the descendants of the original Mand colonists, as the population expanded in the above sample from 21 donors and spouses to 100 offspring. A comparison of transferral patterns in the two colonies is represented in Table 7.4.

Table 7.4
Comparison of Transferrals from Mwalok B and Mand A

	Mwalok B		Mand A	
	n	%	n	%
I. *Transactions by categories of recipients*[a]				
S[1]	15	34.9	16	30.8
AS[1]	5	11.6	1	1.9
Other S	14	32.6	16	30.8
D[1]	5	11.6	14	26.9
Other D	0	0.0	0	0.0
Other	4	9.3	5	9.6
Total	43	100.0	52	100.0

	Mwalok B	Mand A
II. *Integrity of estate and lots*		
Estates:		
divided	9	11
undivided	18	10
Lots:		
divided	1	11
undivided	51	10

a In the case of the Mwalok sample the actual number of recipients was somewhat smaller as there were several cases of more than one source of land.

There is a basic similarity between the two samples (Mand A represents landholders among the original settlers) revealed in the table, in that there is clear preference given sons in the two colonies, though in both colonies this preference is not restricted to first sons. Just as previous discussion showed that the German code did not apply when it came to passing land to brothers and grandsons, such patterns did not pertain for Mand either, in that the "Other" category included only one case of land passing to a wife, one to a cousin, and two to brother's sons. Restrictions against the division of estates which was at least implicit in the German code and Japanese practice does not apply to either group. Part II in the table shows that, especially in the Mand colony, those influences could not have been effective in 1954 when the colony was established. But division of estates is at least implicitly a part of the 1957 code which might be expected to have applied since all of the estate settlement in Mand took place after that date. On the basis of recognition of German deeds on Sokehs Island, it is not surprising that the 1957 code is being violated in Mwalok, but not so that it is being similarly ignored in Mand.

There is a marked contrast in the division of lots, however, that may suggest that in the Mwalok case the impact of German-Japanese strictures are still effective. But it is equally likely that certain demographic contrasts may play a role in bringing about this divergence. One of these contrasts is due to the lack of contemporaneity in the two samples given above. I have used Mwalok B for the figures given above, and the Mand A sample does resemble it in that in both cases the transfers belong to the American period (with the possible exception of a few earlier ones at Mwalok). We can probably assume rough correspondence in ages of the settlers at the time of establishment of the two colonies. There was a possible range of ages from 18-55 or 60 among those males considered adult and getting land, with a probable average age of between 35-40 in each case. But the gap in time between settlement on Sokehs Island in 1911-12 and establishment in Mand (and the cohort labelled Mand A in Table 7.4) in 1954-55 is more than that of one generation. This supposition is supported by the facts that fully 45 percent of the Mwalok Sample B were deceased in 1983, while only 26 percent of the original Mand colonists had died by 1980. As has been stressed at various places in this work, the Japanese period was one of small families, uneven fertility from family to family, and extensive adoption designed to fill out childless families. The American period, on the other hand, when a larger part of the Mand colony was born, has been one of exploding populations and generally even fertility from family to family, and the virtual demise of the adoption system (Damas 1983b). The latter factor relates to the greater number of adoptive heirs in the Mwalok case. It also accounts in part for the smaller number of heirs shown in Table 7.4 for Mwalok where 27 donors transferred land to 43 heirs, a 1:1.59 ratio, while in Mand there were 21 donors and 52 heirs or a 1:2.5 ratio. But the disproportion is even greater when the large number of potential heirs not getting land in Mand is considered.

With regard to the larger proportion of females getting land at Mand, nearly 27 percent as opposed to just under 12 percent in Mwalok B, it might be argued that the provision for females in the 1957 code which was supposed to have affected the former colony may have been involved. It is far more likely, considering the general ignoring of that code, that the Mand colonists were merely trying to approximate the long-standing Pingelapese practice of providing females with land and that they were unaffected by German or Japanese conventions, which had influenced land tenure at Mwalok. Notwithstanding a higher rate of inheritance by women, it is clear, as mentioned above, that those in Mand are disadvantaged compared to the atoll dwellers in this regard. Indeed, female grants in Mand were given in settlement of estates rather than as dowry. There are a few Mand women who were, however, given dowries on the atoll.

I have opined that few if any male offspring of Mwalok B are actually landless when ownership of land on Pingelap is considered, and considering as well, that in a number of cases heirs were the only children or only sons in the Mwalok population of those born during the Japanese period. Such has been proved not to have been the case for the Mand population, despite a greater tendency to divide lots. This condition is due to the rapidly expanding population of the latter colony, with its entire history lying within the American period, a time of great fertility. A similar situation of individual landlessness will surely confront the Sokehs colony of Pingelapese as the generation born during the American period reaches the age at which land is normally inherited, unless lots are subdivided.

While the number of potential but unrealized inheritors of land appears to be on the increase, there are acculturative factors which may reduce the significance of that possibility. The proximity of the Mwalok colony (only three miles by a connecting road) to the capital of Kolonia brought the residents there into the wage economy which developed during the American period, especially beginning in the 1960s when increased funding and greater employment opportunities reached the Trust Territory. With the expansion of the civil service and of service occupations, there his been a parallel expansion of the Mwalok population, largely by immigrants from the atoll who were counted at 253 in 1954 (Emerick 1960: 81) and which I estimated at over 700 in 1983. I further calculated that, if the workforce can be considered to be those men between 20-60 years of age, there was only about a 10 percent rate of "unemployment" (that is lack of wage-earning work) in the colony in 1983. There are as well, a number of women with full-time jobs. Given the typical eight-hour workday and the short tropical evenings year-round, there is little time left for farming and fishing activities. Some of the latter are carried out at night, but the former occupations are largely restricted to weekends. The manager of the local cooperative store in Kolonia complained to me that no more than "a half dozen bags of copra" are traded to him from Mwalok in a year's time. In short, the Pingelapese colony on Sokehs Island can no longer be considered to approach a subsistence economy nor a cash economy based on the copra trade. To be sure, country food items like yams, taro, and breadfruit appear in the diet and are still important for ceremonial events. My impression gained in residence in

Mwalok was that, all in all, they do not match in the diet such store-bought items as flour, rice, and canned meat.

The Mand colony is more distant from the centre at Kolonia, and a smaller number or percentage of the men are employed there, but I noted a brisk week-end traffic of workers returning briefly to the colony. Many of the younger men have moved to Kolonia on a more permanent basis than these commuters. It appears that these younger men, in the second generation of Mand people divide their time between the colony and the capitol, taking part on weekends in certain subsistence activities and products, while the older men continue with farming and copra-making occupations, while maintaining permanent residence there. If wage and salary opportunities keep pace with an expanding population of employable youth, the pressures on land in the colonies may not be crucial, for there is usually ample land available for individual house sites. This assessment is based mainly on considerations of practicalities and the inevitable attraction of quasi-urbanized living and economy. It does not take into account such psychological intangibles as the strong attachment to land above its commercial or subsistence value that was becoming a factor in increasing tensions in the relations between atoll dwellers and colonists in the 1980s.

CHAPTER 8

Pingelapese Land Tenure and External Relations

The establishment of colonies on Pohnpei expanded the property holdings of the total Pingelapese population to outside the atoll itself. But many of the colonists continued to claim land on Pingelap, and in the case of the Mwalok colonists, these claims often endured several generations after emigration from the atoll. I became aware of the stewardship or *kohwa* system in 1976 after I had been taking land tenure histories from informants, and I began to record property held in this way along with land and taro rows claimed through outright ownership. Later, I reviewed the *peliensapw*(s) and *manime*(s) of the entire atoll in terms of both ownership and of stewardship when the latter form of management applied. While subsequent discussion will show that my compilation of land held in *kohwa* was conservative, my survey then showed that about 25 percent of taro rows and 28 percent of land plots were actually owned by people living off the atoll.

As indicated in Chapter 4, according to customary understanding, stewards should send products of the land and the taro rows used to the actual owner with each visit of the field trip vessel. The chief rationale of this procedure is clearly to affirm ownership if not actually constituting rent, but this gesture, when practised, is also useful in terms of dietary complementation, since taro and breadfruit in the case of the Mwalok settlement are rare commodities. In discussion with the Mwalok colonists it became clear that there was a tendency to neglect this obligation, especially when a generation had passed after emigration.

The Nature of the Kohwa System

In looking at the kinds of ties that exist between actual owners and stewards, it is evident that a wide variety of kinship bonds are utilized in contrast to the much more standardized set of ties evident between donors and recipients of

---

The note to Chapter 8 is on p. 252.

land that applied in ownership transferrals. Again, as with transferrals of ownership, almost all individuals involved in *kohwa* arrangements show some sort of kinship connection between steward and owner. This is especially the case for atoll landholders living in the Mand colony. About half of the men living in Mand have brothers on Pingelap. Sharing through *kohwa* is a natural extension of the customary virilocal extended family domestic unit which persists as long as fathers are living. The second most frequent tie involved in *kohwa* arrangements is that between fathers and sons in those cases where the son has been awarded his land at marriage. In most of these cases the sons have migrated, and the father tends the property left behind. There are several cases, as well, where the father lived in one of the colonies and one son has been assigned care of family lands on the atoll. There were also a number of instances where either father or brother looked after lands of female relatives living on Pohnpei or who were otherwise absent from Pingelap. But taken together, the brother/brother, father/son, brother/sister, and father/daughter ties comprise less than half of the *kohwa* pairings. This is not surprising, especially in the case of the Mwalok-Pingelap pairings, since with the passage of two or three generations, kinship ties stretch wider. Examples of other sorts of ties which are exploited in the *kohwa* system are as follows: sister's husband/wife's brother; father-in-law/son-in-law; husband's brother/brother's wife; wife's brother's wife/husband's sister's husband; mother's brother/sister's son; daughter-in-law/father-in-law; father's brother's son/father's brother's son; son/mother; and a number of adoptive relationships. In short, a broad web of kinship, which includes bilaterally connected consanguines as well as affines, is utilized. The large representation of affinal ties is particularly noteworthy and signifies the great extent of marriages between people from Pingelap and those of the greater Pingelapese population which includes people on Pohnpei. This is in sharp contrast to the high degree of endogamy within that total population. It is clear that this is one area where the boundaries of the virilocal extended family, which is the chief land-using unit on the atoll as well as in the colonies, is expanded upon. At the same time my inspection of these cases of *kohwa* arrangements shows that sibling and parent/child ties are employed when they are available and wider sorts of bonds used when they are not.

While the emigration of substantial numbers of Pingelapese which accelerated during the 1970s can be posited as opening more land for use by those remaining on the atoll, the overall effect, when individual cases are considered is not as pronounced as one might expect. In some cases there was indeed a substantial increase in usufruct holdings under the *kohwa* arrangement. For example, there is a case of the youngest of four brothers who served as a steward for the others who lived away from Pingelap. This individual's share of atoll property was only 1 600 square metres of land and 11 rows of taro. His oldest brother, one of the title holders, who lived in Pohnpei as a school teacher, had inherited a fairly large estate which he had also increased through purchases. The youngest brother, the only one of the four living on Pingelap, was left in charge of this considerable holding as well as smaller but still significant land and taro owned by the other brothers. His total of *kohwa* lands contributed over 15 700 square metres of land and 38 more rows of taro, thus increasing his usufruct land area by tenfold and his usufruct taro holdings three-and-a-half times. In another case, a man increased his holdings through *kohwa* from about 6 900 square metres and 17 rows by another 11 800 square metres and 45 rows in the taro patch. Such great accretions for small or medium landholders were unusual rather than typical in my Pingelap Sample B which formed the corpus from which I drew my data. One severely land-poor title holder (chief number 7 in Table 5.7) had, through inheritance and the use of his wife's properties, control of 4 025 square metres and 27 rows. His *kohwa* holdings increased the total of usufruct property by only 2 140 square metres and 5 more rows. This brought him close to the average of Sample B for taro but only a little more than half the actual inherited *peliensapw* holdings for that sample, without counting *kohwa* benefits for others in that sample.

It is apparent, however, that the *kohwa* system often broadened the holdings of already (by Pingelap standards) large owners. I noted in Chapter 5 that the paramount chief increased his inherited total of 22 750 square metres and 46.5 rows, to 45 930 square metres and 101.5 rows as usufruct property through acquisitions from his wife's and son's wives properties, together with *kohwa* holdings. But even if these latter holdings are included, in spite of this increase, he slipped from second to third in total land controlled. The fourth-ranked landholder in terms of land and taro inherited and acquired as usufruct property through marriages, added another 21 500 square metres and 39 rows through *kohwa* bringing his total to 48 500 square metres and 80 rows. Another large land owner doubled his use property through *kohwa* to a total of 41 300 square metres and 110 rows, making him the largest owner of taro plants as well as ranking him fourth as owner of *peliensapw* property. Examples like these suggest that rather than relieving inequalities in the distribution of subsistence and copra-producing property, some such inequalities appear to be aggravated by the *kohwa* system.

If these holdings sometimes appear to be well in excess of what can be properly utilized, it should be considered that, in theory, such usufruct property, as that made available through *kohwa* cannot be passed to one's heirs. But, in practice, there is the tendency to assume possession of such properties and to transfer them as part of one's estate. This is the main problem that the *kohwa* system brings with it. I first became aware of this area of conflict in 1980 when on Pohnpei my chief informant examined my maps of landholdings on the islands of Pingelap and observed that people left in charge of plots as stewards were claiming them as their own property. In 1983, when I began to query informants in Mwalok about their Pingelap holdings, I felt the full impact of this potentially explosive situation. I had planned to compile a complete list of the holdings of the Mwalok people on Pingelap, but after recording only seven such histories, I realized that I had to suspend my investigations due to the consternation expressed by those informants when they examined my maps. Because of this necessary avoidance of a dangerous situation it will be impossible to cover a truly representative range of cases in trying to understand the operation of the *kohwa* system. Examination of the small sample which I did does reveal practices of handling of the stewardship situations which give rise to dispute.

This sample includes the histories of a total of 42 *peliensapw*(s) said by my Mwalok informants to be their property. Of these, my maps show that 20 are listed in the name of the steward, in 6 cases the land plots were identified with the name of a deceased testator; in 3 cases the name of another person other than testator, owner, or steward was given. In 6 cases the plot claimed could not be located on my maps, and only 7 of the 42 plots were identified as being owned by a colonist. Each of these circumstances begs some attempt at explanation. Those cases which are still listed according to deceased testators appear to represent either a breakdown in communication between the island and the colonies or, in a couple of instances, situations where estates had not yet been settled. With regard to plots listed either in the name of persons other than steward, testator, or owner, and probably the plots which could not be located, there seems to be no other explanation than that transferrals from stewards had already taken place. The largest category, that of identification of plot by steward, highlights the chief problem area in the operation of the *kohwa* system. However, while my informants in Mwalok were distressed at seeing names other than their own associated with plots they considered to be theirs, their anxieties might not be justified in every case. Part of the confusion over ownership may be due to the research methods of my field aide and myself. Due to their frequent absences from the atoll, it was not possible to interview owners or stewards of many of the plots and *manime*(s). In these instances we had to rely on information from people who owned plots or sections of the taro patch adjacent to the one being identified. Observations of stewards working these sections might have distorted the true picture of plot ownership. On the other hand, my survey revealed that there was considerable uncertainty regarding ownership in a number of these disputed plots or sections of the patch. It was clear that there was a crisis growing regarding claimants on the atoll versus off-island putative owners. The degree to which this situation reaches crucial proportions depends upon the operation of some acculturative factors on the one hand, or persistence of traditional attitudes toward land on the other. Concern over land ownership on and off the atoll was shared across generations at the times of my studies in the area. Even though older men living in Mwalok had not visited the atoll in years, some claimed property on Pingelap which had been owned by their grandfathers and still placed great value in that property. As well, younger men who appeared to be making no use of their land on Pohnpei in Mand or on Sokehs Island, and who were holding well-paying jobs in the capital also expressed pride in ownership and concern for properties on the atoll. We may be dealing with an attachment to land which is perhaps characteristic of intensive agricultural peoples in general. Most often, concern for properties on Pingelap is expressed either in terms of nostalgia for the old place, and talk of retiring on a piece of their own land or, in terms of a need for security through land ownership. It is difficult to predict, as subsistence occupations fade from the world of these men and their successors in the wage-employment pool, whether or not they will slough off this attachment. It is evident that during the early 1980s employment possibilities on Pohnpei were drying up. Young men with substantial formal education were wandering back and forth between the high island and Pingelap. But some of these men were marrying and settling into the subsistence and copra-based economy of the atoll. Should such a trend continue, the population of Pingelap will again reach early twentieth-century levels, and the value placed on land will be further enhanced. On the other hand, if the flow of U.S. monies expands under the new Compact of Free Association, and at the same time job opportunities expand again, the situation might not arise. There is also the question of whether or not there will be a continuing population expansion among the people who identify themselves as Pingelapese.

Pingelapese Land Tenure and Codification

A second way in which external relations enter into the operation of the Pingelap land tenure system is in its possible articulation in codified laws introduced by nations which have administered Micronesia. In Chapter 4 I outlined both the effects and the limitations of the *Code of the Trust Territory of the Pacific Islands* with regard to internal decisions made in the local court on Pingelap. The local legal organization specified in the *Code* in 1951 was shortly thereafter established on Pingelap, with a justice and an associate justice being appointed, and trials including land trials being regularly held. Cases not settled to the satisfaction of the plaintiffs could be appealed to the district court in Pohnpei. Cases unresolved or appealed at that level could then be sent to the high court in Saipan, presided over by an American judge.

While I did not keep a record of cases tried on the atoll during my stay in 1975-76, I did later obtain a complete record of all cases tried in the local court for the period July 18, 1977, and July 17, 1978, inclusive. I was struck by the fact that, given the assumed tensions created by heavy populations on the atoll, not one case of dispute over property was brought to the local court, and consequently, appealed to higher courts during that time. It is clear that this has not always been the situation during the period of American administration. I was given access to the records of a number of cases from the period 1959-67 at the Pohnpei legal office concerning land tenure disputes on Pingelap which were sent to the High Court. Unfortunately, I was given only limited access to what is likely a more comprehensive corpus of cases and, consequently, my sample cannot represent an accurate guide to the frequency of land-trial cases in American times. It does allow insight into Trust Territory judicial interpretations of, and accommodations to, customary land tenure conventions and practices on Pingelap.

Case 1

This case, tried August 3, 1959, proved to be a precedent-setting one in several respects, and appears to have occurred at the beginning of an especially active period of land trials, a number of which had been festering for some time. This dispute concerned a man who gave land as a gift to a younger son. This land was now being claimed according to the convention of primogeniture by the older son who, however, had moved to the Mwalok colony in 1942. The judgment rendered by the high court was that the plaintiff had no right to land on Pingelap as long as he lived on Pohnpei, with the proviso that if he returned to the atoll and "if he makes his home there in good faith and cannot come to a reasonable understanding with (X) as to the division of the area of the land, he may have a part of this land set off to him to own" (District Court of Ponape, 1959). This provision of course favours rights of use above other considerations. In the preamble to the case an important point is raised which will be seen to have bearing on the subsequent cases discussed here, as well as on the future of Pingelap land tenure. This was mention of the presumed crowded conditions on Pingelap. The judge in this case cites the population on the atoll as 591 people, this estimate coming three to four years after the emigration of the colonists to Mand. He considered the population level to represent an overcrowded condition, but it actually indicates a population of only about 60 percent of that which had peaked about the turn of the twentieth century. The preamble to the case also interjects an interesting interpretation of Pingelapese customary ownership and use practices as follows:

> although the land is regularly referred to as belonging to an individual, it is looked upon as essentially a family asset to be used for and made available to those members of the family present on Pingelap, in rough proportion to their needs, taking into consideration what other lands, if any, are available to them (ibid.).

This statement does give a depiction fairly close to the actualities of land use on Pingelap, if by "family" is meant the virilocal extended family of father and married sons.

Case 2

In this instance the dispute arose over whether a first natal son or an adopted son was the rightful heir to the land in question. Here the first son's mother ran away with another man and the son himself did not look after the father in his old age. The adopted son's right to the land was affirmed by the court in that he was the designate of the oral will and that adoptive status was recognized in Pingelapese custom as legitimate heirship. Also involved is the circumstance that the adopted son had been working the land in question for 17 years before action was taken to dispute ownership. Again, land use was being recognized in support of claim as in Case 1 (District Court of Ponape 1963a).

Case 3

A desertion was invoked here, as well as other complicating factors. The first owner of the land in question left for labour in Nauru and made an oral declaration that his uncle could use the property during his absence, and if he died it would be passed to his sister. The owner did indeed die on Nauru and the uncle carried out the provisions of the declaration and passed the property to the sister. Meanwhile the wife had gone off with another man, taking the daughter who was the plaintiff in this case with her. The property was indeed being used by and was claimed by the daughter of the first sister to whom it had been willed. The judgment was that since the mother had taken the daughter away, the latter could not claim right to the property (in this case 10 rows in the taro patch). As well in this case a Pingelapese had been named Justice for the island by the Japanese and had authorized ownership which had transpired and the judgment of the High Court included the statement that: "private rights in land which were clear under the Japanese administration should be equally clear under the present administration, unless something very specific has happened to change them since the end of Japanese administration" (District Court of Ponape 1965a). A parallel case that had been settled in the same manner for Mwaekil was then cited. Also important in this case was the factor of long-term use of the property in question, since 1918 in this instance, while the dispute was not aired until 46 years had passed. An adoption ruling was also enlisted in this case, with the judgment that adoption recognized in Pineglap custom need not be registered to be valid.

Case 4

In this case two contradictory oral wills were presented. As descendants of an adopted daughter and an adopted son, both plaintiff and defendant claimed right to land on Pingelap. The plaintiff, a woman, was judged to have greater right to the property. This decision was made in Saipan even though the hearing on Pineglap had ruled in favour of the oral will presented by the defendant. The defendant had claimed that since he had acquired land on Sokehs through the same testator, as registered in a German title, this action should validate his claim to Pingelap land. The ruling rejected his claim to an oral will and declared that the German title to land in Sokehs was irrelevant to the claim for atoll land as "Pingelap is unique and was generally unaffected by the German land reforms of 1912" (District Court of Ponape 1965b).

Another factor in the decision was that the defendant had lived in Sokehs and never worked the land, whereas the plaintiff and his father, on the other hand, had planted, and harvested crops and "possessed it for their use for a period of 43 years." It was only after that time had passed that the defendant had returned and tried to claim the land (ibid.). Reading the particulars of this case to my chief informant, I could see that he was becoming upset to a degree which I had never seen in my many interviews with him. When I had finished he proclaimed the settlement as "rotten." His father had been witness for the overruled defendant which made his involvement in the case more than a casual one. Two elements of the case bothered him. First, the judge who travelled to Pingelap received gifts of food from the plaintiff which were seen by my informant as a form of bribery. The second element was that, in his eyes, the settlement violated the principles of *kohwa* by awarding land on the basis of long-term use. He saw the true ownership residing in the defendant living on Sokehs Island. His view of the justice of the *kohwa* system was that those stewards living on Pingelap have the use of the land and get food and copra from it, often for many years. Having had this benefit they should not also be rewarded by getting the land itself no matter how many years or even generations pass without use by the real owner.

Case 5

Here a woman had married three times and her daughter by the second husband was awarded land by that man. This latter woman, long deceased, and her son, who was the defendant in the case, had been between them using the land for 100 years, while the plaintiff claimed that this land had been granted for use only and should, on the death of that woman, be given back to the line of the second husband, the father of the plaintiff. The latter argued that an oral will backed his claim. Since no one except the plaintiff brought evidence for the will, and once again, since the defendant and his mother had used the land over a long period, the high court ruled against the plaintiff. Another complication in this case arose upon the plaintiff's plea that the defendant's mother had not observed the *wesik* obligations, according to which, as a recipient of land, she should provide food to its donor or the donor's descendants if the latter is deceased. This meant that the plaintiff should have been receiving these gifts of food, which he had not. Since the plaintiff's claim to a will was not honoured, the consideration of *wesik* was judged to be not relevant (District Court of Ponape 1967).

Case 6

In this case conditions of adoption were brought to light that may have affected the outcome. The plaintiff claimed right to land of his father's brother on the ground that the present occupant of the land who putatively inherited it from that person was not a legitimately adopted son. At the hearing on Pingelap, the plaintiff indicated that the defendant had indeed been adopted by that man, but that he had been taken back by his true parents, and further, that he had not given the proper attendance to the body of the deceased testator in order to validate his claim. The court did not recognize the adoption and, again, use of the land over a long period, in this case, throughout both the Japanese and American periods, during which the plaintiff had failed to bring action earlier, was also a decisive factor in the judgment (District Court of Ponape 1963b).

Case 7

Here not only was the question of the legitimacy of adoption as raised in the above case involved, but also the validity of oral wills and documents signed by the Japanese administration. The plaintiff and defendant both claimed to have been adopted by the testator who owned land on Sokehs Island and on Pingelap atoll. As the defendant had been borne by the wife of the testator before their marriage, there was some question as to his right to the land, as well as to whether or not he had been adopted. The plaintiff, on the other hand, proposed three different claims to inheritance of the property in question. First, he claimed that the testator had no natural sons, and his position as the son of a brother made him the legitimate heir along patrilineal lines as was consistent with the German-Japanese property route. Second, he claimed to have been adopted by the testator and third, he claimed that the latter had divided land on Pingelap among himself, the defendant, and an adopted daughter. The testator had died in 1921 and had left his Pingelap land to be used by his brother, the father of the plaintiff. But in 1963 the defendant moved from Pohnpei where he had lived for a number of years, back to Pingelap and assumed ownership of the disputed property. Earlier this case had been temporarily resolved by the defendant's agreement that he would return this latter property to the plaintiff; but he had failed to do so. In the event of the new hearing, the plaintiff could produce no evidence or an oral will dividing up the Pingelap land, whereas the defendant exhibited a title document for the land on Sokehs Island signed by the Japanese Governor of Ponape and the Chief Magistrate of Sokehs and dated April 11, 1924. This document showed that the defendant was indeed the adopted son of the testator and was registered as owner of the Sokehs land. Even though this authority could not be openly regarded as relevant to the Pingelap holdings, since the plaintiff could not produce any evidence for division of land on the atoll, the latter property was awarded the defendant. This property had been subsequently transferred to the daughter of the defendant with the knowledge that the plaintiff had continued to use the land. It was also ruled that the plaintiff had not planted on the Pingelap land, thus weakening his claim for ownership in the eyes of the court (District Court of Ponape 1963c).

The above cases illustrate that even in a seemingly straightforward system of land tenure where land is owned by individuals rather than descent units or residential units, so that much ambiguity would seem to be avoided, uncertainty and dispute still arise. In looking at the occasions for dispute as highlighted by these cases, genealogical ambiguity arises principally through adoption, though other kinship relationships bring with them the potential for ambiguity as well. In previous sections I indicated that adoption provided land for otherwise land-poor individuals and provided heirs for those testators with few or no heirs, and can be regarded as one of the mechanisms which worked to even out gross inequalities in the land tenure system as a whole. It is the quality of duplication implied by adoption which gives it the potential for disputation in land tenure cases. Rather than complete transferral into the adoptive family or *keinek*, the adoptee is in some sense a member of both sets of relationships. This duality can be seen especially in cases of returning adoptives at various stages in the life cycle, but particularly in adolescence or adulthood. In theory, the returning children renounce any claim to the land of the adoptive father, but some of the cases cited illustrate that claims often remain on such property. It is noteworthy that the high court accepted demonstrated adoptive relationships as valid bases for land inheritance.

Illegitimacy and step-relationships are other situations which present bases for dispute. Other problems clearly relate to the question of the validity of oral wills. If the number of land disputes increases, it would seem that an effort toward registering written wills will have to be made in order to resolve this area of dispute. In spite of the lack of written wills, custom is said to decree that the eldest male offspring should have the right to distribute the estate when it has not been assigned by a testator. Whether or not such custom will be supported by external legal decisions is not clear. Indeed, there appear to be in these cases some inconsistency regarding acceptance of customary land tenure conventions in court hearings. They leave room for considerable interpretation when applied to specific cases. One dictum which runs counter to the *kohwa* system in particular and was repeatedly upheld in the cases reviewed here was that of long-term use. It is here that I see the demise of the *kohwa* system to be inevitable if the judgments made under the new Federated States of Micronesia government follow the course of those made during the Trust Territory phase of history in the area. There are bound to be a number of hotly contested decisions and considerable reaction to them if they are made according to the criterion of use. While the concept of *derak* is not mentioned in these cases or in the several others which were made available to me, the concept of oral wills was. Unfortunately none of the cases cited here refer to any of the *derak* cases discussed in Chapter 6, so it is difficult to judge whether or not such a ceremony would have validity in the courts of the Trust Territory. It is certain from discussion with Pingelapese that for them such a consideration is paramount in affirming claims to land. In several of the cases cited, however, the long interval of elapsed time made uncertain the memory of actual apportionment of gifts at *derak*(s). This circumstance probably obscured claims as they were presented to the courts.

Another feature of the series of cases cited above is the ingredient that most of them represented long-contested situations, which in one case traced the history of plots back over a century. Decisions were repeatedly made on the basis that the plaintiff did not raise the matter earlier. But it is not clear that the mechanisms for appealing cases above the local level were available either during Japanese, German, or early American times. The fact that a number of the cases which had been smoldering for years before the period of the late 1950s and the 1960s from which these cases come strongly suggests that such recourse was not previously available.

With regard to the decisions of earlier administrations, it is interesting to note that, similar to the Japanese adoption of German land tenure, one decision cited here under the American Trust Territory government referred to a Japanese precedent as well. On the other hand, there was recognition that the German code of 1912 had never been applied to Pingelap and that documents by the Japanese or German governments did not apply to the atoll itself.

In the final analysis, while from German times onward until relatively recently, Pingelapese land tenure has operated according to internal decisions and conventions, it is both in the operation of the *kohwa* system and through appeal to higher courts, and in some cases the confluence of these two factors, that the Pingelapese are being drawn inexorably into a wider universe of decision-making outside their insular situation.

Pingelap and the Copra Trade

The third way in which Pingelapese land tenure relates to external contacts is through the copra trade. In Chapter 2 I indicated that after about 1870, first free-traders, then German firms operating out of the Marshalls brought Pingelap into the world market of copra buying. The trade continued to be carried on under the Japanese and throughout the American period, including that of the Trust Territory, and into the era of the Federated States of Micronesia, as the only commercial activity of importance on the atoll which involves contact with the outside world.

I have indicated that uses of coconuts for such traditional purposes as drinking and food has declined in recent years, but these uses increase when trade items are scarce in the stores on the atoll. While the lands of the islands of the atoll are primarily valued in proportion to the presence or relative abundance of breadfruit trees for food and lumber, as discussed in an earlier section, the ubiquitous coconut palm is the only crop of commercial value. While preparation of copra has been treated in detail by several other anthropologists (cf. Pollock 1970) working in Micronesia, some basic description is appropriately included here with regard to Pingelapese practices.

The nuts are gathered by small groups, but especially by man and wife, a man assisted by a son or sons of varying ages, and in one case at least, by a widow and her daughters. Copra nuts are taken mostly from the ground. After laying out nuts in piles at the site of gathering, the husking commences. A sharpened stick or pointed piece of iron specially designed for the purpose is used to separate the husk from the inner shell. With one of thee instruments set in the ground at an angle, husking proceeds rapidly with the skilled strokes of the husker. Each burlap sack used for carrying nuts and copra can accommodate about 100 husked nuts. If the coconuts are gathered and husked on the main island they are usually moved to the village with hand-drawn carts (*riakas)* several of which remain from Japanese times. The one pickup truck was also used at times to move larger amounts from as far as the end of the road near the deep inlet at the neck of Likin Epin peninsula. If the nuts are gathered on Sukoru or Daekae they are transported across the lagoon in motorized boats or, in times of gasoline shortage, in canoes. Whereas Coulter (1957: 322) in his visit of 1954 noted copra being dried in the sun, this method was seldom being used at the times of my visits to the atoll. Instead, there were a number of drying racks in the village where the process is carried out. These are comprised of screens set on racks about four feet off the ground and sheltered by corrugated iron roofs. There, numbers of people gather for the copra making. Nuts are cracked with the backs of bush knives and then small curved slices of meat about four or five inches long are removed with smaller knives from the inside of the shells. Some husks are carried back from sites of the harvest to be used as fuel for the fires which are lighted below the screens. The shells themselves are also saved for they provide the hottest fires for cooking purposes.

After the cutting, the pieces of meat are laid on the screen, the fires lighted and the drying process commences. Usually this takes about 24 hours or longer. Smoky fires abound in the village in the days just prior to expected visits of the field trip vessel. After drying is complete each bag is loaded with the meat of about 300 coconuts. These bags are then carried to the warehouse near the cooperative store to await the arrival of the ship. They are carefully counted, with the contributions of each man recorded. On the arrival of the ship a number of men carry the 100-pound bags down to the water's edge where most are loaded into the community scow, a craft about 20 feet in length and much broader and deeper than the other boats in use in the waters around Pingelap. The scow when loaded is towed to the ship by one of the smaller boats powered with a large outboard engine.

Coconut products, especially the oil extracted from copra, are associated with cooking oils and margarine, as well as soap and other toilet products (Child 1974: 258-272). The residue or poonac which remains after extracting the oil is also very useful as animal feed, being rich in protein and inexpensive (ibid.: 273-83). Woodruff (1979: 73) notes a seven-year cycle in price trends of copra but also sees the demand extending well beyond the year 2000.

That there is a close correlation between price and intensity of coconut gathering and copra making can be seen in Figure 8.1 which shows the curves of production and copra prices for the period 1975-82.[1] Prices during that period ranged from a high of $21.98 per bag at the very beginning of the period to a low of $6.11 one year later; with another major climb seen in 1979, and with a subsequent fall the following year, and remaining relatively stable after that. (These prices do not reflect the $1.50 per bag deducted for freight costs which reduces the net payment received by the Pingalapese.) Annual copra production during this period varied from the low in 1977 of 2 201 bags to the high in 1980 of 4 380 bags. The graph shows lags in production after price falls and rises, but the response is not immediate. It is evident that the people often continue to produce a high level in the hope that the fall in price is only temporary, and they are also somewhat wary at times when prices show a sudden leap. Continued trends do, nevertheless, have obvious effects on a year-long basis as shown on the graph. In matching price per bag with production, the yearly fluctuations in income from copra during the period ranged from a low of $20 000 in 1981 to a high of $60 000 in 1979. It was fortunate for the Pingelapese that in the two periods of price slumps shown on the graph, 1977-78 and 1981-82, funds became available for work on the airstrip which had been suspended in the period between. Indeed, the majority of families earned substantial incomes from labour on that project. I will deal more with all sources of income below, but with regard to the more usual sole source of income from labour on the atoll, copra production earnings show a range from $37-85 per capita annually during the period covered in Figure 8.1. This is not a great deal, considering the demand for supplies and equipment from the outside world.

Figure 8.1
Copra Production and Copra Prices, 1975-1982

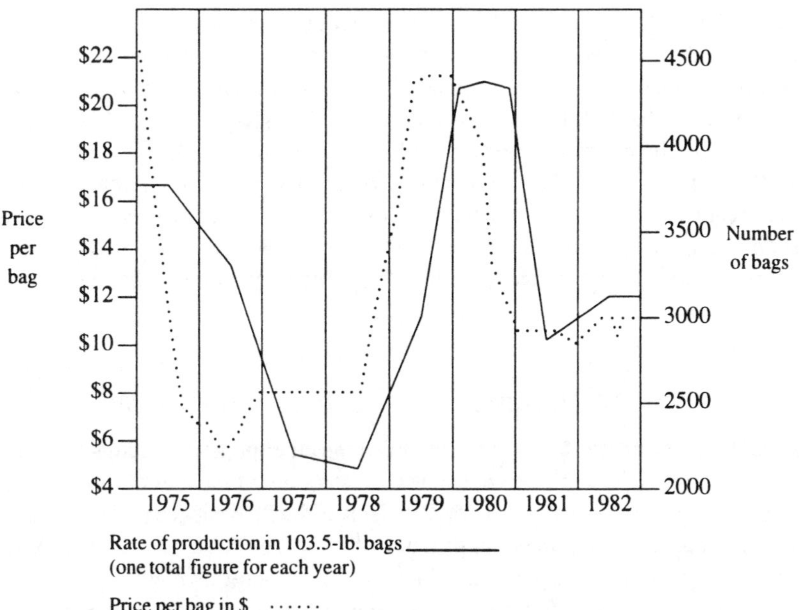

Copra production varies widely from family to family around the village and, consequently, so does income from that source. Unfortunately, the only sample regarding income that I have over any extended period is during the span of time which overlaps a period of lowered prices and relaxed production rates in 1977-78. In this sample the largest producer is also one of the largest landholders, especially when considerable *kohwa* holdings are counted. His income from copra for the year January 1977 to January 1978 was $283.34, but many other workers made less than $100 for that year from copra. A number of men traded only once in that period, and there were also a number of men in the prime of life whose names were absent from the list of copra transactions kept at the store during that time. The combined circumstances of lowered price and alternate source of income through labour on the airstrip undoubtedly curtailed activities to a great extent during 1977-78. Interestingly, I noted that owners of the largest coconut holdings did not necessarily produce the most copra. Correlation between size of landholdings and production of copra in general appears to be very weak. The size of the workforce within extended families was certainly a factor. Such intangibles as differences in individual initiative and motivation to save for a large purchase or investment, as building a new house in particular, seemed to be factors in both individual average production of copra over time, and in steadiness as opposed to spurts of production.

Some idea of the value of labour used in production of copra at a time when prices were near their lowest, in September 1975, appears in my notes. In the first example I have record of a party of 10 men husking 3 000 nuts or 30 bags of husked nuts; or 10 bags of copra meat. The net price per bag after deduction for shipping and handling was at that time $5.00. Thus the work of these men yield $50.00 for 10 men and one day's labour. This is without counting the labour and time needed to carve out and dry the meat which would involve a number of other people and another day's work at least. At the same period I observed that for four men who gathered 1 200 nuts, equivalent to four bags of copra each, the return for their labour for one day was $20.00. When in March 1976 the price slumped to its lowest, I noted that some people continued to make copra. My assistant explained that even though the price was at a very low state, some families had no other source of income with which to purchase kerosene, sugar, flour, and rice, commodities which had come to be regarded as necessities.

Copra Income and Cash Expenditures

It should be clear that while copra has been the chief point of articulation of the land tenure system with outside economies throughout most of the contact history of Pingelap, it has not provided any sort of local affluence or great wherewithal for access to commercial products. I cannot in this study attempt to isolate or control all sources of cash income for the atoll dwellers. Such a task would have value here, for it would provide a close assessment of the extent of reliance of the islanders on outside sources as opposed to the internally generated economy. I do have information on community salaries, but these are very small and are internally provided. The salaries of the school teachers which are derived from United States subsidies, are more significant. I have figures also for the wages paid workers in building the airstrip during the two phases of construction. But I do not have data on a significant outside source of mone, remittances from family members employed in places away from the atoll.

Another way of assessing the extent of involvement in the outside-of-island economy compared to internally derived sources of food and equipment and other supplies is to refer to records which indicate income from copra and expenditures for merchandise for the same periods, so that one can approximate an assessment of the contributions of the copra trade to the total purchasing power of the islanders. The records of the Kolonia Community Cooperative Association (K.C.C.A.), which receives copra from Pingelap, are especially useful in this regard. This agency received copra valued at $31 250 from Pingelap in 1981, but sales of merchandise at the Pingelap Community Cooperative Association (P.C.C.A.) store which emanated from a Pohnpei outlet amounted to $56 000. These figures indicate that about 56 percent of purchases at that store were matched by copra income for that year. For 1982, sales rose to $110 000, but copra income dropped to $25 848 or 23.5 percent of sales. In this latter year two circumstances combined to give copra a far smaller role. The first was a sharp drop in copra prices and the second was the inflow of cash through Trust Territory financing of construction of an airstrip, a project in which the natives were paid for their labour. The 1982 figures regarding copra income and expenditures at the P.C.C.A. store given above probably represent a fairly average situation for recent years in which the store was managed by Pingelapese, for during the year copra prices were at more or less average levels, and production of bags of copra was also at about the mean of their range as given in Figure 8.1. Construction of the airstrip which had begun in 1978 was also halted during 1980 and 1981 due to lack of funds.

Table 8.1
Shipment of Merchandise Received by P.C.C.A., September 13, 1982

No. of pkgs.	Description of commodities	Total price
75 bags	rice 50#	$ 969.00
30 bags	flour 20/50#, 5/10#, 10/5#	438.70
5 cases	Winston cigarettes	841.50
1 case	Benson Hedges cigarettes	168.30
2 drums	kerosene	178.00
5 drums	gasoline	380.00
10 cases	laundry soap	226.80
600	copra bags	330.00
		$3 532.30
	Total price of food items	$1 407.70
	Total price of other items	$2 124.60

In 1979 and 1980 when prices for copra and production were both at high levels, considerable income could be realized by the islanders from that industry, with approximately $60 000 earned in 1979 and $65 000 in 1980. While I do not have sales figures for the P.C.C.A. for those years, the bulk of the purchases there could have been covered by income from copra if the "typical" purchase level for 1981 of $56 000 had prevailed. But two variables confound such correlation. The first is that the store when managed by local natives usually did not provide sufficient inventories to meet normal needs or purchasing power. When, instead, as was the case from 1980 through 1983, Peace Corps volunteers managed the store, inventories were much fuller. The second variable is revealed in the above-cited sales figure for 1982 which shows that when supplies of merchandise are available in the store and wherewithal for their purchase is also at hand, purchasing is hugely expansible.

Table 8.2
Shipment of Merchandise Received by P.C.C.A., October 6, 1982

No. of pkgs.	Description of commodities	Total price
100 bags	rice 50#	$1 186.00
5 pails	flour 11#	44.35
25 cases	flour 6/4.5#	357.25
25 bales	sugar	290.10
10 cases	shortening 12/3#	329.10
2 cases	condensed milk	87.72
3 cases	coffee 12s	143.61
10 bags	kitchen salt 24s	128.60
7 cases	soy sauce 12/pint	81.05
10 cases	ship biscuit	385.47
10 cases	mackeral 48s	350.60
5 cases	cookies	239.42
5 cases	batteries (flashlight)	338.50
5 cases	dry yeast 12s	93.75
5 cases	Spam 24s	51.80
5 cases	sardines 24s	127.10
3 cases	ketchup 15/24 oz.	87.78
3 cases	zorries (Japanese sandals)	262.00
5 cases	assorted candies	201.28
3 cases	bubble gum	275.00
7 cases	mosquito coils	29.50
5 cases	Winston cigarettes	841.50
2 cases	assorted biscuits	129.52
5 cases	powdered soap	185.40
10 cases	laundry soap (bars?)	247.80
50 cases	assorted soft drinks	376.00
1 box	general merchandise?	168.76
800	copra bags	440.00
7 drums	gasoline	539.00
3 drums	kerosene	258.00
		$8 270.96
	Total price of food items	$6 557.50
	Total price of other items	$2 113.46

Invoices from the late summer and autumn of 1982 give some insight into the buying habits and levels of expenditures on Pingelap during a period when the store was being managed by a Peace Corps worker who kept the shelves well stocked according to purchasing demands. It was also a period of some prosperity on the atoll, as wage income from work on the airstrip, which was nearing completion this time, was at hand. During this period four shipments of goods arrived. These came on September 13, October 6, November 13, and December 7, representing one of the periods during which regular monthly sailings were observed. The lists show quite a large variety of merchandise. If the value of cement and rebars used in airstrip construction which were paid for by government funds is excluded, about 52 percent of the monetary worth of the shipments was for items other than food. If confections such as candy, cookies, and soft drinks are included as food (coffee and tea excluded) about 48 percent can be considered as contributing to the calorific needs of the population.

Table 8.3
Shipment of Merchandise Received by P.C.C.A., November 13, 1982

No. of pkgs.	Description of commodities	Total price
100 bags	rice	$561.00
20 bags	sugar 10/2 kilos	420.00
10 bags	sugar 12/5#	280.90
50 cases	assorted soft drinks	396.00
2 cases	Benson Hedges cigarettes	340.00
2 cases	roach killer	43.20
3 cases	Clorox 18 pts.	53.85
2 cases	Clorox 8-1/2 gal.	27.38
4 cases	bath soap	71.56
2 cases	ramen	183.54
3 cases	condensed milk	125.58
2 cases	candy bars	66.74
1 case	mosquito coils	73.82
10 cases	Kendall (motor) oil	283.10
2 cases	sandals	670.80
5 cases	batteries (flashlight)	488.50
1	bicycle	90.80
2 cases	matches	84.00
8 drums	gasoline	608.00
5 drums	kerosene	430.00
500	copra bags	275.00
13 drums	empty	253.50
130 bags	cement	911.30
50 pieces	rebars 1/2″	189.50
25 pieces	rebars 3/8″	53.25
30 sheets	roofing tin 3′ x 8′	257.10
6 each	bed sheets	51.18
30	towels	169.20
16 boxes	thread	204.48
6 cases	toothpaste	43.80
6 dozen	pencils	54.72
2 boxes	yarn(/)ties	34.92
2 boxes	steel wool	44.52

Table 8.3 *(continued)*

No. of pkgs.	Description of commodities	Total price
10 packages	fishing line	432.90
1 package	fishing line	101.55
4 dozen	bandeaux (?)	74.52
3 dozen	lighter flints	20.40
3 dozen	LOCC (?)	52.92
1 dozen	blank tape cassettes	16.08
1 dozen	hasps	6.05
4 dozen	elastic strips	34.84
2 dozen	needles (hand)	17.40
6 dozen	sewing (machine) needles	65.34
1 gross	envelopes	6.98
9 dozen	girl's panties	175.77
4 dozen	boy's briefs	29.28
1 gross	balloons	5.40
20	curtains	146.20
7 dozen	briefs (Pipes)	111.02
3 dozen	briefs (Hanes)	65.40
2 dozen	undershirts	41.44
1 pair	dungaree (Levis) trousers	23.66
1 pair	Sassoon (?)	18.21
17 pairs	knee length trousers	116.45
		$9 613.85
	Total price food items	$2 033.76
	Total price other items	$7 580.09

Among the food items that ranked highest during this period in these purchases for inventory, rice was first, at $2 816, and confections ranked second, at $2 120.06, with sugar next, at $1 335.00; followed by all canned protein foods at $844.41, and flour at $840.30. Granted that the temporary affluence may have elevated the expenditure on luxury foods like soft drinks and sweets, the amounts spent for essential dietary items were not great, especially when it is noted that cigarette orders were the second highest item, at $2 192.10 for the four-month period. This latter figure is especially interesting since church members in good standing were not supposed to smoke.

The inventories of fuel for cooking and light (kerosene) and for outboard motors (gasoline) were kept at unusually high levels during this period. The large orders of gasoline must have strongly affected the fishing activities on the island, if the reader recalls my reference to significant periods in 1975-76 and 1978 when trolling was curtailed due to gasoline shortages. The "other than food items" on the lists give some indication of articles which had become regarded as necessities by this time, including soaps, mosquito coils, sandals, sewing supplies, certain articles of clothing, and fishing equipment.

It would be helpful if one could supply an estimate as to how much of the nutritional needs of the population was being supplied by store foods at this time. As I indicated in Chapter 3 there are too may leaks in the overall picture to arrive at even a rough estimate of calorific needs on Pingelap. The other side of the input-output coin is no more accessible to quantitative analysis. While the above sampling of merchandise acquisitions at the cooperative store might give some rough indication of consumption, there were several other small stores run by Pingelapese which channelled small amounts of food products. These stores were usually run for the purpose of the proprietors getting products at wholesale prices, and most of what they ordered was used for family consumption. There was at this time as well another store run by an American married to a Pingelapese which provided a somewhat greater quantity of goods, including food, but I do not have records of inventory orders or purchases from that source.

Table 8.4
Shipment of Merchandise Received
by P.C.C.A., December 7, 1982

No. of pkgs.	Description of commodities	Total price
30 bags	sugar	$345.00
3 cases	corned beef	126.71
1 case	cookies	176.82
10 cases	lollipops	628.80
5 cases	baking powder	155.10
2 cases	Tang	104.58
1 case	mayonnaise (qts.)	30.33
55 cases	coffee	173.35
5 cases	spaghetti	135.10
5 cases	chicken wings	98.60
20 cases	assorted soft drinks	161.00
10 cases	whale meat	240.00
2 cases	navy biscuits 32/2	120.00
1 case	navy biscuits 64/2	57.84
2 cases	ship biscuits 64/2	102.84
3 cases	tea bags	53.22
5 cases	soy sauce	114.25
28 pairs	women's sandals	193.48
5 cases	bath soap	192.75
10 cases	laundry soap	237.80
5 cases	bath soap	161.25
5 drums	kerosene	430.00
7 drums	gasoline	532.00
600	copra bags	510.00
1 box	general merchandise[a]	559.61
		$5 640.93
	Total price food items	$2 596.97
	Total price other items	$3 043.96

[a] All non-food items.

Over periods of time there have been the fluctuations in purchasing power which I noted above, and I also mentioned large variations in household consumption habits. The supply of such local products as fish also vary widely over a typical year's economic cycle and also from year to year. Crops such as breadfruit also show year-to-year fluctuation in supply. Taking all of these variables into account as far as it is possible to do so, it would be difficult for me to imagine that more than one-fourth of the total nutritional requirements of the Pingelapese population would have come from outside products over any two-year period during the 1970s or 1980s. If one adds wastage, only part of which is consumed by domesticated animals, the balance of locally produced to imported foods swings even further in the direction of internally derived food sources. In this connection I want to stress again that local production of food on Pingelap, as well as some purchases, such as sugar and flour, are not restricted to providing daily human dietary requirements. The ceremonial requirements must be conceded as providing important motivation for local food production and, to a lesser extent, purchasing as well.

Summary

In this chapter I have explored the nature of external relations on the land tenure system of Pingelap during the period 1975-83. Following upon my discussion in the previous chapter regarding land tenure in the Pingelapese colonies, I examined the *kohwa* or stewardship system as it affected the ownership and use of land and taro on Pingelap. Considering the unrecognized (by Pingelap residents) ownership by non-residents, it is likely that fully one-third of the land and taro on the atoll was controlled by stewards rather than by actual owners. This circumstance, along with internal disputes over inheritance of property, seems sure to involve the Pingelapese increasingly in external legal decisions. So far the trend of those decisions has been to favour use and development of land by residents over norms which are considered by many Pingelapese as being part of the *kohwa* system, but pressures from colonists could challenge such decisions in the future.

Aside from the problems inherent in *kohwa* and involvement in outside legal decisions brought on by the implications of that system and by other potential land disputes, the land tenure system of Pingelap drew the islanders into outside economic considerations through the operation of the copra trade. While the contributions of that trade to total cash inflow fluctuated from year to year according to price and presence or absence of other sources of income, it appears destined to continue to play an important part in relations with the outside world. Copra and other cash sources provide for the purchase of equipment and supplies of various kinds, but they cannot be said to have supplied the bulk of foodstuffs for the islanders during the period under consideration. By and large Pingelap continued as a "subsistence plus" internal economy; the "plus" element being the surplus production which supported the heavy schedule of prestation events.

CHAPTER 9

The Pingelap Study in Comparative Perspective

In the foregoing pages I have represented Pingelap as being a "bountiful island" in terms of its having had a high level of subsistence potential which has sustained heavy populations in very restricted space. It has been at least implicit that the land tenure system which has evolved is in some essential way related to having maintained this condition. Yet I must return to questions raised at the beginning in order to clarify this possible relationship. These are: (1) to what degree can the existing system be considered a response to increased pressures on land? and (2) how adequately has the system served to cope with such problems of crowding that may be said to have existed?

In considering the situation that I observed on the atoll during the period of my study, 1975-83, the population level was well below its peak, which had occurred about the turn of the present century, so that pressures on land should have been eased. One could, indeed, argue that certain resources were under-exploited during the time of my visits. Certainly, coconuts had been more widely used in the diet in earlier times. The manufacture of pandanus paste as carried out in other atoll societies could have provided another important source of food. The taro patch appeared to be supplying almost unlimited quantities of corms, and many of the corms were left in the ground long after they had reached harvestable size. A significant number of *peliensapw*(s) were overgrown and showed little evidence of having been used for months or even years. With regard to marine resources, my description of a year's cycle of exploitation showed periodic shortages of certain species and unfavourable weather conditions which resulted in an uneven supply over that period. But the chief limitations imposed on the most important technique, that of trolling, were chronic shortages of gasoline and engine breakdowns. Significant amounts of terrestrial products were seen to be thrown away after the frequent prestation events. To be sure there were limitations on the energy which could be expended by the existing population. In this respect the Pingelapese must be

Notes to Chapter 9 are on pp. 252-54.

regarded on the whole as very energetic, and in times of heavier populations, a larger workforce would have been available for more intense resource utilization. But in spite of an overall picture of calorific affluence and less than complete utilization of existing resources, there were signs that the land tenure system was breaking down. Let me go back in time in order to try to reach an understanding of the possible relationships between that system and the conditions offered by the atoll environment of Pingelap.

The Evolution of the Pingelap Land Tenure System

In Chapter 2, several versions of the development of the existing land tenure system were given on the basis of informant testimony. There did appear to be general agreement that communal land use under the direction of the paramount chief was the initial arrangement. One informant outlined a system of alternating land use under that direction. What transpired later is a matter of some disagreement. While taro holdings were said to have been owned individually for a much longer period, there was a division of land areas a short time before the disastrous typhoon of the 1770s, according to the oral traditions. One version of this division has it that property moved directly into the hands of individual men, while another appears to depict ownership as passing to the level of the *keinek*. After the typhoon another division of lands is said to have taken place. Again there is some disagreement as to whether properties were assigned to individuals or to a higher level of units.

In moving to an era where histories of land transfers are available, about the middle of the nineteenth century, it is clear that individual ownership was well established for men, and that women were beginning to get dowry shares. These histories also indicate that the dowry system was not fully in force until some time later. By about the beginning of the twentieth century, uneven fertility between families stimulated the rise of adoption, which had the effect of levelling family sizes to some degree, providing heirs in the cases of otherwise childless families, and relieving unfavourable land/man ratios in large families. Those adopted out usually received small portions of estates at the times of their adoption.[1] While emigration schemes in the present century did alleviate the apparent gross overcrowding on the atoll, demographic imbalances continued for some time and resulted in ongoing strains on the system. Stewardship of lands of absentee owners who lived in the colonies made available in some cases additional resources for land-poor individuals, but perhaps just as often aggravated existing inequalities, and that system promised to be the source of much conflict involving legal decisions.

If one accepts the general impression of evolution through stages of progressively smaller units of ownership, there is still the question of how intimately such a process is related to conditions of increasing pressures on land, or to ecological-demographic explanation. Regarding the dynamics of such a possible process, oral historians on Pingelap conceive of the motives for instituting individual ownership of property as superiority of such ownership in requiring greater responsibility in managing and harvesting products of the land. One might interject another possible impetus for such a conversion to the level of individual ownership, that increasing populations had put a great strain on the system of communal use and that a more precise system had to be instituted in order to make possible more efficient use of resources. This, to me, is a logical association, but there is little actual evidence to support it. Further, another redistribution is said to have occurred in immediate post-typhoon times, when the population was at its nadir. Rather than reverting to a system of communal property which could be more adaptive in a period of decreased populations, the division took place involving smaller social units. On the face of these accounts, the argument for a movement from larger to smaller units of ownership on the basis of expanding populations would seem to be invalidated. If, however, such division practices had been established at earlier times in response to such conditions of overcrowding, custom might have exerted pressures toward the re-establishment of such a system.[2]

Certainly, land tenure histories reach far enough back to indicate that individual ownership by men was established, and that by women was growing at a time when populations on the atoll had reached only 50 percent of the eventual peak, that is about 450 in 1853 (Eilers 1934: 413). I will leave for the moment this question of the evolution of the system on the basis of ecological-demographic response to move to the second question raised above, that of adequacy of the system in dealing with problems of population expansion.

The system as based on individual ownership of land areas and sections of the main taro patch, with some special adjustments, has some obvious advantages over others. First, there would appear to be fewer occasions for dispute than would be the case where overlapping and conflicting claims would occur in systems based on joint-ownership principles, and the system would provide buttresses against the disputes, which would be expected to grow in number with increased population density. Then there are factors of security. Given an environment where natural disasters can occur periodically and destroy crops in sections of the atoll, the fragmentation of ownership areas which has developed over time has certain advantages. There is also security in terms of social exigencies. For instance, dowry assures women of property in cases of divorce. Gifts of land to children adopted out assures them of property if they return to the natural parents, even though they might lose rights to properties which would be willed to them by adoptive parents. Subsequent discussion will show that one of the solutions to land tenure imbalances in other atoll societies has been expansion of usufruct rights. But the lack of ambiguity in assigning individual ownership rights allows clear processes of conveyance and avoids the sorts of frictions which I have described for the chief expression of usufruct in the Pingelap case, the *kohwa* arrangements.

All in all, the system of individual ownership with the specific form that it has taken on Pingelap has worked through much of the history of Pingelap in delaying what has been conventionally regarded as the end effects of such a system — the threat of reduction of individual holdings to the degree that further divisions among heirs would become meaningless. While I have so far in this chapter considered mainly the gross population-to-land area factors as they appear to relate to the evolution of the existing system, it is, rather, the adjustments which prevent too gross imbalances among individual landholders that is the most crucial question involving demographic-ecological relationships. While the bounty of Pingelap would be unequal to some definite level of population on the atoll, it is not altogether clear that such a level has ever actually been reached. This is especially true if there could have been a time when the intense schedule of prestation events had been curtailed. Figures presented in earlier chapters have revealed considerable inequalities in land ownership, even given biases in sampling which would tend to underplay them. Such imbalances are probably inevitable in any system of land tenure when demographic fluctuations occur, whether on the level of kin groups such as lineages or on those of extended or nuclear families. But it is my conviction that certain ingredients in the system which has evolved on Pingelap have delayed the reduction of individual holdings to a level where subsistence is not possible for the families of such individuals.

The most prominent adjustments to demographic fluctuations that have been employed in the Pingelap case have been dowry and adoption. With regard to awarding women shares, the multiplicity of sources of properties has been implemented. Figures 9.1 and 9.2 should illustrate this process.

Figure 9.1
Routes of Inheritance: Men Only

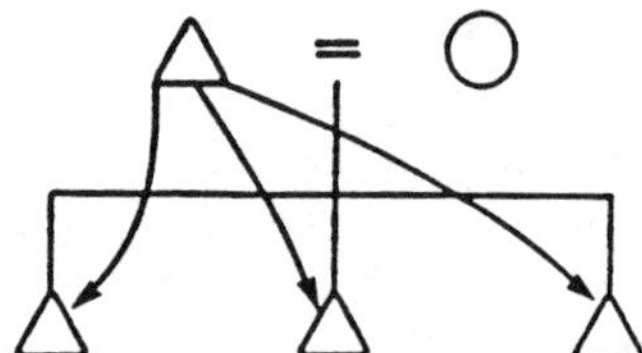

Figure 9.2
Routes of Inheritance: Including Women

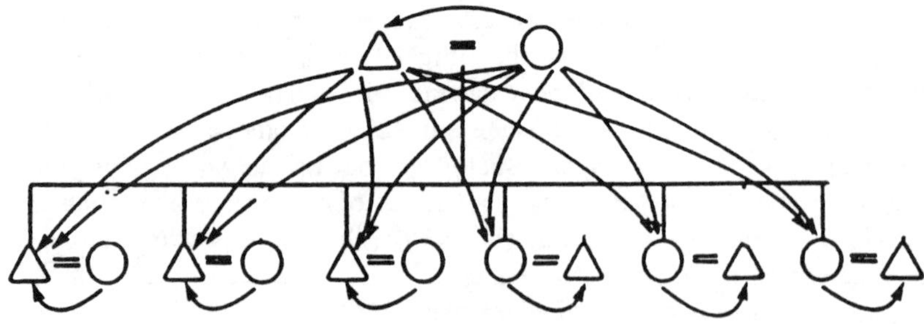

In Figure 9.1, with land division operating on the extended family level, the father of the sibling group shown divides his estate among his sons. By including women, as shown in Figure 9.2, the theoretical sources of land have tripled. In cases where holdings in the family of in-marrying women are substantial, their shares would be, of course, significant, but even if small they increase the options of dispersal. The mother or wife of the testator, the wives of sons as they marry, given the almost exclusive patrilocal residence and formation of land-use units, and eventually, the wives of grandsons of the original couple also bring shares of varying sizes into the usufruct sphere of extended families. Further, these holdings, in most cases, become part of the transferrable property of such units. Dowry shares have been shown to be usually quite small individually, but cumulatively they can and have added significantly to the holdings of certain extended families. But it is only those families which have favourable (from the standpoint of land tenure) sex ratios which do so benefit. This raises the question of the reverse side of the effects of the dowry system on land transferrals.

Figure 9.2 also shows losses from the depicted extended family through dowry. In this hypothetical case, given an equal number of males and females, one would expect the losses and gains brought on by dowry to balance out. In other cases where there are more sons than daughters the gains would be expected to predominate over the losses. Conversely, with more daughters than sons, the losses would be greater than the gains. While the system results in smaller accretions from the various sources than when the father or head of the extended family unit was the only source of property, on balance, the multiplicity of sources assures a better likelihood of more individuals getting some portion of land and taro holdings when women were drawn into the network of land inheritance. In its eventual effect, institution of the dowry system made marriage an institution intimately involved in property transmission, both horizontally and vertically.

The other chief practice which served to balance people-to-land ratios has been adoption. This adjustment worked well during the German and Japanese periods of uneven fertility, but when a better balance in family sizes was achieved in American times, adoption virtually disappeared (Damas 1983b)[3] and could not be relied upon to help equalize imbalances in land ownership. Until that time, however, such factors as dowry and adoption working within the overall system of granting land to individuals had by and large succeeded in warding off the most drastic end results of the system — the eventual landlessness of certain individuals. That contingency was, however, becoming apparent by the 1950s. In the discussion of Chapter 7, I pointed out that, while a number of men in the Mwalok B sample were not acquiring land in that colony, most or all could claim holdings either there or on Pingelap itself, even though the latter property was subject to the uncertainties of the *kohwa* system. The situation was otherwise for the women of that generation, who by and large were excluded from inheritance, and the practice of dowry was also not implemented for them. In the Mand colony some of the men who immigrated in 1954-55 lacked land on the atoll, while about half of their offspring generation were left totally outside the Pingelapese inheritance picture. At this point it is clear that the land tenure system which incorporated the total Pingelapese population was breaking down.

There was a stage in the developmental cycle of the domestic group which offered an option that served to delay the occurrence of actual landlessness. I have mentioned that informants thought that, in cases of severe property shortages within the holdings of extended families, ownership shifted to the level of a fraternal joint family, a unit which represented an alternative cooperative, commensal, and sharing unit on the death of the father. I could document several cases where this situation did occur, rather than the more common splitting into separate units headed by the sons of the testator. But not every one of these cases was one of land deprivation and, further, segments of the estates were still apportioned to some individuals with full rights of conveyance in each case. Eventually it became clear that there was only partial resolution to the seemingly inevitable problem of reduction of holdings to a level where support of individuals would not be possible. That is, a distinction had to be made between nominal ownership, with its right of conveyance, and usufruct privileges. While, in particular, younger sons could use the land and taro resources of such a fraternal joint family, they were not getting land which they could pass on to their potential heirs. It was, then, their children and others who might be expected to inherit land from them who were being pushed off the end of the plank. It might be argued that a sytem of heritable usufruct privileges, as occurs on other atolls, could be established so that one's progeny could be assured some land to work and thus not be greatly deprived with regard to subsistence and copra proceeds. Pingelapese, however, have not adopted such an adjustment, and it is my view that such an arrangement would not sit well with them. As indicated in Chapter 7, so strong is the attachment to land that each man, at least, wants to have the security and the esteem which rests in outright ownership of definite pieces of land and rows in the taro patch.

It would appear that only redistribution of property on the atoll, as well as an increased fragmentation of lands in the colonies, could resolve these problems, but then only if the total population of Pingelapese ceases to expand at the rate it has during the American period. The difficulties of engineering a redistribution of land and taro holdings on the atoll would, in my view, entail such fierce resistance from individual landowners that such a possibility seems to pale from the realm of possibility. In the 1980s, wage labour opportunities in the colonies were in large measure obviating the need for subdividing properties in the colonies, but it also appeared that such opportunities were not expanding to the degree that they would continue to absorb immigrants from the atoll.

In order to place the problems of the Pingelapese in perspective it is useful to compare conditions on a neighbouring atoll which had, and continues to have, problems similar to those found among the Pingelapese.

Land Tenure on Mwaekil (Mokil) Atoll

It has been my good fortune that the most strictly comparable atoll society in terms of geographical proximity and ecological similarity has been the subject of studies which have included a survey of landholdings and an examination of land tenure practices. The anthropologists Weckler (1949, 1953) and Bentzen (1949) and the geographer Murphy (1948, 1949, 1950) worked on Mwaekil in 1947-48 and produced studies of land tenure which together provide a more complete picture than was possible for me to achieve on Pingelap.

Mwaekil is located 52 sea miles WNW of Pingelap and lies in the same moist belt, though the measurement of temperatures and rainfall which I was able to discover for Pingelap were not available for the former atoll. Mwaekil occupies about the same space in the Pacific as does its neighbour, but the land area is only about 70 percent that of Pingelap at .478 square miles while its lagoon is larger, 2.67 vs. .465 square miles for Pingelap. During a brief visit to Mwaekil in April 1983 I observed that there were only a few breadfruit trees on the island where the village is located (Karlap), which was said by Bentzen (1949: 44) to have been the place of greatest concentration of that tree at the time of his study in 1947-48. There were only a very few small canoes made from breadfruit tree trunks in evidence, while there was a large number of locally manufactured whaleboats to be seen, part of the lumber of which they were constructed being imported. By the time of my visit most houses were built of cement blocks, but there were a few constructed of wood still remaining from an earlier building phase that were in ramshackle condition. The village is built on the lagoon shore, and a short distance from the beach a number of open-sided, thatch-roofed boat houses served as lounging and working places during daylight hours. The taro patch lies directly behind and in close proximity to the village. Some activity was devoted to unloading and loading the field trip vessel as it stopped at the atoll, first when coming from Pohnpei and then returning from the East. I noticed torch-fishing at night and preparation of copra during the days of my stay on the atoll.

Aside from these few visual impressions from my own brief visit, there are available detailed accounts from 1947-48 by the above-mentioned workers which include considerable material on economy and land tenure practices that can be compared with the data which have been presented here. Bentzen (1949: 39) and Weckler (1949: 10) report that taro was the most important subsistence crop, as it was available throughout the year, with no tradition of the patch having been closed during the breadfruit season, as was formerly the case on Pingelap. Breadfruit and pandanus have the same periodicity as on the latter atoll, with pandanus being considered, along with sugar cane, as confections rather than important elements in the diet. Coconuts are described by Bentzen (1949: 42) as having a great number of uses, and it is probable that that fruit product has been used more extensively in recent years than on Pingelap, for breadfruit does not play nearly as great a role in the diet. Copra appears to have had at least as important a part in the economy as on Pingelap. For instance, for the calendar year 1969 it has been reported (TTPI 1972) that Mwaekil pro-

Map 7
Mwaekil Atoll

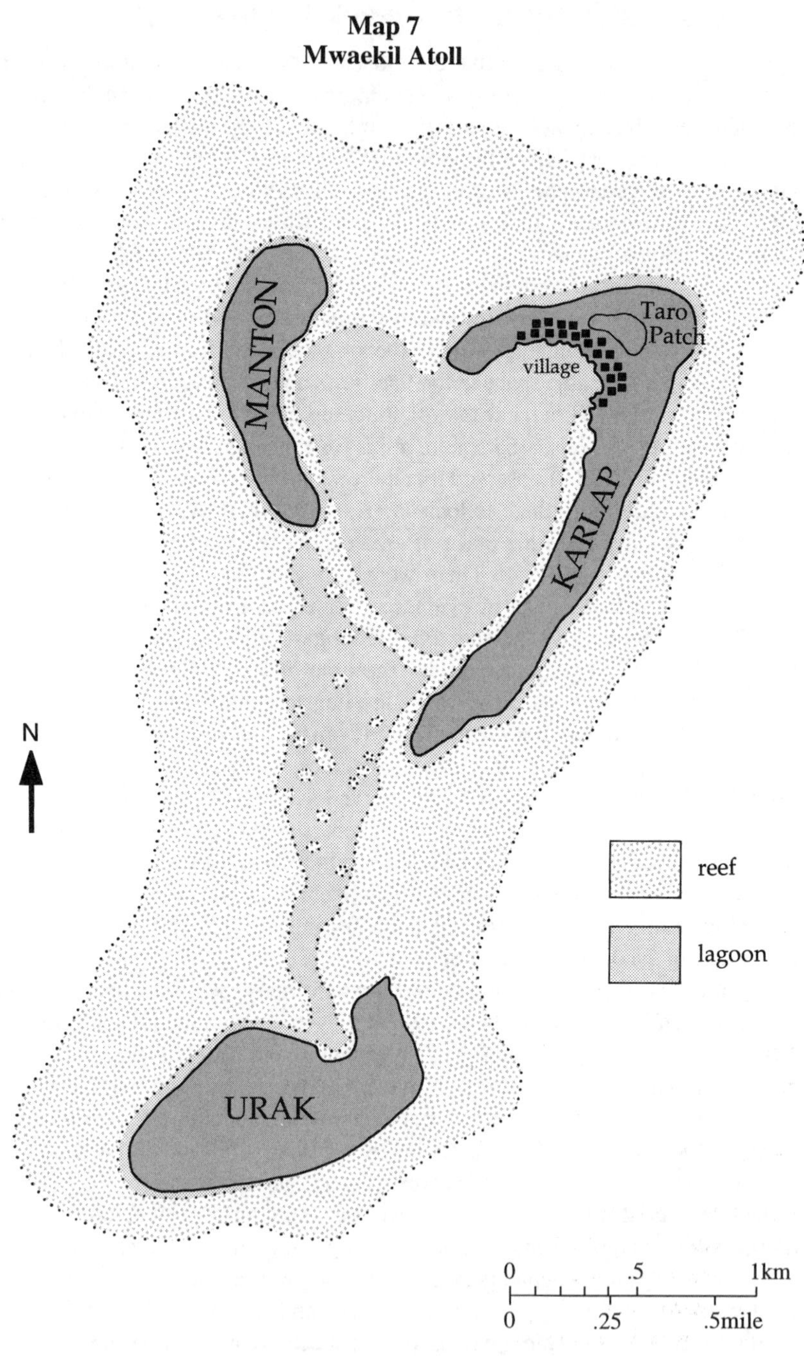

duced $18 679 worth of copra as compared to Pingelap's $20 448, despite having less than half the population of the latter atoll. There was also a more active manufacture of handicrafts both in the time of Bentzen's and Weckler's study and in the 1980s.

Reef fishing appears to have been less frequently practised than on Pingelap, though I observed torch fishing of flying fish which was also described by Bentzen (1949: 58-61) as being a favourite sport, as well as providing substantial amounts of food. None of the sources mention long-lining for tuna, but one informant with whom I talked on the atoll said that technique, called *solong* on Mwaekil, was employed, though I could not determine to what extent.

The islands of Mwaekil atoll are divided into *kousapw*(s), and smaller divisions which appear to correspond to the *lepinsapw*(s) of Pingelap were formerly recognized. The most important divisions with regard to land tenure are, as in the case of the neighbouring atoll, the *peliensapw*(s) (here called *pelienjapw*(s). The taro patch is similarly divided into major sections called, again, *maekah*(s) while individual holdings are called *lolo*(s) rather than *manime*(s). The role of the extended family, or in local parlance, the *paneyney*, as the unit of land use, is also similar to the practice on Pingelap, while the unit of actual ownership is less clear, as will be discussed below. With regard to descent units, the function of the matrilineal clans as exogamic entities has been abandoned to a greater degree than has been the case on Pingelap. The patrilineally based category, here called the *kainek*, has lost its earlier function of title conveyance. Indeed, the political system of Mwaekil never attained the elabouration found on Pingelap (Damas 1983a) with only two titles, one sacred and one secular, formerly existing. But from early in the nineteenth century only the sacred or Nanua title has remained, while taking on secular significance (Weckler 1949: 44). Beginning sometime later in the nineteenth century, this post was more often filled through consensus than through any hereditary right (ibid.: 66). There is a stronger case made by my Mwaekilese informants for the *kainek* being involved in land tenure than was made by my Pingelapese informants for the equivalent unit of the *keinek*. Neither Bentzen, Weckler, nor Murphy identified the *kainek*, whose existence I discovered in working with informants a generation after the visits of those scholars. Weckler (ibid.: 73) does mention three "lineages" based on descent from three males who survived the great typhoon of the 1770s (a disaster which caused as much damage and similar depopulation in its aftermath on Mwaekil as it did on Pingelap). Weckler does not describe the nature of this unit and may have used the term analogously rather than after the strictest anthropological definition. My investigations revealed that the structure of the *kainek* is identical with that of the *keinek*, with its core being based on serial filiation through males to a known ancestor, but with membership also being attained through in-marriage by females and lost through their out-marriage. Both sexes change membership through adoption.[4]

Mwaekilese informants were more definite than those from Pingelap in identifying this descent-based unit with land tenure practices, even though for

Mwaekil that function has been considerably compromised in recent years. There did appear to survive a stronger patrilineal bias to land inheritance at the time of the Bentzen-Weckler-Murphy studies than I had found on Pingelap. There is very little in these earlier reports about the pretyphoon history of Mwaekil, except that land was said to have been used communally, as on Pingelap, and that the practice of individual ownership in the taro patch was established very shortly after that natural disaster. Weckler's (ibid.: 50, 104) land tenure histories support his thesis that dowry was not a part of the original division of the islands among the three surviving adult males, but was instituted in the first transferrals from those individuals and gained in strength thereafter. Weckler's (ibid.: 10) description of Mwaekilese land inheritance points to land passing through males as being of higher status and being in firmer control by heads of extended families than that brought in through dowry or adoption. While permission of women is said to be required for transferral of dowry properties, as is ideally at least, the case on Pingelap, on the latter atoll there is no such sharp separation of lands and taro rows acquired through adoptions from properties gained through patrilineal inheritance. In fact case histories examined in Chapter 5 show indiscriminate transferrals of the various classes of property, that transferrals from women to males are very common, and actually predominate over those between females. Weckler (ibid.: 107), on the other hand, states for Mwaekil that not only are principal *paneyney* properties passed from male to male, but that there is also a strong tendency for dowry properties to pass from mother to daughter, and there appears to be parallel inheritance through patrilineal and matrilineal routes.

While, as in the Pingelap case, individual ownership of sections of the taro patch seems to have had a long history on Mwaekil, the picture of the ownership of *pelienjapw*(s) is clouded in Weckler's and Bentzen's accounts. Consider the following statements: "Aboriginally, all resources were public property and first fruits had to be brought to the king to be 'blessed' before anyone could partake of the year's crop or the season's first catch of migratory species of fish" (Weckler 1953: 563-64) but, "According to modern informants all the land of Mokil was privately owned even before the first contacts with whalers. My accounts of land transferred go back to the original division between the heads of three families that survived the 18th century typhoon" (ibid.: 564). With regard specifically to the advent of the division of the dry land area into plots, Weckler gives two versions. In one of these he (ibid.: 565) depicts an edict by a newly invested paramount chief who, having recently returned from years at sea, sought to emulate white men's conception of property on the islands. The other version attributes this division to the advent of the copra trade and the increased value of the coconut trees (1949: 89-90). In either case the segmentation of dry land areas into *pelienjapw*(s) is said to have occurred during the 1870s. The version which attributes this division to the edict of the chief, Zacharias, contains a contradiction, since "he ruled that henceforth people could gather produce only from *their own land*" (italics mine) (Weckler 1953: 565). Weckler does appear to be aware of a sense of personal property for the years prior to the copra days, for he refers to "pseudo private ownership" as predating contact, though he casts some doubt upon his sources in the matter.

In their surveys of the atoll's islands Bentzen (1949) and Murphy (1948) identify the *pelienjapw*(s) marked on their maps as being owned by the *paneyney*(s) rather than by individuals and they also emphasize the strong role of the *paneyney* heads as managers of lands. However, ambiguous elements creep into descriptions of levels of ownership; for instance, the following:

> When asked the ownership of different parcels of land, as when making a map of land holdings in the field, Mokilese informants will almost always give you the first name of the paneyney head as the owner of each plot. When informants are questioned more closely, however, as in my tracing the detailed genealogy they will then give you the names of the actual individual owners (Weckler 1949: 105).

Bentzen casts some light on this question as follows:

> Individual ownership of coconut lands is recognized in the case of dowry lands brought into the paneyey by marriage or in the case of land that is acquired by a junior member by gift or adoption. Land that has been divided among several brothers . . . may be worked together as one paneyey and the products shared, but here, too, individual ownership is recognized (ibid.: 20).

That source also refers to partitioning the parcels beyond that which is revealed in his maps (Bentzen 1949: 24). During my short stay on Mwaekil I was able to identify the major divisions which the earlier sources had indicated on their maps. They were marked on their boundaries by pairs of coconut trees bending outwardly from each other. While I was becoming aware of subdivisions of such parcels, I could not discern any markers for such divisions as I walked around the island, Karlap, on which the village is located. It was only after I had returned to Sokehs Island and had interviewed Mwaekilese there that I learned of the procedure for marking individual land plots. It seems that at the extreme ends of the strips of properties coconut trees are planted at regular intervals, thus dividing the parcels longitudinally. Finally, with regard to earlier descriptions of land tenure on Mwaekil, Weckler (1949: 97) reports a developmental cycle of the domestic unit which bears close resemblance to that which I have given for Pingelap. At the death of the testator there were, again, two options, dividing the estate among the sons and thus creating separate *paneyney(s)*, or a "partnership" arrangement whereby the brothers would work the property jointly under the direction of the eldest.

The ambiguity found in the earlier accounts of Mwaekilese land tenure could not be fully resolved on the basis of statements of informants interviewed on the atoll and in the Mwaekilese colony on Sokehs Island in 1983. I found contradictions between statements of several informants and even some internal inconsistencies on the part of individual informants. Two thought that the practice of giving the eldest brother control of *paneyney* lands was a custom introduced by the Germans and that the practice of dividing land among all the sons was the true traditional practice. Other informants thought that both options had long histories on the atoll. Still another stated that there had been a definite shift in practice since the time of the Bentzen-Weckler-Murphy studies toward individual ownership. While the *derak* ceremony was known, it has seldom been observed in recent years. As to the degree of control exercised by the *paneyney* head, my information is somewhat at odds with the description of the earlier workers, though change may have occurred since the studies of 1947-48. My informants conceded that while the oldest male might direct activities within that unit, including organization of joint production and distribution of products, he could not control disposal of land in cases where individual plots have been assigned by the testator. In following through two life histories, one of a man of 76, and another of a man in his 80's, both testified that in their cases land had been divided among offspring by the father. In neither case was the *derak* ceremony observed.

In weighing all evidence at my disposal I have concluded that rather than reports of the earlier scholars who worked on Mwaekil being misleading, or my informants being confused, the land tenure situation on Mwaekil has been in a state of flux for some years. At the same time, there does appear to have been a move toward more complete individual ownership and away from *paneyney* control in recent years in the *pelienjapw*(s). Individual ownership of sections of the taro patch was firmly established by the time of the 1947-48 studies and may have had the long history depicted by oral tradition. The actual maps made by Bentzen and by Murphy show less fractionalization of land areas than that which occurred on Pingelap, with 298 acres of land, exclusive of the taro areas, being divided into 379 plots or an average of .79 acre each. On Pingelap 407 acres of such land was divided into about 1100 plots at the time of my studies, or an average of .37 of an acre each. This appears to indicate a larger ownership unit for Mwaekil, and indeed, Weckler (1949), Bentzen (1948), and Murphy (1948) identify ownership of these *pelienjapw*(s) with *paneyney*(s). If, however, the more subtly marked subdivisions indicating individual ownership were to be taken into account there might well be the degree of fractionalization seen on Pingelap.

In taking together the material at hand from Pingelap with that from Mwaekil, the following formulation is suggested, regarding the direction of evolution of their land tenure systems:

Communal use under chief → "Lineage" → Extended family → Individuals

In this process, the division of taro patches to the level of individual owners appears to have clearly preceded that of dry land areas on both atolls. In fact there has to be less conviction that tenure in the wet taro patches passed through each of the stages in this scheme. Indeed, there is no reason why the two different types of land use should display identical transmission patterns.[5]

If the stages depicted in the above scheme do indeed conform to increasing pressure on land, there does not appear to have been any clear-cut break points when each stage was reached. Indeed, the apparent state of flux in levels of ownership seen in Mwaekil suggests that long periods of transition probably transpired between the stages. Table 9.1 shows that while Pingelap began the post-typhoon era of history with only a slightly larger survival population, by the middle of the nineteenth century there was a fivefold difference numerically and a fourfold difference in density between the two atolls. Long before that time individual ownership of both taro and dry land holdings had been instituted on Pingelap, with densities no greater than 600-700 per square mile. In the case of Mwaekil, however, based on the reports of Bentzen, Weckler, and Murphy, the unit of ownership was still ambiguous when population levels on that atoll had reached their maximum of about 800-900 persons per square mile. Table 9.1 also shows that densities on Mwaekil never did reach those seen on Pingelap at the turn of the twentieth century and that, evidentially, pressures on dry land holdings were never as crucial there as they have been at various stages of Pingelap history, though this must be seen as only a very rough comparison.

Table 9.1
Population Estimates for Pingelap and Mwaekil[6]

Mwaekil				Pingelap			
Source[a]	Year	Pop.	Pers./ mi.^{2}	Source	Year	Pop.	Pers./ mi.^{2}
Weckler	1775	25-30	58	Morton	1775	30-40	52
Eilers	1853	90	188	Eilers	1853	450	666
Morton	1901	170	356	Eilers	1899	1 000	1 479
Weckler	1905?	214	448	Bascom	1920	601	889
Weckler	1933?	269	563	Bascom	1925	601	889
Bryan	1935	258	540	Bascom	1930	638	944
Weckler	1948	423	885	Bascom	1935	694	1 027
Morton	1970	393	822	Bascom	1946	639	945
Fitzsimmons	1973	321	672	Coulter	1954	700	1 036
Fitzsimmons	1977	327	684	Morton	1970	815	1 206
				Fitzsimmons	1973	641	948
				Damas	1976	676	1 000
				Damas	1983	753	1 114

a Some of the sources indicated here were secondary because of the difficulty in securing original documents. Figures for Eilers include, for 1853, Hammet, and for 1899, Agassiz. On the basis of conversations with Dr. Morton and my own researches I have expanded the former's estimates for 1775 to range to 40 for Pingelap. Bascom's figures come from Japanese census as apparently are figures cited by Bryan. Weckler's estimates are abstracted from a graph (Weckler 1953: 560) so that precise dates are not available except for 1948. Morton cites Herrman for the Mwaekil 1901 estimates.

Given the acknowledged greater importance of taro holdings, a better comparison might be one based on space given over to that source of food. There are available two estimates as to the supportability of this most intensively cultivated of the agricultural products found on these atolls. Alkire (1978: 30) suggests that from 25 to 27 people can be supported by an acre of Cyrtosperma and Colocasia. Using these figures, on the basis of its 25 acres of taro patch, Pingelap would support 625-75 people, a population corresponding to the censuses of the Japanese period (see Table 9.1). For Mwaekil, Bentzen (1949: 31) wrote that taro areas had been expanded from six to eight acres after about 1940. Eight acres devoted to taro farming would, according to Alkire's formula mean supportability for 200 to 216 people rather than the population of 423 which lived on the island at the period at which that acreage had been achieved. There is, however, another formula offered by Brady (1970: 150, 1974: 167) of one acre of dry land and 1 080 square feet of taro holdings per capita. Application of these figures would yield a population maximum for Pingelap of 1 007 which corresponds closely with its peak population and leaves plenty of margin for later numbers. For Mwaekil a figure of 322 falls short of the peak numbers but does correspond fairly well with the populations throughout most of the American period. With regard to the dry land estimate of one person per acre of Brady, that ratio was markedly less than that found in times of actual peak populations, with Pingelap's 407 acres not devoted to taro, and the equivalent of Mwaekil's 298 acres. Whichever of the two scales is employed, Mwaekil appears to have been decidedly disadvantaged when compared with Pingelap in the immediate post-war period when the studies on that atoll were being made, and this assessment probably justifies Weckler's (1949: 95) and Murphy's (1948: 613) concern with overcrowding at that time.

While the above comparison is suggestive of a degree of crowding which at times might have been critical, a far more significant gauge is the extent of variability in holdings, with the minimums reflecting a truer index of land pressures. In the case of Pingelap, I have reported above that by the time of the founding of the Mand colony in 1954 there were men who were actually landless on the atoll. Extrapolating from later data, it is also probable that certain men controlled over 30 000 square metres of dry land and over 100 rows of taro at that same time. Comparison with Mwaekil is difficult because the early workers expressed ownership on the extended family level. They did provide per capita figures by *paneyney*, and Murphy (1948: 601) found a per capita range among the *paneyney(s)* of from 0.15 acres to 3.29 acres in 1947. For the same period Weckler (1949: 119) found the range to be from 0.24 to 3.22 acres. Bentzen (1949: 21) actually computed running feet of taro rows in his calculations and found the range per capita by *paneyney* [he counted 41 *paneyney(s)* as compared to Murphy's 39] to vary from 55 to 785 running feet. While it is difficult to convert these figures to those provided by Brady, it should be clear that both in the cases of dry land and taro holdings the lower end of the scales for Mwaekil were well below his estimates of supportability.

There is evidence for Mwaekil that the taro areas had been expanded in previous years, particularly at the time of peak populations which coincided with the studies of the late 1940s (ibid.: 31). While I do not have such evidence from Pingelap, it is likely that such expansion also occurred during the nineteenth century when that atoll was reaching peak numbers. With regard to gross per capita taro holdings, Pingelap was in a decidedly more favourable situation after World War II and at the times of my study than was Mwaekil, for its taro area appears to have been expanded to a level to support over 1 000 people, if Brady's estimates are valid. However, even though the population has declined considerably on the atoll itself since that peak, the problem of unequal distribution of individual ownership still persists. Coulter (1957: 328), in his visit to Pingelap in 1954, suggested that pressures could be relieved if the taro patch were to be expanded. Interestingly, an informant opined that this would be a difficult project, since owners of adjacent property would be unwilling to yield dry land ground to such expansion by others.

The preceding chapter reviewed cases of land disputes for the Pingelap population. Such factors as adoption, illegitimacy, the status of oral wills, and absentee ownership, particularly in recent years, and the complications brought on by *kohwa* were cited as sources of dispute. Given the close similarities of the Pingelap and Mwaekil land tenure systems, it is not surprising that most of these sources of dispute are shared between the two atolls. However, at the time of Weckler's study large-scale emigration had not taken place from Mwaekil as it would in later years. Weckler (1949: 113) thought that there would be little problem if those absent from the atoll returned and reaffirmed claims to properties. In contradistinction to this position is the fact that in seven of the twelve cases of land dispute that he examined (ibid.: 124-43), absenteeism was involved. There were, on the other hand, several sources and conditions of dispute which occurred on Mwaekil that were much rarer or absent on Pingelap. One of these was disputes over boundaries. It is clear that the vagueness of boundaries on Mwaekil, as mentioned above, and as compared to their precision and prominence on Pingelap, accounts for this difference. In the Mwaekil cases the paramount chief interfered in decisions and even appropriated properties. With the council of chiefs operating together on Pingelap in traditional times, decision-making in land tenure matters was more diffused. While Weckler cites participation by Spanish, German, and Japanese administrations in land decisions (ibid.), they appear to have been largely ignored. The system of courts in which such decisions were made in the Trust Territory phase of Micronesian history was not yet established at the time of Weckler's study in 1947-48. There are few references to Mwaekil in the oral history of Pingelap, but as I mentioned in Chapter 3, since fishing canoes from the latter atoll would at times sail within sight of Mwaekil, it is more than likely that contacts were made throughout the history of the two atolls, rather than only those which are documented or cited in oral history for the late nineteenth century onward. With regard to possible effects of interchange between the two atolls, several important similarities in the land tenure system can be cited. Both the *keinek* on Pingelap and its cognate unit *kainek* on Mwaekil show evidence of having been involved in land tenure. Further, its structure being basically patrilineal agrees in both places as contrasted to the term being applied to a matrilineal unit on Pohnpei. In both atolls the *peyneyney* or *paneney* is the basic group of land use. In both cases there is a clear trend toward individual ownership of property beginning with the taro holdings and evolving to include land areas. That this latter development represents responses to similar conditions of overcrowding has been argued. On the other hand, the close geographical proximity of the two atolls makes one suspect that diffusion also had a role in this convergence. While the adjustments to conditions of overcrowding are almost identical, they are also highly unusual or even unique in the Pacific. As the following review will illustrate, other Pacific atolls have been confronted with conditions of overcrowding, and responses other than those seen on Pingelap and Mwaekil have developed.

Atoll Land Tenure: A Sampling of Congruity and Variation

Moving from Pingelap's closest neighbour to other Carolinean atolls, Alkire (1974) has presented a detailed study of land tenure in "The Woleai," a group of five atolls in the Central Carolines. Here the matrilineage is the chief unit of land tenure, though control of varying degrees operate on the matriclan, subclan, and inter-island *sawei* levels as well (ibid.: 45-54). There was a variation in population per square mile which ranges from about 300 to over 900 (ibid.: 42) in the inhabited islands of this group at the time of his study in the 1960s, but there is also some evidence for far greater populations in precontact times. For instance, Alkire (1978: 34) estimates an early nineteenth-century population of 1 000 for Lamotrek atoll, a figure which would be equivalent to 2 638 persons per square mile. This is, of course, much higher than even the peak reached in Pingelap. If, as I have argued above, a more significant correlation can be made with taro acreage, the 58 acres given over to that crop, while far exceeding Alkire's range of 25-27 people per acre, is not much above that which could be accommodated by Brady's formula. In this case nearly two-thirds of the patch was not in use at the time of Alkire's study, when there were about 200 people living on the atoll (Alkire 1965: 75). With regard to land tenure practices in the Woleai, while most land was held on the group level, as noted above, certain property was held by individuals:

> This type of fragmentation of land rights seems to involve taro "swamp land" more often than "interior land." This situation probably arises because of the nature of taro-land exploitation. Taro, unlike most "hard land" crops, requires constant care and this is usually the responsibility of the women who received the land as a gift. If help is needed she obtains it from her daughters (Alkire 1974: 55).

The association of individual tenure with taro land is again suggested in this case, though the frequency of such arrangements seems to be rare, according to Alkire's description. Given the long period of contact and subsequent drastic depopulation in this region, we cannot speculate as to the possible association with individual tenure and more extensive taro farming in the past.

Any association between swelling populations and adoption of individual ownership appears to be confounded in the cases of Pis-Losap in the Mortlock Islands, where densities greater than those found on Pingelap have continued.

While our source (Severance 1976) gives little information on the extensiveness of taro acreage, he makes clear that management, including taro property, rests in the hands of lineage heads, though "patrilateral gifts" are common deviations from strict matrilineal inheritance. While such gifts amount to transferral of property between lineages, they actually usually obtain between senior men of the lineage and their immediate kin (ibid.: 81ff.).

By contrast to most Carolinian atolls where taro plays such an important role, the reliance on that series of crops is much less in the Marshalls, and according to Wiens (1962: 379) has shown "a high degree of abandonment" in recent years. There appears to be a complex of factors responsible for this neglect. Certainly, given the comparative aridity of the northern atolls (ibid.: 471), it is doubtful that sufficiently extensive fresh water lenses occur to sustain such crops. But further south where there is ample rainfall, taro still does not attain an important role in the economy or diet. In fact, in her description of land tenure practices on Namu, Pollock (1974) does not even mention taro. Rynkiewich (1972: 331) reports for Arno that while taro was formerly more important than in the time of his visit in 1969-70, it was being neglected because of the extensive labour required. Indeed, he (ibid.: 35) states that Arno's inhabitants were principally fishermen. This distaste for cultivating taro was also expressed by the Bikinians who were moved to Kili, a coral island with substantial taro areas which they chose not to exploit (Kiste 1967: 193). However great a role the cultural factor of distaste for taro cultivation may have become, and whatever the climatic (largely variations in rainfall) conditions exited, there was another factor which probably accounted to a large extent for the neglect of taro agriculture. This was the large lagoon and reef areas enjoyed by most of the Marshall atolls, which made fishing a primary occupation and one preferred to much of the terrestrial industry. Population factors may also have been instrumental in this neglect. Alkire (1978: 131) notes that the Marshalls have had an overall population density of 270 persons per square mile in recent years. This figure can be contrasted to his estimate of 500-1 000 for the Central Carolines (ibid.: 114). It may well be that the Marshallese were pushed to the necessity of cultivating taro in times of greater population densities, whereas more recently, under conditions of relaxed pressures, they have moved from more emphasis on an intensive (taro) economy to a predominately extensive (fishing) economy.

With regard to the units that are most closely associated with land tenure, there has been a basic connection with a matrilineal lineage under the headship of its senior male or *alab*. But Pollock (1974) stresses flexibility on this matrilineal base. Kiste,[7] for the northern atoll, Bikini (1967: 100ff.) and Rynkiewich (1972: viii) for the southern atoll, Arno, indicate that *alabs* were not necessarily lineage heads and that other sorts of landowning units were possible, especially those organized on a patrilocal basis. With regard to the problem of relating types of land tenure systems to degree of pressures on land, Rynkiewich's observations on Arno are particularly interesting. While estimating that the atoll could support much larger populations, he states "by 1970 some people have more land than they can use, others are unable to receive enough rights anywhere on the atoll, and still others have rights in one place but want to live in another place where they do not have rights" (ibid.: 5). Thus, again, the factor of balancing resources evenly across a population rather than gross overall people-land ratios presents the chief demographic problem to be resolved by land tenure systems. In the case of Arno, adjustments were made on a basic matrilineal background with 54 percent of the land being transmitted matrilineally, 24 percent by patrifiliation, and 12 percent by "combinations of alternate inheritance and gift processes" (ibid.: 159).

At this point, having sampled societies from the Central Carolines[8] and the Marshalls, there is little support for the formulation which I posed to describe the evolution of land tenure on Pingelap and Mwaekil. All of the atolls of these former regions had systems which worked on a matrilineal base, though in each case flexibility implemented by patrilateral and other gift arrangements and important usufruct privileges were extended in order to combat problems of internal imbalances. The expedient of individual ownership was not well developed, at least in the period under observation. Weckler (1949: 43-44, 66-67) was much puzzled by the occurrence of prominent patrilineal elements in Mwaekelise society and the weakness of the matrilineal clans there when matrilineality typified societies all around. My own hypothesis (Damas 1979) is that even with the brittleness of matrilineal systems in island groups like the Central Carolines and the Marshalls, the systems are kept alive by the inter-island functions of the clans. Under conditions of extreme isolation like that experienced by Pingelap (and the same can be said for Mwaekil) matrilineality faded and a patrilineal emphasis grew. The extent to which such developments were based on changes in residence as suggested in Goodenough (1955), or on land tenure considerations, is not clear. With greater evidence for involvement of the *keinek* and the *kainek* in land tenure, than formerly available, a case might be made for the latter connection.

Splendidly suitable for comparison with the Pingelap-Mwaekil land tenure system is material from Kapingamarangi atoll, a Polynesian outlier which has been thoroughly studied by several workers (Wiens 1962; Emory 1965; Lieber 1968, 1974). Wiens (1962: 158-62) has tried to address the thorny problem of population pressures in atoll environments by comparing conditions on Arno, Kapingamarangi, Pingelap, and Raroia in the Tuamotus. He dealt with a number of variables similar to those treated in the schemes of Mason and Alkire cited in Chapter 3. He was particularly wary of attempts to assess marine resource potentials at atolls. But Wiens, in agreement with Rynkiewich, thought that the extensive reef-lagoon area of Arno was a distinct asset to subsistence, although he also reported that Kapingamarangi was even better endowed in this respect (ibid.: 460). In comparing the potential of the latter atoll with that of Pingelap, he thought that while the Polynesian outlier has this advantage in marine resources, Pingelap must have superior terrestrial conditions. He concluded that Pingelap must have higher rainfall, though "no actual annual records are known to the writer that give quantitative comparisons" (ibid.: 461). Now, however, with the records cited in Chapter 3 which show an annual range of 106-216 inches for Pingelap, they can be compared to Wiens' (ibid.: 154) estimate of 80-100 inches for Kapingamarangi and confirm his supposition. Wiens also warned that "the mere comparison of densities of population per unit of land or land-and-marine area on different atolls is relatively meaningless" (ibid.: 462).[9] However, a basic comparison of numbers on Pingelap and the Polynesian outlier does bear on some problems of land tenure. Emory (1965: 66) reports a population of 527 for the time of his first visit to Kapingamarangi in 1947. This number declined somewhat in subsequent years, with Lieber (1974: 72) indicating a population of about 400 for 1966. With a land area of .422 square mile this would mean a higher figure ratio of about 1 250 persons per square mile and of the lower figure about 950, or near the ranges found on Pingelap for much of its recent history (see Table 9.1). While the superiority of marine resources seems likely for Kapingamarangi, the assumption by Wiens for a superior land base for Pingelap may need qualification. Since we have argued for the greater importance of taro holdings over other land areas and products, a comparison of wet lands seems appropriate. Wiens (ibid.: 378) took great care in measuring taro areas on the islands of the Polynesian outlier, getting for his result 25.1 acres. My own measurement of the Pingelap main patch was also about 25 acres. If Brady's formula for taro were to be applied to Kapingamarangi, it would imply a sustainable population of about 1 000, though his estimate for dry land acreage falls far below actual populations found on that atoll.

On the face of it, then, given superior marine resources and equal taro potential for support, Kapingamarangi should not be considered disadvantaged to Pingelap in recent years. But, returning to land tenure practices, the latter atoll shares some similarities with Pingelap. Emory (1965: 119) stated that individual ownership was complete at the time of his studies in 1947 and also in 1950, but Lieber (1974: 81) thought that about 52 percent of land plots was so owned in 1947 and that the percentage declined to about 33 percent by 1966, with greater control being exercised by a sibling set by that time. He attributes this shift to a population increase which included those who had migrated to Pohnpei, although they continued to hold land on the atoll. Lieber's conclusion follows that of widely held anthropological thinking and statements by Mwaekilese and Pingelapese informants, that at some point as pressures on land increase within small kin units, individual land tenure must give way to control on higher levels. On the other hand, in an earlier publication Lieber states that for wet taro land there was "unencumbered individual ownership" and that "the kinds of intensive care required to maintain a Puraka (taro) pit are very difficult to coordinate among more than a single individual" (1968: 160). It appears that as in the cases of Pingelap and Mwaekil, the firmest association between individual real ownership rights are with those of wet land taro holdings. It is also significant that on Kapingamarangi usufruct rights are extended only for dry land plots and not for taro holdings where ownership is outright and individual (Lieber 1974: 79). But, returning to the notion of corporate ownership by sibling sets, Lieber (ibid.: 82) indicates that each set has the senior male as steward over the land owned by each set, and that further, each senior male in the apical sibling set of each descent group is also considered to be steward for the whole group. It is not clear that such stewards have as complete control over property as is the case in individual ownership. While Lieber (ibid.) describes the duties of the steward as coordinating use, including rotation of sections used for copra harvesting and provisioning for feasts, the steward does not control inheritance of land. It appears that rights to the land of sibling sets accrues automatically on the basis of genealogical position. Then, too, the steward can be deposed, as Lieber illustrates with a case history (ibid.: 83).[10]

Lieber's work in Kapingamarangi also suggests shifting among various levels of ownership units according to demographic fluctuations. For instance, during a period of depressed populations in the late nineteenth and early twentieth centuries "large amounts of land areas concentrated in the hands of three important families" (1968: 170). Later when "wife swapping, first cousin marriage and polygyny" began to restore birth rates the trend toward concentration was reversed "by the 1920s" (ibid.: 171).

Goodenough's (1955) study of relationships among land tenure, residence, and descent focused on the occurrence of cognatic descent groups in the Gilbert Islands. Lambert (1966) suggested that the ambiguities inherent in assigning land rights with such groups have been resolved in the northern Gilberts through residential associations. Land tenure in the southern Gilberts has been obscured by interaction with British codification (Lundsgaarde 1974a) so that little in the way of generalization can be made regarding an internally derived evolution of land tenure systems as based on the atolls and islands in that region; but the codification is combined in a complex fashion with traditional Gilbertese land tenure custom. While the same difficulties hamper to some extent land tenure studies in the neighbouring Ellice Islands, Brady's (1970, 1974) observations from that group have important bearing on the problems addressed here. I have already referred to the formula which he suggested regarding land and taro areas needed for supportability. While not differentiating between dry land and wet taro holdings, Brady identifies the main landholding unit with "an ambilineal sibling set which is a segment of a larger ramage, a lineal or extended family of from two to sixty members" (1974: 140). On the other hand, Brady (ibid.: 148) also indicates that 28.1 percent of land is held individually "but, however the land is acquired, reversion from individual to joint tenure is in part a natural consequence of population growth in each estate" (ibid.: 148). He sees a pattern whereby, with a high land-man ratio, land-holding groups tend to split and, where the number of inheritors is large, to merge into joint holdings. Again, as in the Kapingamarangi case, "managers" appear to have some control over the use of lands and, indeed, appear to have gained stronger claims in land holdings than others by having land registered in their names in island registers. However, similarly to Kapingamarangi, rights of conveyance are not directly ceded to managers, but rather, inheritance of property is automatic on the basis of genealogical position (1974: 138). Brady

(1974: 168), in agreement with one of my chief arguments, sees the main problem of "land hunger" to be not overall population density averages but rather "maldistribution" of resources. Indeed, he presents considerable documentation from the Ellice Islands (1974: 168-74) to support that view.[11]

Returning to the problems of land disputes, the dearth of cases concerning absentee ownership in the literature dealing with land tenure in the western Carolines or in the Marshalls may be related to the almost universal communal ownership and the ability of land owning units to accommodate use among its remaining members. Exceptions to such arrangements appear to occur in those atoll societies where individual ownership is at least an option. For instance, Brady (ibid.: 165) reports for the Ellice islands where such is the situation, that while absenteeism under joint ownership "poses no real problems," under individual tenure a caretaker has to be appointed, and often there are complaints about maintenance of the land in question. It might be expected that Kapingamarangi would be another place where disputes could result from absenteeism, since, as noted above, individual tenure occurred there too. However, Lieber (1968: 50) reports that after time the colonists in Pohnpei relinquish rights to land on the atoll. Such apparent indifference to attachment to land would be incomprehensible to a Pingelapese and begs comparison of basic values between them and the people of the Polynesian outlier. But in the example of the southern Gilberts from where Lundsgaarde (1974a) also reports individual ownership (though not of the unencumbered variety found on Pingelap), questions of absentee ownership appear among the sources of dispute, as at least one case displayed "a number of conflicting claims involving a written will, adoption, bastardy, a gift for nursing, and the rights of an absentee heir "(1974a: 191). It can be seen that several of these sources of dispute are held in common with Pingelap and might be regarded as being endemic to societies where individual ownership is at least known. This is not to say that such factors as adoption and illegitimacy, in particular, cannot be sources for dispute regarding membership in larger landholding units.

Another source of dispute mentioned for Mwaekil which appears to be common elsewhere is encroachment on boundaries. For example, for the Ellice islands Brady reports that at the root of the problem was the casual system of boundary markings as they were composed of "slash marks made on trees, strategically placed cloth remnants, bottles, rocks, cans, or such impermanent items as palm fronds upended in the ground" (1974: 162). Again, it is well to note that by contrast, the relatively unambiguous and substantial system of marking land plots on Pingelap helps to avoid such disputes. There, chief boundary disputes occur in the taro patch where boundaries between individual holdings are much more subtle, as indicated in Chapter 4.

For Kapingamarangi, lack of use of certain plots for long periods creates uncertainty about ownership, and the familiar problem of adoptive versus natal rights to land appears again. Lieber also cites "stinginess" or "obtuseness" of stewards as cause for dispute (1974: 93). Most importantly for this discussion, that source (Lieber 1968: 239) attributes the general occurrence of disputes to be related to "vagueness" or "inexplicitness" regarding ownership which makes uncertain "who do what on a plot of land at any given time." Indeed, it would seem that such a system as that of Kapingamarangi, where cognatic units of land tenure exist together with individual ownership, and are combined with a complex system of usufruct privileges, the opportunities for ambiguity and concomitant disputes would be frequent.

But disputes over land also occur in the predominately matrilineal systems of the western Carolines and in the Marshalls. One of the common problems cited by sources for those atolls relates to demographic imbalances, which in the western Carolines are attributed to casualties from typhoons (Alkire 1974: 64), and for the Marshalls, at least in part, to casualties in fighting or warfare over land and status (Rynkiewich 1972: 92, 95; Kiste 1974: 59). It should be noted, however, that such fluctuations in kin group size, whether or not they are landholding units, can occur under a broad range of other circumstances. Kili presented a special situation where the Bikini immigrants shifted the land tenure system from overall control by the paramount chief to a council, and from matrilineally oriented lineage control of land to the *bambli* or household or extended family level. Disputes arose over boundaries as well as dissatisfaction with council control and overlapping membership in the *bambli* (Kiste 1974: 115-29).

With regard to settlement of disputes, the various traditional means, including the Pingelapese council of chiefs, the force of public opinion, and in some cases, the failure of sanctions and consequent physical violence, have been replaced in the Ellice islands, the Gilberts, and much of the former Trust Territory by codification and courts. In this regard the people of Woleai were, at the time of Alkire's study, unwilling to have their disputes aired in the court of their district centre at Yap, which they conceived of as representing Yapese laws. According to Alkire (1978: 68) the threat of disapproval by chiefs usually either resolved disputes over land or rendered them quiescent.

The roles of chiefs in settling or avoiding disputes in the Marshalls, arising from demographic imbalances among landholding units, continued strong at the times of the studies cited here, but there is doubt expressed regarding the equity of such attempted settlements. Rynkiewich reports that such redistributions engineered by chiefs "are random in their selection of recipients" (1972: 96) for Arno. Likewise, Kiste, writing about the situation on Bikini, indicates that such redistributions do not result in equal distribution of land but rather "individuals who control land allocate it in a manner which contributes to the welfare of themselves and/or the kinsmen with whom they share common interest" (1967: 126). Whatever the means of attempted resolution of land tenure disputes or conditions which may produce them, there appears to be a consensus among students of atoll land tenure systems that most disputes are never really resolved and continue to fester and reappear over periods of generations.

While cases of disputes from Pingelap have been mentioned here, I have argued that the system of individual ownership which has evolved there has the advantage of avoiding much disputation. It may well be that the *derak* ceremony which validates claims to land has had similar effect. Accounts from other atolls are lacking in description or discussion of such ritual, so it is difficult to judge whether or not there are present equivalent mechanisms for validating claims to land. We do have available samples of case histories from several sources besides our own (Weckler 1949; Lieber 1968; Lundsgaarde 1974a; Alkire 1974; Kiste 1974), but it is not clear that those compilations of cases are exhaustive for any given period. Whatever differential rates of disputes for the various atoll tenure systems may exist, it should be apparent that the character of disputes will vary from place to place according to such factors as the nature of landholding units, demographic characteristics of populations, relative precision of boundary markings, and kinds of dispute-settlement mechanisms.

In summarizing the preceding pages which have been devoted to a sampling of Micronesian and neighbouring Polynesian atoll society populations[12] and land tenure systems, several points should be emphasized, as follows: (1) a range of adjustments to atoll land tenure problems have been made, including deviations framed within basically matrilineal systems, cognatic adaptations, and in both of these circumstances, various usufruct adjustments; (2) while gross people-land ratios give some general notion of potential for support, the imbalances in holdings by groups or individuals is a far more crucial sort of manifestation of pressures on land; (3) as populations increased there has been a tendency toward expanding wet taro areas as the most prominent manifestation of intensification of cultivation; (4) together with that tendency there are also examples where individuation of taro landholdings show greater antiquity and more persistence than in dry land holdings; (5) there is some evidence to suggest that individuation of holdings does not provide the ultimate solution to pressures on land and that a reversion to control by larger units is a possible solution under some circumstances; (6) disputes seem to be endemic in atoll land tenure systems, but their character and means of resolution vary according to several factors.

Conclusion: Land Tenure in Restricted Space

Returning to the discussion raised in Chapter 1, Collier's (1975) *curvilinear hypothesis* posits first, the strengthening of unilineal control of land under conditions of population pressures, followed by a weakening of such emphases with further pressures, accompanied by moves toward individual ownership; and, finally under still more severe pressures, the eventual collapse of land tenure systems with other solutions including, in the case of his Mayan examples, adoption of family industries and emigration (ibid.: 49-78). There appeared to be support for this hypothesis in the histories of Pingelapese and Mwaekilese land tenure systems. But while in those cases, as in Collier's Tzotzil example, at least temporary resolution to the problems of pressures on land could be seen in emigration and wage employment, there was also the suggestion not seen in Collier's cases, of examples of atoll reversion to larger landholding units, at least on the usufruct level. This process appeared to have been manifested more strongly in such places as Kapingamarangi and in the Ellice Islands than on Mwaekil and Pingelap, but where it appears it suggests an "S curve" to the profile of land tenure evolution under conditions of population pressures.

There may be a broad sort of application of Collier's hypothesis to other atoll situations if one assumes a level of pressures on land that has compromised strict unilineal control. For example, modifications on matrilineal bases occurred in the Central Carolines and the Marshall Islands, as well as utilization of cognatic forms in the Gilberts and several Polynesian examples. But this sampling of atoll land tenure systems did not produce any examples of exclusive control by unilineal descent units. Whether or not the absence of such examples from my sample can, indeed, be attributed to advanced stages of land pressure existing in each case is not clear.

Collier hoped to apply his hypothesis broadly, but he also outlined some of the difficulties in doing so and emphasized that its most successful application has been controlled comparative situations (ibid.: 52) such as his Mayan study. Certainly, having seen the variation of practices within atoll societies, I am reluctant to extend any generalizations made here to other economic situations. One of the difficulties in applying any scheme of land tenure relationships or evolution to atoll societies is the variant role that marine resources have among the atoll or coral island economies.

In attempting the perilous task of extending generalization further, I will suggest that there may be a broad sort of similarity between the situations on the atolls considered here and certain societies practising shifting cultivation. Referring again to Chapter 1, Brown and Podolefsky in their survey of New Guinea societies found a correlation between intensification of agriculture and land tenure, specifically, that individual tenure is found in "societies where agriculture is permanent or fallow is less than six years" (1976: 221). A similar association is noted by Netting (1969) for another society with shifting agriculture, the Kofyar of Nigeria. Returning to a possible application of this principle to atoll economies, the chief means of agricultural intensification has been taro cultivation, and while the two societies which have been the foci of study here, Pingelap and Mwaekil, also show the relationship with individuation in ownership in that crop, the comparative material from other atolls is ambiguous.

Further studies of land tenure on atolls and elsewhere will be largely concerned with changes under conditions of contact and of migration. The groundwork which has been laid by students of land tenure in these societies, some of whom have been referred to in this study, will provide firm bases from which such studies can proceed.

Appendix

Catalogue of the Flora of Pingelap

Scientific Name	Pingelapese Term	Remarks
Polypodiaceae		
1. *Asplenium nidus* (L.)	*seilik*	Fernlike growth on rotten logs or coral. Leaves wrapped around breadfruit for baking.
2. *Nephrolepis biserrata* (Sw) Schott	*pwe*	A fern mixed with grass and used as fertilizer for taro.
3. *Polypodium phymatodes* (L.)	*kitew*	A medicinal fern chewed or pounded to a liquid and used for open wounds.
4. *Vittaria elongata* (Sw) common fern	*lit*	Known but has no special use. St. John (1948: 106) says grows on mossy bases of coconut trees. Very rare for an atoll.
Pandanaceae (Pandanus)		
5. *Pandanus* (Sp.)	*Kipar*	Generic term for pandanus.
	1. *asibuirek* 2. *nangaisal* 3. *sonumeireia* 4. *nanagasak* 5. *aisesewil* 6. *makosokosok* 7. *musamuis* 8. *esies* 9. *suioibueibuei* 10. *arawan* 11. *muisigel* (has no flowers - no fruit) 12. *meikilikil* 13. *luaram* (from Marshalls) 14. *sobodin*	Informant Albert. This list (left) confirms the 14 varieties noted by St. John (ibid.) but alters spelling in some cases. Pandanus leaves are used for mats and hats; also for thatching roofs. Trunks used for rafters when split into sixths for subsidiary support for thatched roofs. The sap or juice of pandanus roots squeezed for juice is used for stomach or other internal ailments.
Hydrocharitaceae		
6. *Thalassia hemprichii* (Ehrenb.)	*walaht*	This flowering weed which grows in or close to water was used chiefly to "wave around to chase away evil spirits."

Catalogue of the Flora of Pingelap *(continued)*

Scientific Name	Pingelapese Term	Remarks
Gramineae (Grasses)		
7. *Eragrostis amabilis* (L.) Wight & Arn.	*rosaki*	Seems to be the generic term for grass. Albert (chief informant) knows two kinds while St. John (ibid., 107) lists three.
8. *Lepturus repens* R. Br.		Designated *roskais*, including 8 and 9.
9. *Saccharum officinarum* (L.) Cultivated	*seu*	Sugar cane. St. John (ibid.) lists 5 but Albert adds two more (6 and 7).
	1. *kala* 2. *owesasa* 3. *palau* 4. *teimos* 5. *ieseng* 6. *seni* 7. *parmosa* (Formosa)	Grown chiefly in *inepwuel* but also near houses. *Palau* and *parmosa* are named for islands of origin and introduced during Japanese times. Tradition has it that those on the atoll were introduced from far to the west.
10. *Thuarae involuta* (Forst. f.) R. & S.	*mokarak*	In contrast to *rosaki* grows close along ground. Used only as fertilizer.
11. *Cyperus javanicus* Houtt	*sapasak*	This plant is described by St. John (ibid.) as growing at edge of fresh swamp and being used to *remove* the odour from the body. Flowers were used for perfume.
12. *Fimbristylis cymosa* R.Br.	*rosaki*	In woods by lagoon beach. Not clear as to which of the *rosaki* this is. Possibly a softer variety. Harder varieties (above) used to clean ears and to pick specks from eyes.
Palmae (palms)		
13. *Cocos nucifers* (L.) Cultivated and Spontaneous	*nih*	Albert says only palm on Pingelap is the coconut. He names nine stages (left) as compared to four given by St. John (ibid.).
	1. *kiripw*	Smallest nut stage.
	2. *uhpw*	All soft shell edible.
	3. *ah*	Bottom of shell still soft and edible, top hard.
	4. *pin*	Drinking nut. St. John (ibid.) says 2/3 grown.
	5. *langas*	Nut is now brown, still on trees, can be drunk still, milk is effervescent.

Catalogue of the Flora of Pingelap *(continued)*

Scientific Name	Pingelapese Term	Remarks
	6. *aring*	Fallen brown coconut used in copra making.
	7. *par*	Nut has grown embryo and germinated.
	8. *wayat*	Sprout now more than three feet tall, but still using nutrition from shell.
	9. *nih*	Shell now is used and tree steadily growing; now recognized as a coconut palm.

Araceae(aroids)

Three lists of this species are available, St. John's (ibid.) and those of two informants. These are combined here, but there is a possibility of other varieties occurring on the atoll.

Scientific Name	Pingelapese Term	Remarks
14. *Colocasia esculenta* (L.) Schott var. antiquorum (Schott) Hubb & Rehd Cultivated	*sawa* 1. *bokor* 2. *tawang* 3. *mesawsol* 4. *koso* 5. *sawa pingelap*	St. John (ibid.) says true taro is a crop of minor importance which agrees with my observations (except see text). He lists all seven recognized by informants.
	6. *sauk* 7. *pemeru*	Albert refers to these as "soft taro." A wet taro.
15. *Cyrtosperma chamissonis* (Schott) Merr. Cultivated[1]	1. *Meyung am ngatik* (named for atoll of presumed origin) 2. *Meyung dontol* 3. *nein pwekilamen* 4. *simiden* 5. *seriseng*	As St. John (ibid.) states, the major food crop. First five named in St. John (ibid.) with some orthographic alterations. These are "wet taros" grown in the inepwuel.
	6. *sounpwung walnu*	Means "six months," but more often harvested after one to one-and-one half years.
	7. *nein aikem*	Named for discoverer (Aikem). Flowering takes three to four years.
	8. *pisop*	Largest variety, used in annual competitions. Doesn't need fertilizer.

1 Albert says that *nein aikem*, *nein seria* and *nein silington* are named for grandfather, son, and grandson who accidentally each discovered these varieties are all planted from the flower rather than from the stalk and cap. They attain the largest sizes of any of the aroids with a record corm of the *silington* variety being marked on the wall of the municipal building said to be 10 feet above ground. The largest roots of these types extend well above the level of the mud and coconut husks and other fertilizer is piled upon them.

Catalogue of the Flora of Pingelap *(continued)*

Scientific Name	Pingelapese Term	Remarks
	9. *ne silington*	Named for discoverer (Silington) said by second informant to be largest, with plant attaining ten feet in height.
	10. *nesira*	Named for man (Nesira) who introduced variety from Ponape.
	11. *epawn*	
	12. *nein seria*	Named for discoverer (Seria).
The following three variables are "dry taro" grown at various places on the atoll.		
	1. *wat*	Perhaps the generic name.
	2. *wotiruk*	Introduced from Truk.
	3. *wisilik*	Named for man who introduced it from Hawaii in 1951.
Amaryllidaceae		
16. *Crinum asiaticum* (L.) Cultivated	*kiepw* (lilies)	These two used only in decoration. Grow cultivated near houses.
17. *Zephyranthes rosea* (Sprong) Lindl. Cultivated	*kiepw*	
Taccaceae		
18. *Tacca leontipetaloides* (L.) Ktze.-Rev. Gen. Pl. 704, 1891. *Leontice leontopetaloides* (L.), (Sp). Pl. 313, 1753 *T. pinnatifida* Forst., Char. Gen. 70, t. 35, 1776.	*mwekemwek* (Arrowroot)	St. John (ibid.: 108) says both cultivated and spontaneous and used in plaiting hats as well as a source of food. Albert says that the seed is dried in sun and mixed with bananas, coconut milk, and sugar to make a favourite dish called *pilobo*.
Dioscoreaceae		
19. *Dioscorea ? korrensis* R. Knuth	*kehp* (yams)	Edible yams said to be grown and cultivated in village by by St. John (ibid.) but I think at times of my visits chiefly growing wild as vines in the forest. Albert says it can grow as long as a man's arm. St. John (ibid.) — 1 mm and 3 dm in diametre.
Musaceae		
20. *Musa paradisiaca* (L.) Cultivated in village and *inepwuel*	*wis* (bananas)	First 10 listed by St. John (ibid.) others added. Can be eaten either raw or cooked.
	1. *latin*	Probably introduced from South America by whalers, according to informant.

Catalogue of the Flora of Pingelap *(continued)*

Scientific Name	Pingelapese Term	Remarks
	2. *america*	Introduced by whalers. (medicinal according to informant).
	3. *usigaras*	A very small native variety.
	4. *teymyan*	Native (ibid., Iyeman).
	5. *lakatan*	Native.
	6. *taiwan*	Probably brought by Japanese.
	7. *kudul*	Native.
	8. *panilo*	Native.
	9. *manila*	Japanese introduction (from Phillipines).
	10. *wisiak*	Native.
	11. *inek*	Recent. Introduced by native Inek from Pohnpei.
	12. *fiji*	Introduced earlier, from Truk (medicinal).
Piperaceae		
21. *Peperomia ponapensis* C. DC.	*wahnin*	Called "warin" by St. John (ibid.). A bushlike tree. Roots grow through crevices in coral. Fruit yellow, both fruit and leaf used for medicine. St. John (ibid.: 109) says poultice for boils.
Moraceae[2]		
22. *Artocarpus incisus* (Thunb.) (L.) f., Suppl. 411, 1781. Cultivated.	*mei* (breadfruit)	St. John (ibid.) says trees attain 20 m. or more.
	1. *mei sabarek*	St. John's (ibid.) information incorrect. This is not a seedless variety.
Rademachia incisa Thunb., Vet Akad.Stockholm, Handl. 37: 254, 1776.	2. *mei mokil*	Not named by St. John, also seedless.
	3. *meipa*	Error in St. John (ibid.). This variety *with* seeds.
	4. *mei si*	This variety *with* seeds contrary to St. John (ibid.: 110).
A. communis Forst., Char. Gen. 101, 1776.		

2 All varieties harvested from late May into September. Very few ripen at other seasons. *Mei pa* most abundant. *Mei sabarek* and *mei mokil* most abundant on Meseirong (main part of main island of atoll), while the other two are mostly growing on Daekae and, formerly, Sukoru as well.

Catalogue of the Flora of Pingelap *(continued)*

Scientific Name	Pingelapese Term	Remarks
Sitodium-altile Parkinson, Jour. Voy, Endeavour 45, 1773.		Not described by informants.
A. altilis (Parkinson) Fosberg, Wash. Acad. Sci., Jour. 31:95, 1941.		Not described by informants.
23. *Ficus* (Sp.)	*kawain*	Native. Fruit cooked and eaten. Bark formerly used in fish nets.
Urticaceae		
24. *Pilea microphylla* (L.) Liebm.	*re*	Adventive weed (ibid.). Albert says very hard to remove from stone walls and foundations. Grows along ground. Used as fertilizer for bananas and in taro patch.
25. *Pipturus argenteus* (Forst. f.) Wedd.	*oroma*	Used in fish lines. Thought to be superior to commerical lines because it remains soft after use in salt water. Tuna also said to bite better with *oroma* used at forepart of line. Also, leaves are medicinal when squeezed in water. Becomes slippery and when drunk said to ease childbirths, by numbing pain as well as "smoothing the way." Used as laxative as well.
Nyctaginaceae		
26. *Ceodes umbellifera* J.R. & G. Forst.	*mas*	Leaves best taro fertilizer. Fibre for nets. Has flower. Because branches are soft they are used for backing when umbilicus is cut with shell. Dangerous to climb because of brittle branches. Not good for lumber because of spaces in fibre. Trees to 10 m. in height by 3 dm. in diametre. Seen in village by St. John (ibid.).
27. *Mirabilis jalapa* (L.) Cultivated	*pesikulck*	"Ornamental flower commonly cultivated in village" St. John (ibid.: 111).
Crassulaceae		
28. *Bryophyllum pinnatum* (Lam.) Kurz-Cultivated in village	*limalam*	A bush yielding small oval leaves about 5" long by 1/10" thick. Used as "letter paper," written on by ribs of coconut leaves. Word related to lamalam or "thinking."

Catalogue of the Flora of Pingelap *(continued)*

Scientific Name	Pingelapese Term	Remarks
Leguminosae		
29. *Derris trifoliata* Lour	*kainipil*	A vine which is pounded and sap used on fresh wounds.
30. *Vigna marina* (Burn) Merr.	*nimelitop*	Vine which glosses as *litop* = woman; having recently given birth/*nime* = something to drink. This vine drunk after childbirth to heal the wounds of the womb.
Euphorbiaceae		
31. *Acalypha grandis* Benth. var. *genuina* Muell. Arg. Cultivated	*kurulong*	An ornamental flower grown around the village. Introduced during German times (ibid.: 111).
32. *Euphorbia atoto* Forst.	*pelepel*	Flower. "Tufted, erect; leaves glaucous beneath. In grassy thicket."
33. *Phyllanthus niruri* (L.)	*limaimeripung*	Last syllable *pung* added to St. John (ibid.: 111) version. A flower-bearing "weed" with leaves that open in daylight. Used as a fungus remedy.
Sapindaceae		
34. *Allophylus timorensis* (D.C.) Bl.	*kitahk*	Can grow to 15 feet in height. Saplings used for handles of flying fish nets.
Tiliaceae		
35. *Triumfetta procumbens* Forst. f.	*konop*	Vine creeping on ground. Pounded flat to be used in plaiting and mats.
Malvaceae		
36. *Sida fallax* Walp. Cultivated in village	*kao*	Shrub St. John (ibid.) says 2 m tall. No use given.
37. *Thespesia populnea* (L.) Soland.	*penne*	Wood of good quality, used for breadfruit pole (*pilet*), axe handles, and flying-fish net handles. The trunk of tree used for lumber. Bark used for fish nets. A very hard wood.
Guttiferae		
38. *Calophyllum inophyllum* (L.)	*sepang*	St. John (ibid.) in error, not related to island of Saipan, but native. His description 15 m tall by 1 dm in diametre apparently correct. Used for walking sticks for boards, knife handles, furniture, etc. Not used for canoes as stated by St. John (ibid.) because of knottiness of wood. The nut squeezed for oil and used by shaman "to give power."

Catalogue of the Flora of Pingelap *(continued)*

Scientific Name	Pingelapese Term	Remarks
Caricaceae		
39. *Carica papaya* (L.) Cultivated	*kaineap* (papayas)	Grown mainly around houses to avoid theft. Eaten cooked or raw.
Lythraceae		
40. *Pemphis acidula* Forst.	*kaini?*	Albert calls "hardest wood in the Pacific." Grows in water. Must be cut with axe. Some attain one foot in diametre. Japanese used for pipes.
Sonneratiaceae		
41. *Sonneratia alba* (Smw)	*kosa*	Mangrove which sends its shoots above water. Roots in mud.
Lecythidaceae		
42. *Barringtonia asiatica* (L.) Kruz.	*wi*	White-flowering tree. Seed mixed with ashes and used as fish poison.
Anacardiaceae		
43. *Mangifera indica* (mango)	*kaingit*	One tree on island. (Not mentioned in St. John).
Rhizophoraceae		
44. *Rizophora mucronata (Lam)*	*al*	Called *ah* in St. John (ibid.). A mangrove with prop (above water level) roots in low tide. Found in shallow salt water of lagoon. Grows about 8m tall.
Combretaceae		
45. *Terminalia catappa* (L.) Cultivated	*tepop*	No reference by informants.
46. *Terminala litoralis* Seem	*win*	Tree 9 m tall. Fruit 15-18 mm long, edible. Wood used for tool handles (ibid.). Flower greenish.
Onagraceae		
47. (St. John's 46) *Jussiaea suffruticosa* (L.) var ligustrifolia (HBK) Griseb.	*kuri*	Introduced weed, seen by St. John (ibid.) growing in taro patch.
Apocynaceae		
48. (St. John's 47) *Plumeria acutifolia*	*pomaria*	Introduced, ornamental and cultivated (ibid.).
Asclepiadaceae		
49. (St. John's 48) *Asclepias curassavica* (L.)	*kimeme*	Introduced weed, grows in village (ibid.).
Boraginaceae		
50. (St. John's 49) *Messerchmidia argentea* (L.f.) I.M. Johnson	*seseni*	Tree 8 m tall, common (ibid.).

Catalogue of the Flora of Pingelap *(continued)*

Scientific Name	Pingelapese Term	Remarks
Verbenaceae		
51. (St. John's 50) *Clerodendrum inerme* (L.) Gacrip	*ilau*	Shrub with arching branches 2-4 m long. Seen in forest near lagoon beach by St. John (ibid.).
52. (St. John's 51) *Premna integrifolia* (L.)	*sokok*	Tree 8 m tall and 2 dm in diametre, flower white, fruit black (ibid.).
Acanthaceae		
53. (St. John's 52) *Pseuderant bemum atropurpureum* Bull (Radik) Cultivated	*sarinairam*	Cultivated in village. Introduced by Germans. Shrub 1-4 m tall. White flowers with magenta spots.
Rubiaceae		
54. (St. John's 53) *Guettarda speciosa* (L.)	*eles*	Tree 7 m tall by 2 dm diametre. Logs used for canoe hulls and flowers for ornaments or to perfume coconut oil according to St. John (ibid.).
55. (St. John's 54) *Ixora carolinensis* (val.) Hosokona	*kalesu*	Shrub about 5 m tall. Cultivated in village (ibid.).
56. (St. John's 55) *Morinda citrifolia* (L.)	*obul*	Growing away from village, apparently not native. Eaten or used as a medicine (ibid.).
Goodeniaceae		
57. (St. John's 56) *Scaevola fructescens* (Mill.) Krouse Cultivated	*ramek*	Shrub 8 m tall by 2 dm in diametre, flowers with edible fruit (ibid.).
Compositae		
58. (St. John's 57) *Wedelia biflora* (L.) D.C.	*kisuwell*	Half scandent shrub found in moist areas.
59.	*apus*	A small green fruit.

Glossary of Micronesian Terms

auwalait: A prestation event usually held in the month of July if and when great prosperity in subsistence pursuits is realized. The term derives from the Pingelapese expression for "waiting for the fishermen."

daekae: Pingelapese term for "island" also used to designate the second largest island of the atoll (sometimes also *Daekaelu*), which lies north of the lagoon.

delawan: Two meanings are attributed, either a corruption of "Tarawa" or the supposed origin of Gilbertese who settled on Pingelap; or, *dela* — "to go" *wa* — "canoe" applied to any foreigner who arrived at the atoll.

derak: The ceremony of distribution of pigs and taro which validates divisions of land. When held during lifetime of testator referred to as *derak mehla*. If held after testator's death, as *derak mour*.

eketar: A fishing method employing a feather and float attached to line and pole, used in catching reef fish.

ilarak: Describes trolling for fish from boats or canoes.

ilik: The east shores or windward sides of the islands of Pingelap, especially of the main island.

inepwuel: The main taro patch on Pingelap.

irirpwe: A celebration, including food distribution, which occurs when the paramount chief recovers from an illness or serious injury.

kahil: A fish which is featured in an origin myth of Pingelap.

kahlek: The method of catching flying fish at night from canoes by torchlight. Derived from the term for dancing.

kahnihmw: Pingelapese for "village."

kamadipw: The generalized term for "feast" or prestation event. Derived from "*kama*" and "*dipw*" or "to kill" and "to waste."

kasapwasapw en peyneyey: Describes a gift of land from sister's husband to wife's brother. The term *kasapwasapw* is combined with several other terms to describe various other land transactions.

katella (also *kateri*): Men's house where formerly boys and unmarried men slept. Also used as a meeting place.

keinek (Mwaekilese *kainek*): A descent unit based on a core of patrilineally linked males but with a periphery of in-marrying females and adoptees of both sexes. Traces to a known apical ancestor.

keliek: Term for "basket," but also applied to a legendary system of rotating land use on Pingelap.

kohta mweniap: Ritual which occurred after the first catch of the flying fish season wherein a representative of each canoe presented the paramount chief with a string of fish.

kohwa: The system of stewardship of property of absentee owners.

koso: Term for pig in Pingelapese: said to mean "cut" in Mwaekilese.

kounen kousapw: Chief representing each major division of the main island (2), and Daekae.

kousahkis: The act of erecting a plank upon which to measure corms of Cyrtosperma at the contest called *umwanpahdah* which marked the closing of the taro patch.

kousapw: Division of main island into northern and southern sections, and also Deakae into an eastern and western half.

kumangen um: The outer circle of participants in *derak*.

lam: Term used to designate the lagoon of Pingelap atoll.

lepinsapw: One of the subdivisions of the land areas of Pingelap. May have had some land-owning significance in earlier times, but today used mainly as a general locative designation.

lepous: Term designating inland direction.

lolo: Mwaekilese term for ownership divisions in main taro patch. Equivalent to Pingelapese *manime*.

lompwei: Member of the lower house (*muten kas pa*) of chiefs. Represented one of four major divisions (*pwekil*s) of the village.

maekah: One of the major named divisions of the main taro patch on both Pingelap and Mwaekil, separated from each other by open spaces of mud.

maesdah: The shore facing the village of Pingelap.

maeyung: Term for Cyrtosperma.

manime: Pingelapese term for sections of taro patch which comprise individual ownership divisions.

mar: Breadfruit fermented in the ground.

medau: Pingelapese term for the deep sea.

mesieni en keinek: Oldest living male in each *keinek*.

muten kas pa: The traditional "lower house" of the council of chiefs, which included representatives from each of the four *pwekils*(s) who served as police for their respective sections of the village.

muten kas piete: The traditional "upper house" of the council of chiefs composed of priest of the sea and of the land as well as the heir apparent and the paramount chief.

Mwoalen Wahu: Council of High Chiefs in bicameral legislature of the state of Pohnpei.

mwol: A gift of land from grandparent to grandchild.

mwungamwung: First-fruit ceremony which marks the opening of the breadfruit season on Pingelap.

mwurilik: Funeral ceremony sometimes held together with *derak* or *pwakamar*.

nahlaimw: The Pingelapese "priest of the sea."

nahlik: Member of lower house of chiefs. Represented one of the four *pwekils*.

nahnawa: Title holder replaced washai in upper house.

nahneken: Member of upper house (*muten kas piete*) of chiefs served as "talking chief" or intermediary between paramount chief and other chiefs.

nahnmariki (Pohnpeian *nanmariki*): The paramount chief.

nahno: Members of lower house of chiefs. Represented one of the four *pwekils*.

nahpwusak: New title for heir to paramount chief position; changed (from about 1870) from wasahi — no longer member of upper house.

nanapas: Formerly the "priest of the land." After the establishment of the Sokehs colony this title holder became paramount chief there.

nanit: New title added in twentieth century modelled after Pohnpeian usage. Function unclear.

nanpei: New title added in twentieth century modelled after Pohnpeian usage. Function unclear.

nansaho: New (twentieth-century) title — designated as "chief of police."

pelienenmwar: Pingelapese term for dowry.

peliensapw: (Mwaekilese *pelienjapw*) individual land-owning strips of land areas of Mwaekil and Pingelap.

perau: The reef.

perumw: apparently a loan word from English which describes a fishing method where a number of men drive fish toward a net held by two men.

peyneyney (Mwaekilese *paneyney*): The extended family of virilocal orientation which is the chief land-using unit. Also a general term for "relations."

pirap: Term for stealing from or trespassing on property of others.

pong: One of the minor taro pits found on the *peliensapw*(s) of the main island of Pingelap and on Daekae.

pongolikilik: A method of reef fishing employed at night with poles and hook and with bait of crabs strewn on the surface.

pulliculliculli: One of the numerous markers of *peliensapw* boundaries which on Pingelap are composed of long piles of coconut palm fronds, husks, and near the village, various garbage.

pwakamar: The ceremony which celebrates transferral of a title after the death of a title holder.

pwekil: One of the four politically significant divisions of the village of Pingelap.

sadek: The Pingelapese word for "kind" their most highly prized personality quality.

saksawa: The contest for determining the largest corm of *sawa* or Colocasia marks the reopening of the taro patch about the end of August.

sawa (Mwaekilese *jawa*): Term used to designate true taro (Colocasia).

secon kipar: Ceremony which marks the beginning (twice a year) of pandanus seasons.

seilululak: A form of trolling for fish where the line is dragged deeper in the water than is the case of *ilarak*.

selong (Mwaekilese *solong*): Deep-water fishing for tuna where a line is dropped with a sinker of lead or stone to great depths in order to hook the yellow fin tuna.

siwih perian: An inner circle of relatives who engage in the *derak* ceremony.

songmar: Ceremony at which the first *mar*, fermented breadfruit, is dug up, eaten and distributed. This marks the end of the ripe breadfruit season.

sou: The matrilineal clan.

sounpwong walnu: Quick-growing species of aroid said to be ready for harvesting six months after planting.

souwel: Member of lower house of chiefs. Representative of one of four *pwekils*.

sukor: A muddy space which transects the main taro patch and which serve to separate *maekah(s)*.

uhkesik: A method of reef fishing which employs small hand nets.

umwahpahdah: Ceremony which marks the closing of the taro patch and included the contest for the largest corm of Crytosperma (*kousahkis*).

wael: Pingelapese word for the forests of the atoll.

waliempo: Ceremonial gift-giving by *keinek* receiving title shifted from another major

wasahi: Formerly member of upper house of chiefs as heir apparent to paramount chief.

weteke: Literally "piece of wood." Refers to the two balsa which act as floats in this method of fishing with a pole.

wesik: One of several ceremonies involving recognition of membership as, for instance, the *wesik en keinek*, or of sources of land as the *wesik en sapw*.

Notes

Chapter 1

1 I have adopted new spellings of the names of these high islands which were formerly known as Ponape and Kusaie, according to the preferences of their present-day inhabitants. However, in instances when usages are contained in quotations or references from earlier sources I have retained the previous spellings.

2 Dimensions of the atoll are taken from Bryan (1971). This source gives the land area as .676 and the lagoon area as .478 square miles, respectively.

3 For convenience I have used the term "taro" as a generic term for all aroids (*araceae*). Botanists point out that among those species which are grown on Pingelap only the *Colacasia* should be termed a true taro.

4 Dr. Douglas Russell, leprologist, indicated to me, however, that similar depigmentation occurs with certain tropical skin diseases, which makes it difficult to diagnose leprosy in such cases on that basis alone.

5 On my last visit to Pingelap in May 1983, I noted that church attendance had fallen off and that some people, especially young men, could be seen in the village or at other places during Sunday church services. This occurrence is probably related to two factors. One of these was a certain relaxation of strict control by the church with the virtual defeat of the rival Seventh Day Adventist mission attempt to become established on the atoll. The other appeared to be a certain rebelliousness against the strictures of the church by youth who had spent some time off the island and had developed some skepticism regarding religion as practised on Pingelap.

6 The suspension of cooking on Sundays meant that it went on throughout Saturday nights, often until dawn, when the new day was considered to begin. In these cases families often sat round the hearths in outdoor cooking shelters and talked long into the night without any attempt to tone down conversations. This was another example of the apparent indifference to a need for sleep or concern for silence during the night hours.

7 My original treatment of the Pingelapese descent system (Damas 1979) was lacking in a number of respects. Dr. David M. Schneider (1980), expressed some doubts about my representation of double descent on Pingelap. Later, I was able to get a great deal more information, especially regarding the nature of the *keinek* and tried to clarify my position on that basis (Damas 1981), though Schneider and probably other anthropologists will continue to hold views divergent from my own regarding the nature of descent and probably as well what I see as a system of dual reckoning on Pingelap.

8 That others are concerned with this trend in anthropology is seen in Salzman (1988) who describes in detail the "demi-decadal trade-in of models" and the condition that "anthropology has come to content itself with performance rather than progress, with novelty rather than deepening understanding" (1988: 32).

9 In my analysis of Pingelapese residential patterns I cited Bordieu (1977) and Linares (1984) as representing my own views on the notion of norms as often being principles, or schemes, which, as I understand them to mean, must be built from a combination of informant statements and inferences.

Chapter 2

1 Morton's estimate appears to be made largely on linguistic evidence which employed a glottochronological formula that showed Pingelapese-Pohnpeian divergence at .708.

2 "This lack of external verification does not mean that no inferences at all may be drawn as to what may have happened in Tikopia society during the period to which the traditions refer, or that no inference has any higher degree of plausibility than any other. But it does mean that the probability value of any particular set of inferences must be low" (Firth 1961: 5). Notwithstanding this pessimism, Firth devotes a section of his book to interpreting what he calls the "quasi-history" of the traditions (ibid.: 27-154).

Regarding use of traditions in Micronesia, Lessa's (1961) study is the most comprehensive. While analyzing the tales of Ulithi atoll in terms of psychological revelations and similarities and probable diffusion between other Micronesian islands, he casts serious doubts on their value as history. Regarding what he calls "the euphemistic doctrine of the supposed historicity of all folklore" he states that while some tales and myths may be true or based on fact "in the face of what seems to be the absence of necessary fact euphemism is a 'will-o-the-wisp' " (ibid.: 454).

3 Eilers (1934: 424) reports on the typhoon of 1905, while Wiens (1962: 182) describes the effects of the 1957 typhoon on Pingelap as follows: "In November 1957 the centre of typhoon Lola passed by Pingelap Atoll about 120 miles to its north but the 60 to 70 knot winds blew down or snapped off many breadfruit trees and coconut trees. The year's copra output was cut by an estimated 50 percent, the taro was ruined by salt water, and 25 percent of the houses and canoes were damaged."

A report on the 1972 typhoon (also called Lola [TTPI 1972]) estimated damage on Pingelap as total destruction of the taro patch, 80 percent destruction of breadfruit trees, 10 percent of coconut trees uprooted, with 35 percent burned. There was also reported to be an 80 percent loss of bananas, 70 percent loss of pandanus, and 85 percent loss of papaya trees. In addition 24 houses were destroyed in that storm as well as 17 boat houses and 70 other structures. Most dramatic was destruction of the cement pier which had aided unloading of supplies and loading copra by the field trip vessel. The damage to Mwaekil atoll was significantly less but still substantial.

4 The estimate is based on Hammet's report (Eilers 1934: 413) that 150 men and boys, but no women or girls, appeared on the beach at his arrival, with the projection being based on Morton (personal communication) whose genealogical evidence supports such a figure. For a complete listing of estimates of Pingelap's population see Table 9.1.

5 At the time the chief products of trade appear to have been trepang and coconut oil and Restieaux is reported to have collected 200 gallons of the oil during his stay on Pingelap (Hezel 1983: 251). Shortly, the main trade was to shift to copra itself since a couple of years before it had been discovered that in this form spoilage could be avoided by shipping the meat in well-dried form. This meant that native labourers could be spared the tiresome work of pressing the oil out of the copra with the crude devices that had been used for this purpose; not only would the merchants have purer

oil but they had the caked meat as a bonus to sell for animal food and fertilizer (ibid.: 212).

6 The Thilenius expedition of 1908-10 purported to provide information on all German possessions in the Pacific including islands and atolls in Micronesia, Polynesia, and Melanesia. Krämer headed the party which visited the atoll briefly in 1910. The account, however, was drawn together some years later by Eilers (1934).

7 The siege by German warships of Pohnpeians on Sokehs Island which resulted in their deportation is described in Bascom (1965) and Ehrlich (1978) in greatest detail, though a number of other accounts appear in the literature.

8 In an earlier publication (Damas 1979) I had confused what I assumed to have been a survival of the Ten Man Council with the body known as the Seven Men which had been established during the German period as mentioned earlier in this chapter. This confusion arose over the fact that this latter body had been expanded to 10 as discussed in Chapter 4. Certainly, while several of the members were title holders, membership was not congruent with, and indeed, did not totally replace, the title system on Pingelap.

9 This version of the frequency of ship visits during the Japanese period comes from informants. Peattie (1988: 148) gives "twelve times a year" as the frequency with which "the Ponape line touched at the easternmost atolls of the Carolines," but based partly on the above testimony and on general skepticism about schedules of sailings in this part of the Pacific derived from field experiences, I rather doubt this high rate of contact by ship during the period.

Chapter 3

1 I am fortunate in having available the report of Dr. Harold St. John (1948) who, though spending only one day (December 27, 1945) on the atoll, was able to collect an impressive list of Pingelapese flora. Additions have been made on the basis of statements of native informants (see Appendix).

2 Wiens (1962: 21-22) gives the diametres of the reefs of Pingelap as 2.3 by 1.3 miles with a maximum depth of lagoon of 162 feet, while these dimensions for Kwajalein are 66 by 15 miles and 198 feet.

3 There has not been any attempt to develop commercial fishing on the atoll. Indeed, given the heavy population it is doubtful whether the reef and surrounding deep waters could produce a volume of fish much beyond subsistence levels. Certainly some of the difficulties present in fishing that I saw during my visits to the atoll, especially supply of gasoline and engine breakdowns, make commercial development doubtful. For a meticulous and throughgoing study of a Pacific Island commercial fishing industry, see Rodman 1989.

4 For an account of the career of John Higgins, see Weckler 1949: 74-79.

5 On the basis of contradictory statements from my informants there appears to be some uncertainty as to whether harvesting and planting yams are, or were at some time, prohibited activities for women.

6 According to my chief informant, dogs were exterminated periodically after their introduction "but always seemed to come back after a few years" with a rapidly growing population.

7 With regard to seasonal supplies of food, it could be argued that storing breadfruit and the former closing of the taro patch might be regarded as insurance for lean periods in the year, or for longer stretches of time. It was my observation, however, that fermented breadfruit was eaten or distributed mainly at the "feasts" and was regarded as being a luxury food. The massive destruction of crops including arboreal,

taro swamp, and breadfruit pits that accompanied the floods and high winds of the periodic typhoons made it impossible for the Pingelapese to provide for such catastrophes. As noted earlier, it was only through outside help that they were able to avoid famines after the storms of 1905, 1957, and 1972, according to my informants and the documented accounts of these disasters. Over the year's cycle, with the enormous amounts of taro and coconuts available, there would be normally enough food of some sort. On the other hand as the description of the yearly fishing cycle showed, the uncertainties of maritime sources of food probably at times brought on protein famines in the otherwise well-nourished population.

Chapter 4

1 The terms "homestead" and "estate" are used for land parcels elsewhere in Micronesia, but the equivalence is far from exact. These terms seem to connote continuity and totality to the extent that usually does not pertain on Pingelap. Seldom do these strips of land by themselves amount to total holdings for individuals due to the fractionalization of land on the atoll. Total *estates* are usually spatially split.

2 In their definitive work "Bridewealth and Dowry in Africa and Eurasia" Goody and Tambiah outline "variables in bridewealth and dowry payments" listing the following characteristics of dowry: (1) All property (as contrasted to only moveable property for bridewealth) can be transmitted through dowry; (2) the recipient is the bride; (3) the givers are the kin of the bride; (4) returnability is always a possibility; (5) always occurs; (6) always payable at marriage; (7) used as part of a familial fund (1973: 21). All of these characteristics fit the Pingelap example. Also applicable is the concept of "diverging devolution" (ibid.: 17) in this case as applied to downward bilateral transmission. However, as Tambiah notes in a later article this bilateral transmission need not involve a premortem inheritance which implies equal shares (1989: 420). Indeed as the following chapter will show, the ideal of a patrilineal bias is realized in most cases of downward transmission.

There are, however, two points upon which the Pingelap system differs from those of India and Africa. On the one hand it is not associated with plow agriculture as in the former areas, and as well, it is not associated with marked status differentiation or attendant hypergamy. While there is a council of chiefs on Pingelap, their families do not form a special social stratum, and it is questionable whether or not marriages were formerly arranged according to considerations of any sort of quasi-nobility, though land ownership considerations were probably always important when marriages were arranged in the past.

3 In another place I (Damas 1983b) considered adoption on Pingelap in detail. Briefly, the chief conclusions of that study were as follows: the main features of adoption included the existence of two types, general adoption and adoption of grandchildren; change in kin group affiliation with shift in membership in the *keinek*(s) as well as extended and nuclear family of adopted child; usual accompaniment of land with child from donor family; absorption in land tenure holdings of recipient family and eventual rights of heirship; preference for males in adoption; the intention of permanence of the arrangement, though cases of return were reported.

Motives for adoption related to the filling out of small families, which implied eventual expansion of the workforce as adoptees reached maturity, as well as provision of successors to titles where applicable. More specifically expressed, and germane to the present study, was the wish to provide an heir to property. While it was not surprising to find that most recipient families were those without, or with few offspring especially of males at least at the times of adoption, it was surprising that the donor families were also small or not yet formed. That is, often couples donated their first-born. Clearly kinship obligations, especially those contingent upon younger siblings, who were the principle donors, were in operation in those cases. As Goody (1976: 95) points out in writing of adoption in Greece, "until the present century, the heir-producing aspects of adoption showed a straight ascendancy over the child-welfare ones." A similar point is made by Carroll (1970: 6) for Oceania in general, but child welfare or care of illegitimate children is also an important secondary function of adoption on Pingelap (Damas 1983b: 331).

Adoption appears to have reached substantial proportions about the turn of the present century and continued at high rates throughout the German and Japanese periods. I have related the high rates during these times to uneven fertility due probably to the introduction of and continuance of venereal disease. With the advent of the American period and the use of antibiotics, fertility increased and balanced after 1945 and the practice of adoption, except for grandparent-grandchild adoption, has disappeared in the Pingelapese population. The notion of "old age insurance" associated with the latter form of adoption appears to have a long history on the atoll.

4 As in the case of dowry, Goody's concept of "diverging devolution" applies to all property which is celebrated at *derak* rituals. With regard to the Pacific in general, however, I find some difficulties with Goody's (1976: 12-13) compilation of data and interpretations regarding the frequency and function of this process. He relates the opposing convention of "homogeneous" devolution or, simply put, unilineal inheritance, to those societies in the Pacific "outside the major traditions i.e. tribal societies of various kinds, especially those without advanced agriculture" (ibid.). In the first place, my survey of Micronesian atolls (see chap. 9) reveals that almost always there is deviation from strictly unilineal inheritance. This is especially true of matrilineally based ones, while the very nature of the cognatic societies implies "divergence" of inheritance.

While the notion of association of this vertical bilateral inheritance with plow agriculture alone does not fit for Pacific islands, the concept of "advanced" or intensive agriculture might in part bear such an association, at least in Micronesia. As Goody (ibid.: 20) points out, the adoption of "advanced agriculture" allows expansion of the population, making for scarcity of land. In the case of Pingelap and other Micronesian atolls, the chief means of intensifying agriculture is through digging, maintaining, and expanding taro patches. I am arguing in this study that the involvement of women in the inheritance scheme of Pingelap can be associated with population expansions of the nineteenth century, and that individual ownership by men predated that time. Even earlier, ownership of taro holdings had been organized on an individual basis, but later, after crowding increased, the individuation of landownership, including inheritance by both sexes, was extended to the land areas devoted to the less-intensive arboricultural pursuits.

5 This raises the possibility of postmortem inheritance by females in the absence of male heirs. Considerable efforts were made to provide male heirs (chiefly through adoption when natural offspring were not present). The rarity of such cases in my records of earlier periods (but see case 2 in chap. 5) make generalizations highly conjectural. It seems to be logical that the testator would not yield all of his properties to daughters at times of their marriages in order that he might retain land of his own to work and to reap from. As discussion in Chapter 7 will show, the practice of awarding daughters property in wills rather than as dowries has taken hold in the Pingelap colonies on Pohnpei in recent years.

Chapter 5

1 Results of surveys like my own which have been submitted to district Land Commission Offices by anthropologists have met with mixed reactions. Although the head of the local commission in Pohnpei requested copies of my maps, other members greeted my identification as an anthropologist with reactions ranging from amusement to derision. Our maps are suspect because of the roughness of our measurements and our alleged use of biased informants.

In marking off the boundaries of individual plots I found that while I employed a Brunton compass, that instrument was useful mainly in sighting along coastal stretches and in the village where open space allowed sightings. In the forest it was impossible to sight along the boundaries because trees and undergrowth obscured them. Nor did I use a tape measure for my measurements. It may seem that pacing off lengths and widths of the plots is a highly inexact method. Members of the Ponape Land Commission office told me that they measured plots on the high island by clearing trees at the corners of plots and photograph them from the air. Given the small size of Pingelap plots, such a method would require cutting down a third or more of the trees. While a tape-measure survey could be attempted this would require a large crew and more time than I had available. While more accurate methods might be employed, I doubt that whatever improved degree of accuracy that would be achieved would seriously alter the conclusions of this study.

With regard to the other chief objection directed toward the surveys of anthropologists, questionable assignment of ownership to plots as mapped, I have no doubt that some of the assignments which I made can be, and have been, disputed. Such disputes are an integral part of the problems of land tenure on the atoll. My original maps include names of putative owners. I have chosen to avoid identification of ownership on the maps used here since my objectives are academic rather than legalistic.

2 The Pingelapese kinship terminology of reference employs a large number of descriptive terms in the ascending generations. Thus, father's brother, father's sister, mother's brother, mother's sister all have separate terms which indeed correspond to their English equivalents. This arrangement forms the Bifurcate-Collateral Aunt-Uncle system (Murdock 1949: 224-26). Similarly, the parents of each parent are set off terminologically as father's father, father's mother, mother's father, mother's mother.

On Ego's generation, however, a basic Hawaiian arrangement is apparent, though with some modification. Cousins are equated with male siblings and female siblings respectively, though there is also a term which is sometimes used for a sibling of the opposite sex. In addition, the eldest male and eldest female of sibling group of Ego is designated, *meseini*, together with identification of male and female sex.

On the first descending generation the Bifurcate-Collateral system again applies with separate terms used for children of Ego, for male siblings, and for female siblings. The latter two terms are extended to children of male and female cousins respectively.

Affines are simply referred to as "spouse of," together with Ego's term for appropriate mate.

In address, members of all ascending generations are called by parental terms which are, however, different from parental reference terms. Persons in descending generations are addressed by the reference terms for children of each sex while those on Ego's generation are called by name (cf. Morton et al. 1973).

3 Crude adoption rate is a measure which matches the number of named children born in a generation to the number adopted during that time span (Damas 1983b: 336).

4 Considering the importance of taro patch holdings, it is unfortunate that there was insufficient information regarding such properties for them to be included in this case study.
5 One of the reasons for the further weakening of the powers of the council of chiefs that had been manifest by the time of my visits to the atoll was the frequent absence of members. In Chapter 3 I noted that only four of the title holders were present at a *Mwungamwung* ceremony held in 1976. At that time frequent visiting of relatives in the new colonies absented several of the chiefs. Others had moved to the colonies. Most important was the often long-term absences of the paramount chief himself, so that the traditional practice of periodically drawing together the officers of the council had been largely abandoned during the period of my study, 1975-83. Certainly there were no such meetings reported to me during the times of my actual residences on the atoll. Probably due also to this problem of suspended or delayed communication among the titled, I noted that decisions about selecting successors when title holders died were delayed for a year or more. In fact, at any given time during my study there would be perhaps an average of two vacancies in the roster.
6 In Chapter 3 I noted that seepage from tides occurs around the margins of the lenses so that there is greater salinity much of the time in such places. The relative freshness of the water of the lenses of the atoll islands is also affected by the amount of rainfall. It would appear that normally the lenses of the Pingelap islands would be quite low in salinity, though the drought of 1983 must have increased that quality.

Chapter 6

1 The existence and proliferation of funeral ceremonies are widespread throughout the Pacific. Rodman (1987: 43-48) describes a *bongi* cycle of feasting and prestation of pigs which covers 100 days in a Vanuatan society. But this Longanan system is based on competition of conflicting claims to the lands of the deceased, given a marked flexibility in land-inheritance practices. In contrast, the *derak* ceremony confirms previously agreed upon divisions of properties. Also, the Longanan cycle does not specify numbers of pigs to be contributed by claiments, and indeed, claims appear to be strengthened by presenting larger numbers of pigs to the brothers of the deceased, whose claims are automatic. In *derak*, the numbers of pigs and taro corms are supposed to be in direct proportion to the amount of land (and taro holdings) acquired.

Chapter 7

1 An anonymous reviewer suggests that this practice of adopting sons-in-law could have been inspired by Japanese contact as a common Japanese practice. However, the fact that this practice was successfully applied to disguise passing land to daughters implies that the Japanese administration must have been unaware of its application on Pohnpei.
2 That there are similar percentages of adoptive fathers represented in Pingelap A and Mwalok B is coincidental, as they concerned different stages in the history of the rise and fall of adoptions in the total Pingelapese population. In Pingelap A the rise of adoption was overrepresented in the sample of its cohort group. In the case of Mwalok B the nearly normal representation 19 percent (as opposed to 15 percent overall) of adoption frequency for Mwalok as compared to its total Pingelapese cohort draws a lower figure than the Pingelap B sample, which is contemporaneous and atypical of the total sample.

3 I am dealing here only with the more obvious of possible economic motivations for immigration to Mand. Certainly there must have been less tangible motives if their full range could be explored. With regard, however, to certain quite apparent motives exhibited or inferred regarding emigration from Pingelap in the 1970s and 1980s, those of educational and occupational opportunity could not have been much in evidence in 1954-56 when the colonization at Mand took place. It was mainly after the expanded flow of funds that began in the Kennedy administration that such opportunities became highly manifest. In this regard those Mand people who had taken up employment in Kolonia or had left the colony for education or training outside Micronesia at the time of my studies were not representatives of the original colonists of adult ages. Rather, they were the children of that element.

Chapter 8

1 This pattern contrasts to that reported in Rodman's Vanuatan study where it is only in the early stages of price rises that increased production takes place. She (Rodman 1987: 96) indicates that small producers, in particular, show increases in copra production when they are building funds in order to make specific purchases, after which production falls off regardless of price increases. I noted a similar pattern for poorer Pingelapese, particularly those who have no other income. However, such sources of fluctuations are swamped in the overall picture of copra production which, as the graph shows, is definitely linked to price changes.

Chapter 9

1 It should be mentioned, as noted by an anonymous reviewer, that Pingelapese adoption is related to land tenure functions, in contrast to that relationship in other Micronesian societies. On Pingelap, adoption provides individual heirs, whereas in other Micronesian regions adoption provides alliances among larger landholding units.

2 A reader suggests that "land use, especially in the taro areas, was still intensive (at this time) and with crops that had to be mulched and that matured over long time periods, a reallocation of land within the *keinek* would have resulted in individuals losing value of their investment." This seems a logical possibility and provides an alternate and more functionally oriented explanation, though I do not have any informant statements regarding this possibility.

3 As noted in this previous publication, this generalization applies to most cases of adoption, but not to adoption of grandchildren, which has continued throughout the period of my studies.

4 It is clear that the *keinek* and *kainek* bear close similarity, if not identity, with Murdock's (1949: 65-78) clan. While Lingenfelter (1975) has used this designation for an apparently similar unit for Yap, I have chosen to use the native terms or "lineage." Murdock (1949: 67, 78) concedes the difficulty in assigning a term to such "compromise kin groups," and there are problems implicit in such alternate usages as "localized lineages" and "localized clans" (cf. Steward 1955). My own difficulty with the term "clan" so applied is that at least two levels can be incorporated in this usage, units of demonstrated descent and those of putative descent. Since there has been a tendency to equate "sib" with "clan" on a higher level of unit, and since the *keinek* and *kainek* are based on actual descent from a known apical ancestor, I am reluctant to class them as clans.

Further to my own hypothesis regarding the evolution of double descent on Pingelap (Damas 1979), the priority which Murdock (1949: 77) attributes to such compromise kin groups in such evolutionary processes appears to be consistent with such units or categories being halfway stations in the shift from predominately matrilineal systems towards patrilineality.

5 Netting (1976), basing his formulation on his study of a Swiss alpine village, distinguishes between the types of property which are owned communally and those which are owned individually as follows: Those which are owned communally are characterized by low values of production per unit area, frequency and dependability of use or yield, possibility of improvement or intensification; and by large areas required for effective use and large labour forces. Those properties which are owned individually are high in the first four of these qualities and require only small areas for effective use and small workforces, such as families or individuals. In applying this scheme to Pingelap and Mwaekil, the priority of individual ownership in the taro patch certainly appears to conform to Netting's list of characteristics for that type of ownership and use. The dry land areas perhaps show some correspondence with his criteria for communal tenure, but even so, under conditions of population pressure in limited space a shift to individual tenure appears to be one solution.

6 Lessa (1962: 339-40) indicates that early population estimates for the Carolines tended to be overestimates, and Alkire's (1978: 32-340) analysis of early figures for Lamotrek and Woleai seem to bear this out. On the other hand the sampling of Micronesian and Polynesian atolls represented in Carroll (1975) does not show a clear-cut tendency of that sort. Exceptions include estimates based on beachcomber reports in the Gilberts (Lambert 1975: 214, 277) and an early misleading number for Ontang-Java (Bayliss-Smith 1975: 430). Clearly the estimates of Weckler and Morton for post-typhoon survival populations cannot be said to be such. While the nineteenth-century estimates are few, they appear to show that by the end of the century a 2-3 percent growth rate was maintained over the long run for Pingelap.

7 Kiste associates "status and authority" with control over land "in most island and atoll communities in Micronesia and Polynesia where land is limited in quantity" (1967: 249). This is probably true for several societies whose sources Kiste cites, but it is not true for Pingelap and Mwaekil, at least during the current period. I have argued that chieftainship does not guarantee ownership of large properties. While first-fruit ceremonies are present, or have been on these two atolls, the chiefs control neither land ownership nor the use of the products of the land. Perhaps the existence of individual, or in the case of Mwaekil, quasi-individual ownership manages to a greater degree to avoid the "intra-societal conflict, discord and tensions between individuals and groups over land" (ibid.: 250) than is the case in other societies where Kiste sees such problems to be endemic. On the level of island or atoll chiefs, *iroij*(s), in the Marshalls, Kiste (ibid.: 33) indicates that their power rested not only on the amount of land controlled but also on the number of commoners, *kajur*(s), and on their reputations as war leaders. This latter attribute was clearly important in such cases where *iroij*(s) extended power over several of the Marshall atolls, forming political units which Alkire (1978: 131-34) calls "coral complexes."

8 In expanding this survey briefly beyond Carolinian atolls to the high island of Yap, some similarities might be noted with the situation on Pingelap in the depiction by Labby (1976) of a shift from predominately matrilineal land tenure practices to an injection of important patrilineal elements. I have addressed this possibility in an earlier publication as follows:

In the case of Pingelap it is futile to posit such an intricate series of probable events to account for such a shift, as has Labby for Yap. The patrilineal emphasis in land tenure is far more solidly established on Pingelap. Oral traditions do not suggest earlier matrilineal emphasis in either land tenure or in succession to titles. In fact, so firmly established is the idea of patrilineal land inheritance on Pingelap that oral history contends that it was only during the early part of the nineteenth century that daughters received small plots of land for their dowries (Damas 1979: 193).

Land tenure histories presented here (chap. 5) point to a probably even later advent of the dowry system, with its full establishment being accomplished only at the end of the nineteenth century or the beginning of the twentieth. Further, even in the cases of dowry there is no clear-cut pattern of mother to daughter transmission of properties.

9 While Wiens (1962: 458) notes the lack of quantitative data regarding the extent of population pressures on atolls and points to the difficulties of gathering such data, Bayliss-Smith has attempted such a chore. In incorporating such factors as important subsistence crops (especially taro), area of land potentially available for production of staples, minimum consumption level of each staple, and mean calorific requirements per person per year, he develops a formula aimed at computing carrying capacity (1974: 285). While this formula lacks consideration of marine resources, application to Polynesian outliers is impressive and thought-provoking. Bayliss-Smith (ibid.: 288-89) also compared population densities of various atolls and concluded that the atolls of the eastern Carolines "have rather higher densities, higher even than the carrying capacity densities."

10 The ownership and usufruct networks on Kapingamarngi are enmeshed in cognatic kinship, which allows for a number of acquisitions as well as use options for each individual. The selection of which of a series of rights is exploited depends on the kinds of land resource needed, the degree of control which is exercised over plots, and the social relationship one has with the steward, in cases of corporate ownership situations (Lieber 1974: 89-90). With regard to usufruct rights, it is usually genealogical distance which governs exercise of rights. The relationship between stewards and those granted usufruct privileges is likened to the parent-child tie. The "parent" gains prestige in the community and the "child" loses prestige "for this reason, usufruct tends not to be utilized with great frequency by anyone" (ibid.: 91).

11 Shifting outside atoll situations, O'Meara's (1990) Samoan study also reports individual ownership and inheritance of land. In that case the acculturative factor of cash-cropping is cited. In one version of the beginning of individual ownership on Mwaekil, its inception is associated with the copra trade, but, as above, the evidence is ambiguous. The other atoll sources cited here do not make a firm association between individual ownership and the copra trade and certainly the history of land tenure on Pingelap shows much greater antiquity in both taro holdings and dry land plots. It should be noted again that individual ownership of taro areas had closer relationship to individual ownership in several cases cited here and thus was not related to cash-cropping.

Another contrast seen in the Samoan case is the breakdown of the extended family as a usufruct unit, a situation not seen on Pingelap or reported for the other atoll societies cited here.

12 While we do have available the two collections of chapters on Pacific land tenure of Crocombe (1971) and Lundsgaarde (1974), as well as Kiste (1974) to draw upon, to a great degree my survey had to rely on unpublished theses and reports. It is unfortunate that the great bulk of material on atoll land tenure systems remains in this unfinished state.

Bibliography

Alkire, William H.

1965 *Lamotrek Atoll and Inter-island Socioeconomic Ties*. Urbana: University of Illinois Press.

1968 Porpoises and Taro. *Ethnology* 7: 280-89.

1974 Land Tenure in the Woleai. In *Land Tenure in Oceania*, edited by Henry P. Lundsgaarde, Honolulu: The University of Hawaii Press.

1978 *Coral Islanders*. Arlington Heights: AHM Publishing.

Bascom, William R.

1965 *Ponape: A Pacific Economy in Transition*. Berkeley: University of California Anthropological Records, No. 22.

Bayliss-Smith, Tim

1974 Constraints on Population Growth: The Case of the Polynesian Outlier Atolls in the Pre-Contact Period. *Human Ecology* 2(4): 259-95.

1975 The Central Polynesian Outlier Populations. In *Pacific Atoll Populations*, edited by Vern Carroll. Honolulu: University of Hawaii Press.

Becke, Louis

1894 Ninia. In *By Reef and Palm and the Ebbing of the Tide*. Philadelphia: J. B. Lippincott Co.

Bentzen, Conrad

1949 Land and Livelihood on Mokil, Part II. Unpublished manuscript. Los Angeles.

Best, Elsdon

1924 *The Maori*: 2 vols. Wellington: Vol. 5 of Memoirs of the Polynesian Society.

Bordieu, Pierre

1977 *Outline of a Theory of Practice*. Cambridge: Cambridge University Press.

Brady, Ivan, A.

1970 Land Tenure, Kinship and Community Structure: Strategies for Living in the Ellice Islands of Western Polynesia. Ph.D. dissertation. Eugene: University of Oregon.

1974 Land Tenure in the Ellice Islands: A Changing Profile. In *Land Tenure in Oceania*, edited by Henry P. Lundsgaarde. Honolulu: University of Hawaii Press.

Brookfield, H. C., and Paula Brown

1963 *The Struggle for Land*. London: Oxford University Press.

Brown, Paula, and Aaron Podolefsky

1976 Population Density, Agricultural Intensity, Land Tenure, and Group Size in the New Guinea Highlands. *Ethnology* 15(3): 211-38.

Bryan, E. H., Jr.
1971 *Guide to Place Names in the Trust Territory of the Pacific Islands*. Honolulu: Pacific Science Information Center, Bernice P. Bishop Museum.

Buck, Peter H. (Te Rangi Hiroa)
1934 *Mangaian Society*. Honolulu: Bernice P. Bishop Museum Bulletin 122.

Carroll, Vern
1970 Introduction: What Does Adoption Mean? In *Adoption in Eastern Oceania*, edited by Vern Carroll. Honolulu: University of Hawaii Press.
1975 *Pacific Atoll Populations*. Honolulu. University of Hawaii Press.

Child, Reginald
1974 *Coconuts*. 2nd ed. London: Longmans.

Christian, Frederick, W.
1899 *The Caroline Islands*. London: Methuen and Co.

Collier, George, A.
1975 *Fields of the Tzotsil*. Austin & London: University of Texas Press.

Conklin, Harold C.
1957 *The Study of Shifting Cultivation*. Washington: Pan American Union.

Connell, John
1986 Population, Migration and Problems of Atoll Development in the South Pacific. *Pacific Studies* 9(2): 41-58.

Coulter, John, W.
1957 *The Pacific Dependencies of the United States*. Putney: Tuttle.

Crocombe, Ron, G.
1971 *Land Tenure in the Pacific*. Melbourne: Oxford University Press.
1974 Land Tenure in a Test Tube: The Case of Palnerston Atoll. In *Land Tenure in Oceania*, edited by Henry P. Lundsgaarde. Honolulu: University of Hawaii Press.

Damas, David
1969 The Study of Cultural Ecology and the Ecology Conference. In *Ecological Essays*, edited by David Damas. Ottawa: National Museums of Canada Bulletin 230.
1979 Double Descent in the Eastern Carolines. *Journal of the Polynesian Society* 88(2): 177-98.
1981 The *Keinek* of Pingelap and Patrilineal Descent. *Journal of the Polynesian Society* 90(1): 117-22.
1983a The Title System of Pingelap and the Diversity of Atoll Political Organizations. *Culture* 3(1): 3-18.
1983b Demography and Kinship as Variables in Adoption in the Carolines. *American Ethnologist* 5(2): 328-44.
1985 Pingelap Politics and American-Micronesian Relations. *Ethnology* 24(3): 43-55.
1986 Residential Group Types, Virilocality, and Migration: The Pingelap Case. *Ethnology* 25(4): 241-56.

Dana, Julian
1935 *Gods Who Die: The Story of Samoa's Greatest Adventurer*. New York: Macmillan.

District Court of Ponape
1959 Civil Action No. 59. Kelemend Plaintiff, Mark Defendent.
1963a Civil Action No. 217. Mark Mareke Plaintiff, Nerios Dikson Defendant.

1963b Civil Action No. 216. Mark Modekai Plaintiff, Iosua Soswel Defendant.

1963c Civil Action No. 235. Aram Peres Plaintiff, Inderal Rehab Defendant.

1965a Civil Action No. 240. Neli Mwokin, Plaintiff, Suli Sairenius Defendant.

1965b Civil Action No. 234. Poronika Interes Plaintiff, Aminis Sehson Defendant.

1967 Civil Action No. 232. Inek Sehk Plaintiff, Ohana Sohn Defendant.

Dolgin, Janet, David S. Kemnitzer, and David M. Schneider, eds.

1977 *Symbolic Anthropology*. New York: Columbia University Press.

Eggan, Fred

1954 Social Anthropology and the Method of Controlled Comparison. *American Anthropologist* 56 (5) Part I: 743-63.

Ehrlich, Paul M.

1978 The Clothes of Men: Ponape Island and German Colonial Rule 1899-1914. Ph.D. dissertation. State University of New York.

Eilers, Annaliese

1934 Inseln um Ponape. *Ergebnisse der Sudsee-Expedition* 1908-1910, edited by G. Thilenius. Hamburg: Friederichsen, de Gruyter.

Emerick, Richard G.

1960 Homesteading on Ponape: A Study and Analysis of a Resettlement Program of the United States Trust Territory Government in Micronesia. Ph.D. dissertation. Philadelphia: University of Pennsylvania.

Emory, Kenneth, P.

1965 *Kapingamarangi*: Social and Religious Life of a Polynesian Atoll. Honolulu: Bernice P. Bishop Museum Bulletin 228.

Feil, D.K.

1987 *The Evolution of Highland Papua New Guinea Societies*. Cambridge: Cambridge University Press.

Firth, Raymond

1929 *Primitive Economics of the New Zealand Maori*. New York: E. P. Dutton.

1961 *History and Traditions of Tikopia*. Wellington: The Polynesian Society.

Firth, Stewart

1978 German Labour Policy in Nauru and Anguar, 1906-1914. *The Journal of Pacific History* 13(1): 36-52.

Fischer, John L.

1951 Contemporary Pohepean Land Tenure. Mimeographed report. Ponape, June 5, 1951.

1958 Contemporary Ponape Island Land Tenure. In *Land Tenure Patterns, Trust Territory of the Pacific*, Vol. 1: *Guam: Trust Territory of the Pacific Islands*.

________, and Anne Fischer

1957 *The Eastern Carolines*. New Haven: Human Relations Area Files.

Fitzsimmons, Jim

1982 Federated States of Micronesia Yearbook of Statistics, 1981. No. 1, February 1982. Office of Planning and Statistics. FSM National Government.

Frake, Charles

1962 Cultural Ecology and Ethnography. *American Anthropologist* 64(1) Part I: 53-59.

Goodenough, Ward H.

1955 A Problem in Malayo-Polynesian Social Organization. *American Anthropologist* 57(1): 71-83.

1961 *Property, Kin and Community on Truk*. New Haven: Yale University Press.

Goody, Jack R.

1958 *The Development Cycle in Domestic Groups*, edited by Jack R. Goody. Cambridge: Cambridge University Press.

1973 Bridewealth and Dowry in Africa and Eurasia. In *Bridewealth and Dowry*, edited by Jack Goody and Stanley J. Tambiah. Cambridge: Cambridge University Press.

1976 *Production and Reproduction*. Cambridge: Cambridge University Press.

Greene, Sandra E.

1981 Land, Lineage and Clan in Early Anlo. *Africa* 51(1): 451-64.

Hallpike, Christopher R.

1977 *Bloodshed and Vengeance in the Papuan Mountains*. Oxford: Clarendon Press.

1986 *The Principles of Social Evolution*. New York: Oxford University Press.

Harris, G. T.

1985 Motives for Migration and Land Pressure in Simbu Province, Papua New Guinea. *Pacific Studies* 9(1): 1-12.

Harris, Marvin

1968 *The Rise of Anthropological Theory*. New York: Crowell.

Hecht, Robert M.

1984 The Transformation of Lineage Production in Southern Ivory Coast, 1920-1980. *Ethnology* 23(4): 261-78.

Hezel, Francis X.

1983 *The First Taint of Civilization*. Pacific Islands Monograph Series, No. 1. Honolulu: University of Hawaii Press.

________, and Maria Teresa Del Valle

1972 Early European Contact with the Western Carolines: 1525-1750. *The Journal of Pacific History* 7: 26-44.

Hurd, Jane N.

1977 A History and Some Traditions of Pingelap, an Atoll in the Eastern Caroline Islands. Unpublished M.A. thesis. University of Hawaii.

Johnson, Allen

1974 Ethnoecology and Planting Practices in a Swidden Agricultural System. *American Ethnologist* 1(1): 87-101.

Kenichi, Sugiura

1944 *Land Tenure of the South Sea Islanders. (Nanyo gunto Genjumin no tochi Seido)* Tokyo: Minzoku Kenkyujo. (Translated from Japanese by Chris Pearce.)

Kiste, Robert C.

1967 Changing Patterns of Land Tenure and Social Organization Among the Ex-Bikini Marshallese. Ph.D. dissertation. Seattle: University of Washington.

1972 Relocation and Technological Change in Micronesia. In *Technology and Social Change*, edited by Russell Bernard and Pertti J. Pelto. New York: Macmillan.

1974 *The Bikinians: A Study in Forced Migration*. Menlo Park: Cummings Publishing.

Knudson, Kenneth E.

1977 Sydney Island, Titiana, and Kamaleai: Southern Gilbertese in the Phoenix and Solomon Islanda. In *Exiles and Migrants in Oceania*, edited by Michael D. Lieber. Honolulu: University of Hawaii Press.

Labby, David

1976 *The Demystification of Yap*. Chicago: University of Chicago Press.

Lambert, Bernd

1966 Ambilineal Descent Groups in the Northern Gilbert Islands. *American Anthropologist* 68(3): 641-64.

1971 The Gilbert Islands: Micro-individualism. In *Land Tenure in the Pacific*, edited by Ron Crocombe. Melbourne: Oxford University.

1975 Makin and the Outside World. In *Pacific Island Populations*, edited by Vern Carroll. Honolulu: University of Hawaii Press.

Lessa, William A.

1961 *Tales from Ulithi Atoll*. Berkeley and Los Angeles: University of California Press.

Lieber, Michael D.

1968 The Nature of the Relationship Between Land Tenure and Kinship on Kapingamarangi Atoll. Unpublished Ph.D. dissertation. Pittsburgh: University of Pittsburgh.

1974 Land Tenure on Kapingamarangi. In *Land Tenure in Oceania*, edited by Henry P. Lundsgaarde. Honolulu: University of Hawaii Press.

1977 *Exiles and Migrants in Oceania*. Honolulu: University of Hawaii Press.

Linares, Olga F.

1984 Households Among the Diola of Senegal: Should Norms Enter by the Front or Side Door? In *Households*, edited by Robert McC. Netting. Berkeley: University of California Press.

Lingenfelter, Sherwood G.

1975 *Yap: Political Leadership and Culture Change in an Island Society*. Honolulu: University of Hawaii Press.

Lowie, Robert

1915 Oral Tradition and History. *American Anthropologist* 17(3): 597-99.

Lubbock, Basil.

1931 *Bully Hayes South Seas Pirate*. London: Martin Hopkinson.

Lundsgaarde, Henry P.

1974a The Evolution of Tenure Principles on Tamana, Gilbert Islands. In *Land Tenure in Oceania*, edited by Henry P. Lundsgaarde. Honolulu: University of Hawaii Press.

1974b Pacific Land Tenure in a Nutshell. In *Land Tenure in Oceania*, edited by Henry P. Lundsgaarde. Honolulu: University of Hawaii Press.

1974c *Land Tenure in Oceania*. Honolulu: University of Hawaii Press.

Malinowski, Bronislaw

1929 *The Sexual Life of Savages in Northwestern New Guinea*. New York: The Eugenics Press.

Mason, Leonard

1968 Suprafamilial Authority and Economic Process in Micronesian Atolls. In *Peoples and Cultures of the Pacific*, edited by Andrew P. Vayda. Garden City: The Natural History Press.

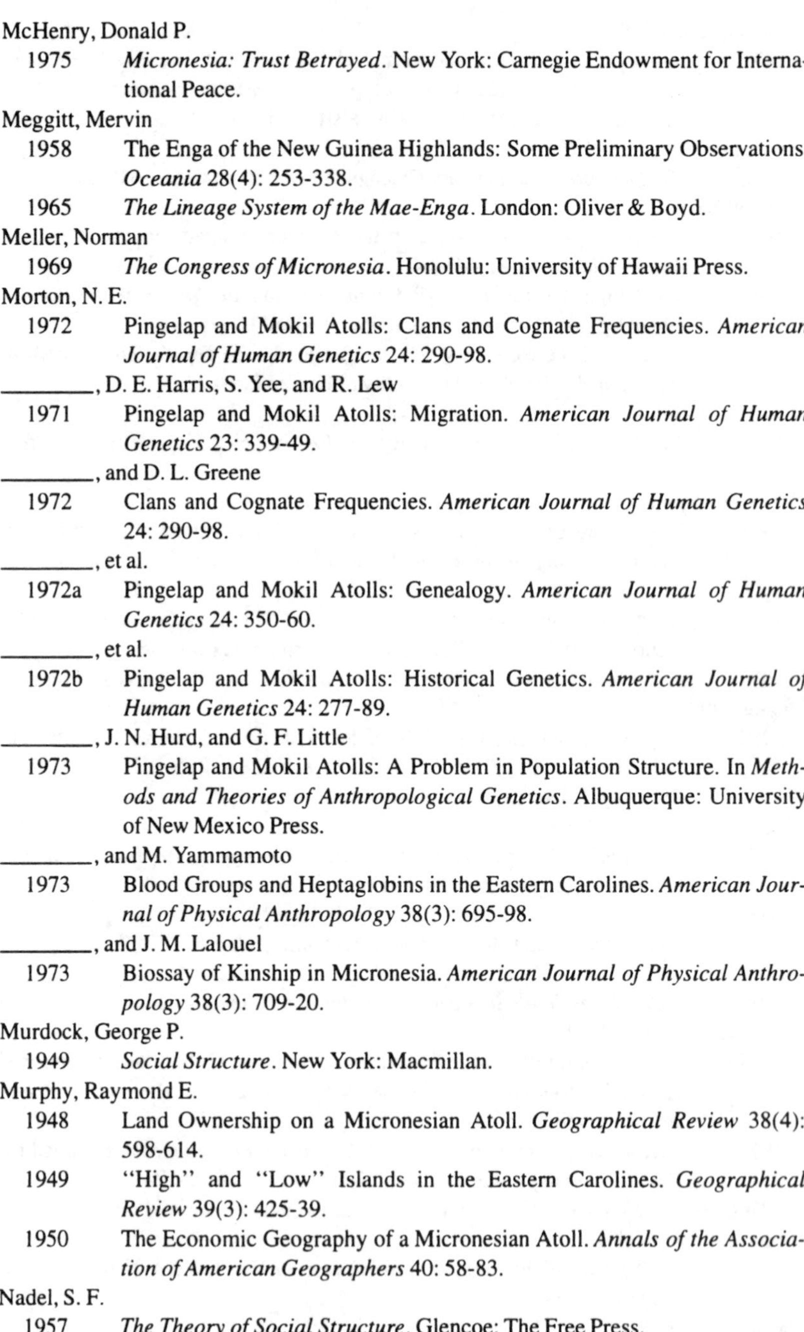

McHenry, Donald P.
1975 *Micronesia: Trust Betrayed*. New York: Carnegie Endowment for International Peace.

Meggitt, Mervin
1958 The Enga of the New Guinea Highlands: Some Preliminary Observations. *Oceania* 28(4): 253-338.
1965 *The Lineage System of the Mae-Enga*. London: Oliver & Boyd.

Meller, Norman
1969 *The Congress of Micronesia*. Honolulu: University of Hawaii Press.

Morton, N. E.
1972 Pingelap and Mokil Atolls: Clans and Cognate Frequencies. *American Journal of Human Genetics* 24: 290-98.

________, D. E. Harris, S. Yee, and R. Lew
1971 Pingelap and Mokil Atolls: Migration. *American Journal of Human Genetics* 23: 339-49.

________, and D. L. Greene
1972 Clans and Cognate Frequencies. *American Journal of Human Genetics* 24: 290-98.

________, et al.
1972a Pingelap and Mokil Atolls: Genealogy. *American Journal of Human Genetics* 24: 350-60.

________, et al.
1972b Pingelap and Mokil Atolls: Historical Genetics. *American Journal of Human Genetics* 24: 277-89.

________, J. N. Hurd, and G. F. Little
1973 Pingelap and Mokil Atolls: A Problem in Population Structure. In *Methods and Theories of Anthropological Genetics*. Albuquerque: University of New Mexico Press.

________, and M. Yammamoto
1973 Blood Groups and Heptaglobins in the Eastern Carolines. *American Journal of Physical Anthropology* 38(3): 695-98.

________, and J. M. Lalouel
1973 Biossay of Kinship in Micronesia. *American Journal of Physical Anthropology* 38(3): 709-20.

Murdock, George P.
1949 *Social Structure*. New York: Macmillan.

Murphy, Raymond E.
1948 Land Ownership on a Micronesian Atoll. *Geographical Review* 38(4): 598-614.
1949 "High" and "Low" Islands in the Eastern Carolines. *Geographical Review* 39(3): 425-39.
1950 The Economic Geography of a Micronesian Atoll. *Annals of the Association of American Geographers* 40: 58-83.

Nadel, S. F.
1957 *The Theory of Social Structure*. Glencoe: The Free Press.

National Union, The
1983 FSM Ratifies Compact. September 15, 1983.

Netting, Robert McC.

1969 Ecosystems in Process: A Comparative Study of Change in Two West African Societies. In *Ecological Essays*, edited by David Damas. Ottawa: National Museums of Canada Bulletin 230.

1976 What Alpine Peasants Have in Common: Observations on Communal Tenure in a Swiss Village. *Human Ecology* 4: 135-46.

1981 *Balancing on an Alp*. Cambridge: Cambridge University Press.

1982 The Ecological Perspective: Holism and Scholasticism in Anthropology. In *Crisis in Anthropology*, edited by E. Adamson Hoebel, Richard Currier, and Susan Kaiser. New York: Garland.

Nevin, David

1977 *The American Touch in Micronesia*. New York: W. W. Norton.

Nufer, Harold F.

1978 *Micronesia Under American Rule*. Hicksville: Exposition Press.

Oliver, Douglas

1971 *Planning Micronesia's Future*. Honolulu: University of Hawaii Press.

O'Meara, Tim

1990 *Samoan Planters*. Fort Worth: Holt, Rinehart and Winston.

Peattie, Mark R.

1988 *Nanyo*, Pacific Islands Monograph Series, No. 4. Honolulu: University of Hawaii Press.

Peoples, James G.

1978 Dependence in a Micronesian Economy. *American Ethnologist* 5(3): 535-52.

Pollock, Nancy

1970 Breadfruit and Breadwinning on Namu Atoll. Ph.D. dissertation. Honolulu: University of Hawaii.

1974 Landholding on Namu Atoll, Marshall Islands. In *Land Tenure in Oceania*, edited by Henry P. Lundsgaarde. Honolulu: University of Hawaii Press.

Purcell, David C., Jr.

1976 The Economics of Exploitation. The Japanese in Mariana, Caroline and Marshall Islands, 1915- 1940. *Journal of Pacific History* 11(3): 189-11.

Rappaport, Roy

1967 *Pigs for the Ancestors*. New Haven: Yale University Press.

Redfield, Robert

1955 *The Little Community*. Chicago: University of Chicago Press.

Riesenberg, Saul H.

1965 Table of Voyages Affecting Micronesian Islands. *Oceania* 36(2): 155-70.

Rodman, Margaret C.

1987 *Masters of Tradition*. Vancouver: University of British Columbia Press.

1989 *Deep Water*. Boulder & London: Westview Press.

Rogers, Edward S.

1969 Historical Factors. In *Ecological Essays*, edited by David Damas. Ottawa: National Museums of Canada Bulletin 230.

Rosaldo, Renato

1980 *Ilongot Head Hunting, 1883-1974: A Study in Society and History*. Stanford: Stanford University Press.

Rynkiewich, Michael A.
1972 Land Tenure Among Arno Marshallese. Ph.D. dissertation. Minneapolis: University of Minnesota.

St. John, Harold
1948 Report on the Flora of Pingelap Atoll, Caroline Islands, Micronesia, and Observations on the Vocabulary of the Native Inhabitants: Pacific Plant Studies. *Pacific Science* 2: 96-113.

Sahlins, Marshall
1958 *Social Stratification in Polynesia*. Seattle: University of Washington Press.
1981 *Historical Metaphors and Mythical Realities*. Ann Arbor: University of Michigan Press.
1985 *Islands of History*. Chicago: University of Chicago Press.

Salzman, Philip C.
1988 Fads and Fashions in Anthropology. *Anthropology Newsletter* 29(5): 31-33.

Schneider, David M.
1953 Yap Kinship terminology and Kin Groups. *American Anthropologist* 55(2) Part 1: 215-36.
1962 Double Descent on Yap. *Journal of the Polynesian Society* 71(1): 1-24.
1972 What Is Kinship All About? In *Kinship Studies in the Morgan Centennial Year*, edited by P. Reining. Washington, D.C.: Anthropological Society of Washington.
1980 Is There Really Double Descent on Pingelap? *Journal of the Polynesian Society* 89(4): 521-28.
1984 *A Critique of the Study of Kinship*. Ann Arbor: University of Michigan Press.

Severance, Craig
1976 Land, Food, and Fish: Strategy and Transaction on a Micronesian Atoll. Ph.D. dissertation. Eugene: University of Oregon.

Shankman, Paul
1986 Review of *Islands of History* by Marshall Sahlins. *American Anthropologist* 88(3): 766-68.

Steincipher, John R. (ed.)
1970a *Trust Territory Code*, Vol. I. Seattle: Book Publishing Company.
1970b *Trust Territory Code*, Vol. II. Seattle: Book Publishing Company.
1975 *Code of the Trust Territory of the Pacific Islands, 1975 Cumulative Supplement*. Seattle: Book Publishing Company.

Steward, Julian H.
1955 *Theory of Culture Change*. Urbana: University of Illinois Press.

Strathern, Andrew
1959 Descent and Alliance in the New Guinea Highlands: Some Problems of Comparison. *Proceedings of the Royal Anthropological Institute* 1968, pp. 37-52.

Sturtevant, William
1964 Studies in Ethnoscience. *American Anthropologist* 66(3) Part 2: 99-131.

Tambiah, Stanley I.
1989 Bridewealth and Dowry Revisited: The Position of Women in Sub-Saharan Africa and North India. *Current Anthropology* 30(4): 413-35.

Tobin, Jack A.

1967 The Resettlement of the Enewetok People: A Study of a Displaced Community in the Marshall Islands. Ph.D. dissertation. Berkeley: University of California.

TTPI

1972 Survey of Damage to Mokil and Pingelap Atolls by Tropical Storm Lola. Memorandum from Field Trip Party to Mokil and Pingelap to Acting District Administator. Ponape: Trust Territory of the Pacific Islands.

Vayda, Andrew P., and Roy Rappaport

1976 Ecology, Cultural and Noncultual. In *Human Ecology*, edited by Peter Richerson and J. McEvoy. North Scitaute: Duxbury Press.

Weckler, Joseph E.

1949 Land and Livelihood on Mokil, An Atoll in the Eastern Carolines, Part I. Unpublished manuscript. Los Angeles.

1953 Adoption on Mokil. *American Anthropologist* 55(4): 555-68.

Wiens, Harold J.

1962 *Atoll Environment and Ecology*. New Haven and London: Yale University Press.

Wilson, Walter Scott

1976 Household, Land and Adoption on Kusaie. In *Transactions in Kinship*, edited by Ivan Brady. Honolulu: University of Hawaii Press.

Woodruff, Jasper G.

1979 *Coconuts: Production, Processes, Products*. 2nd ed. Westport: AVI Publishing.

Yanaihara, Tadao

1976 *Pacific Islands Under Japanese Mandate*. Westport: Greenwood Press.

Index